ONYE-NKUZI
TEACHER, STATESMAN, ICON OF EDUCATION
A Historical Biography of REUBEN IBEKWE UZOMA, "RI"

ONYE-NKUZI
TEACHER, STATESMAN, ICON OF EDUCATION
A Historical Biography of REUBEN IBEKWE UZOMA, "RI"

by

ADAOHA C. OKWUOSA
NONYE NNAMEZIE

Safari Books Ltd.
Ibadan

Published by
Safari Books Ltd.
Ile Ori Detu 1, Shell Close
Onireke, Ibadan.
Email: safarinigeria@gmail.com
Website: http://safaribooks.com.ng

© 2018, Adaoha C Okwuosa, Nonye Nnamezie
First Published 2018

All rights reserved. This book is copyright and so no part of it may be reproduced, stored in a retrieval system, or transmitted, in any form or by any means, electrical, mechanical, electrostatic, magnetic tape, photocopying, recording or otherwise, without the prior written permission of the author.

ISBN: Paperback- 978-978-55448-5-5
Cased- 978-978-55448-6-2

DEDICATION

To:
Anii, Ukachi, Ocy, Ndubuisi, Eby, Chinyere and Chuks,
Beloved siblings of Adaoha, Ugochi, Okechukwu,
Elewechi and Ijeuru

TABLE OF CONTENTS

Dedication .... *v*
Acronyms .... *xi*
Foreword .... *xiii*
Preface .... *xvii*
Acknowledgements .... *xxi*

| **INTRODUCTION** | **1** |

| **CHAPTER ONE: LIFE FOUNDATIONS** | **5** |

Nkwerre; R.I. Uzoma's Hometown 5
Family Roots and Antecedents 13
Childhood and Early Schooling 19

| **CHAPTER TWO: MAKING OF AN ICON OF EDUCATION** | **25** |

Higher Education and Training.................................. 25
- St. Paul's College, Awka, 1931-1934; 1939-1943 27
- Achimota College, Ghana, 1939-1939 32
- Institute of Education, University of London, 1946-1947 34

Teacher and Educational Administrator 37
- Onye-Nkuzi, Pupil Teacher, School-Master 37
- Tutor, Dennis Memorial Grammar School (DMGS), Onitsha, 1936 39
- Principal Okrika Grammar School (OGS), 1944-1946 47

CHAPTER THREE: LAYING FOUNDATIONS IN FORMAL EDUCATION POLICY — 51

Minister of Education, Eastern Region (1951-1953) 51
A Wealth of Experience 59
The R.I. Uzoma 1953 UPE Blueprint and After 61
- The 1952 Cambridge Conference 61
- A Measured UPE Plan 63
- 1953 Political Disruptions 65
- The Post-R.I. Uzoma Challenges to UPE 68

CHAPTER FOUR: BUILDING EARLY EDUCATIONAL INFRASTRUCTURE — 71

Return to Voluntary Agency Service 71
- The Ngwa High School Model 73
- The Birabi Memorial Grammar School (BMGS), Bori-Ogoni Example 77
Upsurge in Voluntary Agency Schools and Colleges 80

CHAPTER FIVE: SERVICE TO CHURCH AND COMMUNITY — 85

Lay Prince of the Church 85
'Father' of the Diocese 88
Serving Nkwerre Community 93
Post-Retirement Public Service 102

CHAPTER SIX: THE MAN AND HIS PRINCIPLES — 105

First Normative Influences 105
Early Campaign for Girl-Child Education 109
Humane, Impartial, Unassuming 114
A Principled Stand; the Nkwerre Chieftaincy Affair 120
The R.I. Uzoma Educational Foundation 125

CHAPTER SEVEN: A PARTNER IN SERVICE; JEMIMAH CHINYERE UZOMA **131**

Family Roots and Antecedents 132
From Childhood to Queen's College, Lagos 138
From School-Mistress to Pivotal Teacher 146
Service to Women and Church 150
- Nkwerre Aborigines Union/Women's Section (NAU/WS).. 150
- Nzuko Ekeukwu and Mother's Union........................... 154
- Young Women's Christian Association (YWCA)............ 156
- National Council of Women's Societies (NCWS).......... 159

Appendixes: From the R.I. Uzoma Papers............................ 163
Bibliography... 325
Glossary.. 329
Index... 333
About the Author... 347
About the Co-Author... 349

ACRONYMS

ABSU	Abia State University, Uturu, Nigeria
ACMGS	Archdeacon Crowther Memorial Girls' Secondary School Elelenwa, Nigeria
BDGS	Bishop Dimieari Grammar School, Yenagoa, Nigeria
BMGS	Birabi Memorial Grammar School, Bori-Ogoni, Nigeria
CCB	Cooperative & Commerce Bank
CCN	Christian Council of Nigeria
CMS	Church Missionary Society
DC	District Commissioner
DMGS	Dennis Memorial Grammar School, Onitsha, Nigeria
ECS	Ekwulobia Central School, Ekwulobia, Nigeria
ECOWAS	Economic Community of West African States
ENRAC	Eastern Nigeria Rural Activities Committee of the CCN
FRGS	Fellow of the Royal Geographical Society
FUTO	Federal University of Technology, Owerri, Nigeria
IMSU	Imo State University, Owerri, Nigeria
KJW	Knight of John Wesley
KSC	Knight of Saint Christopher
MHA	Member, House of Assembly
MHR	Member, House of Representatives
NAU	Nkwerre Aborigine's Union, Nkwerre, Nigeria

NAU/WS	Nkwerre Aborigine's Union, Women's Section
NCNC	National Council of Nigeria and the Cameroons
NCWS	National Council of Women's Societies of Nigeria
NYM	National Youth Movement
OAU	Organization of African Unity
OBE	Officer of the Magnificent Order of the British Empire
OFR	Officer of the Order of the Federal Republic of Nigeria
OGS	Okrika Grammar School, Okrika, Nigeria
OON	Officer of the Order of the Niger
RCM	Roman Catholic Mission
RIUEF	Reuben Ibekwe Uzoma Educational Foundation
SAGS	St Augustine's Grammar School, Nkwerre, Nigeria
SDA	Seventh Day Adventist Church
TTC	Teacher Training College
UNEC	University of Nigeria, Enugu Campus
UNESCO	United Nations Educational, Scientific & Cultural Organization
UNICEF	United Nations Children's Fund
UNN	University of Nigeria, Nsukka, Nigeria
UPE	Universal Primary Education
WAFF	West African Frontier Force
YWCA	Young Women's Christian Association

FOREWORD

It is with much pride and pleasure that I write this foreword to a historical biography of the late Sir Reuben Ibekwe Uzoma, BA London (1943), Dip Ed. London (1947), LL.D (UNN)*Honoris Causa* (1990), FRGS, OBE, OFR. Reuben Ibekwe Uzoma was a pillar of the Anglican Church in Nigeria, and an icon of education, particularly in the former Eastern Region.

"Nnanyi RI" as he was affectionately known by his many admirers, was like a colossus that bestrode the frontiers of educational development and of management of educational institutions by the voluntary agencies. This was in the period from late colonial rule up to the end of the Nigerian civil war, and the government take-over of schools, beginning with the East Central State in 1970. He was the first Minister of Education for the Eastern Region of Nigeria from January 1952 to December 1953, following the granting of self-rule to the Colony and Protectorates of Nigeria under the MacPherson Constitution of 1951.

As Minister of Education, R.I. Uzoma established a milestone in terms of government's first attempts at formulating a coherent policy for formal education. This was in sharp contrast to the situation in the colonial period in which education policy was left largely to the whims and caprices of the voluntary agencies, which consisted largely of the missionary churches. The ideology of a Universal Primary Education Policy (UPE) as the bedrock for formal education was first introduced for the former Eastern Region by R.I Uzoma in December 1952. From then on, the UPE as a principle which sees access to education as a universal right for all, became an accepted norm in Eastern Nigeria. The UPE concept introduced in 1952 by R.I. Uzoma in the Eastern Region, and by S.O. Awokoya in the Western Region, marked a significant departure from the elitist approach to education in the colonial period in which education was regarded as a privilege for a few. It was an approach that had the sole objective of producing a small crop of literate and skilled individuals that would man the colonial public services. R.I. Uzoma also pioneered the idea of a formal policy of government sponsorship for tertiary education in the former Eastern Region. He did so by starting the first Eastern Region Scholarship Scheme of 1952-1953 which benefitted candidates from all the administrative divisions of the old Eastern Region including Southern Cameroons.

R.I. Uzoma also served as Education Secretary and Supervisor of Schools for the Anglican Mission in the Niger Delta and Owerri Dioceses of the East from 1948 to 1951 and from 1954 to 1967. The Anglican Mission was at the time one of the major voluntary agencies that instituted and managed the majority of the schools and colleges across the then Eastern Region. In his capacity as Education Secretary, R.I. Uzoma left his footprints in the establishment of a wide network of secondary schools and teacher training colleges (TTCs) in the territory that is present-day Imo, Abia, Rivers and Bayelsa States of Nigeria. As Supervisor of Schools, he became famous for the efficient and disciplined inspection and monitoring of grassroots educational institutions and a familiar figure whose unscheduled visits, made teachers and heads of institutions to sit up.

R.I. Uzoma was equally a major player in the public service of government, after the civil war, in the former East Central State and subsequently in Imo State, following his retirement from the education system of the Anglican Mission. As Teachers Service Commissioner and later Public Service Commissioner in the East Central and later Imo states, "Nnanyi R.I" made immense contributions to the rehabilitation of the teaching profession, as well as to the transparent recruitment, appointment and discipline of public servants in the East in the period following the civil war up until 1981. His working-life in government public sector was a period which so eloquently portrayed the symbiotic impact on his work, by the great Anglican-church traditions of integrity, honesty, and deep sense of justice, with which he had been trained. These were the values which he brought to bear on the public service, as a professional and a technocrat.

This historical biography is a highly recommended reading, and reference material for all who wish to have an informed insight into the important contributions of the Anglican Mission as a voluntary agency, in the early development of education in the former Eastern Region. Against the background of the numerous challenges that have beset the education sector in our contemporary society, this book also provides a view into a past and admirable age of formal education operations, and the teaching profession. It is equally a contribution regarding the strength and calibre of the great men and women like R.I. Uzoma who pioneered that regrettably now bygone age.

Once again, I am proud as well as honoured to be associated with this volume on "Dede R.I.", for his breed laid the foundation on which the type of me stood and rose to national academic and professional excellence. I wish to congratulate those who put together this erudite volume, especially Dr. Ada Okwuosa, a chip of the old block, a true daughter of "Dede RI" and Mama. I expected no less a scholarly production, and they all did a fine job.

PROFESSOR. O.C. NWANA *KSC, KJW*
Emeritus Professor of Education
of UNN, ABSU and IMSU

PREFACE

This biography is aptly described as historical for two reasons. Firstly it adopts a style that documents the life and times of an iconic figure of our society within the context of an incisive narrative on events, places and situations which in terms of chronology have assumed the character of history. Secondly, it seeks to do so with the objective of demonstrating the important pioneering role of an individual in the early development of two key sectors of human endeavor in our society, in this case, education and the Church. The understanding is that history is about events that have either been made by people as key players, or were experienced by people as spectators.

A historical biography has the intention of providing a record that is more than a tunnel-narrative on the personality who is its subject. Historical biographers have tended not to receive deserved attention in Nigerian academic production because of the preference for auto-biographies, and the fast-track biographies that are written to coincide promptly with the obsequies of personalities. In other words, a historical biography is designed to portray a truly composite picture of a person's "life and times". It is rather like putting together the many interrelated pieces of a jig-saw puzzle, in order to create a portrait with a background. This work is also designed to serve as a useful reference source on collateral social, political and other phenomena which unfolded in the course of the subject's lifetime. That is the intention of this biography of Reuben Ibekwe Uzoma, a leading educationist, public figure and Anglican Church-leader of the former Eastern Region of Nigeria, from the 1940s to the 1990s.

Adopting a largely descriptive and narrative writing style, the life and times of R.I. Uzoma is utilised to provide an insight into aspects of the history of the Anglican Church as one of the voluntary agencies that initiated early educational development in the Eastern Region. Of particular interest is the role of the CMS Mission of the Anglican Church in driving the emergence of the first crop of educated leaders in the first few decades of the 20th Century. It is also utilised to take an informed look at some of the early efforts of those leaders in the former Eastern Region in establishing foundations for universal education, within the framework of honest and disciplined public service.

The public education sector in Nigeria today is plagued by many problems. Principal among these are the decline of deserved emphasis on teacher-training and teacher-education, as well as on inspection and monitoring of schools. The hindsight view of an earlier stage in our development when these challenges were absent, which is provided in this biography, could serve as a stimulus in the search for solutions.

This work on R.I. Uzoma's active and productive career is equally an example of fruitful academic collaboration between different disciplines in the Arts and Social Sciences. Different perspectives from History Studies, Sociology and Political Science have been brought together to analyse the vast amount of material available for this biography, especially from the private archives of R.I. Uzoma himself. There was also a significant amount of reliance on oral sources.

The sheer quantum of organised and well-documented material by way of file records, addresses, sermons, memoranda and reports which were found in R.I. Uzoma's private archives, was indeed a testimony to the character of the man. These materials cover a period of about 50 years from the 1940s to about 1990. They relate to issues ranging from the first indigenous government of the Eastern Region of Nigeria, contribution to national political issues, community development projects in Nkwerre, and the growth and functioning of the Anglican Church in the Eastern Region. There is also material on grassroots management of schools and teachers as well as on the Public Service Commission of Imo State in its early days.

All through his busy working life, R.I. Uzoma was popularly known as "Onye-Nkuzi" or by his initials as "RI", and will be referred to as such in much of this book. However, he was also honoured with two chieftaincy titles of *Ukeje Nkwerre* and *Ochonma-Oha* of Orlu, and also with the Knighthood of St. Christopher of the Anglican Church. Nevertheless, he continued to cherish the simpler affectionate titles of "Onye-Nkuzi" and "RI", which had no connotations of power or flamboyance.

The job of researching for this biography was made so much easier by R.I. Uzoma himself, and the authors would therefore like to place their appreciation on record in this regard. The organisation and content-details of most of the papers from his private archives, quite a number of which were in his famous legible, cursive handwriting, was remarkable. It was such that one sometimes had the feeling that R.I. Uzoma was speaking out about himself to the authors, and knew that his private papers would be needed some day. Happily, a selected number of that vast collection is available as part of this publication, in the Appendices Section.

ACKNOWLEDGEMENTS

The inspiration for writing this biography was always there in my years as an academic, before joining the Federal Civil Service. It however became more compelling from 2010, the tenth year anniversary of the passing of Sir R.I. Uzoma. The opportunity for seriously taking up the assignment came from 2012 when I became free from the hectic diplomatic schedule of a five-year service as Nigeria's Commissioner to the Economic Community of West African States (ECOWAS). By that time, it was clear that writing on the life and times of R.I. Uzoma would be best done by way of a historical biography, which requires painstaking field-research.

    I am therefore immensely grateful to Sir Walter Ofonagoro, PhD, KSC the distinguished Professor of Economic History and former Minister of Information, who connected me with an energetic young academic, Nonye Ihuoma Nnamezie of the Department of History and Strategic Studies, University of Lagos. She has quite some experience as a biographer, in addition to being an indigene of Nkwerre, the hometown of the subject. She was therefore an ideal person for the field-research and oral interviews required to write on the family roots, childhood, early education and teaching years of Sir R.I. Uzoma. I am immensely grateful to her. The first few years were spent on field research and collection of literature and making of copious notes. Hence, serious writing did not start until 2015.

    I will always owe a debt of gratitude to a number of prominent former colleagues and Nkwerre citizens who gave invaluable support in that regard. Among them are Ambassador Godwin Onyegbula KSC, who patiently went through an initial draft and articulated very useful ideas, Professor of Political Science Elochukwu Amucheazi, formerly of University of Nigeria, who not only responded promptly to requests for information, but also sent in useful publications, and Emeritus Professor of Education, O.C. Nwana KSC, KJW, who without hesitation accepted to write the foreword to the book and also provided materials.

The huge reliance on oral interviews was made quite easy by ready cooperation of those whom I refer to as the "pillars of the home front", Mrs. Roseline Nwanu Uzoma (Daa Nwanu), followed by Dee Ndukwe Akano and Nze Edwin Asugha, both cousins of R.I. Uzoma, and Madam Margaret Iheme (nee Uzoma) "Daa Maggie", his only surviving sibling. Their incisive and intelligent narration on the oral history of the subject's Nkwerre kindred and family made one to appreciate even better, what a blessing it is to have such healthy and supportive senior citizens attending to the home front.

In addition to these "pillars of the home front", very special thanks also go to other decent Nigerians who readily granted oral interviews from their personal knowledge of the life and times of R.I. Uzoma, or the institutions he influenced. These interviews were graciously granted in Port-Harcourt by Professor Godwin Nwoke, and Chief Jack Gogo, an Old Boy of OGS from Yenagoa in Bayelsa State. In Lagos, we interviewed Madam Dinah Erinne, who for many years taught at the CMS Central School in Ezeoke and was a close family friend of the Nwachukwu and R.I. Uzoma families. Interviews were also granted by Sir Martin Ilona, a retired Chief Lands Officer from Ozubulu, Anambra State, and Dr. D.G.C. Onwuneme of Anambra State University, Uli. Chief Magnus Nkemdilim, son of a retired teacher of Ekwulobia Central School was also interviewed.

In Nkwerre, we relied on Elder Geoffrey Chinaka, an Old Boy of OGS in the tenure of R.I. Uzoma, Elder Timothy Ikoroha, Elder Augustine Esonwanne (Dee Iheanyi), personal driver of R.I. Uzoma for over ten years, Daa Rhoda Tasie and Daa Augustina Olenwanne, both of R.I. Uzoma's maternal kindred, Kaka Ihegboro and Joekwes Onwukwem of Amaegbu and Umunachi respectively, and Chief Ikeaghalam, a retired teacher from Eziama Obaire. In Emekuku we relied on Chief Maxwell Ahaneku. In Owerri, Madam Josephine Ezue, Matron at the YWCA offices and facilities, also gave invaluable research data. We thank them all immensely.

An immense gratitude goes to my great friends outside Nkwerre, Dr. Timiebi Koripamo-Agary, Ambassador Nkem Wadibia-Anyanwu, Nwadia de Souza (nee Okediadi), Ijeoma Eronini (nee Ekeocha), Princess Gloria Nwoyibo Iweka, Dr. Bennett Birabi, Elelaonu Okoro (nee Amadi), who were often called at odd hours to confirm various information from field-research on their own parents or other family member, who were either close friends, colleagues or school mates of R.I. Uzoma, or of his wife, Jemimah C. Uzoma. Special thanks also go to Chiedu Ofodile, the lawyer-poet and prolific writer, who showed special interest in the work and gave most useful tips on the chapter on Queens College, Lagos, Mrs. Jemimah Uzoma's alma mater.

Coming closer to home, I cannot fail to appreciate my two "housemates" at the time of writing, Barristers Uchechi Okwuosa and Charles Uzoma, grand children of R.I. Uzoma, whom I refer to as my in-house legal advisers, for their patience and understanding all those days that I would "switch off" from domestic interactions and become a recluse and almost anti-social. They were always ready to operate the temperamental in-house desktop and printer for me on demand at awkward times. Equally deserving of special thanks, is another grandchild, Barrister Onyinyechi Amy Onwumere, the patient and meticulous "secretary." Fresh from just completing her Masters in Law in the United Kingdom, she patiently went beyond word processing to correcting and editing my style on footnotes and references.

Ultimate deep appreciation however, goes to Sir R.I. Uzoma himself, for leaving behind so huge a treasure trove of archival material in his private study that it was sometimes quite difficult to decide what to use and what to leave out. The authors are gratified to have been able to complete this project, with so much support from so many people, based on the goodwill that is the legacy of the man Reuben Ibekwe Uzoma, KSC, OBE, OFR, LL.D (Honoris Causa) 1912-2000, and of his wife, Lady Jemimah Chinyere Uzoma, 1922-2003.

DR. ADAOHA .C. OKWUOSA, *KSM, OON*

INTRODUCTION

This work represents one more contribution to Nigerian academics, of a historical biography as an important academic tool. Historical biographies have tended to be relegated to the background in Nigerian academic documentation, even though they serve as useful reference material in academic research. Historical biographies essentially provide an insight into past events by utilising the life and times of a major player in those events, as matrix. In the case of this work, the life and times of a pioneering personality whose life was a catalyst over an important period of social and political change in Nigeria, is examined. The contributions and achievements of Reuben Ibekwe Uzoma who lived between 1912 and 2000 are incisively portrayed within the context of the growth of formal education and of the Anglican Church, particularly in the former Eastern Nigeria.

Obviously, historical biographies are predicated very much on biographical research. This is research that is largely based on the acceptance that biography is a social construct. In this sense, biography is conceived as a social construction which constitutes both social reality, and the subject's world of knowledge and experience. That world is constantly affirmed and transformed within the dialectical relationship between life history, knowledge, experiences and social patterns. The main questions of interest to biographical-theoretical research are how people produce a biography in different cultural contexts, and how social conditions, rules and patterns of construction can be observed in that process. Hence, the concept of biographical work is significant in relation to these questions. For theoretical and empirical reasons, in the context of biographical research, the concept of biographical construction is often used instead of the term identity. However, identity is conceptualised as the accomplishment of building and maintaining continuity and coherence through changing situations.

At the turn of the 20th Century in Colonial Nigeria, the Church could not be separated from the unfolding system of formal education. The history of schooling went hand in hand with the history of Christianity in Nigeria. The Anglican Church undertook the educational enterprise as an initial means for facilitating the proselytisation mission of the Church. Education at this time was used for evangelism to achieve salvation and to spread the Christian faith. To achieve this initial goal, the Church set up schools alongside church buildings. The primary aim at the time was to equip the beneficiaries for active and meaningful participation in church activities. This explains why men like RI who were products of mission education, dedicated much of their lives to the work of the Church which raised them from their early stages of schooling. Many products of this early stage also became no more than teachers or clerks servicing the colonial government.

However, this period saw a number of the early products of the basic primary education, breaking the glass ceiling, and going further than the literary and rhetorical acquisition of the basic skills of reading, writing, arithmetic and catechism. Over time, they excelled beyond this limited stage through their desire and capacity for real educational development. Developments on the colonial political scene, as a result of the emergent nationalist pressures, also created a need for a highly educated class of indigenous leaders, who could support the system, and possibly substitute the colonials in governance (Nwadialor & Umeanolue, 2012:112-127). The missionary education system found it necessary to establish what could be regarded as centres for education.

Introduction

This work also opens a discourse on the role of Church Missions which became known as Voluntary Agencies, in the important social development platform of primary, secondary and teacher-training tertiary education in Eastern Nigeria. Reuben Ibekwe Uzoma was a leading actor in this process. He was also, a pioneering personality whose childhood and youth coincided with an interesting period of modernity in relation to the concept of "modern childhood."

In reference to the concept of modernity, the colonial period ushered children into the civilising mission which in other words is called "modern childhood". Modern childhood is better understood within the context of the "Mission Houses" that sprang up along the southern fringes of the West African coastline in the first half of the nineteenth century. Several historical works have effectively examined the introduction of Christianity into West Africa and the numerous anti slave-trade activities. These studies have however, not dealt with the far-reaching effects of mission education on the conception of modern childhood in Igboland, a gap this biography can perhaps help to fill.

This biography also identifies the fact that in the early stages of colonialism, mission education was not universal within the traditional communities, even though it was free. Families preferred their children to continue to help them on their farms and other domestic and commercial activities. They desired that their children's exposure to the new Christian morals and teachings should be accompanied by respect for traditional norms and conventions. They also wanted their children to continue to learn the evening games and moonlight stories and to receive competent traditional education in cultural activities and customs. Hence, they saw formal mission education, not as a substitute but as a supplement, an apprenticeship that exposed their children to additional skills such as reading and writing which could become useful for handling commercial transactions. From the foregoing, it is apparent that it was not the British colonial government but the missionaries who spearheaded the introduction of Western education in Nigeria. However, the colonial government did much to facilitate and establish western education as a major instrument of modernisation. This was done through the institutions of imperialism and their infrastructure of colonialism and social transformation.

Observably, the period of schooling in the colonial times, introduced new and additional forms of children's financial dependency on their families, and decreased their contributory economic role within the traditional family. That economic role was one reason for the high number of children born to families in the past. They were needed to increase the family's workforce on farmlands since wage labour was not the norm. Formal schooling also elongated the progression from childhood to adulthood. In contrast to the nineteenth century, when missionary education was largely free, the twentieth century saw most mission schools in Eastern Nigeria beginning to charge fees. This made education the most expensive investment for most families. Hence for those who desired formal education for their children, but could not afford it, the answer was to have those children serve a schoolmaster or mistress, in order to have their fees paid. R.I. Uzoma did not need to serve any master to go to school, but his outstanding brilliance stood him out and qualified him for various CMS scholarships. His family welcomed innovation and accepted the belief that children were primary change-agents. This gave him the necessary support to become a part of the colonial civilising mission.

As the icing on the cake, it is expected that this historical biography will meet the need to document the important life contributions and achievements of a foremost individual in our history for reference purposes and for posterity. This work is also expected to afford readers the opportunity of appreciating some of the cardinal principles of leadership and service embodied in the personality of one of Nigeria's pioneers.

1

LIFE FOUNDATIONS

Nkwerre, RI's Hometown

Sir Reuben Ibekwe Uzoma was one man whose name cannot be omitted in any study of the history and development of formal education in Nigeria, particularly in the erstwhile Eastern Region of Nigeria. He acquired early fame as the first university graduate from Nkwerre and from the old Orlu Division as a whole.[1] The old Orlu Division was the most populous division in the former Owerri Province, in the erstwhile Eastern Region of Nigeria. Today, Orlu town is the second largest city, after Owerri, in Imo State, Southeast Nigeria.

The old Orlu Division has, however, today been broken down into several local government areas which include Orlu, Njaba, Oru East, Oru West, Orsu, Isu, Ideato North, Ideato South, Nkwerre and Nwangele in Imo State. Orlu Division has a long history and played a critical role as the headquarters for the Organisation of African Unity (OAU) Humanitarian Relief Agency during the Nigerian civil war. The Nigerian headquarters of the British Cheshire Homes was also in the city. R.I. Uzoma was therefore among the first iconic personalities that highlighted the name of Nkwerre and Orlu on the map of Nigeria.

The people of the old Orlu Division have made important contributions towards the educational, sporting and political growth of Nigeria, and the narration of these may never be complete without Sir R.I. Uzoma, who set the pace for educational

---

1 Oral interview with Nze Edwin Asugha, RI's cousin, Obinuhu Village, Nkwerre, Imo State, 24th March, 2016.

scholarship in the zone. It should be recalled that he was the Chairman, Zonal Education Management Board, housed at the former Teachers' Training College Umuna in Orlu, now Urban Secondary School in Umuna.[2] R.I. Uzoma's hometown, Nkwerre is one of the local government areas in Imo State of Nigeria, with council headquarters in Nkwerre town. Since the advent of modern society and modern government, the history of Nkwerre town began to record the successful transition of one Igbo community from the traditional lucrative occupations of war, gun-making and migrant trade to modern commerce and business, as well as white and blue collar jobs (Isichei, 1976).

A well-travelled people, the Nkwerre people have been acknowledged as a good example of successful long distance Igbo traders in West Africa dating from the 17th, 18th and 19th centuries. Long before 1590, at the height of the slave trade and at the time when venturing beyond one's village was fraught with great danger, Nkwerre people were already found in settlements in different coastal towns such as Kalabari, Okrika, Bonny Ogoni, Brass, Gabon and Equatorial Island of Fernando Po (Panya). They were the trading link between the coastal towns and the people of the central Igbo area including Mbano, Mbaise, Orlu, Okigwe, Oru, Orsu, and Ideato. Many outward-looking communities preferred to have Nkwerre people residing amongst them because it gave them important links to other distant communities. With the white merchants on the coast, Nkwerre traders showed exceptional skills. They discussed business proposals with the Portuguese, Spanish and British sea captains and traders and the European merchants recognised them for driving hard bargains (Isichei, 1976).

Nkwerre town is located on the southern part of Igboland and situated in the heart of Nkwerre Local Government Area in Imo State. Nkwerre is situated on table-land overlooking a valley that separates it on the eastern side from a downhill slope towards

---

2   Oral Interview with Dr. D.G.C. Onwuneme, RI's neighbor in Owerri, and a retired lecturer, Anambra State University, Uli Campus, April 12, 2016.

Umuna-Isiaka. It is bounded on the west by Amaigbo, on the north by Ama Okpara/Eziama and on the south by Umudi and Owerre Nkworji. Nkwerre town is inclusive of over thirty-one interdependent villages formerly known as Nkwerre *Ohuebe*. There are only two rivers in Nkwerre with more than twenty streams or water-holes. These are *Iyi Bekee* flowing southwest wards and Orashi River with its source at Dikenafai and flowing northwards through Okija to Oguta. However, some of the streams or water-holes have in recent times dried up because of population growth and spread. Gun-smithing was a traditional occupation of Nkwerre people. Various types of guns, such as dane guns, cap-guns, rifles, pistols, revolvers and double barrel shot guns were being manufactured by Nkwerre blacksmiths in the past. It was this industry that gave the town the name Nkwerre *Opiaegbe*. Unfortunately this essential industry has today gone extinct.(Obialor, 2006:167-168).

Nkwerre has a history as an independent town whose local authority was never limited by any outside powers, long before the advent of British Rule, and ever before it became a government station by about 1910. From the 1966 Constituent Assembly convened at Enugu, Lt Col. Odumegwu Ojukwu, then Military Governor of Eastern Region, had adopted recommendations to administer the region on the basis of provinces. These were Onitsha, Enugu, Nsukka, Abakili, Awka, Owerri, Orlu, Okigwe, Aba, Umuahia, Calabar, Uyo, Ikot-Ekpene, Ogoja, Port-Harcourt, Brass and Degama. Each province was to be divided into Divisions. Then "Orlu Province" was composed of Nkwerre Division with headquarters at Nkwerre, and Mgbidi Division with headquarters at Mgbidi.[3] However, this arrangement ended with the end of the civil war in 1970 and there was a move by Orlu people for the divisional headquarters to be returned to Orlu. This gave rise to the Anyaegbunam Enquiry and the result was the creation of

---

[3] From R.I. Uzoma's biographical notes on his role in the creation of Local Government Areas after the civil war. R.I. Uzoma Archives.

more government areas within Orlu zone.[4] In 1967, Late Murtala Mohammed's administration created more local government areas and attached the "Isu" to Nkwerre and it then became "Nkwerre-Isu" Local Government Area.

In 1989, the Gen. Ibrahim Babangida's regime yet again created new local government areas. The administration then excised the "Isu section" to grant Isu a separate local government council. Thus, Nkwerre returned to its former status as Nkwerre Local Government Area with headquarters in Nkwerre. It is important to mention however, that the Nigerian civil war between the federal forces and the defunct Biafra, ended in Nkwerre town on January 12, 1970.[5] As the federal troops entered Owerri, Mbano, Anara and up to Amaigbo and Owerri Nkworji, the communities living in these areas fled to hide for their safety in order not to be attacked by the federal troops. But Nkwerre people never fled, rather the people came out in their numbers to receive and welcome the soldiers by shouting "One Nigeria". This singular wisdom prevented any attack by the federal forces on the town.[6] This is one reason why Nkwerre people are said to be natural diplomats.

From 1958, the *Eshi* stool (the traditional ruler of Nkwerre) was instituted as the traditional head of the entire community, Okwaraeshi was the head of the kingmaker family, and there are Chiefs and Ndi Nze who perform their own role in the politics of Nkwerre. Before then, a good number of Nkwerre sons and daughters had served in one way or the other in government for example, R.I. Uzoma, as the first Minister of Education in the Eastern Region, Barrister Willie Onyejiaka who was the Commissioner for Industry in Imo State in the 80s, Sir G.A Onyegbula who was an Ambassador before the war, just to mention a few.

---

4   Ibid.
5   Oral Interview with Joekwes Onwukwem, (Akwukwonatouto), a knowledgeable Nkwerre historian and researcher from Umunachi Village, Nkwerre, Imo State, June 15 2016.
6   Ibid.

Originally, Nkwerre had fourteen villages which were broadly divided into two major groups of Ebe-Asa North and Ebe-Asa South. Ebe-Asa North was principally made up of Onusa-Ama-Ato and Umukor Amanano kindred groups. Onusa comprises Umuagu, Umuogbo and Umuezike, while Amanano comprises Umukor, Umuokpu, Ubah (now extinct) and Okwu. The Ebe-Asa South was principally made up of Nnanano and Nnanato kindred groups. Nnanano comprises the villages of Umuoforolo, Umueze, Umunaga, Isiogwugwu and Alaekwe. *Umuerom* later joined Isiogwugwu, while Nnanato includes *Umunubo, Umugara* and *Umunachi*.[7]

About 1989, there was a need for further splitting of the existing 14 villages for economic and political reasons. The Nkwerre Aborigines Union (NAU) under the presidency of the Late Francis U. Ihekwaba gave conditions for which more villages could be created. One of these conditions was that any group which was able to pay the sum of one hundred pounds to the community would be recognised as a separate village.[8] It was during this time that some village sections became full separate villages. These were Durumba, Umukalu/Okwaraji from former Umukor village, Umunyem, Ukwube, Umukabia and Ukwuinyi from the former Umunubo villages, then Duruenereji from Onusa Nkwerre. As a result of death, Umuerim people were reduced to a small population and this made them join Isiogwugwu (now Umuchukwu). It was after this splitting exercise that the number of villages in Nkwerre increased to twenty over the period from 1989 to early 1990s. Subsequently, on historical and lineage affiliation reasons, the 20 villages are today grouped under the traditional four-kindred group as follows[9];

Onusa made up of *Umuagu, Umuogbo, Umumezike and Duruenereji.*

---

7 Ibid.
8 Ibid.
9 Ibid.

Nnanano made up of *Ukwube, Ukwuinyi, Umuyem, Umukabia, Umueze and Umunaga, Isiogwugwu and Alaekwe.*

Amanano made up of *Durumba, Umuokpu, Okwu, Umukalu and Okwaraji.*

Nnanato made up of *Umuduruaji, Amorji (Ugwu na agbo), Amaegbu, Umunachi, Umugara, and Amangwu.*

Christian religion arrived in Nkwerre in 1913, through the Church Missionary Society (CMS), a year after RI was born (Obialor, 1995:133). Ironically, while most of the Anglican communities in the present Imo State received their first mission influence through evangelists operating from Egbu or Onitsha, early Christian influence came to Nkwerre from the Niger Delta area (Obialor, 1995:133). Most of the early evangelists in the Niger Delta area were Nkwerre traders and blacksmiths who had settled in various parts of the present Rivers State and parts of Abia State. While there, they came in contact with missionaries and were converted to the Christian faith. Traditionally, as traders, Nkwerre people are quick to bring innovation into their land from wherever they settled. These settlers saw how Christianity was transforming the riverine areas in the Niger Delta and decided to introduce the same into their home community.

The Roman Catholic Church, on its own part, was introduced into Nkwerre in 1917 four years after the CMS. While smaller churches also sprang up in private compounds and sitting-rooms, there was no serious co-ordination or organisation until July 1918. That year the first permanent church, the present-day St. Paul's Anglican Church was established at Mbara-Nwakpa. This used to be regarded as a meeting place of evil spirits and evil men, an uninhabitable area called Okoro-Eto which nobody dared make a place of abode.[10] It served as a dumping ground for the community rejects such as the remains of those who died of

---

10   Oral Interview with Kaka Ihegboro, Amaegbu Village, Nkwerre, Imo State, 23rd May, 2017.

infectious diseases. There was a consensus that Mbara Nwakpa be chosen as the permanent location of the church at Nkwerre.[11]

Late Rev. J. Ibeneme was the first Anglican (CMS) Mission priest in Nkwerre following his transfer from Ndi-Izuogu. The Nkwerre community had to pay an outstanding assessment-fee of twelve pounds, ten shillings, to make that move possible. At that point, the headquarters of what was known as Okigwe (Ecclesiastical) District, which covered the present Orlu and Okigwe North Dioceses, was in Nkwerre. Barely a year after the take-off of the St. Paul's CMS Church, Nkwerre, Onusa and Umukor people introduced the Roman Catholic Mission (RCM) from Orlu area. This was in 1919. Chief Anyiam, the Nkwerre warrant chief, was reported to have directed that the church be set on fire using court messengers.[12] He was vexed over not being consulted formally before the establishment of the church. However, after receiving apologies, he gave authority for the Catholic Mission to take-off in 1919 and the Catholic Mission was established.

Other smaller church denominations sprang up in the Nkwerre environs after the establishment of CMS and RCM. In 1936, the First African Church Mission was introduced by Amorji indigenes, pioneered by Mark Achigbu Obiefule, Isaac Iheanetu, James Okparaocha, Thomas Okwara and Matthew Anyaegbu who was the first teacher. These early converts pulled out of St. Barnabas' NDP Church, Omoba on account of double payment of "class-fees" which involved paying at Omoba, a neighbouring community, and at Nkwerre-proper simultaneously (Nnamezie, 2006). The "class-fee" is like a registration fee paid for membership of the Christian-teaching class in churches at the time. It was used for basic development and maintenance of the churches. If indigenes wished to be identified in Nkwerre as members, they were expected to pay fees in Nkwerre. The NDP church metamorphosed

---

[11] From a Magazine of the St. Paul's Church, Nkwerre Centenary Celebrations, 2013.
[12] Oral Interview with Kaka Ihegboro, Amaegbu Village, Nkwerre, Imo State, 23rd May, 2017.

in name and became African Gospel Mission (AGM), but has today stabilised as First African Church Mission. It is assumed that this church appealed to polygamous Nkwerre families because it allowed the marriage of more than one wife.

The AGM was christened *Chochi ama ghere oghe* depicting its support for polygamy, while the Anglican CMS Church which advocated the marriage of only one wife was known as *Amachie*. Daniel Uju Okparaocha, Nzewuba Okparaocha, young Ukegbu and other well to do Nkwerre polygamists including many others, migrated from the CMS Church to African Church. The church soon spread to Owerre Nkworji, Amaigbo, Amandugba and Amike (Nnamezie, 2006). Chief Nwankpa Nwosu became a staunch member of the African Church, so also was Madumere Igbani and Agbarakwe Merenu, Da Nweke of Amaegbu, and many other idol worshippers who were converted. The first church building of African Church was at Amaegbu near Atuma Ashiegbu's residence before moving to its present site (Nnamezie, 2006).

The Seventh Day Adventist Mission (SDA) was also introduced in 1936 through Chief Ezekiel Uzoma Emeto. He was a houseboy to one Pastor Leonard Edmonds, a Briton and manager of SDA schools in Eastern Nigeria, with headquarters at Aba. Nkwerre people showed some enthusiasm for this church, hence the establishment of a branch of the church in Nkwerre. The four villages of Umuoforolo showed much interest and support for the SDA church, so much that they donated a piece of land, Ohia Ofoma where the mission was built. Chief Anyiam Emeghara, the traditional ruler of Nkwerre at that time, gave his approval for this (Seventh Day Adventist Mission) to be established in Nkwerre.

Today, the zonal headquarters of the SDA Mission is located in Nkwerre. Until recently, the teachers were mainly drawn from Ngwa area with Mr. Marcus Nwankwo Anchor of Abayi-Umuocham as the first teacher/evangelist. In 1953, the Assemblies of God Mission was called *Chochi-Dick-Na-Ugoagwu*, because it was introduced by Dick Ibezim and Ugoagwu

Obiajunwa, both of Umugara village. This church was established in Umugara, Nkwerre (Nnamezie, 2006). A few other small church denominations have been introduced to Nkwerre people and each has its group of ardent followers. After the Nigerian civil war, there was an explosion of new churches as several pentecostal churches sprang up with varying degrees of continuity due to private disagreements. The interesting thing is that most of the churches in Orlu zone have their headquarters in Nkwerre, which is recognition of the lighthouse-effect of St. Paul's (CMS) Anglican Mission, Nkwerre.[13]

The rapid influx of various churches into Nkwerre in the first decades of the 20th century may sound like a fairy tale today, but the development marked a traumatic period of social change for the people. It was a period that brought in so many new ideas in terms of behavioural expectations and economic demands on the indigenes. It is against this background of the rapid "Christianisation" of Nkwerre and Orlu area in general, that R.I. Uzoma was born and experienced his early childhood. This is a fact of history that very much shaped his early development both practically and normatively.

Family Roots and Antecedents

RI or "Onyenkuzi", as Reuben Ibekwe came to be popularly addressed, was born in May 1912 as the first son of the late Uzoma Ibekwe and his wife, late Janet Nwannedie Ibekwe. Unknown to Nkwerre people, his birth was to mark the acceleration of an era of social change through advanced formal education as a quick overview of his roots will show. His father, Uzoma Ibekwe, was from Obinuhu village in Nkwerre in the present-day Nkwerre Local Government Area of Imo State. His place of birth, Obinuhu, is one family out of the seven kindreds that make up Umuduruaji, a component part of Umunubo. The seven kindreds are, in no

---

13. From a Magazine of the St. Paul's Church, Nkwerre Centenary Celebrations, 2013.

particular order, Umu-Chigbo, Umu-Okeka, Umu-Ndikam, Umu-Durueshikaodu, Umu-Ike, Umu-Ekwegbara and Umu-Onwunwuru Ogu. In Nkwerre, Obinuhu and Obinocha made up Umu-Duruogharaibe known today in Nkwerre as Obinuhu.[14] In the past, Obinuhu lived in Uhu-Duruaji and Obinocha resided in Uhu-Durueze before they both moved to their present place of habitation.

When RI was born, Obinuhu and Obinocha were regarded as one endogamous village and therefore could not intermarry until the 1950s when the generational bond was considered distant enough to be broken. RI was born into the Enwerem family, one of the four families that make up his kindred known as Umu-Durueshikaodu. This is the eldest among other families that make up Obinuhu and as such holds the Ofo-Ajimiri on behalf of Umuduruaji. Other families in the Eshikaodu kindred are Okehielem, Nwokoro and Nwobi. Eshikaodu is one family out of the seven families that make up Umu-Duruogharaibe. Obinuhu village, as earlier mentioned, is a component part of Obinocha. Both Obinocha and Obinuhu are called Umuduruaji.[15] Umu-Duruaji is one of the villages that make up Nnanato kindred group. Before the advent of Christianity, the Obinuhu families enjoyed the special status of being performers of the Upo Ritual. This meant that they had the right to eat *Upo* before any other village, and any non-Obinuhu individual that violated this rule would be sanctioned. *Upo* is a traditional delicacy prepared with okro, pepper and oil, usually used in eating yam especially during the new yam festival in Nkwerre.

Obinuhu was one of the four children of Nubo known in Nkwerre as Umu-Nubo, other children of Nubo being Amaegbu, Amorji, and Amangwu. Obinuhu was believed to be a more obedient son than Obinocha and this earned him their father's love. Their father, Duruaji, had therefore handed over the staff of

---

14   Oral interview with Nze Edwin Asugha, RI's cousin, Obinuhu Village, Nkwerre, Imo State, 23rd May, 2017.
15   *Ibid.*

authority known as *Aro-Ozo* to Obinuhu and this gave Obinuhu the right to become their father's heir ever since. The grand children occupied the land close to the father's Obi on Ufo-Duruaji or Uhu-Duruaji and this gave them the name Obinuhu. Nubo who was the father of Obinuhu, is one of the children of Okeh, whose three children, Umunubo, Nachi and Gara make up Nnanato. Umunubo, to which R.I. Uzoma's kindred belongs, has been described as the most enterprising village in Nkwerre. Obinuhu, RI's specific kindred within Umunubo, is bounded on the east by Amangwu, on the west by Isiogwugwu, on the north by Umuko and on the south by Obinocha.[16]

At the turn of the 20th century, many Obinuhu indigenes were settled in Aba, Owerri and Mbano as traders and farmers. Reuben Ibekwe's father, Uzoma Ibekwe, as a migrant merchant, lived in Umuopara community of present-day Mbano, as well as in Umunede in present-day Delta State for many years. Reuben Ibekwe's mother, Janet Nwannedie, was from Umunyem village also in Nkwerre. Umunyem village is bounded on the east by Umueze, on the west by Isiogwugwu and on the north by Umuchoke in Amaigbo. The village is made up of three families namely, Okwaraije, Okwaraji and Okwaraekwe and each of them holds *Ofo Umunyem*. Many *Umunyem* people lived and engaged in various businesses in Asa and Ngwa in the past, and they were traditionally well-known for the Nguma festival which entails clearing the Nguma shrine and tying fresh palm fronds on the shrine. The feast is said to be observed on every eighth Orie market day. Umunyem is however, one of the villages that make up Nnanano. Janet Nwannedie was known among her people as *Daa Acha-Ama,* this is because she was a petite beautiful with a fair complexion. She was born into the Olenwanne family in Okoro Duruokwara of Umunyem village and was the only child of her mother. Her father had other children from his other wives

---

16   *Ibid.*

and notable among them are Tasie, the eldest son, Osuala, Nnadi and Oguamanam, all children of Olenwanne (Onyedum, 2000).

Daa Acha-Ama has been perfectly described as a lover of her siblings, generous to a fault and not carried away by the outstanding achievements of her children, especially her son RI. In his maternal home, RI was regarded as *Nwanwa-Ukwu* [17] Obviously, the love for *Daa Acha-Ama* and RI's record-breaking achievement as the first university graduate in the Old Orlu Division, made him indeed *Nwanwa-Ukwu* in Olenwanne's family. RI's maternal kindred respected him so much that they gave a large portion of their land, on his request and persuasion, for the construction of the first girls' secondary school (St. Catherine's Girls Secondary School) in Nkwerre. They also made sure that harvests of his favourite products such as his favourite pawpaw tree in the maternal home remained reserved only for him.[18] His siblings include brothers, Dr. James Uzoma who is recorded in history as the first medical doctor in Nkwerre, Bertram, Johnson, and sisters, Margaret Iheme who married into a family in Umu-oforolo, Susan Ajoku, Beatrice who married into a family in Amorji Ugwu.[19]

Even before western education became the norm in Nkwerre families, the children of Uzoma Ibekwe had since embraced formal education and this made them the first among their equals. After RI, the next son Bertram, followed his older brother to Okrika, and attended the Grammar School (OGS). He later became the first veterinary officer in Nkwerre. Dr. James Uzoma who attended Dennis Memorial Grammar School (DMGS) was one of the first medical doctors in Nkwerre as earlier noted. The next son, Johnson attended Wisconsin University in the USA, and

---

17   Oral Interview with Daa Rhoda Tasie, RI's maternal cousin, Umuokwaraekwe Kindred, Umunyem village, Nkwerre, Imo State on 10th June, 2017.
18   Oral Interview with Daa Augustina Olenwanne, RI's maternal cousin, Umuokwaraekwe Kindred, Umunyem village, Nkwerre, Imo State on 10th June, 2017.
19   Oral Interview with R.I. Uzoma's daughter, Dr. Adaoha Okwuosa (Mrs) in Abuja, 9th December, 2016.

became a university lecturer. The youngest son, Eric Chinyere, studied Accountancy at the University of Nigeria (UNN) and became a banker.[20] RI's uncle, Nze Ezekiel Ihedioha Asugha was known to be the first Nkwerre man to have obtained the first Standard Six Primary School Certificate. He received his primary education in Benin City in the present-day Edo State, and was the first court clerk in Orlu Division. Nze Ezekiel Asugha was therefore, a motivator and role model for the young RI within his extended family, and he played that role in his life time.[21]

RI's father, Uzoma Ibekwe was the only son of his parents and as a result, became engaged to Janet, his first wife, when he was still very young. Though a polygamist, he loved his four wives and had special names for each of them. He named the first wife *Nwannediya* and the second *Omasiridiya*. The special name given to his first wife was inspired by the fact that he was an only son, a status which Nkwerre people refer to as *'Okpuolu"*; hence the wife is regarded as a sister to her husband. RI was the first son of his parents and was raised in a polygamous setting in which love, unity and discipline were the foundation of the child's upbringing. His father, a hard-working tobacco trader died quite early in life when RI was just about 28 years old while his mother died in 1986 when RI was 74years old.[22]

Before Ibekwe Uzoma passed away, he settled and carried out commercial activities in Umuopara, a neighboring community to Ezeoke-Nsu, Ehime Mbano. Ezeoke-Nsu is the community from which RI later chose his bride, as a result of the good relationship his father had with his host community. In particular, RI's father was well-known to the man who later became his father-in-law, Eze Daniel Nwokocha Nwachukwu. RI married Jemimah Chinyere Nwachukwu in January 1942 a few months to his 30th birthday. Jemimah became the first female trained and certificated teacher

---

20   *Ibid.*
21   Oral interview with Nze Edwin Asugha, RI's cousin, Obinuhu Village, Nkwerre, Imo State, 23rd May, 2017.
22   *Ibid.*

in Nkwerre. RI respected education and scholarship immensely, hence, he demonstrated this by choosing a life partner who was exposed to the highest level of formal education available for most women at the time. In this respect, RI again was different from most of his peers. Together, he and his wife had twelve children of whom they were able to raise ten, five sons and five daughters, to adulthood, and all as university graduates.[23]

The first son of R.I. Uzoma and his wife, Anele Nwachukwu, was a consultant paediatric surgeon, while their first daughter, Adaoha Chibuzo, became the first female university graduate and female doctoral degree holder from Nkwerre. The second son, Onuoha Chijioke, had a Masters degree in Petroleum Geology and the third son, Ndubuisi Chigozie graduated with a Bsc in Business Administration and an MBA from South-Eastern University in Washington DC, USA. The next daughter Ugochi Eziaha, qualified with a Bachelor's degree in Zoology from UNN, followed by an Advanced Diploma in Education from the University of Glasgow in Scotland, UK. Her younger sister, Ebere Obioma, studied Medicine at UNEC and was a Senior Registrar, Obstetrics & Gynaecology at ABSU Teaching Hospital. The next son, Okechukwu Madueke, is a Howard University graduate of Political Science and a Masters degree holder, while the last son, Chukwukere Ihetu, was an ABU graduate of Industrial Design. The last two girls, the twins, Ijeuru Okwuchi and Elewechi Uzonna, both graduated in Marketing from the UNN before relocating to the USA to become Masters' degree holders in Nursing and Nursing Administration.[24]

"Daa Jemimah" as RI's wife became popularly known, was the first secretary and subsequently president of the Nkwerre Aborigines' Union (Women's Section) as will be discussed in a subsequent chapter. However, RI declined to take up too many positions in the Nkwerre Aborigines' Union due to his very busy schedule, but he continued to play important support roles and

---

23 Ibid.
24 Oral Interview with R.I. Uzoma's daughters, Dr Adaoha Okwuosa (Mrs) and Mrs Ugochi Onwumere, in Abuja and Enugu respectively, January, 2017.

was consulted constantly, especially on issues concerning relations with government. He influenced members of his Obinuhu kindred with the same academic zeal, making them to have a preference for formal education and white-collar public service jobs, even when their contemporaries were engaging in commerce and business.

R.I. Uzoma clearly set the pace for academic scholarship in Nkwerre and the Nkwerre people in turn saw in him, a worthy ambassador. He was respected and admired by many academics, scholars and public servants from within and outside Nkwerre. He was frequently consulted by these admirers who sought guidance from him either for themselves, or for their children. Many Nkwerre sons and daughters attended schools where he either taught or had connections, and parents who had their children in those institutions never worried about the well-being of their wards. Above all, he was a very humane public servant, especially in relating to requests from people with problems, those in need and also his domestic staff. He largely used his many public service positions to assist Nkwerre citizens and other Nigerians to further their own educational development, and careers.[25]

Childhood and Early Schooling

R.I. Uzoma, who became a self-made icon of education and pillar of the Anglican Church, was opportuned to start his giant academic exploits, from the humble beginnings of a local village school built of mud and raffia, located a short walking distance from his home. He was one of the pioneer pupils of Nkwerre Central SchoolI when it started classes in 1922 (Uzoma, R.I., Undated, Education in Nkwerre). This epoch-making experience, namely primary education, started with the arrival of Mr. Andrew Onubuogu (later

---

25 Oral Interview with Elder Augustine Esonwanne, RI's personal driver for over 10 years, Umukor Village, Nkwerre on 9th June, 2017.

Reverend), an enthusiastic and certificated school master from Ogidi in the present-day Anambra State. He was the first headmaster and the number one teacher of RI in Central School. The establishment of the Nkwerre primary school is one of the major benefits of the arrival of the CMS Mission in Nkwerre.

The Central School, Nkwerre, was originally situated at the site of the present church hall in the St. Paul's Pro-Cathedral compound. It was later moved to its permanent site in Obinocha Umuduruaji in 1927, by which time the school was the first and only Standard Six School in the entire Okigwe Division, an area which covers the present Okigwe and Orlu Zones (Uzoma, R.I., Undated). The result was that boys from quite distant communities such as Ezeoke, Anara, Uli, Ubulu, and Ndizuogu resided in Nkwerre, where they attended school from Monday to Friday. They usually trekked back home after school on Friday to bring raw food for the following week. Obviously, it would have been difficult for small boys from humble homes like RI to attend school in those days if the school had been located far from his home and he had had to do the long trekking to and from school each day (Uzoma, R.I., Undated, "Education in Nkwerre").

In one of his many archival papers, RI recorded that the first set of boys to pass the Government Standard Six Examinations from the school did so in 1927. Two of the Nkwerre boys among them were Daniel Nwosu Onuoha (RI's cousin) and Reuben Ibekwe Uzoma, both from Obinuhu. Before the primary school at Nkwerre became a reality in the early twenties, some notable Nkwerre gentry who had heard of Hope Waddell Training Institute, Calabar, Methodist Uzuakoli and Bonny Government School, had sent their sons to those schools. Others sent their sons to government schools in Aba. Thus, even before Daniel Nwosu Onuoha and Reuben Uzoma passed the Standard Six at the Nkwerre Central School, men like Ezekiel Asugha, late Silas Ihiekwe, late Thompson Ohagwa and the late Timothy Onwukwe had passed Standard Six in institutions outside Nkwerre. Later, Chief Fred Anyiam and the late Barrister U.U. Anyiam passed the same examination from the Government School in Aba and went from there to Government College, Umuahia (Uzoma, R.I., Undated, "Education in Nkwerre"). RI did not see education for evangelism as being sufficient, and his tutors did not expect a child with his potentials to stop at Standard Six. Apart from his extraordinary brilliance, he was very respectful and humble. He did not distance himself from his classmates despite the fact that he excelled over them. This won him the admiration of his classmates and the love of his tutors. He humbly and dutifully participated in manual labour, carrying bricks, stones and mud for the building of Central SchoolI, Nkwerre. [26] It should be recalled that in those days, mud buildings were the norm and most of the seats in the classrooms were constructed with mud. Central School I, Nkwerre was a typical traditional building and the building materials for this school were taken from the immediate environment. They were principally mud, wood, straw, palm fronds and raffia matting with the roof of the school being made out of a mix of straw and mats from raffia palm leaves. Most of these building materials were collected by the students and parishioners who were ever willing to have the first "white man's school" established in Nkwerre. Provisions were made for buildings which were converted to boarding houses to accommodate children from faraway communities.

    The children from neighbouring communities such as Amaigbo, Amaokwara, Owerre Nkworji, Eziama-Obiare, Eziachi, Amucha and others also joined hands with Nkwerre people to fetch materials for the building of this school.[27] One of the foundation students of the school who attended from Amaigbo, was Chief Gabriel Obioha Ofonagoro, the *Ugochinyere* of Amaigbo and *Durueshimbu* of Umuanu, Amaigbo. Among his many children

---

26   Oral interview with Elder Timothy Ikoroha, Nkwerre historian, Umunachi Village, Nkwerre, 28th April, 2017.
27   *Ibid.*

is the eminent historian and former federal minister, Sir Walter Ibekwe Ofonagoro. Chief Gabriel Ofonagoro like a few of the Standard Six candidates was also appointed a pupil-teacher following his brilliant pass at the examination. He was then posted to another CMS primary school in Okohia-Mbano. A few years later, he opted out of the CMS-education system when he was admitted into TTC Ogwashi-Uku, preferring instead to go into a successful career in the colonial commercial and business sector in Port Harcourt.[28]

At that time, RI was one of the youngest of the students who were registered in the primary school. Many of the other students were much older than him, nonetheless they all coexisted peacefully, under the watchful eyes of the church-teachers and missionaries, without any form of bullying by the older ones or any acts of disrespect from the young students. Even as a younger student, RI took it as a great privilege to help out his classmates with any topic they didn't seem to understand. It was great fun for him and his classmates to trek from Umugara to Obinocha, fetching local building materials for the construction of the school. Sometimes, they trekked from distant communities like Amaigbo, Amaopara and other neighbouring communities, sourcing for building materials. The ultimate goal was for them, the prospect of acquiring formal education and speaking *'Bekee''* (English language). One major feature of Central SchoolI, Nkwerre, at this time (1922), was the glaring absence of female students. It took almost another decade before families became convinced of the necessity to send their daughters to primary school, and that decision quickly paid off in Nkwerre.[29]

RI was not raised with a silver-spoon, and his childhood was not a luxurious one. In his lifetime, he often told his children

---

[28] Oral Interview with Chief Walter Ofonagoro, KSC, PhD, Professor of History and former Minister of Information, Lagos, January 2016.

[29] Oral interview with Elder Timothy Ikoroha, Nkwerre historian, Umunachi Village, Nkwerre, 28th April, 2017.

stories of how most mornings, he would wake up early for school without having much to eat for breakfast. He was being raised by his paternal grandmother known as *"Baabá"* who was only a subsistence-farmer and petty trader. He had plenty of affection from her but resources were limited, hence he often stuffed his pockets with palm-kernel nuts which served him as food all day. But in the midst of all odds, he was able to make very good grades because he enjoyed schooling and looked forward to his lessons.[30] When RI passed out with flying colours from primary school in 1927, he was quickly appointed to serve as a pupil-teacher, along with his cousin Daniel Nwosu Onuoha who also passed the Standard Six examinations. It was natural for him to choose a career in teaching, especially when he was soon awarded a scholarship for further training at CMS College, Awka in 1931, after only 2 years as a pupil-teacher. Having established primary and secondary schools, the need for manpower to staff the schools, became a priority for the CMS Mission and educational development in the area of teacher-training, became a prime need.

---

30 Oral Interview with R.I. Uzoma's daughter, Dr. Adaoha Okwuosa (Mrs) in Abuja, 9th December, 2016.

2

MAKING OF AN ICON OF EDUCATION

Higher Education and Training

R.I. Uzoma was one of the early Nigerian leaders who benefitted from the scholarships of the CMS Mission education system throughout their formal education. This made it possible for him to become one of the rare breed of Nigerians who acquired a university degree before the Elliot Commission of 1943 which culminated in the establishment of the University College, Ibadan (UCI) in 1948 (Fafunwa, 1974:158). The University College, Ibadan was started as an affiliate of University of London, making the Elliot Commission a high point in the history of university education in Nigeria.

The UCI remained an affiliate of the University of London until 1962. UCI was saddled with a number of problems at inception ranging from rigid constitutional provisions, poor staffing, and low enrolment to high dropout rate. In April 1959, the Federal Government of Nigeria commissioned the Ashby Commission to advise it on the higher education needs of the country for its first two decades. Before the submission of the report, the Eastern Region government in 1960 established its own university at Nsukka (UNN) (Fafunwa, 1974:167-168). Before this time, RI already had a university degree by 1943, and was recognised as an educationist already serving the country in various capacities from the pre-independence period. He was being rightly described as a beacon of education in Nigeria and was already well-known in the Orlu communities for his achievements as *Onye-Nkuzi*. [31] Other early holders of university degrees from the former Eastern Region were men like Alvan Ikoku, E.I. Oli, Akanu Ibiam, Eyo Ita and F.O. Iheanacho.

The opening of the first set of universities in Nigeria from 1958 marked a new phase in tertiary education as more and more graduates followed. The British colonialists had instituted a formal education system in Nigeria which had emphasis on reading, writing and arithmetic, followed by teaching as the main profession with only a few joining the white-collar professions. The first institution set up to train teachers opened in 1896, when the Church Missionary Society (CMS), now the Church of Nigeria (Anglican Communion) established St. Andrew's Teachers' College in Oyo. This improved the quality of teachers who hitherto had been mainly Standard Six Certificate holders.

After 1896, many more TTC's were started. Baptist Training College, Ogbomosho opened as early as 1897, followed by St. Paul's Training College, Awka in 1904. In 1905, Oron saw the start of the Oron Training Institute, just as Ibadan got Wesleyan Training Institute in 1928. In 1929, St. Charles Training College, Onitsha was established. Grade III teachers were subsequently produced, following the establishment of these first Teachers' Colleges (Fafunwa, 1974:211).

In Northern Nigeria, the colonial government was directly involved in the funding and managing of their teachers colleges (Fafunwa, 1974:211-214). Teachers Training College, Katsina and Toro Teachers Training College, founded in the same period, are clear examples. Teaching was clearly the dominant profession for educated citizens of colonial Nigeria, at least for the opening of their working careers.

---

31 Oral interview with Nze Edwin Asugha, RI's cousin in Obinuhu Village, Nkwerre, 24th March, 2016.

St Paul's College, Awka 1931-1935, 1939 - 1943

R.I. Uzoma's admission into the CMS Teachers Training College, known then as Awka College, was for what became equivalent to secondary education for him. It followed after a couple of years of his deployment as a Pupil Teacher following his brilliant pass in the Standard Six Certificate as the first pupil to do so at the first attempt in Nkwerre. In 1988, RI wrote as follows:

> I went to Awka Teachers Training College after serving as a Pupil Teacher in 1931. The selection committee of the Diocese on the Niger selected me, I was top on the entrance examination list, and even though many thought I was too young, the expatriate principal of the college, the Rev. A.M. Gelsthorpe and a few others convinced the committee that it was the younger people like me that the college wanted because we were going to start the four-year course instead of the former three-year course. (Uzoma, R.I., 1988)

RI's admission into the Awka TTC before the age of 20 was a masterstroke of fate because it served as his springboard to other accelerated professional qualifications. He was encouraged by the confidence that the expatriate principal had in him to aspire beyond the Higher Elementary Teachers' Certificate which was the end-goal of the four-year programme at the college. While only in his second year at the college, the principal in 1932 entered RI along with a few other bright trainees, for the Cambridge Junior School Certificate Examination and arranged for private lessons in Latin and Mathematics for them (Uzoma, R.I. 1988). RI passed the examination and was poised for the Bachelor of Arts Degree in Geography which he later easily obtained when he returned to Awka College as a tutor in 1939 after Achimota College.

RI wrote that in those days, there was no university in Nigeria and the only graduate from the Eastern part of the country was Dr. Alvan Ikoku from Arochukwu. One could obtain a degree within Nigeria only by studying for the London Matriculation Examination which was the precursor to a Bachelor of Arts Degree. Dr. Alvan

Ikoku followed by Dr. Enoch Oli, were the first gentlemen from the Igbo-speaking part of Nigeria to obtain London University degrees without going through any tertiary institution (Uzoma, R.I., 1989).

St. Paul's College, Awka, commonly referred to as Awka College but which later became St. Paul's University College, was established in 1904 in Awka, present-day Anambra State. The historical origins of the famous Awka College lie in the CMS missionary efforts towards the training of church workers, teachers and clerics in the Niger Mission Area at the turn of the 20th century. A training institution for catechists and school teachers was first opened in Asaba in 1896, and then moved to Onitsha when that town became the seat of the Niger Mission, before finally being permanently relocated to Awka in 1904. Awka College soon came to be regarded as the "power-house" of the Niger Mission Group of Dioceses of the Anglican Church (Nwankiti, 1998:29-30).

Strategically, Awka is located midway between two major cities in Northern Igboland, Onitsha and Enugu which has informed its choice as an administrative centre for the colonial authorities and today as a base for the Anambra State Government. According to Chinua Achebe, Awka has a certain kind of aura about it, because it was the place of the blacksmiths that created implements which made agriculture possible. Awka is one of the oldest settlements in Igboland established at the centre of the Nri civilisation which produced the earliest documented bronze works in sub-Saharan Africa around 800 AD, and was the cradle of Igbo civilisation (Basden, 1966:30). The earliest settlers of Awka were the *ifiteana* which translates into people who sprouted from the earth. They were farmers, hunters, and skilled iron workers, an occupation Nkwerre people shared with them. Many have argued that blacksmithing started in Nkwerre but because of lack of written sources to back it up, Nkwerre lost that position in historical analysis to Awka. The early settlers lived on the banks of the

Ogwugwu stream in what is now known as Nkwelle ward of Awka (Basden, 1966).

The deity of the *Ifiteana* was known as *Okika-na-ube* or the god pre-eminent with the spear, and the *Ifiteana* were known as *Umu-Okanube* or "worshippers of Okanube", which eventually became shortened to Umu-Oka and eventually Oka, and its *anglicised* version "Awka". In ancient times, Awka was populated by elephants with a section of the town named *Ama-enyi* (haunt of elephants) and a pond, *Iyi-Enyi* which was the elephant's watering hole. The elephants were hunted for their prized ivory tusks (*okike*) which was kept as a symbol to the god, *Okanube,* in every Awka home, with hunting-medicine stored in the hollow of the tusk.

Awka lies below 300 metres above sea-level in a valley on the plains of the Mamu River. Two ridges both lying in a North-South direction form the major topographical features of the area. The ridges reach the highest point at Agulu just outside today's Awka Capital Territory. The geography of Awka obviously made it a very convenient choice for the establishment of the Anglican Teachers' Training College in 1904 after it was moved from Onitsha. The college assumed responsibility not just for training classroom teachers only, but also for producing clergy-support staff known as catechists and seasoned tutors who later metamorphosed into academic administrators like RI (Nwankiti, 1996:30; Uzoma, R.I., 1991).

It is noteworthy that Awka College for RI, was also the platform on which he met and became friends with a good number of other CMS-trained pillars of education in the then Eastern Region. The educational profile and careers of these notable pioneers closely mirrored each others, both in terms of institutions attended, and of positions subsequently held. In Awka College, RI's roommate and close friend was Samuel Iyasele Okediadi from Aboh in present-day Delta State, who later married Eunice Chinelo Onyeabo, one of the daughters of Rt. Rev. (Bishop) Alphonso Chukwuma Onyeabo, the first Igbo Bishop of the Anglican Church. Mr. and Mrs. Okediadi later became parents to, among others, Nwadinafor Chinyelu de Souza (nee Okediadi) an ace conference interpreter, international civil servant and expert in mediation and workplace conflict management. Like RI, Mr. Okediadi subsequently furthered his education abroad under CMS sponsorship at King's College, London.[32]

From 1939 to 1943 after Achimota College, R.I. Uzoma returned to Awka College as a tutor in Geography, Principles and Method of Education, English, ChurchHistory, and Mathematics. At the same time, he was the principal of the Awka College Practising School, the training ground for future teachers in the system. By his second coming to Awka College, RI had earned both the Cambridge School Certificate in 1938 and the London Intermediate Bachelors Degree (Intermediate BA) in 1939 from Achimota College. It was during this second tenure at Awka that RI worked with his friend, Jonathan Uwakwe Ekeocha of Ubomiri, Mbaitoli in present-day Imo State. Before RI, Sir Ekeocha had attended Achimota College earlier from 1935-1937 before being deployed to Awka College as a tutor in 1938. Prior to Achimota, he was a foundation student and later tutor at DMGS for some years from 1925. Sir Ekeocha was father to, among others, Mrs. Ijeoma Adaoha Eronini mni (nee Ekeocha), who became the first female head of the Civil Service of Imo State, from 1999 to 2003. She also chaired the Board of the National Centre for Women Development from 2005 to 2006 before representing Imo and Abia States as Federal Civil Service Commissioner from 2007 to 2012. The Ekeocha and R.I. Uzoma families were so close, that Sir Ekeocha named his first daughter Adaoha, after the first daughter of RI.[33]

---

32   Oral Interview with Nwadia de Souza (nee Okediadi), in London, September 2016.
33   Oral Interview with Ijeoma Eronini (nee Ekeocha), daughter of Jonathan Ekeocha, in Abuja, May 2016 and November 2017.

Another Awka College graduate whose path crossed with that of R.I. Uzoma was Sir. E.C. Ezekwesili, foundation principal of St. Augustine's Grammar School (SAGS), Nkwerre from 1949 to 1958. Sir E.C. Ezekwesili, who obtained a Diploma in Education from the University of London in 1948, had also attended the DMGS for three years from 1929 before doing two years at Awka College from 1934 to 1936. He later served the CMS Mission as Education Secretary and Manager of Schools in the Owerri Diocese from 1959 to 1969, before he was replaced by R.I. Uzoma in that position in 1969. From 1969, E.C. Ezekwesili went on to become principal of his alma-mater, the Awka College, which is today's St Paul's University in Awka, Anambra State (Animalu & Onwurah, 1997:19-20).

Mr. E. O. Enemuo was another notable contemporary of RI, who was also a CMS-sponsored student of Achimota College in the late 1930s. He later served the CMS Mission also as Education Secretary of the Niger Diocese in the 1960s at the headquarters in Onitsha. Within that period, RI was occupying the same position of Education Secretary in the Delta Diocese and later in Owerri Diocese. This was indeed the golden age of teaching when the profession was held in high esteem and teachers were a proud army of friends and colleagues across the land, contrary to what the situation has become today. The criss-crossing of career paths of these pioneer graduates of the early CMS institutions and sponsorship, underscored the huge impact of the Anglican Mission as voluntary agencies' power house for future leaders of the Eastern Region. In several instances, the careers of these pioneers also ventured into the government service, thus illustrating how much the late colonial administration and immediate post-independence government depended on the voluntary agencies for manpower.

Achimota College, Ghana 1937-1939

R.I. Uzoma graduated with flying colours in the Higher Elementary Teaching Certificate from Awka College in 1934. After one year as tutor at DMGS in 1936, he was sent on a CMS scholarship to Achimota College in the former Gold Coast for further studies. The Achimota College was founded in Achimota, Gold Coast (now Ghana) in 1924 by Dr. James Emman Kwegyir Aggrey, Rev. Alexander Garden Fraser and Sir Gordon Guggisberg, the British governor of the Gold Coast (1919-1927). The school was an elite secondary school based on the British model of public education. Governor Guggisberg urged local Gold Coast residents to create the institution to provide teacher-training, technical-training, and secondary-schooling for the colony. The governor's request came after a committee he appointed in 1920 to closely examine educational needs in the Gold Coast, recommended the establishment of a secondary boarding school for boys. The committee also recommended its location in the coastal town of Achimota, about ten miles from Accra, the capital of the Gold Coast. Born and raised in the Gold Coast Colony, Dr. Aggrey served as a teacher and secretary of the Aborigines Rights Protection Society before going on to the United States where he earned a Bachelor of Arts at Livingstone College, a small African American institution in North Carolina, and subsequently, a Ph.D. from Columbia University (Williams, 1962).

Eager to have the involvement of Dr. Aggrey in founding Achimota, Governor Guggisberg acceded to all three conditions set forth by Dr. Aggrey namely, that African members of staff should occupy an equal position to Europeans, that appointments would be at the discretion of the principal rather than the colonial government, and that the school would teach children as young as six. Even though Guggisberg's committee recommended that girls not be admitted, Dr. Aggrey and Rev. A. G. Fraser stipulated that Achimota should be co-educational (Williams, 1962). In the spirit of these recommendations, Achimota College hired indigenous staff even before it had buildings, so that teachers could study the local languages, establish local interest, and gain experience teaching in Gold Coast schools. On January 28, 1927, Achimota was formally opened with 120 students. The college was government-funded and in a unique break from missionary-education tradition, it was interdenominational, with students and staff practicing their own denomination of Christianity. Additionally, attending religious services was optional. In 1948, Achimota College became three separate institutions, the University College of the Gold Coast (now the University of Ghana), the Achimota Teachers' Training College, and Achimota School. Achimota College proper still operates today as Achimota School under the oversight of the Ghana Education Service, providing a senior high school education to young women and men (Williams, 1962).

The school has educated many African leaders including Kwame Nkrumah, the father of African nationalism, Edward Akufo-Addo, Jerry John Rawlings, and John Evans Atta Mills, all of whom are former heads of state of Ghana. Former president of Ghana, John Dramani Mahama had his primary education there, while former prime minister, Dr. Kofi Abrefa Busia, was a teacher at Achimota. Also included in Achimota's list of African heads of state, are former Zimbabwean president, Robert Mugabe, and Sir Dawda Jawara, first head of state of The Gambia (Daniel, 1996:649-656). An alumnus or alumna of Achimota is known as an "Akora".

Achimota College, which was originally known as the Prince of Wales College and School, occupies more than two square miles (525 hectares) of prime real estate in the middle of the Achimota Forest Reserve in the Accra Metropolitan Area. The school's colonial architecture and planned landscape blends with its wooded surroundings to make the campus conducive for academic enterprise (Daniel, 1996, 649–656). It is therefore not surprising that the long list of former heads of state is accompanied by an Africa-wide network of Old Boys of Achimota College. This is a large body of notable African leaders and professionals, including politicians, academics, scientists, doctors, lawyers, engineers, architects, diplomat, computer scientists, agriculturalists, accountants, artists, business leaders and educators, one of whom was R.I. Uzoma of Nigeria.

Within his first year at Achimota College, R.I. Uzoma passed the Cambridge School Certificate Examination in Division One, in the same year, earning him an exemption from what was known at the time as the London Matriculation. It is noteworthy that he won the form prize for Best Student of the Year, and prizes in five subjects including Mathematics and Latin. In 1938, he was accelerated into the second year of the London Intermediate Bachelors Degree (Intermediate B.A.) class, and passed out successfully in 1939. In 1943, he became the first university graduate from the Old Orlu Province on earning the full degree following his return home at the outbreak of the second world war in 1939.

Institute of Education, University of London, 1946-1947

In August 1946, R.I. Uzoma left for the United Kingdom to study for a one year Post-graduate Diploma in Education at the Institute for Education of the University of London. He achieved this through a CMS scholarship. At this time, he had to leave his young family of a pregnant wife and two toddlers. Before leaving, he made an arrangement to relocate his young family from Okrika to Elelenwa which was not too distant, where his wife Jemimah would be a teacher at the CMS Archdeacon Crowder Memorial Girl's Secondary School until his return. Having had secondary education at Queens College, Lagos, along with two years of teaching experience from St. Bartholomew's Primary School Enugu, Jemimah did not have to return to the home community to be idle for the one year that her husband would be away in the United Kingdom.

R.I. Uzoma's course of studies at the Institute of Education, University of London was on the Theory and Practice of Education, with special reference to the Colonial Dependencies. In July 1947, he was examined in the following subjects:[34]

i. The Principles of Education
ii. Educational Psychology
iii. The Present Educational System
iv. Comparative Education and Administration
v. Special Method
vi. The Study of Society: An Introduction to Social Anthropology
vii. Tropical Hygiene

The course on the Principles of Teaching was centered on Special Methods for Teaching of English as a Foreign Language, Geography, New Media Mathematics, Teaching the Three Rs in Primary School, and Special Method for Tropical Areas. He passed all his examinations with flying colours. All these were outlined in the Diploma Certificate that he was issued at the end of the course. In that document, the director of the institute, G.M. Jeffrey had this to say about RI in the section for Remarks:

> Mr. Uzoma is a good teacher, possessing a pleasant disposition, exhibiting consistency of effort in preparation, and a thoughtful attitude towards his exposition and material. He gets on well with pupils and staff and is constructive in his attitude towards criticism. His participation in discussion is shrewd, timely and reasonable. His written work is marked by clarity of expression, carefulness and selection of facts and a sound exercise of powers of judgment. Mr. Uzoma has made excellent use of his opportunities and should carry back to Nigeria a widened experience and increased capacity for the successful direction of his school.[35]

---

34 Taken from Diploma in Education Certificate issued to R.I. Uzoma, by the University of London, Institute of Education, September 1947; R.I. Uzoma Archives: See Appendix 19.
35 Ibid.

Soon after his arrival at the University of London, in November 1946, R.I. Uzoma was elected as a Fellow Royal of the Geographical Society (FRGS), and this constituted a huge incentive for him. In his constant search for academic improvement in the one year of Postgraduate Diploma Studies, R.I. Uzoma made different efforts to add to his knowledge and qualifications. From his modest students' accommodation at 5, Lidlington Place, London NWl in June 1947, he applied to be registered as an external student for the degree of Master of Arts (M.A.). The application was however accepted by 23rd September 1947, at which time he was already back in Nigeria. It was to be a 3-year course that would end in 1950. It was a great disappointment to RI that he was unable to complete this programme due to his extensive duties as General Manager of schools for Niger Delta Diocese, a position which he took up in order to continue to serve his sponsors, the CMS Mission, immediately he returned from the United Kingdom in early 1948.

While at the University of London, he also applied in November 1946 to be registered as a special user of the private library of the Royal Empire Society then located at the Northumberland Avenue, London WC2. It was a library that did not lend out books but RI received the necessary support in terms of materials. He also communicated with and received positive response from the World Association for Adult Education, looking for materials on adult education from other parts of the world such as India and Latin America which could benefit his comparative studies of adult education.[36] He was also engaged as one of the external examiners for Igbo language examination at the School of Oriental and African Studies of the University of London. 1946 and 1947 were indeed quite intensive for RI, a period in which he sharpened his academic interests and his appetite for research and writing.

---

36 See the correspondences to R.I. Uzoma from the World Association for Adult Education, 35 Woodsfield Avenue, Ealing, London W5, 19th and 23rd June 1947; R.I. Uzoma Archives. See Appendix 52.

This led to the successful publication of his first two academic works. The first one titled "Adult Literacy Work at Okrika in the Delta of the Niger" was published in 1948 in *Overseas Education,* Volume 19(4) pages 737-741. This paper was the outcome of an adult literacy project which R.I. Uzoma personally executed while he was principal of the Okrika Grammar School from 1944 to 1946. The second work titled "Universal Schooling in Ngwa Clan of Aba Division" was published in 1952, also in *Overseas Education,* Volume 23(2), pages 234-236. By that date, R.I. Uzoma was listed as General Manager and Supervisor of Anglican Schools on the publications. He had already returned home to Nigeria and moved on to the Eastern Regional Assembly, to be appointed Minister for Education for the Eastern Region.

Teacher and Educational Administrator

Onye-Nkuzi, Pupil Teacher, School Master

After two years at Achimota College, R.I. Uzoma naturally went home to serve the CMS system that had so generously sponsored all of his education. He did not go into government service. Rather, while serving the CMS system, he continued to improve his educational qualifications, thus gaining for himself a reputation among peers as a "bookworm". However, he remained at heart, an *Onye-Nkuzi* (a teacher) and later an administrator of schools.

RI cut his teeth in the teaching profession as a young pupil teacher first at St. Paul's Nkwerre CMS Central School from February 1928 to December 1928, his primary school alma mater and then at St. Paul's Ezeoke-Nsu CMS Central School, in present-day Ehime-Mbano in Imo State from January 1st 1929 to December 31st 1929. The postings were usually tenured to coincide with the school year from January to December of the year. These dates were meticulously documented in RI's record of service on his retirement. In an undated handwritten paper by RI roughly sometime in the 1970s and titled "Education in Nkwerre

Town", RI explained how he became a pupil teacher so early in life in the following words,

> The normal thing in those days for a boy, who passed Standard Six, was either to take up a job with the Government, a firm, or to be appointed a pupil teacher by the Church. Both Chief R.I. Uzoma and Nze D.I. Onuoha started as pupil teachers after passing Standard Six, and entered the famous Awka College in 1931 to train as teachers. They were the first to obtain any approved qualification higher than Standard Six. That was in 1934 when they passed the Teacher's Higher Elementary Certificate exam. From then the floodgate for Nkwerre boys and girls to obtain higher qualifications followed (Uzoma, R.I., Undated: *Education in Nkwerre*).

The posting to Ezeoke as a C-Teacher, which was the same as pupil teacher, was a uniquely significant experience for RI. He was an adolescent, so modest in height that he had to be supported with a raised platform to enable him write effectively on the chalk board.[37] RI was at Ezeoke Central School for a two-year period, yet the impact on his life was far-reaching and significant. Within that brief period, he became close to the family of the powerful warrant chief, Eze Nwachukwu Nwadigo on whose land the school was located. No one could have guessed that the young confident pupil teacher, who endeared himself to the school community, had crossed the path of the family which would become his future kith and kin through marriage, as a subsequent chapter will show. From Ezeoke, he was admitted into Awka College for the four-year programme towards the Higher Elementary School Certificate. It was directly from Awka College that RI was sent to Ekwulobia Central School (ECS) in Aguata as second master. ECS Ekwulobia as it was popularly known, was one of the earliest primary schools opened by the CMS in present-day Anambra State. At this stage in the early development of voluntary agency schools, the frequent movement of the few capable trained hands in the CMS school

---
37 Oral Interview with Mama Dinah Erinne, a former teacher at Ezeoke Central School and a family friend of the Nwachukwu and R.I. Uzoma families.

system was normal, as careers continued to grow with additional qualifications and new postings. At Ekwulobia, RI approached his duties with a great deal of enthusiasm because it was his first deployment as a certificated teacher.

As the only primary school of note in the administrative division at the time, the Ekwulobia school attracted pupils from a wide network of neighbouring communities which included Nanka, Ugah, and Oko. Teaching at ECS brought RI into contact with some of the brightest future stars who were indigenes of today's Anambra State, and who became giants in academics and other fields. Among these were James Okoye Chukwuka Ezeilo from Nanka, a 1953 first class graduate of the University of London, who became the first professor of mathematics in Nigeria, Emeritus Professor and former Vice-Chancellor of UNN.[38] Another notable pupil of RI was Bertram Ikedinachukwu Okpala from Ugah who rose to become a professor of zoological sciences and a former Dean of the Faculty of Biological Sciences, also at UNN. Ekwulobia was therefore a brief but impactful tenure, for RI had to leave in 1937 for Achimota College in the Gold Coast on CMS scholarship.

Tutor, Dennis Memorial Grammar School (DMGS), Onitsha, 1936

In 1936, RI was deployed from Ekwulobia to the famous Dennis Memorial Grammar School (DMGS) as a tutor. His students eulogised him and remember his strong expertise in the dissemination of knowledge, especially his ability to make them do a quick sketch of the world map in Geography. His stay at DMGS was again short, lasting from January to December of that year, but it was memorable because 1936 became the year for one of the best results that the school recorded in the Senior Cambridge

---

38 Oral Interview with Dr Adaoha Okwuosa, daughter of R.I. Uzoma, in Abuja, on 9th December 2016. Dr Okwuosa was a lecturer at UNN in the tenure of Prof J.O.C. Ezeilo.

Certificate Examinations. That year's set became known as the "Glorious Set of 1936". R.I. Uzoma joined the ranks of proud teachers in a school that already developed a remarkable history in less than a decade from 1925.

The two factors which stimulated the founding of the Dennis Memorial Grammar School were the presence of the Holy Ghost Fathers at Onitsha, and the thirst of the Igbo people for education. Although the Church Missionary Society began its activities at Onitsha in 1857, it took her sixty-eight years to build the first grammar school in Igboland. This long delay indicated that it was not the initial intention of the early missionaries to introduce grammar school education into Igboland. Their first aim was to spread the gospel to the people, and they at first, did not believe that secondary education was necessary for the propagation of Christianity (Ekechi, 1972: 27).

Bishop Crowther began his evangelisation work in the Niger Mission with yeomen who had little or no formal education, but were farmers, carpenters, bricklayers, shoemakers, messengers and stewards on board ships. Therefore, such pioneers laid emphasis on vernacular-based education. They were satisfied with bush-schools and junior elementary schools, where vernacular could be the medium of instruction. This policy naturally led to the production of vernacular agents, catechists and clergymen, to whom the teaching of English language and secular subjects was strange (Ekechi, 1972: 27).

The arrival of the Holy Ghost Fathers, a Roman Catholic Church missionary organisation at Onitsha, was ultimately to change the situation. These fathers opened schools at Onitsha in which the English language became the medium for their instruction. The products of their schools very easily secured jobs in the British government offices and in the commercial houses. When the local people realised the economic advantages of literacy in the English language, the CMS Mission also clamoured for it. In January 25, 1925, the Dennis Memorial Grammar School (DMGS) was established. A light in the educational development in Igboland was lit by the Church Missionary Society which since then has never been quenched. The first intake consisted of nineteen boarders and forty-six day students. Most of the students came from Onitsha and the surrounding towns where the missionaries had worked for over half a century, and where people had begun to appreciate the economic value of "English education".

In one of the papers in RI's archives, he wrote that one foundation student of DMGS was an Nkwerre youth named Ezekiel Emeanuru, younger brother of a certain Mr. Uzoukwu Emeanuru who was his guardian and sponsor. This young man unfortunately, died in the same 1925 that the school was opened. According to reports about his illness, it was believed that his death was as a result of malaria, a disease feared in those days because of inadequate access to a cure. His relations and people from his community attributed his death to foul play and it created fear and panic. The result was that for some years after the death of Ezekiel Emeanuru, no family from the Nkwerre area allowed their son to sit for the entrance examination into DMGS Onitsha or for any other secondary school for that matter, until several years later. (Uzoma, R.I. Undated: Education in Nkwerre). However, students from other parts of the Igbo territory continued to attend the school.

Others among the first set of DMGS students were Harford Anierobi (retired senior administrative officer), Isaac Iweka (the distinguished pioneer civil engineer, who later became the Igwe of Obosi), Wilfred Mbonu (retired Rev. Canon of the Anglican Church) Isaac Nwangwu (retired civil servant), Alfred Ogbolu (a retired civil servant), Jonathan Uwakwe Ekeocha (a retired educationist), and Walter Onubogu (a well known medical practitioner). The foundation staff comprised the principal, the Rev. H. Taylor, and three Africans who were the late Mr. Mark. Anyaegbuna, Mr. Samuel Achebe, who retired later as a civil servant, and the renowned Venerable. Dr. B.C.E. Nwosu, a retired Archdeacon of Onitsha (Otonti, 1976:69-92).

The curriculum was initially modelled after that of the English grammar school of the period, and was essentially designed to provide a literary type of education. It was meant to produce highly accomplished elites who would be expected to perform their professional jobs efficiently and become effective leaders. The DMGS curriculum was divided into two sections; first was the compulsory subjects; Arithmetic, Religious Instruction, English Literature and English Language (Composition, Dictation, Reading and Colloquial English). The secondary subjects were: Algebra, Geometry, Geography, History, Drawing, Science, Hygiene and Latin (Otonti, 1976:69-92). Of the compulsory courses, RI taught Arithmetic and English Language, and in the secondary category, he was what one of his students referred to as "a Geography expert" while also teaching Latin.

For the first ten years of her history, with this curriculum, DMGS provided educated personnel for the ever-increasing activities of the Anglican Church and the colonial government, following the "pacification" of the hinterland of Southern Nigeria in the 1930s. These personnel were in great demand and up to 1935, most of the pupils left after secondary year two, to take up appointment in government departments and mercantile houses or as teachers in schools. Teaching this curriculum was not easy because teachers were not readily available. The chief source of the supply of staff for the school was Awka (C.M.S.) Training College, the institution in which RI was trained.

The first set of pioneer staff, from 1925 to 1929, did not attend secondary school and had not studied any secondary school subjects, yet they were called upon to teach them. These were highly motivated pioneers who, while their companions slept, worked hard in the night. They were devoted and gave their best to raise the standard of their pupils above their own. Like the biblical John the Baptist, they were prepared to decrease in order to make their pupils increase. The first Nigerian public examination by pupils of the school was an entrance examination into the School of Agriculture in 1926. Two candidates, Louis Asika and T. Weekes were successful. Unfortunately, Weekes died soon after from drowning, the first bereavement suffered by the school. By the end of this decade, the DMGS had laid a solid academic foundation and set the pattern for its future successes in examinations (Otonti, 1976:69-92).

Reporting to the 1936 Synod of the Diocese on the Niger on the 1935 examinations, the principal, the Rev. C. A. Forster, recounted that 34 boys passed the Cambridge Junior, giving the largest number of passes in Nigeria: 7 boys passed the Lower Middle II, 2 boys gained scholarships to King's College, Lagos: 1 boy gained a scholarship for the new scholarship course at the Higher College, Yaba and 2 boys passed the qualifying examination for the African technical staff of the P.W.D. (Public Works Department). In spite of the diverse careers which DMGS graduates later followed, during this first decade of the school, great care was taken to build its training on a solid religious and moral foundation. To this end, religious worship was insisted upon.[39]

The first principal of DMGS was Rev. A. M. Gelsthorpe (November 1925 - Feb.1926), who later went on to open OGS, followed by Mr. R.E. Walter (February 1926-April 1927), Mr. E.I. Ohia (April – July 1927), Rev. S.H. Chelds (April-November 1933) and Rev. C. J. Patterson in 1935. Other members of staff include Messrs R. D. Ogori, B. Onwuchekwa, H. L. O. Okechukwu, Albert Okechukwu, C. A. Jos Omonegbuzia, G.U. Njoku, S. C. Anadu, Andrew C. Okocha, Mbonu Ojike, Walter Anionwu, Jonathan Ekeocha, Ernest Okeondarue and E. R. D. Jaja. A few of the staff were pioneer students, for example Jonathan Ekeocha.

R.I. Uzoma became a tutor in DMGS during the period described as the Vintage Age which followed immediately after the school's

---

39 See "A Brief History of Dennis Memorial Grammar School" in DMGS Golden Jubilee Anniversary Magazine, October 1975.

10th anniversary in 1935. This period in the history of DMGS which covering about thirty years or a generation, is regarded as the most memorable and important part of her history. Each of the years in that period constituted a significant landmark in the history of the school. In 1936, DMGS presented her first set of candidates for the Cambridge (Overseas) School Certificate Examinations. There were twelve candidates. Twelve passed, eight were exempted from the London Matriculation. This was another impressive and encouraging record, and sure evidence that a solid foundation had been laid in the pioneering period. It also clearly demonstrated that among the few grammar schools in Nigeria, DMGS had taken a pride of place.[40]

The 1936 set for the Cambridge Examinations became known as the "Glorious Set". Among the candidates who set this enviable record was Kenneth Dike, who was the first African Vice-Chancellor of the first Nigerian university, and later Andrew W. Mellon, Professor of African History at the celebrated American University, Harvard. Edmund Ekwulugo, a retired chief magistrate, C. O. Odiakosa, well known agriculturist, Alfred Bovi, a retired educationist, Theophilus R. Yirenki, a Ghanaian pharmacist, and Daniel Onwuegbuzia, a retired customs officer,[41] were also candidates. All were tutored by R.I. Uzoma.

With the improved trend in educational development in the 1930s, the DMGS took the major decision to introduce science subjects into its curriculum. The first, Laboratory Sciences, was designed by Dr. E. H. Duckworth, a government inspector of science education. Then in 1935, Dr. J. B. Miles, a specialist in organic chemistry, joined the staff as the science master and the study of science subjects began in earnest. Under his successors, Rev. F. E. Drinkwater, Mr. J. W. L. Thompson and Mr. D.C. Erinne, assisted by Messrs Nathaniel Ohaeri, Clement Ikejo, Sammy Ogwo and former students that had already graduated, sciences courses gained momentum.[42]

---

40   Ibid
41   Ibid
42   Ibid

Making of an Icon of Education

The founding fathers of DMGS had several objectives. One of them was to build an institution which would help to produce the manpower required by an emerging independent Nigeria, the fact that DMGS was a CMS-Mission school notwithstanding. In that regard, DMGS easily became one of the leading institutions that contributed to the critical manpower required by a developing Nigeria from the early thirties. DMGS produced a large number of civil servants, workers in the commercial houses, teachers in the primary schools and technicians who have helped to build up this country. Many distinguished medical and legal practitioners, educationists, administrators, army officers, engineers and pharmacists, owe their secondary school career to DMGS. Among the Vice-Chancellors of federal universities of Nigeria as at 2017, the time of writing, DMGS produced two, namely the Vice-Chancellors of the University of Nigeria, Nzukka and the University of Jos. DMGS has also produced some leading clergymen, among whom are three Anglican Bishops, namely Bishop Benjamin Nwankiti, formerly of Owerri Diocese, who was at DMGS from 1943-1946, Bishop Gideon Otubelu of Enugu Diocese, a student of DMGS from 1943-1947, and Bishop James Onyemelukwe of the Niger Diocese. Of no less significance is the large number of old boys who have become leaders of their churches as priests, lay readers, members of parochial committees, and in other significant church roles.

DMGS has also produced some of the distinguished 'firsts' of Nigeria. Examples are Professor K.O. Dike, the first Nigerian professor of History, who was directly tutored by RI. The first Nigerian professor of Mathematics, Professor J.O.C. Ezeilo, whom RI also taught at the primary school level at Ekwulobia Central School, and the first Igbo civil engineer who was also the second in Nigeria, and others. That civil engineer was Isaac Iweka, the pioneer "Dengramite" who became Igwe of Obosi. He was sponsored by his own father and not by Mission scholarship, to study at Imperial College, London in the late 1930s. Among his many accomplished children is a daughter, Princess Gloria Nwoyibo Iweka, OON, who served the Federal Government of Nigeria as Senior Special Assistant to two Heads of State, General Olusegun Obasanjo and Musa Yar'Adua, from 2000 to 2008.[43]

It is important to note that from 1925, DMGS served as a flag-bearer in opening the way for more boy's secondary schools in the Igbo-speaking territory of Eastern Nigeria. Hope Waddell Institute which is much older than DMGS is located in Calabar. More secondary schools followed suit in the East after DMGS, in the goal of providing educated manpower for emerging Nigeria. One example is the Methodist Boys College, Uzuakoli, later known as Methodist Boys High School. This institution was founded by the CMS missionaries (Methodist group) first as an Institute in 1923, and converted into a full Boys College in 1931. The founding missionaries were led by Rev. Herbert Lewis, with Octavia Williams as first principal. Even as an institute, the school succeeded in producing many notable leaders. Among its prominent graduates who went into public service or church roles, were Dr M.I. Okpara, Former Premier of the Eastern Region, Sir Udo Udoma, the eminent jurist, Sunday Mbang, prelate of the Methodist Church and Clement Isong, a former governor of the Central Bank of Nigeria.

A prominent Uzuakoli graduate of the 1930s who equally dominated, but in the world of business was Chief James Chukwuma Okeke, the *Ogbunechendo* Nnewi, the first Nigerian Railway contractor East of the Niger and prime National Council of Nigeria and the Cameroons (NCNC) financier in his political days.[44] His daughter, Ebele Okeke, CFR is the first female civil engineer in Nigeria, and also the first female Head of Civil Service of the Federation. She is also currently the Pro-Chancellor of Gregory University, Uturu in Abia State.

---

43 Oral Interview with Princess Gloria Nwoyibo Iweka, daughter of Igwe Isaac Iweka, a foundation student of DMGS

44 Oral Interview with Engr. Ebele O. Okeke, CFR, daughter of Chief J.C. Okeke, in Abuja on 10th February 2017

R.I. Uzoma was indeed a participant eye-witness to the glorious days of CMS Mission contribution to human development in the last stages of 20th century Colonial Nigeria. The year that he was at DMGS remains a landmark date in academic excellence at that school. As usual, when duty called during his tenure in DMGS, he returned in December 1936 to his base at Awka Practising School, and from there on scholarship to Achimota College in 1937.

Principal, Okrika Grammar School (OGS), 1944 - 1946

After DMGS, R.I. Uzoma attended Achimota College for two years, and from there returned to Awka College as tutor from 1939 to 1943. It was while he was at Awka, that Rt. Rev. A. Morris Gelsthorpe left Okrika Grammar School in 1942 and there was a need for a substantive principal for the school. In the absence of any, the eminent Enoch I. Oli, who was a senior staff at the school, acted as the principal and held the position of principal for an interim period of two years until the arrival of RI in 1944. RI at this point became the first substantive African principal of Okrika Grammar School where he left his footprints on the sands of time. It was during this period that RI and his wife had their second child and first daughter Adaoha Chibuzo, who became baby sister to the first son Anele Nwachukwu, born in December 1942 before RI left Awka for Okrika. The third child Onuoha Chijioke, was on the way by the time RI left Okrika for further studies in the United Kingdom in July 1946.[45] RI's vice-principal and right-hand colleague was Timothy Naaku Paul Birabi, a distinguished son of Ogoni who was the first university graduate from Ogoniland. R.I. Uzoma and T.N.P. Birabi later met each other again as elected members of the Eastern Regional House of Assembly, under the MacPherson Constitution in December 1951.

St. Peter's School, Okrika and Okrika Grammar School, Okrika (OGS) were forerunners of the first primary and secondary schools

---

45 Oral Interview with Dr. Adaoha Okwuosa, daughter of R.I. Uzoma, in Abuja, on 9th December 2016.

in Okrika, situated in present-day Rivers State. Close collaboration between the chiefs and peoples of the community and Christian Missionary Society (CMS), the dominant Christian mission in Kirikese at the time, led to the establishment of Okrika Grammar School. This was twenty years after the first primary school in the community, St. Peter's School Okrika, had commenced. St. Peter's School, Okrika (Primary) opened around 1920 and had trained a number of pupils to Standard Six before the establishment of OGS in 1936.[46]

The idea of a secondary school in Okrika was first mooted in 1938 by the late Rt. Rev. A. Morris Gelsthorpe, then an assistant Bishop on the Niger. Major problems had to be overcome, with land having to be donated by the Ado Royal House of Okrika and finances, syndicated from multiple sources. The CMS Mission sourced £300; the Okrika Community sourced £347, and the Okrika Native Authority, £337. The school was however, named by the Okrika people themselves although it was originally to be named Gelsthorpe Secondary School. The idea was dropped because Bishop Gelsthorpe was still living at the time the school opened. The motto of the school, *Perseverantia Vincit* (Perseverance Conquers), was coined by the institution's first principal. The school commenced classes on April 2nd 1940 and remained a single-stream school until 1962. Okrika Grammar School is known to its old boys as the "Coastal Varsity", and like DMGS, has had a most impressive record.[47]

The school was established through the tremendous foresight of the Chiefs and people of the kingdom of Okrika, and the commitment of the missionaries. Even though most of the locals were not literate at the time, they were able to appreciate the value of sound formal education and so, offered immense

---

[46] "Okrika Grammar School, How it all Started", a paper presented by Tekena Nitonye Tamuno on the occasion of the OGS 60th Anniversary Celebration, 12th April, 2000.

[47] Oral interview with Chief Jack Gogo, Old Boy, Okirika Grammar School, in Yenagoa, Bayelsa State, 27th March, 2017.

support for the establishment of the school in their community. They voluntarily gave up their communal land for construction, contributed financially, ensured community participation and encouraged their children to attend school. In no distant time, a crop of educated and informed men and women had emerged from the locality and joined wider society. They became globally competitive and contributed substantially to society through various fields of human endeavour. The school has produced many prominent Nigerians such as the late William Pikibo, late Emeritus Professor Tekena Nitonye Tamuno, Admiral Promise Fingesi, Chief Rufus Ada George, the late Professor Abiye Obuforibo II, and Chief Emmanuel Akwiwu, SAN, who was one of the students of RI in 1944. He was also a house prefect of Gelsthorpe House and later married the younger sister of RI's wife, Lady Jemimah Uzoma. Nkwerre students who attended OGS include Abraham Nwachukwu, Christopher Asugha, Lawrence Onyegbula, his younger brother Godwin Onyegbula, a seasoned diplomat, Bertram Uzoma, RI's younger brother and Geoffrey Chinaka and Jason Ihetu, among others.[48]

RI has been described as a natural and dedicated teacher by his students, particularly his ability to mix academic depth with an approachable manner. Many wished they were students from Nkwerre town because RI made out time occasionally to privately host Nkwerre students in OGS[49] and stood in as their "parent" in the school. Socialising with Nkwerre students did not stop RI from being a disciplinarian. He didn't spare them whenever they erred because for him, charity must begin from home. He also did not discriminate against any students in order to favour others including those from his home town, Nkwerre.[50] Partiality for RI was totally an unacceptable behaviour because for him,

---

48   From Okrika Grammar School at 50, Golden Jubilee 1940-1990, A booklet published for the Golden Jubilee Celebrations of OGS 21st-27th May 1990, pp 2-8

49   Oral interview with Elder Geoffrey Chinaka, Ex Student, Okirika Grammar School in Umueze, Nkwerre, 10th May, 2017

50   *Ibid*

merit must always take precedence in academic administration. Although he was a strict disciplinarian, when RI left OGS for further studies in London in 1946, he was greatly missed, especially for the brotherly counsel he provided and his personal touch which enabled him to know each student by his first name.[51] In order to commemorate his stay in OGS, a House was named after him as Uzoma House.

---

51   Ibid

3

LAYING FOUNDATIONS IN FORMAL EDUCATION POLICY

Minister of Education, Eastern Region

A landmark development in the political history of Nigeria, which impacted on the evolution of formal education policy, was the enactment of the MacPherson Constitution in 1951. That constitution became perhaps the most important instrument of colonial rule, apart from the 1960 Independence Constitution itself, in the process towards independence.[52] The MacPherson Constitution granted the three regional governments, partial self-rule by indigenous citizens of the then Colony and Protectorate of Nigeria under a quasi-federation arrangement. The key elements were the election of Members to Regional Houses of Assembly (MHA). In turn, the Houses of Assembly were empowered to legislate on and appropriate funds in the key areas such as agriculture, education, health and local government. The regional governments, by the same constitution, thus had the powers to appoint ministers of indigenous origin in those designated areas of executive authority from the assembly. A number of those representatives were selected to represent their region as Members of the House of Representatives (MHR).

---

[52] The political structure of three Regions for the Colony and Protectorates of Nigeria had earlier been adopted under the 1946 Richards Constitution. However, opposition to that framework from some of the major nationalist figures led to a Review Constitutional Conference and the 1951 MacPherson Constitution.

The MacPherson Constitution marked a watershed in the transition from colony and protectorate to full independence. It provided for pioneering achievers from the indigenous population, the opportunity to become ministers, and to serve as catalysts in development and change. R.I. Uzoma became one such pioneer. Aged thirty-nine years at the time of his appointment, he was one of that select group of eminently qualified leading lights for the Eastern Region. They were all products of the rather eclectic colonial education system which, for a few of them was followed with foreign tertiary education. All aged in their thirties and forties, they were motivated by nationalistic zeal, and a sense of pride in their newly-acquired training as professionals.

The Eastern Region Cabinet was made up of men who were already household names in their various constituencies due to their careers, either in early nationalist leadership, or in community development initiatives. More especially, and in line with the British parliamentary system, they had been elected through an experimental electoral process, which was put in place under the new constitution. That polling system has been described as a "multi-stage electoral college system with a tax-payer suffrage at the primary level" (Abernethy, 1969: 125). It was more of a "popularity poll" based on personal merit, rather than on partisan political alignments. The candidates have in fact been described as independents, inspite of some latter-day misconception of their political status as that of NCNC politicians (Udoma, 1994: 113-114), (Usman & Abba, 2000). The actual position was that the NCNC political party made overtures to adopt these popularly-elected individuals into their ranks after they were already in government. The exceptions were perhaps Eyo-Ita and M.I. Okpara, who had been part of the National Youth Movement and Zikist Movement of the NCNC respectively.

The Eastern Region Cabinet whose members have been described as "the first crop of educated Eastern Nigerians"

Laying Foundations in Formal Education Policy

(Amucheazi, 1986: 35,160) had in its ranks, Prof. Eyo-Ita as Minister of Natural Resources, Mr. S.J. Una, for Public Health, Mr. R.I. Uzoma for Education, Mr. E.I. Oli for Local Government, Mr. S.W. Ubani-Ukoma for Lands and Survey and Mr. S. T. Muna for Ministry of Works. There were three ministers without portfolio, the equivalent of what is known today as cabinet ministers. These were Mr. M.C. Awgu, Mr. R.J.E. Koripamo and Dr. M.I. Okpara.

Prof. Eyo-Ita of Creek Town Calabar, who was also Head of Government, was educated in the United Kingdom and the United States of America where he graduated in 1934 from Columbia University, New York. Like Nnamdi Azikiwe, he became one of the first Nigerians to have American tertiary education. In 1934, Eyo-Ita founded the Nigerian Youth Movement (NYM) which became one of the forerunner organisations to the NCNC (National Council of Nigeria and the Cameroons). He also became the Deputy national president of the NCNC. Dr. Michael Iheonukara Okpara (1920-1984) was later appointed Minister of Health in 1954. A medical doctor trained at the premier Yaba Higher College in Lagos, Dr. Okpara, popularly known as M.I., was also a product of the Nigerian Youth Movement, and the Zikist Movement. Much later he became Minister for Agriculture, a leader of the NCNC in the Eastern Region and subsequently premier at the age of thirty-nine years, after Nnamdi Azikiwe from 1959 to 1961.

Another colleague of R.I. Uzoma, Mr. E.I. Oli, was Minister for Local Government. He became famous as founder of a foremost pioneer secondary institution, the Merchants of Light Secondary School, Oba, in present-day Anambra State his home community. Mr. E.I. Oli's profile was almost exactly similar to that of R.I. Uzoma, with about ten years head start. Like RI, he was a CMS-educated protégée who started as a pupil teacher after primary education and ended up in 1922, as a tutor, first at the CMS Awka College, and later at DMGS Onitsha as acting principal from 1927. Without having any secondary school education, Mr. Oli became the second Igbo-speaking university graduate in 1936 after Alvan Ikoku. Like RI, his degree was in Geography and from the University of London. He subsequently also received a Postgraduate Diploma in Education in 1944 from Oxford University, whereas R.I. Uzoma received his from the University of London in 1947. Mr. Oli became Minister for Local Government in the Eastern Regional government following his election to the House of Assembly for the Onitsha Division, while R.I. Uzoma was elected for Orlu.[53]

Mr. R.J.E. Koripamo, Cabinet Minister, was a well-known educationist and opinion leader from Odi in present day Bayelsa State. Like R.I. Uzoma and Enoch I. Oli, he was elected in 1951, as a Member of the Regional House of Assembly, by the Electoral College which met for his constituency (Brass Division) in Toru, Angiama.[54] It was an election which was largely based on personality and not on party politics, as was the case for R.I. Uzoma in Orlu Constituency and E.I. Oli in Onitsha. The candidates for membership of the House of Assembly (MHA) were already popular pioneers who had served their various communities significantly. Among Rowland Koripamo's children is Dr. Timiebi Koripamo-Agary, OON, an accomplished science and technology administrator, who is a former Director-General of the National Centre for Women Development in Nigeria, and a retired federal permanent secretary.

Together with R.I. Uzoma and E.I. Oli, Rowland Koripamo was one of the many like-minds in the Eastern Regional Cabinet, who in late 1953, resisted pressure from the NCNC party leadership to truncate their elected positions prematurely without due respect for constitutional process. This was following the defeat of the NCNC in the 1952 Western Region elections which denied the party leader, Nnamdi Azikiwe, the position of head of government

---

53 From an unpublished March 1982 booklet titled, "Epitaph of a Great Educationist, Patriot and Philanthropist, Biography of Chief Dr. Enoch Ifediora Oli, MFR, MBE, BA Hons, MA London, Dip. Ed (Oxon), D.Litt.(UNN), The Ide of Oba, 1902-1982."
54 Oral Interview with Dr. Timiebi Koripamo-Agary, daughter of Rowland Koripamo, Abuja, 9th August 2017.

in the Western Region. There was insistence on respect for the rule of law, by a sizeable group of ministers in the Eastern Region. In the heated political atmosphere of the time, this was misconstrued as a "sit-tight" attitude to political position on their part. These gentlemen however were not party politicians, but rather mission-trained technocrats with a strong belief in principles. They simply wanted to get on with the ministerial duties for which they had been elected and appointed. In the end, with the formal dissolution of the Regional Assembly in December 1953, they comfortably returned to their fulfilling careers in the CMS Mission and voluntary agency education system.

Mr. S.T. Muna was the Minister from the then Southern Cameroons, which at the time was administered as part of the Eastern Region. He soon left to return home following a plebiscite in 1953 in which the Southern Cameroons Protectorate voted to join with their kin in French–controlled Northern Cameroons, in the march towards independence.[55] It was a move that S.T. Muna had to make in the middle of the 1953 school year, requiring him to leave two of his older sons behind in Enugu, in the guardianship of his friend and colleague R.I. Uzoma and his wife. The two Muna boys thus continued their primary schooling with the three older R.I. Uzoma children at St. Bartholomew's Primary School in Asata, Enugu, until the end of the school year. This was the early stages of a friendship between the two families that continued for several decades.

R.I. Uzoma's ministerial tenure was an integral part of a period of fateful collision of events in Nigeria's political history, with the pioneering careers of some of Nigeria's early icons. In an interview which RI granted to the editorial board of a magazine in his home state in 1984, he aptly summarised his important achievements in the two-year period in which he was minister. It is a summary

---

55   Hon. E.M.L Endeley, 1916 to 1988, was another notable member of the Eastern House of Assembly from the Cameroons, and he led the movement for the Southern Cameroons to opt out of the Eastern House in 1954.

which leaves no doubt as to his primary focus and discipline. It also brings out clearly, the sense of solidarity and team spirit which motivated the cabinet members, a solidarity which was borne out of the fact that they were "like-minds" as well as partners on the ship of fate. They were a team of pace-setters in terms of educational qualifications, as well as the opportunity they had to determine the direction of government policy at the threshold of Nigeria's independence. For R.I. Uzoma, this chance was in the field of education, his other contributions in the executive team and the regional legislature notwithstanding.

R.I. Uzoma's pioneering role in social development found greatest expression with his appointment as Minister of Education. It gave him the opportunity to articulate the first proposals for a Universal Primary Education (UPE) policy for the Eastern Region. That policy was designed to broaden formal education away from the limited scope of the voluntary agency network, and the elitist government school's system of the colonial government. He also had the opportunity to initiate the first policy of Eastern Regional Government scholarships for Tertiary Education. In RI's words in 1984,

> I was the Minister of Education of the former Eastern Region between January 1952 and December 1953. During this period, some achievements were made... First, the planning of the Universal Primary Education was laid out. The idea was to make the first two classes free for the first year, and in the second year extend to the third class. This plan was carefully drawn up taking into consideration the financial resources of the Region which were not as immense as those of the Western Region, which made a lot of revenue out of cocoa and tobacco, under the principle of derivation in Revenue Allocation. In 1955/56, after the House had been dissolved, the NCNC Government (in the East) introduced free education in all the classes at once and by 1957, the financial burden nearly caused the collapse of the government. Secondly, we introduced a scholarship scheme by which a good number of men and women with requisite qualifications were helped to obtain higher academic

qualifications. This enabled them to fill places in the government service left by expatriates when independence came to be in 1960 and the expatriates left after taking their lump sum gratuity.

Thirdly, we entrenched the principle of probity and accountability to shun bribery and corruption. It was during our time, that the area of Enugu called Uwani, was laid out and demarcated into plots. We the Ministers decided that no Minister should apply for any piece of land, or benefit directly from the scholarship scheme. Consequently, none of us had a plot (in Uwani), or a scholarship for a son or daughter... in fact one of the main causes of the 1953 crisis was our firm stand against corruption, political jobbery and nepotism. We tried to uphold the Christian ethics of integrity and honesty. I remember a contractor reporting to another that we, the ministers, did not know 'how to do businesses' because we refused to accept bribes to offer scholarships or award contracts... to incompetent people who might be waving party badges. Finally, I personally sponsored a Bill banning nudity in the old Abakiliki province (Uzoma R.I., 1986).[56]

Prior to the enactment of the MacPherson Constitution, the approach of the colonial government to public education was an eclectic and uncoordinated one. There existed no coherent policy for the regulation of public education from primary to secondary level. It was a situation in which that important area of human development was largely left in the hands of a number of private voluntary agencies, such as church organisations, local community groups, and a few individuals. Leaders among the church organisations in the provision of primary and secondary education were the Church Missionary Society of the Anglican Church (CMS) and the Roman Catholic Mission (RCM). The Presbyterian and Methodist Churches were also active in education. These agencies operated across the protectorates, each with their own different ethical and philosophical directions, with minimal

---

56 A written, unpublished 1986 Interview with Chief R.I. Uzoma, former Chairman Zonal Education Board, Orlu, conducted by Messrs I. Umezurike, P.N. Abamara, Ifeanyi Ekenasi, and Anene Ogidi, of the Orlu *Zonal Educator* Editorial Board on 14th April, 1986. R.I. Uzoma Archives; See Appendix 9

interference from the colonial authorities. Primary education, in particular, suffered this fate, while secondary education received some targeted attention from government.

The main concern of the colonial government was the maintenance of political control and effective administration across the colonial space, economic exploitation of resources, and the maintenance of peace and security in the territory. Government's targeted involvement in education from 1990, consisted of the establishment of a small number of elitist secondary schools and institutions. Examples were King's College, Lagos established in 1909; Katsina Teachers College, now Barewa College in 1921, and Queen's College, Lagos in 1927.[57] The driving force behind the establishment of these institutions was either the colonial government itself, or private groups of colonial elite working hand in hand with government. These schools were unapologetically elitist in nature. For Queen's College, Lagos, it was the New Era Ladies Club in Lagos that pushed for the opening of the school in 1921 as a match to King's College, Lagos. Kings College had earlier in 1909 been established, originally as King's School, by an Act of the Parliament of the colonial power, Great Britain. The goal was not education for the masses, but the production of a crop of future leaders for Nigeria, who would go into government service, or into "Mercantile Service", the term for the colonial private business sector, dominated by trading and exploitation of raw materials.

The Katsina Teachers College, which is today's famous Barewa College, for its own part was established in 1921 by the governor–general himself, Sir Hugh Clifford. The idea was equally to ensure the emergence of an elite crop of indigenous citizens who would be qualified to man the colonial civil service in the vast North. Hence, in 1929, its focus was further extended beyond teacher–

---

57 *Pass on the Torch: The History of Queen's College, Yaba, Lagos*(1927-1997) Commemorative Book on 70 years of the College published in 1997, by Brands International Company, Lagos, which gives a detailed history of Queen's College, Lagos.

training to manpower development and it became Katsina Higher College. Ultimately, the contemporary name of the institution, Barewa College, was adopted in 1971 from the native name for the gazelle. This is the animal symbol on the institution's logo, depicting the more fast-track progress that the college was expected to expedite.[58]

It was against this background of limited government intervention in education policy that R.I. Uzoma became the first Minister of Education in the Eastern Region. It is necessary to reiterate that although they were first elected in December 1951 as the representatives for their constituencies to the Regional Assembly, R.I. Uzoma and majority of his colleagues were not partisan "politicians" in today's sense of the word, but young technocrats and community icons who could be better described as "nationalist pioneers". This determined their mindset on the job.

A Wealth of Experience[59]

Reuben Ibekwe Uzoma came to the job of Minister for Education with relevant experience that was already extensive for those days, as has been outlined in the previous chapter. His educational qualifications clearly identified him as a product of the two systems of education, which co-existed in the colonial period. The more extensive system was made up of primary, secondary and teacher–training institutions managed by the voluntary agencies and missions on one hand. The less extensive was the network of a few colonial government–instituted secondary and tertiary institutions on the other hand. Before 1952, R.I. Uzoma had already graduated after training as a teacher at the CMS St. Paul's College, Awka in present-day Anambra State, between 1931 and

---

58 For more information on the history of Barewa College, see https://en.wikipedia.org>wiki>Barewa.
59 Information for this section is taken from RI's CV and autobiographical notes found in his Archives; R.I. Uzoma Archives.

1935. This was after his primary schooling at another mission-run school, the St. Paul's (CMS) Central School in his home community of Nkwerre, between the years of 1921 and 1927, followed by his initiation into teaching as a pupil-teacher from 1928 to 1930. After obtaining the Teacher's Higher Elementary Certificate from Awka College in 1935, and without benefit of a formal secondary school education as it is known today, he had a brief stint as a tutor at Dennis Memorial Grammar School (DMGS) in 1936. Following that, he proceeded on CMS scholarship, to Achimota College in the then Gold Coast colony in 1938, where he furthered his dreams for a university qualification.

Within his first year at Achimota College, R.I. Uzoma passed the Cambridge School Certificate Examination in Division One, earning himself an exemption from what was known at the time as the London Matriculation. It is noteworthy that he won the form prize for Best Student of the Year, and prizes in five subjects including Mathematics and Latin. In 1938, he earned a fast-track into the second year of the London Intermediate Bachelors Degree (B.A) class and passed out successfully in 1939. This placed him on the last step to becoming the first university graduate from the Old Orlu Province and was able to return home at the outbreak of the second world war. In 1943, while serving as a teacher at the Awka Teacher's College, he sat for the London BA Honours degree in Geography, and became one of the first Nigerians at the time to have passed this examination as an external candidate at the first attempt. In the period that he was a tutor at Awka College, R.I. Uzoma was also a practitioner of primary educational administration, as principal of the Awka College Practising School, the training ground for future teachers which was annexed to the college.

In terms of work experience, at the time R.I. Uzoma came to the job of Minister of Education, he had not only acquired a broad background of teacher-education, but had also gained important experience in the higher-level management of schools. After two years at Achimota College, R.I. Uzoma naturally went home to serve the CMS system that had so generously sponsored all of his education. At the same time, he continued to improve his educational qualifications as earlier indicated, thus gaining for himself a reputation among peers as a "bookworm". From 1939 to 1943, he was a tutor at the Awka College, teaching Geography, Principles and Method of Education, English, Church History, and Mathematics. To add to his educational management experience, from 1944 to 1946 R.I. Uzoma served as principal of the famous Okrika Boys Grammar School, a foremost CMS secondary education institution in the Eastern Region. That deployment made R.I. Uzoma the first substantive African principal of Okrika Grammar School, a posting that was followed in 1946, by his departure to the Institute of Education, University of London to study for a Postgraduate Diploma in Education. It was a period of study that brought him together at the institute, with such icons of pre-independence Nigeria as Mallam Aminu Kano of Kano State, and Pa Michael Adekunle Ajasin of Ondo State, the latter obtaining the Postgraduate Diploma the same year as R.I. Uzoma. It was also a period of academic growth that further developed his confidence in seeking to apply education as the panacea for all-round development in his home country.

The R.I Uzoma 1953 UPE Blueprint and After

The 1952 Cambridge Conference

As earlier stated, the provisions of limited self-rule under the MacPherson Constitution opened the way for a number of educated pioneers in colonial Nigeria to contribute significantly to history and social change as ministers. R.I Uzoma was an ardent disciple of the belief that a sound primary and secondary education is the building block for solid development at all levels.

If he were still around today he would certainly have seen the commonly held notion of poor standards of public education and teaching at all levels, as being predicated on the abject neglect of the grassroots school system. It was therefore not a surprise that the primary attention of R.I Uzoma in the period that he served as Minister of Education, was on universal education.

In September 1952, R.I Uzoma and his colleague, the Minister of Education for the Western Region, S.H.O Awokoya attended the Cambridge Conference convened at King's College in Cambridge University, United Kingdom. Other colleagues from the then Colony and Protectorates of Nigeria, were the Hon. Shettima Kashim MHR, Minister, Social Services; the Hon. Aliyu MHR, Makaman Bida, Minister for Social Services, Northern Region; Mallam Ahmadu Coomasie, provincial education officer, Northern Nigeria; Mr. E.E. Esua, General Secretary, Nigerian Union of Teachers; Mr. F.O. Awoshika MHR, Western Region; Mr. U.U. Okure assistant vice-principal, Methodist Boys High School, Ikot-Ekpene, Eastern Region.[60] It should be noted that by 1952, education was not a distinct portfolio of its own in the colonial government of Northern Nigeria and in the central government in Lagos, but was subsumed under Social Services. For the House of Representatives in Lagos, members were selected from among those who were already elected into the Regional Houses of Assembly (Abernethy, 1969:125).

The Cambridge Conference was organised by the Colonial government to provide a forum for the final review of a survey of African Education conducted under the sponsorship of the Colonial Office and the Nuffield Foundation (Otonti, 1973). The colonial authorities at this point had become increasingly open to the idea of eventually relinquishing power in the colonies to Africans. They

---

60 The list of delegates from the Colony and Protectorates of Nigeria, to the 1952 Cambridge Conference, has been obtained from a group photograph of them taken at the occasion in the grounds of Kings College, Cambridge and carefully captioned at the back. The photo is from the R.I. Uzoma's Archives and is part of this publication.

were beginning to consider what would be the preferred education policies that could produce a stable educated class to whom such powers would be transferred. The conference was one of the sources of inspiration that emboldened the two Ministers, from the Eastern and Western Regions, to, initiate a policy for early Universal Primary Education (UPE) in their respective regions. Both men correctly felt the pulse of their populations, who were fired by a nationalistic hunger for education, in those years of heightened anticipation for political independence. For them, a successful UPE scheme would constitute a bold step towards what was tantamount to a revolution at that time, considering the numerous hurdles encountered before the UPE succeeded in the Western Region in 1955 and in the Eastern Region in 1957.

A Measured UPE Plan

By December 1952, after the Cambridge Conference, R.I Uzoma had returned to his desk in Enugu and developed policy papers for a Universal Primary Education (UPE) for the Eastern Region. His colleague from the Western Region, Hon. S.O. Awokoya had done the same in 1952 with a "bold call for a programme of free universal primary and compulsory education to be introduced in the region not later than January 1955" (Abernethy, 1969: 127). Hon. Awokoya's UPE plan for the Western Region was popular and sweeping. Apart from the earlier target date of 1955, it proposed a rapid increase in teacher training facilities, introduction of secondary-modern schools similar to the British model, as a parallel outlet for the anticipated large army of primary school leavers, as well as ten new secondary schools. Awokoya held a strong view of educational development as being "imperative and urgent". He sought to treat it as a "national emergency, second to war", which was to proceed with "the momentum of a revolution" (Abernethy, 1969: 161). He was indeed passionate about it.

R.I Uzoma's proposals for the Eastern Region were more measured and "participatory" in terms of involving local communities. He anticipated several challenges starting with funding, because the Western Region was more economically buoyant than the Eastern Region. He was also mindful of the strong values of individualism, community independence, and respect for participatory consultation which were prevalent in the segmentary communities of the Eastern Region. He also considered possible resistance from the voluntary agencies and churches who largely owned and managed primary and secondary education in the Eastern Region at the time. He was after all, a product of such schools. R.I Uzoma therefore did not call for a totally free Universal Primary Education. As a matter of fact, he held the view that the term "Free Education" was a misnomer, arguing that there is no education that can be provided cost-free, only one that can have a no-fee provision for the beneficiaries (Abernethy,1969:161).

He considered all these possible challenges and proposed that the local government bodies had to be part of the scheme by contributing forty-five (45) percent of the cost. The no-fee schooling would be put in place only for the first 4 years of junior primary namely Infants I and II as well as Standards I and II, as they were designated at the time. His anticipated target-date for the entire Eastern Region was the end of 1956, one year after the date projected by the Western Region.

R.I Uzoma's plan portrayed a caution that was the outcome of his field experience and training. He was concerned that the programme should have enough grassroots community support as well as adequate technical inputs. The programme should not simply be "popular" in political terms. He therefore made a proposal for the gradual increase of trained teachers from 1,500 to 2,500 "over the next few years, and for a secondary school to be provided in every division that lacked one." In summary, the highlights of the R.I Uzoma blueprint were, firstly, a no-fee primary schooling system for the first four foundation years. Secondly, a compulsory attendance requirement was to be introduced only when each community felt ready to put it into practice (Abernethy, 1969: 162). Thirdly, funding was to be tied to the local government contribution of 45 percent through education rates in order to ensure sustainability. The R.I Uzoma plan was a systematic but a more cautious UPE programme. It was similar, in terms of the basic principle of "universality", to that initiated by Hon. Awokoya in the Western Region a few months earlier. Awokoya's plan aggregated to six years of free UPE. The main difference between the two plans was in terms of funding and community participation. In summary, R.I Uzoma tailored his proposals to the circumstances of the Eastern Region, around his reasoned position that there can be no such thing as a "free" education, but only a no-fee paying one. His style was also not that of political populism and sloganeering, but of a more professional and technocratic approach to issues. He was equally mindful of the fiercely independent spirit of the people of the Eastern Region.

1953 Political Disruptions

Subsequent political developments in the Eastern Region however resulted in a delayed implementation of the Eastern Region's UPE. They also led to its largely unsuccessful execution, in contrast to what occurred in the Western Region. Several scholars of the history of education and of educational management in Nigeria have examined the main elements of the R.I. Uzoma proposals, as against the provisions that were actually implemented thereafter under the Akpabio UPE program (Abernethy, 1969; Fafunwa, 1974; Oni, 2008; Anero, 2011). There is a consensus that political developments which followed in quick succession from 1954, along with other factors such as poor funding and instability in the local government structures, combined to derail the success of the UPE in the Eastern Region. According to Anero, with the change of government in the Eastern Region in 1953, leading to a change of ministers, primary education became the "greatest casualty" (Anero, 2011:100). Under the new administration, from 1954, Nnamdi Azikiwe became head of government/Premier while I.U. Akpabio took over as Minister of Education, replacing Eyo-Ita and R.I. Uzoma in those two respective positions. The Regional government proceeded to make policy changes in education that placed a priority on populist political considerations. In Anero's view, the changes were a "fire brigade" approach which manifested in "failures in almost all dimensions" (Anero, 2011:100). J.O. Oni made a similar assessment of the state of the UPE programme in the Eastern Region under the new administration. According to him,

> In 1954, Dr. Nnamdi Azikiwe... replaced Prof. Eyo-Ita as the leader of the government. In like manner, Mr. I.U. Akpabio now occupied the position of the Minister of Education, which had been vacated by Mr. R.I. Uzoma. The government in a wave of political promises now changed the UPE project from modest and cautious expansion to a more ambitious programme. Free UPE education in the Region would now be for all of eight years, covering junior and senior primary years. The government also expressed its intention to bear all financial responsibilities all alone without local government contributions. The resultant effect... was a total failure (Oni, 2008: 28).

Fafunwa had in the same vein in 1974, attributed the failure of the UPE programme in the Eastern Region to the abandonment of the R.I. Uzoma proposals following the crisis generated by the NCNC leadership in 1953. As demonstrated previously, the crisis led to the dissolution of the House of Assembly and the departure of most of the ministers. The subsequent government of 1954 under Azikiwe and Akpabio adopted a rushed and inadequately planned set of proposals which ended in massive failure by 1957 and 1958. In Fafunwa's words,

> The major changes that took place in the Eastern Region in 1953 seriously affected the proposed free primary education scheme... The new government, led by Dr Nnamdi Azikiwe, rejected the former government's modest proposal, preferring the rapid introduction of universal primary education on a large scale... The Eastern Regional Government had less time than the Western Region to plan its own scheme. In February 1957, the universal primary education scheme was launched. Practically all the new schools were staffed by untrained teachers as there was not enough time to train... As expected the scheme ran into difficulties right from the beginning, and from 1958 many teachers were laid off and many schools were closed due to lack of funds (Fafunwa, 1974: 185-186).

It could be argued that Fafunwa, Anero and Oni's assessments are those of academic experts in Educational Administration, who were naturally being concerned about their chosen professional fields. However, a fourth study by Abernethy has equally posited similar views on what constituted the Achilles heel of the Universal Primary Education programme in the Eastern Region of Nigeria, after R.I. Uzoma. Implementation of the more ambitious and populist UPE plan that was ushered in by 1954, clearly exposed a weaker planning and financial base as its major problem. By 1956 it was apparent that special education rates from the local governments as a source of funding could not carry the more grandiose plan of eight years of totally "free" primary education. With the departure from R.I. Uzoma's cautious UPE plan, the new regional government put itself under immense financial pressure towards achieving its target of eight years of "free" primary education. That target was intended to match that of the more buoyant Western Region which started under Awokoya by January 1955. Funding became a major issue in the East. In Abernethy's view,

> By 1956, it became clear that local education rating, the expedient on which Uzoma had relied in his initial proposals was "in a state of collapse". Widespread poverty, corrupt practices by Local councilors and inadequate tax collection machinery, all severely limited the amount that could be collected from local resources

and popular resistance to paying education rates intensified with each increase in the rates" (Abernethy, 1969: 162).

Abernethy's 1969 study thus, provides the most comprehensive analysis of the crisis that ensued in the attempted implementation of the Eyo-Ita/Akpabio UPE plan in the Eastern Region. Abernethy also reported that the 1956 Education Law was passed without the input of the Nigerian Union of Teachers (NUT) and the Voluntary Agencies, mainly Presbyterian, Methodist and Catholic Missions. In 1955, they openly raised issues with Akpabio and in 1956, the NUT threatened a strike action. His study thus provides an unwitting confirmation of the challenges which R.I. Uzoma had considered in 1953, a consideration which he brought to bear on what could be described as his more "gradualist" and "participatory" proposals. That approach by RI was the result of his background training and antecedent work-experience.

The Post-R.I. Uzoma Challenges to UPE

The Eyo-Ita UPE program put a stop to the idea of joint-financing with the local government councils, irrespective of the weak funding base of the regional government. Populist sloganeering of the NCNC politics became more important. A new era of partisan politics had arrived, and the need for populist support, over and above professional planning and technocratic expertise, had taken over. These factors combined with a growing lack of sense of ownership and involvement in the programme by local communities. It was a frustration which they were more ready to voice in the atmosphere of party politics that rode the land from 1954. These trends also evoked an undercurrent of grassroots opposition to the government's free UPE programme from the local communities. Local people were encouraged to oppose government by the previous "owners" of the schools system, such as the Roman Catholic Missions, who controlled more than half of the primary and secondary schools of the region. The local communities complained of inadequate consultation, especially in funding and planning. So also did the voluntary agencies that saw themselves as stakeholders in the management of schools. This was the nightmare scenario which the R.I. Uzoma plan had envisaged. The Azikiwe/Akpabio government which took over in 1954 committed itself to a target date of January, 1957 for the launching of its more grandiose UPE scheme. They therefore put themselves under political pressure to meet that date, because of the impending regional elections.

The political pressure on the Azikiwe/Akpabio government over the UPE programme intensified after January 1955 when Awokoya's vision materialised. That year, the UPE in the Western Region under the Action Group government became a reality. It was a well-celebrated launching in Ibadan at which January 17, the opening date of the school year, was dubbed Education Day (Abernethy,1969:127-128). February 1957 witnessed the eventual launching of the scheme in the Eastern Region in a highly politicised event. Nonetheless, many technical problems continued to plague the programme, thereby exposing the inadequate ground work. These included first and foremost, shortage of funding since education rates could no longer be imposed, shortage of trained teachers, buildings and basic equipment, compounded by lack of much-needed cooperation from the former proprietors of the schools, the voluntary agencies.

By 1958, after a life-span of only one year of UPE headaches, the new regional government saw the need to appoint one committee after another to "review" the UPE programme. The scheme was already in serious trouble having become an object of the high wire politics of the later 1950s. The first 1958 UPE Review Committee headed by Professor Kenneth Dike, came out with recommendations that advised government to put emphasis on "quality" education rather than "quantity" education. It was followed by a second committee, also in 1958, known as the Ikoku Committee (Fafunwa, 1974: 188). This committee made recommendations which even more bluntly, advised that government should return to the original R.I. Uzoma idea of involvement of local government councils in primary–education funding. That committee also advised a return to a more measured and cautious approach by recommending the consolidation of the bloated number of primary schools, many of which were not viable, and their placement under government control. It also recommended the reduction of the primary school tenure from seven (7) years to six (6) years, just as the R.I. Uzoma plan had proposed in 1953.

In the meantime, R.I. Uzoma had returned to working for the Anglican Church Mission whom he had previously served. From 1954 to 1962, he was the Education Secretary and Supervisor of schools in the Niger Delta Diocese, with offices in Old-Umuahia in present-day Abia State. This was followed by a transfer to Owerri Diocese in the same capacity, from 1963 until retirement in 1967. With the departure of R.I. Uzoma from ministerial duties and his return to the Missions education system, the government's loss became the gains of the Anglican Church in the field of education. It was in the establishment and management of schools and colleges under the auspices of the Anglican Church from 1954 to 1961, that R.I. Uzoma used his skills as a technocrat to perfect and put into practice the systematic ideas that he had penned for government in his UPE blueprint.

4

BUILDING EARLY EDUCATIONAL INFRASTRUCTURE IN THE EAST

Return to Voluntary Agency Service

What government lost, in terms of policy formulation as a result of the departure of R.I. Uzoma from the cabinet of the Eastern Regional government, the voluntary agency sector, specifically the Anglican Church Mission, gained. This was in terms of proficient education policy-making and implementation. For a period of over one decade, from 1954 to 1967, R.I. Uzoma was opportuned to continue service in a field that he clearly felt at home, as Education Secretary and Supervisor of Schools, in two separate dioceses of the mission. He had a hectic schedule involving the management of schools and development of educational infrastructure. This he did on a platform that had already established itself as a major transformational vehicle in pre-independence Nigeria, namely the Anglican Church Schools System. The two dioceses he served cover the territories of present-day Bayelsa, Rivers, Imo and Abia States.

The actual development of educational infrastructure in the 1950s and 1960s, much of which is still in existence today, became one area in which R.I. Uzoma made his greatest mark. Many of the schools and colleges that he was involved with are located in rural hinterland communities, where the AnglicanMission had its furthest outreaches. Not all the institutions were secondary schools or colleges. There were also, a few trade schools and hospital projects, depending on the identified priority of the communities.

R.I. Uzoma's involvement in the establishment of these institutions, consisted largely in an intricate role, which harnessed the local community development initiatives of the people, with the local council authorities. It also brought in the professional management skills of the Mission's education system. The latter provided professional advice, while the local government councils gave logistic support wherever needed, particularly at the stage of construction, and provision of necessary approvals for each project. The local community development initiatives in almost all cases, took the form of granting land and raising funds through levies. This would later be supplemented with government's financial support in the form of grants-in-aid to each school after completion. Responsibility for management of each project on completion, was given to the Anglican Mission education department in each case, while the communities remained the initial proprietors. In most cases however, there followed a full handover of the completed project to the voluntary agency, in this case the Anglican Mission.

A unique characteristic of the role of the Education Secretary and Supervisor of Schools, was the combination of administrative office duties with field duties in the host communities. These field duties took the form of negotiations with community leaders, awareness creation, conflict resolution, inspection of projects and all manner of 'jack-of-all-trades' assignments. R.I. Uzoma was so often on tour in far-flung rural areas that his young family became quite accustomed to it. Not being a priest, he was seen as a 'lay-missionary', by the leaders of host communities with which he interacted. As Supervisor ofSchools, he was also a sort of community public relations officer for the CMS Mission. Local leaders felt at home with him and often consulted him on a myriad of other issues, ranging from cultural disputes, to career choices for their sons and daughters. Two examples of the schools whose establishment R.I. Uzoma was involved with, will be examined here, to illustrate the winning model that he operated.

The Ngwa High School Model

A close look at the process behind the founding of a majority of the premier secondary schools and colleges in present-day Imo, Abia, Rivers and Bayelsa States, will reveal that delicate interplay of participatory decision-making, with public-private agency cooperation at the grassroots level. This was the key to the success of the Anglican Mission education system, until the 1970 takeover of the schools and colleges by the state government, at the end of the Nigerian civil war. Ngwa High School, in Aba, in present-day Abia State is a case in point. That secondary school for boys was formally opened in 1954 after only two years of the type of intense collaborative effort described earlier. The bodies involved were the Ngwa Educational Cultural Assembly, the Anglican Mission Education Secretary's Office of the Niger-Delta Diocese, and the Okpuala-Ngwa Native Authority, as well as the Aba-Ngwa County Councils.

The process was straight forward. First of all the grassroots community development platforms, in this case the Ngwa Cultural Assembly, would convince itself of a need for the project. The community leaders, namely the chiefs and opinion leaders then take up the idea to the level of inviting the Anglican Mission to assist them towards their goal. The Ngwa hinterland was already home to a wide network of predominantly Anglican Mission primary schools. Hence, it was easy for the education department of the Diocese to establish a working relationship with the Ngwa Cultural Assembly. R.I. Uzoma as Education Secretary and Supervisor of Schools for the Diocese, easily became a familiar figure in the educational hopes and aspirations of Ngwa land.

RI's special interest in education among the Ngwa people, started as early as 1948, after his University of London training, when he assumed duties over a territory that included Ngwa land. His first academic paper published in *Overseas Education* in January 1952 was titled "Universal Schooling in Ngwa Clan of Aba Division, Nigeria" (Uzoma, R.I., 1952). In the paper, RI showed his keen interest in the special mechanisms which the Ngwa village unions applied, in order to increase the primary school enrolment of their children, especially the girl-children. He recognised their organised reliance for financial self-help on the harvesting of communal palm forests. RI equally noted the early efforts of Ngwa people in addressing the gender disparity in school enrolment. That disparity was caused by such factors as early marriage and the preferred use of girl-children for farming and household work. One of the remedies which the Ngwa villages adopted, as was reported in RI's paper, was the granting of loans from the village union purse, to parents who were tempted to marry off their girl-children before their completion of primary education. Such loans were made refundable when the girl-child had passed Standard Six. This was something that quite excited R.I. Uzoma's zeal for education (Uzoma, R.I, 1952).

The special mechanisms adopted by the Ngwa people for primary school enrolment resulted in a phenomenal increase in school enrolment from 1948 to 1952 (Uzoma, R.I., 1952). It was a development which RI was only too happy to share with researchers and students of growth of education in Nigeria, who approached him for information (Adiele, 2014: 84-86). By the 1950s Ngwa land had already recorded an impressive level of primary school enrolment, hence the people began to aspire towards having a secondary school of their own. The Ngwa Educational Cultural Assembly was an umbrella body which covered the territory that was then known as Northern-Ngwa and Eastern-Ngwa. Its leadership was made up of highly respected traditional rulers and other prominent Ngwa sons, while the extensive influence of the Anglican Mission in Ngwa land acted as a powerful matrix for action. On the part of the community, the notable actors were late Chief Hon M.W. Ubani, Ezeoha of Southern Ngwa, Chiefs Nwachukwu, Nwannunu, Chief Olum and Mr. Ogwuma from Northern Ngwa and Chief J.N. Ogbonna, Chief Nwaigwe and John Nosike from Eastern Ngwa.[61] On the part of the Anglican Mission, the principal actors were the Rt. Reverend E.T. Dimieari, Bishop of the Niger-Delta Diocese from 1952 to 1961, Mr. R.I. Uzoma, the Education Secretary and Manager of Schools for the Diocese and the Rev. Cockin who was the Senior Supervisor of Schools.[62]

With the cooperation and involvement of the traditional rulers, it was easy to mobilize levies, and also acquire land from the communities for the siting of the schools, first from Umuocham village, and later from Abayi Village. It must be noted that this was not done forcefully, because when Umuocham village decided to withdraw their initial donation of land due to some internal constraints, there was no ill-feeling about it. Abayi village readily took over that responsibility.[63] With the singular act of donation of land by some villages, the subsequent agreement to raise funds from the people through what became known as the "Ngwa College Rate", was easily implemented.

The community levy was fixed at a rate of five shillings from every adult Ngwa male. However, the women of the community, led by Mrs. Mary Ubani on the platform of their own grassroots association, the Ngwa Women Association, refused to be left out, and made a contribution of five hundred pounds at the launching of the school project. These amounts were quite significant by the standards of those days considering the fact that the Ngwa people were predominantly small-scale farmers. Apart from peasant farming, the Ngwa people were producers of a major cash-crop of the Nigerian export economy, the palm oil and palm

---

61 S.I. Amadi (Venerable), History of Ngwa High School, Unpublished Speech given at the Schools' first Prize-Giving Day on 12th September 1964. S.I. Amadi was the schools' Principal from 1961 to 1967.
62 Ibid.
63 Ibid.

kernel. Large palm tree plantations thrived across Ngwa land and the palm fruit and its harvest, became a major factor in the raising of the "College Rate" levy for the Ngwa High School project. It became logical that the palm fruit was adopted as the icon on the logo of the School when it was opened in 1954.

Aside from the facilitatory role of the local government authorities, it was initialy in connection with the regular collection and security of these funds that the local government council, namely the Okpuala Ngwa Native Authority, had to be brought into the picture.[64] To start with, the "College Rate" was collected from the people alongside the regular Aba Ngwa District County Council Rate in order to ensure proper accounting records. However, later on the "College Rate" was removed from the council accounts and placed under the management of the Financial Secretary of the Anglican Church Mission. This was logical, considering that the overall responsibility for construction and maintenance of the school buildings, as well as the eventual management of the schools, were ceded to the Anglican Mission.[65]

The managerial role of the Anglican Mission included recruitment and discipline of staff, and selection and welfare of students. It also included decisions on curriculum and administration of examinations according to approved standards, as well as general liaison with the host communities. These were all within the ambit of the responsibilities of R.I. Uzoma as Education Secretary and Schools Supervisor for the Niger-Delta diocese at the time. Ngwa High School became his first major project on his return from ministerial duties and presented the model which was followed for many more such projects. Rapid progress on these projects was, to a large extent, made possible

---

64   *Ibid.*
65   The Anglican Mission had the responsibility for providing the contractor for the construction of the school in the person of M.I. Ugorji of Owerri who did the job in record time from November 2nd 1953 to the opening of the school by the start of the school year in 1954. He became the much trusted-contractor used by the Education Secretary for many of the Mission's projects.

by the fact that the Education Secretary had substantial executive latitude in the day-to-day performance of his duties. His reporting line was the Church hierarchy of the Synod and the Bishop. The Ngwa High School was formally opened on 22nd September 1954 with one first-year class of 29 boys, and a House named after R.I. Uzoma. The first Principal, the Rev. W.G. Pollard was a well-known British missionary member of the Mission's education team, who later served for many years as Bursar at the Archdeacon Crowder Girls' Secondary School (ACMGS) in Elelenwa.

The Birabi Memorial Grammar School (BMGS) Bori-Ogoni Example[66]

The Birabi Memorial Grammar School (BMGS) in Bori, Rivers State is another case in point. This secondary school for boys was actually completed in 1953 but did not take off till January 1957. The delay was due to the death in 1953 of the prominent community leader and driving force behind the school, late Timothy Naaku Paul Birabi. His loss in 1953 threw the community in mourning because he was the founder and President of the Ogoni Representatives Assembly. This body served as the community development platform responsible for mobilizing the entire Ogoni community towards building the school. From the 1940s till his death in 1953, Mr. Birabi was a leading light of the Ogoni community in more respects than one. He was the first university graduate from Ogoniland, having obtained a combined Honours Degree in Geography from the University of Southampton in the UK. He then worked closely with R.I. Uzoma as Vice-Principal, at the time the latter was Principal of Okrika Grammar School for Boys, from 1944 to 1946.

---

66 All information on BMGS is based on an oral interview with Senator Bennett Nweizor Birabi, medical doctor and son of the late icon of Ogoniland, T.N.P Birabi in whose memory the school was named. At a youthful age, Dr. Birabi followed his father's public service footsteps to become a Minister of Youth and Sports in the 1983/84 tenure of Shehu Shagari's government and was later elected Senator in the 1992/93 3rd National Assembly of the Babangida transition programme. He was interviewed on 4th June 2017.

Mr T.N.P. Birabi, some years later, was elected to represent the Ogoni Constituency in the Eastern House of Assembly, following the enactment of the 1951 MacPherson Constitution. From that position, he became one of the elected members picked to represent the Eastern Region in the House of Representatives in Lagos. Mr Birabi's passion for greater education for his people, naturally found understanding and support in his former colleague R.I. Uzoma, when the latter became the Education Secretary for the leading voluntary agency in Birabi's territory. It was a support which continued even after the death of Mr. Birabi and saw the final launching of the Ogoni Grammar School project in his blessed memory in 1957.

Similar to the process in respect of Ngwa High School, the new secondary school in Ogoni was also founded on the basis of a tripartite collaboration between the community, local council and the Church Mission. The community organisation, in this case the Ogoni Representatives Assembly, had Mr. Birabi as its president up to 1953. Another energetic Ogoni leader, Mr. Fiito N. Saronwiyor was General Secretary. Together the two had no difficulty in acquiring land and raising funds for the construction of a secondary school, through levies imposed on all adult males of Ogoniland.[67] Construction was completed in record time from 1951 to 1953. Ogoniland was at this time, a rich agricultural community not yet devastated by the ravages of pollution from the upstream oil industry. This was a period in which communities reposed total confidence in the enlightened and sincere leadership of their few educated heroes, while the Missions were the ever-present agents of social transformation at the rural level. Partisan politics and unhealthy political competitiveness had not yet disorganised Nigeria's rural communities.

---

67 *Ibid.* As MHR in 1951-1953, T.N.P. Birabi had fellow young politicians who later became Nigerian leaders, such as Shehu Shagari and Maitama Sule.

In the case of BMGS, the community leaders brought in the Methodist Church Mission to be part of the management of the school, alongside the Anglican Church. This was the result of a close and shared history that existed between the two missions in Ogoniland. In the 1950s the Anglican Mission and the Methodist Mission, having arrived in Ogoni about the same time, were the two most influential voluntary agencies in Ogoni territory. It was therefore an easy working relationship for both missions.[68] There was equally a close working relationship with the Ogoni County Council in the running of the school once it took off in January 1957. The collaboration was arranged in such a way, that the Methodists and the Anglicans provided teaching staff for the school, while appointment to the post of principal was alternated between the two Missions. Hence from about 1963, Mr. S.M.O. Nwosu an Anglican teacher took over as principal from the Rev. P.G. Collingwoods, a Methodist priest who managed the school in its teething years. Mr. Nwosu headed the school until the start of the Nigerian civil war in 1967. Since the end of the civil war, BMGS has continued to function as a Grammar School under the Rivers State government.

The Birabi Memorial Grammar School has remained in contemporary times, one of the few schools in Rivers State that continue to retain their original identity and name. This is due to the strong sense of ownership in its existence within the Ogoni community. It has been spared one of the major changes that came with the government take-over of voluntary-agency institutions after the Nigerian civil war, which is change in function and identity for most schools. Several schools, particularly the Teacher Training Colleges, were either closed down or converted into secondary commercial schools or trade schools. In a

---

68 The Roman Catholic Church Mission is known to have arrived late in Ogoniland, long after the two Protestant missions, Anglican and Methodist, had established a foothold.

particular case in neighbouring Abia State, the former Northern-Ngwa Teacher Training College at Nsulu, Nbawsi was converted into a Games Village for training of sports men and women, by the East-Central State government. Nonetheless, it still ended up being abandoned and over grown with weeds for many years.

Upsurge in Voluntary-Agency Schools and Colleges from the 1950s to the Start of the Civil War

The success of the Ngwa High School and BMGS model, encouraged the Anglican Mission to further replicate the same approach, with a few local variations, in the founding of more community institutions from the 1950s to the start of the civil war in 1967. As stated, the key to that success were joint decision-making, grassroots consultation, and initial local community funding. These three factors ensured a continued sense of proud ownership of each project by the community. It was not a surprise that several other secondary schools and colleges followed in quick succession, in the period of R.I. Uzoma's tenure as Education Secretary. Significantly, he was in a position to see the need for making several of those institutions Teacher Training Colleges (TTC). This was based on his recent role in the Eastern Region's vision for a UPE programme that required a vast increase in the number of trained teachers. The list that follows, shows institutions in the then Niger Delta Diocese and Owerri Diocese, in whose establishment and early management R.I. Uzoma was involved between 1954 and 1967. At least seven of them were Teacher Training Colleges (TTCs).[69]

---

69   From R.I. Uzoma's curriculum vitae and autobiographical notes sent to the Brochure Committee for the 1989 NAU 50 years Anniversary Celebrations; see R.I. Uzoma Archives.

In Present-Day Rivers and Bayelsa States

1. Bishop Dimieari Grammar School (BDGS), Yenagoa
2. Anglican Grammar School, Port Harcourt
3. County Grammar School, Ikwerre-Etche, Igritta
4. West Ahoada County High School, Ahoada
5. B.M.G.S., Bori, Ogoni
6. Nyemoni Grammar School, Abonema
7. Isiokpo Women's Training College (WTC) (Now Girl's Secondary School)
8. Umuobiakani T.T.C. (Now Secondary Commercial School)
9. Oporoma T.T.C. (Now Secondary Commercial School)
10. Okordia Zarama T.T.C., Brass
11. Okrika Joint Hospital, Okrika

In Present-Day Imo and Abia States

1. Ngwa High School, Aba
2. Anglican Grammar School, Umuahia
3. Anglican Grammar School, Nbawsi
4. Anglican Girls' School, Ovom, Aba
5. Anglican Girls' Secondary School, Amumara, Mbaise
6. Asa Grammar School, Asa, Imo River
7. Ndoki Grammar School, Obohia
8. Abayi-Umuocham Girls' Trade School
9. Ohanso Girls' Trade School, Ohanso
10. Osusu Teacher Training College (T.T.C.) (Now Delta Trade Centre)
11. Umuobasi-Amavo (W.T.C.) via Aba, (Now Girl's Secondary).
12. Northern Ngwa (T.T.C.), Nsulu, Nbawsi (Now Games' village)

13. Atta Girls' Secondary School
14. Ezeoke Girls' Secondary School, Ezeoke
15. Akabo Girls' Secondary School
16. Owerri-Nkworji Girls' Secondary School
17. Ogwa Community Hospital, Ogwa

One of the sad commentaries of the state of education in Nigeria today, is the minimal attention given to the specialised training of teachers for the primary and secondary school institutions. There is a fallacious assumption that any individual with some tertiary education in a particular discipline can be a teacher in that field. The conversion of so many Teacher Training Colleges to other functions, after the Nigerian civil war, is surely a policy-decision which R.I. Uzoma would have objected to in the period of his watch. With hindsight, it is possible that RI's time was a golden era of balanced development of educational infrastructure. R.I. Uzoma was as equally mindful of the need for some gender-balance in institutions because, he was guided by a deep social conscience. Two premier secondary schools were established in this period in R.I. Uzoma's hometown of Nkwerre. They were both placed under the Anglican CMS Mission and naturally benefitted from his experience. The two schools are the St. Augustine's Secondary School for Boys founded in 1948, and the St. Catherine's Secondary School for Girls founded in 1955. The antecedent to both schools followed the same unique formula that worked for the CMS Mission across the Eastern Region. Working hand in hand with a strong town union and dedicated community leaders, R.I. Uzoma and his wife, Jemimah C. Uzoma, provided invaluable support to their community in the establishment of both schools, as will be demonstrated in the next chapter.

The period in which so many communities in the former Eastern Region were able to come together to fund their own educational infrastructure, was an era of hunger for formal education. There was also enormous respect for the practitioners of education themselves, the teachers. It was equally a period of extensive rural development by community development organs. The rural populations were not yet factionalised by partisan politics and debilitating materialism. It was in that golden era that R.I. Uzoma became popularly known in his Nkwerre community and beyond, as "Onye-Nkuzi", a name which hitherto, had only been used to address him affectionately by his immediate family.*Onye-Nkuzi* which in Igbo simply means "Teacher", came to be attributed to R.I. Uzoma as a badge of honour, in the broader sense of "Scholar", "Leader". *Onye-Nkuzi* became a cherished title for R.I. Uzoma throughout his life, such that for a long time, he declined offers of chieftaincy titles from several communities.

5

SERVICE TO CHURCH, COMMUNITY, STATE

Lay Prince of the Church

There was an awareness among those who knew the man R.I. Uzoma, that his contributions to the Anglican Church of Nigeria were extensive. Clergy and Laity both acknowledged this and gave him due deference for it. However, while many of his contemporaries added the cassock to their personality, R.I. Uzoma chose to remain a "Lay prince of the Anglican Church in Nigeria without the mitre, even when it was within his grasp."[70] He did so in order to be able to equally render service in the public sector especially in the field of education, as administrator and technocrat. Quite early in his career, he became a Life Member of the Church Missionary Society (CMS) due to his admiration of their goals. However, he chose to pursue those goals as a layman through a 'civilian' career of teaching and educational administration. In the end, R.I. Uzoma straddled the two worlds of government and church comfortably.

Indeed the hallmark of R.I. Uzoma's working life was a bi-lateral career of dedicated service to the public sector through government institutions on one hand and church institutions on the other. For example, he will forever be remembered as a "father"

---

[70] An eminent Nkwerre citizen and one of RI's mentees, Ambassador Godwin .A. Onyegbula KSC, has aptly described R.I. Uzoma in these terms in an interview he granted this author sometime in 2016.

and facilitator of the Orlu/Okigwe Diocese of the Anglican Church of Nigeria in Imo State which was established in 1984. That diocese was at the time, carved out of the rather large Owerri Diocese after several years of negotiation and groundwork. Yet RI was in that same period, functioning as a high-ranking official of the Imo State public service, precisely as a Commissioner in the Public Service Commission. This chapter summarizes the contributions of R.I. Uzoma to the Anglican Church in Eastern Nigeria in particular, and also to the church as a corporate organisation within and outside Nigeria. Those contributions were mainly in the form of boardroom policy-making, administrative management in the field of education, and in local support through various committees.

It can be said that R.I. Uzoma's professional growth epitomized the early stages of development in education in pre-independence Nigeria. The church agencies were the first institutions that impacted on the civil populations, more extensively than the agencies of government. The Colonial government itself was largely dependent on the churches and missions for the production of the critical manpower, which it required to establish effective governance over society. R.I. Uzoma became one of those early leaders in the professions in Nigeria who were at home in the two milieux of the church as a social movement, and the public service bureaucracy as an agent of governance. Both worlds benefitted from his expertise which he provided to the best of his ability. The values which R.I internalised from his CMS training and early work-experience were applied positively to his subsequent work in government positions. In turn, the bureaucratic and managerial skills that he acquired while in government roles, served him well in his contributions to the Anglican Church. A previous chapter has already outlined some of those contributions which R.I. Uzoma made to the development of education in Eastern Nigeria.

The earliest opportunity which R.I. Uzoma had to contribute to management of education for the Anglican Church was as

General Manager of schools in the Niger-Delta Diocese from 1949 to 1951, from his Old Umuahia base in present-day Abia State. This was soon after he returned from the University of London, and before he was elected into the Eastern House of Assembly, to serve as Minister of Education in the Eastern Region from 1951 to 1953. From 1954 to 1962, RI returned to Old Umuahia in his earlier position, but for a longer stint, this time with greater responsibilities as Education Secretary and Supervisor of Schools. As indicated in an earlier chapter, this was a position which involved wide-ranging managerial duties over secondary and teacher-training institutions, together with a great deal of field responsibilities. In 1959, the Diocese of Owerri was created partly from the rather sprawling Niger-Delta Diocese. From 1963 to 1967, RI was moved from the Niger-Delta to the Owerri Diocese, where he took over the same responsibilities from his colleague and friend, E.C. Ezekwesili. The latter was then transferred to serve as principal of the famous Awka College from 1963 (Amucheazi, 1986:79; Animalu, Onwurah, 1997: 41).

It is noteworthy that at the same time that RI was serving in these positions in the period up to 1967, he was also a member of the Provincial Synod of the Province of West Africa, as well as of the Standing Committee of the House of Laity. He was equally a member of the Christian Council of Nigeria (CCN) at the level of its Executive Committee, both at the national level, and at the Eastern Regional level. Particularly, he found time to provide valuable service as the Secretary of the Eastern Regional Education Advisory Council of the CCN, a capacity in which he was the vital link between the Education Secretaries of all the various Missions belonging to the CCN, namely the Methodist, Presbyterian and Anglican.

The meticulous administrative skills, intellectual energy and patient approach of R.I. Uzoma to official duties, was such that he found himself being relied on for a wide cross-section of lay ad-hoc responsibilities in the CCN. For instance up to 1966, he was the CCN representative on the Extended Scale Committee of the Board of Education mandated to look into the payment system in the schools. At about the same time, he also chaired the Eastern Nigeria Rural Activities Committee (ENRAC) of the CCN, followed by more work as a member of the Anglican Church Committee that was responsible for designating Bishops for the new dioceses in the proposed Anglican Church of Nigeria. The Church of Nigeria became independent from the larger Church of the Province of West Africa with an inaugural ceremony held on 24th February, 1979 (Nwankiti, 1996: 25).

"Father" of the Diocese

In the period after his retirement from formal public sector employment in 1967, particularly at the end of the Nigerian civil war in 1970, R.I. Uzoma focused his attention on the growth of the Anglican Church closer to home. Having travelled extensively in his younger days as a minister, and later as an Education Secretary, he considered that it was time to re-channel his energies. It was in this period that a good example of the commitment for which he was known, in his work for the Church, presented itself. This was in the pursuit for the establishment of the new Okigwe/Orlu Diocese in Imo State between 1977 and 1984.

The idea of creating a new Diocese of Okigwe/Orlu out of the rather large Owerri Diocese, was first conceived in 1977 by R.I. Uzoma and Eze J. Ovuike of Umuihi in Etiti Local Government of Imo State. The new diocese was to be constituted out of the Okigwe/Orlu Archdeaconry which had been carved out within Owerri Diocese in 1959. These two leaders behind the idea, started by convening a meeting of stakeholders in R.I. Uzoma's residence in Nkwerre. In attendance at the meeting, were leading church delegates, chiefs and other opinion leaders of the Anglican denomination. The rationale behind the idea was presented by RI and Eze Ovuike and was immediately welcomed. The meeting easily transformed into what became, the Okigwe/Orlu Christian Association, covering the two Archdeaconries of Okigwe and Orlu. Thereafter, a set of proposals was agreed on and were put forward to the sitting Bishop of Owerri, then the Rt. Rev. B. Nwankiti on September 30th 1977. Leadership of the Okigwe/Orlu Christian Association continued under R.I. Uzoma as chairman and Eze Ovuike as deputy, until the diocese became a reality an entire seven years later in 1984 (Uzoma, R.I., 1984).

To R.I. Uzoma the need for the new diocese was not only obvious, it was also historically, sociologically and politically imperative. The motivating factors were strong. The Owerri Diocese had not only become too large in comparison to dioceses in other parts of the Church of Nigeria, it had become administratively awkward to manage the sheer number of its members, its churches and other institutions. In the words of R.I. Uzoma,

> As far back as 1971 at the Owerri Diocesan Synod held at Obizi, Mbaise, we had "prophesied" that with the improvement in the economy of the country, the consequent recovery of the churches from the ravages of the civil war, the archdeaconries of Owerri Diocese would develop into full-fledged autonomous dioceses. It was not, until 1977, during the funeral of the Late Dr. Aaron Ogbonna in the same Obizi that the stark reality of the enormity of numbers stared us in the face. The crowd from the Owerri Diocese was so great that both the church building and the compound could not take them – men and women, big and small, rich and poor, young and old, school children etc. (Uzoma, R.I., 1984).

Having to convince other stakeholders and opinion leaders of the original Owerri Diocese was not an easy task. After the first initial delegation to Bishop Nwankiti of the Owerri Diocese on the matter, there were several more years of delegations, debates and meetings. However R.I. Uzoma's dogged intellectual arguments helped to carry the day. His paperwork involved comparative research into the creation of new dioceses in other parts of the

Church in Nigeria. It also provided data and statistics on numbers of parishes in each diocese, and spatial distribution with costs. Several memoranda and other correspondence, signed by members of the Okigwe/Orlu Christian Association under the leadership of R.I. Uzoma, were forwarded to the Bishop of Owerri Diocese. The major ones were those of September 30th 1977 and another of early January 1980. The Bishop initially raised objections to the request, preferring instead that a few more Archdeaconries be created. The Okigwe/Orlu Christian Association persisted and its Chairman, R.I. Uzoma, continued to support the argument for the new diocese with documented facts and figures. He drew from his broad experience and knowledge of the history of the Anglican Church all over Nigeria. According to him,

> The Owerri Diocese by 1983 was one of the largest numerically (not spatially) in the Church of Nigeria (Anglican Communion). It had about 57 parishes, 29 of which are in the new Okigwe/Orlu Diocese. In terms of the senatorial zones of the era of party politics, the new diocese embraces the whole of the Okigwe senatorial zone except the Oguta-Egbema-Ohaji Local Government Area. At present the diocese is made up of two large archdeaconries namely: Okigwe, with headquarters at Ezeoke-Nsu in Mbano Local Government Area and Orlu, with headquarters at Nkwerre/Isu Local Government Area. By some accident of history, the Anglican Communion for many years had only one church in Orlu Urban and none in Okigwe Urban before 1977. Since then, Okigwe has become the headquarters of a new virile parish which includes not only churches on the southern side of the Imo River, but also churches in Okigwe Urban, Isuochi and Isuikwuato on the northern side of the Imo River (Uzoma, R.I., 1984).

In February 1980, the Lord Bishop of Owerri finally acceded to the wishes of his Okigwe/Orlu parishioners at a meeting of the diocese by stating as follows:

> I want to make it clear that I am not in principle, against the splitting of Owerri Diocese. No Bishop will block the legitimate wishes of the people of God in his care...[71]

---

71 See "History of Orlu Diocese" (2018) Retrieved 1st February 2018, from http://orludiocese.com/history.html.

The Bishop followed through by appointing a 24-member Advisory Committee with R.I. Uzoma as chairman. The committee was charged with the responsibility of recommending on the way forward for the creation of the new diocese in terms of administration, logistics and other needs, and in line with the guidelines of the Church of Nigeria. The committee's report was adopted, and R.I. Uzoma found himself having to play a key role in meeting targets for the requirements towards provision of a suitable Bishop's court and offices in Nkwerre. He later personally facilitated the acquisition of land from Nkwerre villages for the Bishop's court and offices, and personally supervised construction work for these infrastructure. The years of delay in the take-off of the new diocese soon came to an end, and all efforts culminated in a celebratory inauguration at the St. Paul's Pro-Cathedral Church in Nkwerre on November 6th 1984. RI became known as "Father" of the Okigwe/Orlu Diocese for the rest of his life.

The new Diocese was more or less the last bastion of service for R.I. Uzoma and his wife in the 1980s and 1990s. For many years from the inception of the diocese, R.I. Uzoma provided valuable advisory support as a member of the Synod and Chairman of the Okigwe/Orlu Laity Council as well as its Standing Committee. He also functioned as Education Adviser to the diocese. An extension of that responsibility was his role as Chairman of the Management Committee of the Okigwe/Orlu seminaries and other educational institutions. Beyond the Diocese, RI also represented Okigwe/Orlu on the Joint Council of Anglican Dioceses of Eastern States of Nigeria, from 1985. As the name implies, this is a platform which brings together the Bishops, Archdeacons, Knights, prominent lay-members including academicians, of all the dioceses located east of the Niger. The platform covers the five ecclesiastical provinces of the Anglican Church. In the 1980s, it included the Dioceses of Owerri, Okigwe/Orlu, Awka, Aba, the Niger, Enugu, the Niger-Delta, Uyo and Calabar among others. Within the Joint Council,

R.I. Uzoma chaired the Committee on Higher Education. In 1991 that committee made a case, and put forward proposals for the conversion of St. Paul's College, Awka, the famous alma mater of RI and many members on the joint council, into a tertiary institution focused on theological studies. This was at the time the Anambra State government had returned that institution to the Anglican Church, after it was utilised as a College of Education. The work of RI's committee, after some years, led to the college being elevated, first to St. Paul's University College (of Theology), and presently to a full university known as the St. Paul's University, a private Christian institution.

The dedication, with which R.I. Uzoma served the new diocese even at the lowest level, was legendary. No duty was too low for him and no demand on him was too great, because he felt a compelling need to contribute his best to the success of the new diocese. In his retirement and into the mid-1990s, RI sat on the Pastoral Committee of the diocese which had the responsibility for recruitment and deployment of catechists and priests for various parishes. He also chaired the Junior Staff Employment and Promotions Committee whose duties sometimes involved thorny disciplinary cases. One such example was the Mount Carmel '92 Investigative Panel whose report was finally resolved by RI's committee. This was an incident in which an unusual form of radical pentecostalism found expression in the actions of an overzealous church teacher, who doubled as a laboratory assistant at the Junior Seminary in Osina. Without due authority from the supervising priests, the said staff had organised a "Revival" which agitated the young people with new ideas and new language which caused some concern among the priesthood.[72] RI's remarkable understanding as an educationist as usual did not fail to settle the issue and calm frayed nerves.

RI continued to show deep commitment to service even in his later years, such that he became an institution in the Diocesan

---

[72] Report on Meeting of Diocesan Junior Staff Employment and Promotions Committee of November 26th, 1992; R.I. Uzoma Archives.

offices at Nkwerre. It was therefore not a surprise when the first meeting-hall constructed in the Cathedral grounds was named after him after his passing on April 4th 2000. Following that, the second Bishop of the Diocese, the Rt. Rev. Dr. B.C.I. Okoro, also started a Diocesan Scholarship Scheme in his name for children of struggling families in the diocese.

Service to Nkwerre Community

According to available records, the Nkwerre Aborigines Union (NAU) was inaugurated in 1939, following a spirited fund-raising drive by four wealthy Nkwerre merchants, namely Chief Francis Ihekwaba, Chief Abel Nwakanma, Samuel Chinaka, and Daniel Udeagu Ukegbu. The fund-raising exercise was undertaken in an effort to meet a condition which had been imposed by the CMS Niger Mission Authorities in 1935, for the establishment of a college for boys in any suitable location in the Old Owerri province. According to Obialor (2006:143) that condition required that "any town or group which could produce between three thousand and four thousand pounds" would be considered first as a location for a proposed CMS College for Boys. This was the background history to the establishment of St. Augustine's Grammar School for Boys (SAGS), in Nkwerre in 1948. The fund-raising drive towards getting a college became the stimulus that gave birth to the Nkwerre Aborigine's Union (NAU), a powerful organ of development in Nkwerre (Obialor, 2006: 143-145).

Following the success of the fund-raising drive, the wealthy elite of Nkwerre, in their wisdom realised the need to galvanize a more broad-based group with varying expertise, in order to achieve the goal of founding an educational institution in Nkwerre. The project obviously needed those who could reach out to the CMS authorities and speak their language. In 1939, they convened a meeting of all the nascent elite of Nkwerre in Aba. Due to his rising profile as an educated Nkwerre son, R.I. Uzoma was part of that meeting and came to be one of those young emergent leaders whose skills would become indispensable in the actualisation of the vision of the NAU.

While in his late 20's, R.I. Uzoma was recognised as one of the founding fathers of the Nkwerre Aborigines Union along with such established Nkwerre citizens as Nze Francis U. Ihekwoaba, Chief Abel N. Nwakanma, Lazarus Ihekwoaba, Nze Daniel Udeagwu Ukegbu, Samuel Chinaka, John Nwogu, Daniel Uju Okparaocha, Marcus Onyejiaka, James Idiwogu Nwosu, Chief Fred. U. Anyiam, Uriah Anyiam Osigwe, Benneth Agugua, Eze J.O. Ugochukwu, Francis I. Osunkwo, Chief S.N. Ohanka, Nze James Iheme Nwosu, Joseph O. Nnajuba, Nze M.C. Emenike, Nze Okwara Oji, Nze Jonathan A. Emenike, Isaiah Amaechi, Jimanze Ihedioha, Nze Paul Enwereobi Egbuchu, John Ihekwoaba, Dickson Ukegbu, James Onyeagiri, Rufus Egwuekwe, and others (Obialor, 2006: 91).

However, by deliberate choice and in deference to his many older 'brothers,' R.I. Uzoma did not from the start seek to hold any formal positions in the leadership hierarchy of the town union. He largely chose to provide valuable technical advice and professional support, from behind the scenes. This turned out to be a wise decision as he grew in his career into many strategic positions especially in the CMS Mission, and later in the government public service. After serving as National Treasurer for 10 years from 1957 to 1967, R.I. Uzoma did not occupy any other office in the executive committee of the NAU. The hectic nature of his schedule in the various positions he held either in the Anglican Church or in government, made it difficult for him to effectively occupy positions in the town union. He was a perfectionist who always wanted to put in his best in any assignment. He however, accepted nomination as one of the patrons of the NAU and remained so all through his life.

The contributions of R.I. Uzoma to the development of Nkwerre remain quite significant in terms of human and social development, even when they may not always be calculable in physical and material terms. One early contribution of R.I. Uzoma to human development in Nkwerre was the increase of awareness among Nkwerre youth towards being physically mobile in search of formal education outside Nkwerre. From the time RI became principal of Okrika Grammar School (OGS), from 1944 to 1946, Nkwerre saw a discernible increase in the number of its sons who as pioneers, went into secondary education to that distant institution, as well as elsewhere. By 1944, Okrika Grammar School was only five years old having opened in 1939. Prior to that date, Nkwerre parents had suffered a scare which made them reluctant to send their children for secondary education in distant locations. Although a few of them had attained Standard Six primary education in locations quite far from Nkwerre, secondary education was another matter.

As earlier reported, in 1925 one of the first pupils of Nkwerre Central School had been admitted into the pioneer mission secondary school then, the Dennis Memorial Grammar School (DMGS) in Onitsha. His name was Ezekiel Emeanuru and he unfortunately fell ill at that school and died. Nkwerre parents became frightened of encouraging schooling for their children in distant communities where boarding would be necessary. With the deployment of R.I. Uzoma to Okrika Grammar School (OGS) from Awka College in 1943, that fear receded and their confidence returned. From 1940 and 1941 one or two students from Nkwerre and the neighbouring town of Abba were already at OGS, but the arrival of R.I. Uzoma as Principal gave them the courage and impetus to complete their studies during his tenure. These were Abraham Nwachukwu, Christopher Asugha and Emmanuel Akwiwu. More students from Nkwerre enrolled at OGS during R.I. Uzoma's tenure (1943-1945). These included Jason Ihetu, Bertram Uzoma,

Benson Ogbonna, Silas Onwumere, Lawrence Onyegbula, Benson Nwakanma and Nathan Nwakanma.[73]

By the time RI was leaving OGS in Okrika Grammar School for further studies in the UK, the jinx was broken and a floodgate of Nkwerre students studying at OGS, was opened. Between 1946 and 1949, more Nkwerre pioneers followed. These were: Julius Madumere, Sunday Nwankpa, Geoffrey Chinaka, Timothy Nnadi, Ndubueze Ukegbu, Emmanuel Anumnu, Udeze Azodeh, Godwin Onyegbula, Abraham Nwachukwu, Emmanuel Onyejiaka, Christopher Madumere, and Harold Asugha.[74] It was the establishment of St. Augustine's Grammar School for Boys in 1948 that stemmed the tide of Nkwerre youth seeking secondary education at OGS. In 1946, R.I. Uzoma left OGS for the University of London for roughly one year. Before his departure, he ensured that the Nkwerre Town Union (NAU) was able to clear all the hurdles towards the siting of the proposed Boys College in Nkwerre. The College had been designated for the old Owerri province. At that time in Colonial Nigeria, the rather large Owerri province covered what were Okigwe, Bende and Owerri Divisions, with Orlu as part of the Okigwe Division. Nkwerre town was within the Orlu District.

R.I. Uzoma was a life member of the CMS, and while at Awka College, he had become quite versed with the administrative procedures of the CMS authorities. He was therefore in a position to advise on the establishment and eventual take-over of the proposed Boy's College by the CMS mission. Apart from financial contribution to the project under the auspices of the NAU, RI utilised his position as the only Nigerian graduate school principal in the CMS Niger Diocese education system at the time, to push for the Boy's College project. He successfully lobbied the CMS authorities to accede to locating the school in Nkwerre and to

---

73 From Okrika Grammar School at 50, Golden Jubilee 1940-1990, A Booklet published for the Golden Jubilee celebrations of Okrika Grammar School, 21st-27th May, 1990, with a comprehensive list titled, Prefects and Students' Roll Call from 1940 to 1974. Pp 2-8.
74 Ibid, 2-8

do so "at a time the Diocese was complaining of a shortage of graduate teachers."[75] By the time R.I. Uzoma returned home from the UK in 1947, the final approval for the Boys' College in Nkwerre, had been granted to the NAU. The site was inspected and approved by the Inspector of Education. The NAU quickly moved into action to raise more funds and mobilised the relevant committees for construction of the first buildings of the college.

In 1948, the college which was named the St. Augustine's Grammar School (SAGS) started off on a temporary site at the old Church hall of St. Paul's Church before moving into the permanent site in 1949 (Obialor, 2006: 145). It is noteworthy that by a happy coincidence, both the CMS officer appointed as the first principal of SAGS in 1948, and the Senior Master who acted for him until his return from postgraduate studies in the UK, were colleagues and friends of R.I. Uzoma. These two pioneer heads of SAGS were Mr. Mark Anyiam, Acting Principal in 1948 and Mr. E.C. Ezekwesili, Substantive Principal from 1948 to 1959 (Obialor, 2006: 145). Within the next decade, the impact of OGS and SAGS was felt in Nkwerre as the town became a leader, not only in commerce and business, but also in terms of its sizeable population of educated professionals.

R.I. Uzoma continued his facilitatory and technical support role, into the establishment in Nkwerre, of the oldest girls' secondary school in present-day Imo State, the St. Catherine's Girls' Secondary School. This was in 1955 seven years after the St. Augustine's Boys School had taken off. At that time, RI was resident in Old Umuahia as the Education Secretary and supervisor of schools for the CMS Niger-Delta Diocese. Similar to SAGS, the school was handed over to the Anglican CMS Mission for management. St. Catherine's Girls' Secondary School became one of the many schools and teacher training colleges whose establishment was a major part of R.I. Uzoma's hectic schedule

---

[75] From R.I. Uzoma's autobiographical notes forwarded to the Brochure Committee for the 1989 NAU 50 years Anniversary Celebrations; R.I. Uzoma Archives

in the 1950's. R.I. Uzoma's involvement with the founding of St. Catherine's had special meaning for him given his well-known commitment to girls' education. Also important was the role of his wife, Mrs. Jemimah Uzoma, who at the time was the National Secretary of the women's wing of the NAU. The NAU/Women's Section single-handedly funded and supervised the construction of the Girls' School. Mrs. Uzoma, herself the first female certified teacher in Nkwerre, worked hand in hand with her husband, and the then President of the NAU Women's Wing, Da Sarah Akaose, a dynamic and highly charismatic business woman who refused to be hindered by her lack of formal schooling (Obialor, 2006:147).

From 1957 to 1967, RI served the NAU as the National Treasurer. Fund-raising within the NAU was not a difficult matter. This was the era of strong town unions across the Igbo territory. Communities were highly motivated by the spirit of nationalism and solidarity sweeping across the land. It was in this period that Nkwerre people built for themselves most of the projects that should have been provided by government. They could not wait for government patronage, having started the practice of self-development as early as 1948 to 1950 with the construction of a post office (Obialor, 2006:92). After the two secondary schools in 1948 and 1955, the NAU went further to develop the Nkwerre Water Scheme, a High Court complex, a public library, a general hospital and later, a civic centre. In the ten years that he was National Treasurer, in addition to his official duties as Education Secretary and Manager of Schools R.I. Uzoma was a very busy man indeed.

Before the civil war, and while he was NAU treasurer, R.I. Uzoma opened correspondence with the Regional government in Enugu on the "Nkwerre Water Scheme". He used his knowledge of government officials to facilitate the project by contacting the then Minister of Works, Mr. Ururuka, and the Water Engineer Mr Okpofabiri. He went further to pay the first deposit of £2000 raised and approved by the NAU and later a further £1000 raised by the NAU, Women's Wing. As a result of these deposits, the Nkwerre local government had running water all through the civil war. In addition, Nkwerre community did not have to pay any water rates for over ten years following the successful take-off of the scheme. After the civil war, the water scheme which was serving the entire local government area became a subject of local politics in the newly re-designated Nkwerre/Isu Local Government Council. The Isu communities raised issues and argued that the water scheme should be renamed the "Isu Water Scheme". R.I. Uzoma rose in defence of Nkwerre and tendered all the documents which had led to the execution of the project in the area. These included letters and payment receipts issued to NAU. The Isu leaders had no documents to back their case and the name "Nkwerre Water Scheme" remained.[76]

In 1967 when he was appointed Administrator for Orlu Province in defunct 'Biafra', R.I signed off from elected executive committee positions in the NAU and handed over to his brother, Nze Nwosu-Iheme, as National Treasurer. He chose to remain in the background as an elder and kingmaker in town union matters. However he could not hide from call to public office and civic duties of an ad-hoc and sometimes quite political nature. In 1966 he had been appointed by the Eastern Regional Military Government of Lt. Col. Odumegwu Ojukwu to represent Orlu Province as a member of the Constituent Assembly. That Assembly was to decide on new administrative divisions in the Eastern Region. The subsequent creation of Nkwerre Division, by the Edict of December 10th 1966, would not have been possible but for the efforts of Chief R.I. Uzoma as a member of the Constituent Assembly during the regime of Lt. Col. Odumegwu Ojukwu. Together with Ambassador G.A. Onyegbula, then the Secretary to the Military Government, both men successfully made the case for Nkwerre. By the 1966 Edict, an Orlu Province was created with headquarters at Orlu and

---

76   *Ibid*, for the start of the Nkwerre Water Scheme Project.

was made up of two divisions, namely Nkwerre with headquarters at Nkwerre, and Mgbidi with headquarters at Mgbidi.

At the end of the civil war, the provincial system was abolished and there was an agitation to move the headquarters from Nkwerre. This led to the appointment of the "Anyaegbunam Local Government Re-Organisation Committee" in July 1971. R.I. Uzoma spent two weeks personally preparing the memorandum on the case for Nkwerre. He was the spokesman for Nkwerre and proved all his points with documented facts. In 1976 another committee, the Agada Local Government Panel, was set up, this time over the renewed agitation for the name of the Local Government and whether it should be "Nkwerre" or "Isu" or some other name. R.I. Uzoma again took the responsibility for preparing a memorandum putting forward the Nkwerre case before the panel. The result was the retention of Nkwerre as the name for the local government area.[77]

RI's main concern in the NAU remained the promotion of enlightened and honest leadership in the Union. Hence in 1978, with other elders of the Union, namely Chief B.C.U. Agugua and Chief Emma Nwosu, RI persuaded a reluctant Ambassador Godwin A. Onyegbula to contest and take up the post of President-General of the Union, following the successful end of Chief Nwosu's tenure. Again in 1988, RI was one of the main supporters of the same eminent citizen of Nkwerre, G.A. Onyegbula for successful election into the Constituent Assembly which was appointed by the Federal Military Government to draft a new constitution for Nigeria's return to civilian rule (Onyegbula, 2005:232). At this time RI's goal was clearly the involvement of the younger educated crop of Nkwerre citizens, into as many strategic public office positions as possible.

The special interest of RI in the development of Nkwerre continued in all the public offices or political dispensations he found himself in. During the civil war and while serving as Administrator for Orlu Province between 1967 and 1970, he facilitated the opening

---

[77] *Ibid*, for RI's role in the various local government creation efforts.

of a police post in Nkwerre, the first ever of such a security post in the town. In order to ensure speedy installation of that facility, he convinced his kindred to offer to the police authorities, a building that served as family meeting hall in Obinuhu. This became the first location of the police post. Thereafter Nkwerre has continued to have a police station, particularly since Nkwerre became the seat of a local administrative unit after the civil war. The erstwhile Biafra Police Charge Office in Nkwerre, is today a full police station of the Nigerian Police Force with a DPO in charge. With these antecedents, it was not a surprise that R.I. Uzoma served as a key member of the Police Public Relations Committee of the Nkwerre/Isu Local Government throughout the 1980s. He performed this function in the company of traditional rulers and other opinion leaders of the communities in the local government area, and received special appreciation from the Inspector-General of Police at the time.

In 1964/65, while resident at Owerri as Education Secretary, RI also took up the assignment of seeing a bank sited in Nkwerre. He made contact with a Mr John Otagburuagu, Manager of the Owerri Branch of the then Cooperative and Commerce Bank (CCB), and Mr B. Nwachukwu, the General Manager at Aba. They applied for a branch of CCB to be opened in Nkwerre. RI personally went to Nkwerre with these bank officials for an inspection. The Nkwerre residence of Nze D.I. Onuoha in Obinuhu, was found suitable as the best location because it was a large structure and had adequate parking space in its forecourt. A prominent Nkwerre contractor, Chief C.C. Ugochukwu, was engaged by the bank to make the required structural adjustments on the building, and the bank was able to take off in a few months. Through this development, Nkwerre citizens were saved from much hardship caused by currency crunch during the civil war and in the immediate period thereafter.[78]

---

78   *Ibid*, for the introduction of a branch of the Cooperative and Commerce Bank into Nkwerre.

Post-Retirement Public Service

R.I. Uzoma's retirement from formal employment with the Anglican Church Missions in 1967 was followed by the civil war (1967 to 1970). It marked a watershed in his extensive service in the direct management of schools and colleges. After briefly serving as a member of the governing council of the University of Lagos from 1965 to 1967, the outbreak of the civil war ironically gave him a breathing space. He had travelled so much on field duties from 1953 to 1967 that he felt that some scaling down had become necessary. During the civil war he was appointed as Administrator of the Orlu Province. No sooner had the war ended in January 1970, that R.I. Uzoma found himself being called upon to continue service in several tenured political assignments under the post civil-war federal structure.

From 1970 to 1973, R.I was compelled to do a "second-coming" or gradual return to public service in the government of the then East Central State (ECS) of Nigeria. The glaring need to rebuild nearly all public-sector institutions in the territory of the former Eastern Region, compelled the state government to seek out men of experience and integrity like R.I. Uzoma. In 1970, RI was appointed Chairman of the Nkwerre Divisional School Board with offices in Orlu, a position he was initially reluctant to accept. Thereafter, from 1974 to 1976 he moved on to Enugu, the capital of the new East Central State as one of the pioneer commissioners in the newly-created Teachers' Service Commission (TSC). He was motivated to take up these two positions first in Orlu and then in Enugu, because of the sorry state of schools and the teaching profession in the East Central State (ECS) following the devastations of the civil war. It was a state of affairs that gave R.I. Uzoma quite some concern, due to his love for that profession.

At the end of the civil war, the East Central State government, by Military Decree, took over control of all the schools and colleges in the state that had belonged to the "Voluntary Service

Agencies." This was a wide network of secondary and teacher-training institutions previously under the management of the church missions, with only a few belonging to local communities and private proprietors. The Church Missions found themselves confused as to how to handle the situation, especially in view of the huge investment they had made into the schools system in the Eastern Region in terms of human and material resources. It was at this time that the then Bishop of Owerri Diocese, the Rt. Rev. B.C. Nwankiti, wrote an urgent letter to R.I. Uzoma inviting his input on the matter into the Synod Report of 1970. Specifically RI was asked to make a submission that could "sound a note of hope and encouragement and to help the diocese to understand the important part which the church must play in a state-controlled education system."[79] R.I. Uzoma at the time was a principal member of the Owerri Diocesan Synod. His submission to the Synod did much to chart a way for the Anglican Mission to positively integrate their educational vision into the government's management style.

Two years of hectic duties for RI on the Nkwerre Divisional Education Board, were followed by another equally tedious year as Commissioner on the State Teachers' Service Commission (TSC), managing the careers of traumatised teachers from the civil war. On January 30th 1976, R.I. Uzoma was moved from the TSC to the Public Service Commission (PSC) of the East Central State where government felt he could apply the same expertise to the wider platform of civil servants in general. Before that move, he had to double for a few months as Commissioner in the Public Service Commission of the East Central State, in addition to his duties at the Teachers Service Commission.

In early 1976, the federal government restructured the country from twelve states to twenty-one states. The carving out of Anambra and Imo States from the ECS which followed, gave

---

79   From a letter from the Bishop of Owerri, Rt. Rev. B.C. Nwankiti to R.I. Uzoma, dated June 22nd, 1970; R.I. Uzoma Archives. See Appendix 59

some relief to RI from his hectic double schedule in Enugu. With the creation of new states, RI found himself serving in the East Central State for a few more months only. On March 12th 1976, he received yet another appointment letter requiring him to report in Owerri as Public Service Commissioner for the new Imo State. Thereafter, R.I. Uzoma served out the full tenure of four years in the Imo State Public Service Commission from 1976 to 1980. In that period, together with his equally eminent fellow commissioners, in the persons of Dr. D.W. Emutchay (Chairman), Chief H.K. Offonry, Chief D. Akuneme, Chief E.N Ukpabi and Sir J.B. Onyia, they were a formidable team that helped to put the civil service of the new state on the right footing.

It was as though government was reluctant to allow R.I. Uzoma to truly retire and rest, especially in matters that had to do with public service discipline and education. In 1980 after his four-year tenure on the Imo State Public Service Commission, he was yet appointed by the federal government to serve as a member of the inaugural governing council of the Federal University of Technology in Owerri (FUTO) from 1982, while also serving as Chairman of the Orlu Zonal Education Board for three years. He eventually signed off from post-retirement public duties, as Chairman of the State Teachers' Disciplinary Committee from 1984 to a few years later. Thereafter, RI had to put his foot down and reject further calls to public service, a privilege he had so often been denied.

6

THE MAN AND HIS PRINCIPLES

This biography would be incomplete without a chapter that profiles strictly the personality and character of the man R.I. Uzoma, and some of the core principles which guided his life of service. Given the historical style which has been adopted so far, such a chapter would be necessary for a deeper understanding of this uniquely iconic leader from a transformative era of Nigeria's development. The style of embedding the life and times of R.I. Uzoma within the context of a wide range of interrelated events such as early missionary education and its principal actors, gives room for the possibility that some readers may lose sight of the biographical element, which is the man, R.I. Uzoma himself. This chapter is therefore intended to refocus the interest of the reader on the main subject, that is the individual whose life and contributions have had immeasurable impact on the lives of many, and on the period in which he lived.

First Normative Influences

When he set foot on the grounds of CMS Central School, Nkwerre, Reuben Ibekwe Uzoma exhibited traits which made his peers and teachers alike to see him as a child prodigy. As earlier stated, RI was among the first set of students to start their formal education at the school when it was established in 1922. He was then aged about ten years old. It was an age much higher than six years which is today's standard for the start of primary education in

Nigeria, yet R.I. Uzoma was easily the youngest in his class. Many of his classmates were already in their early teenage years or older. The church teachers and missionaries took notice of the young Reuben because of his quick response to questions in class, as well as his constant interest in reading and mathematics.

One of the early pre-requisites for primary school registration at the time was the baptism of children with "English" first names, often of Biblical origin. Such baptism became the proud mark of conversion to Christianity. As he got older, RI took this experience beyond the school into his family. Hence, this period of early missionary education sowed the seed of many of the principles that guided him in his life. With time, he became a harbinger of the Christian values of self-discipline, truth and justice, standing on one's beliefs and promoting fair play and equity. By the time RI left CMS Central School in Nkwerre, and went into teacher training at Awka College, he had become his family's shining light, a leader whose advice was often sought and needed. This situation arose particularly in relation to the numerous social innovations that swept across Igbo communities in this period, in the form of Western education, colonial economy, new religious practices and other social norms. RI found himself taking decisions in matters concerning the education and upbringing of his siblings, a huge responsibility that fell on him, particularly after the death of his father in 1940.

R.I. Uzoma was in his late 20s when his father Uzoma, son of Ibekwe, died early in his forties. From then on, the young Reuben had to grow up quickly in order to assume responsibilities as a head of family. In any case, his father Uzoma Ibekwe was frequently away from Nkwerre during much of RI's childhood. He was a typical Nkwerre migrant trader, whose polygamous nuclear family was strategically split between his home-community and his distant host community of trade (Uzoma, A.C., 1971). In Ibekwe's case, these communities included Umuopara in present-day

The Man and his Principles

Mbano, Imo State and Umunede in Delta State.[80] RI's childhood years in Nkwerre were spent largely under the care of his paternal grandmother *'Baabd*. She did her best to see that RI went through school on the best of her meagre resources from farming and local trade. As previously reported, it was not a silver-spoon existence for Reuben, even though he was pampered in terms of love and affection.

Notwithstanding his youthful years, by the time he became a trained teacher, after passing through Awka College with flying colours, RI had acquired so much charisma, due to the awe in which teachers were held in those days. The young R.I Uzoma quickly came to be respected in his family and community at large as *Onye-nkuzi*, and as a big brother to all in his family. By then he had developed a passion for formal education. In his view, it was only formal education that turned his life around from an ordinary childhood, to a career of professional promise. He embraced it not only for himself, but also for his siblings and any extended family kindred who came to him for advice.

In an interview which he granted to the Editorial Board of the Orlu Zonal "Educator" in 1986, R.I. stated that,

> The CMS Central School, Nkwerre, the oldest "Standard Six" School in Orlu Zone, happens to have been situated in my village at Nkwerre – a pole or two from my compound. My father sent me to school at a tender age; if I had to trek six or more kilometres before getting to school, I don't think I would have gone to school at all. Probably, I would have been a trader like other Nkwerre people. My father was a busy tobacco trader. He rather left me with my grandmother who so pampered me that today, I wonder how I managed to do well at school. My grandmother at any given time had two or three of her nieces to live with her and serve her. As my father was her only son and I, her first grandson, I was not allowed to do any serious work.

---

80   The practice in the past for Nkwerre migrant traders was for them to leave a section of their usually polygamous families behind in Nkwerre, in the charge of one or two of their wives or of their mother. The home branch of the family would then carry on with the home farming and local trade. See Uzoma, A.C. 1971

> I was admired by my teachers for being particularly good in Arithmetic and I had a relatively good retentive memory. In fact, I did little or no home work nor any private study after school. It was only when I went to Awka College in 1931 that I developed the habit of reading.
>
> I can say that at the Primary School stage, I pursued education by the sheer incident of being born in a village that had a Central School planted in it as far back as 1922, and the next motivation was the interest my Headmaster and my teacher had in me for my good memory and ability in figures. I think I was the "darling" of the teacher."[81]

It followed naturally for RI, that he should introduce his family into the Christian way of life which had put him on the new path of western education. That introduction started with baptism at St Paul's Church Nkwerre, and the adoption of new names. Thus his mother, Nwannediya (Nwannedie) became Janet, his immediate younger brother Azuatalam became Bertram, and the next brother, born Agbarakwe became James Chikwe. The other brothers were Johnson Nduweze and Eric Chinyere. The girls were the older sister Nwaigbe baptized as Sophia Nwaigbe, Elechi as Christiana, Ikwuoma as Margaret, Nwanyiwunwa as Susanna, Ubakanwa as Eunice, Ikechi as Blessing, Nwaobiaraku as Beatrice, Ahuzuru as Comfort and Nwanyimba as Emilia also called Nwamba.[82]

For RI, the adoption of western names for himself and his siblings in the early formative years was only the symbol of adoption of western education in his youth. As he matured into a more single-minded adult, he came under the influence of some of the nationalist ideals which influenced the first educated Nigerians of the 1940s. He saw the need to balance western values with a pride in the positive elements of his own culture. By

---

[81] 1986 Interview with Chief R.I. Uzoma, former Chairman, Zonal Education Board, conducted by Messrs I. Umezurike, P.N. Abamara, Ifeanyi Ekenasi and Anene Ogidi of the Orlu Zonal Educator Editorial Board, 14th April, 1986; R.I. Uzoma Archives

[82] Oral Interview with Dr Adaoha Okwuosa (Mrs), R.I. Uzoma's daughter, October 2017

the time he married in 1942 and started his own family, RI and his young wife made it a point of principle to give their children only vernacular names. This decision was different from the practice for many educated elite of the time. Mr. and Mrs R.I. Uzoma baptized their children with Igbo names only. Each child as a rule, was given a vernacular name that has in it "Chi" or "Chukwu", either as a prefix or as a suffix, in reference to the Christian God.

Thus the first son of RI was named Anele Nwachukwu, the next child the first daughter, became Adaoha Chibuzo, followed by another son Onuoha Chijioke and then, a girl, Ukachi Nwaobiara. The fifth child another son, was named Ndubuisi Chigozie, followed by another daughter Ugochi Eziaha, after whom came another girl, Eberechukwu Obioma followed by another son, Okechukwu Madueke. The last four children of RI and his wife are two sets of twins. The first set, two boys, were named Chinyere Iheanacho and Chukwukere Ihetu. They were followed by another set of twins, two girls born in December 1961, and named Elewechi Uzonna and Ijeuru Okwuchi. By choosing only native names for his children, R.I. Uzoma was demonstrating his firm belief that vernacular names in themselves are not anti-thetical to Christianity. It is their meaning and origin that is important. He held the view that carefully chosen vernacular names, whose meaning the parents and children fully understand, are better than the many fancy European names, whose origins and meaning are unknown to Igbo culture.

Early Campaign for Girl-Child Education

The fact that R.I started early to shoulder responsibilities in his family, gave him the early opportunity to put into practice the guiding principles that molded his life. He was still a student when his older sister, Nwaigbe Sophia, whom he was very fond of, was married off as a teenage bride to a wealthy Port Harcourt merchant, Chief Nzewuba Okparaocha. Nzewuba was brother to

Chief Achonu and Chief Uju of Ukwuinyi village in Nkwerre. The three brothers were a well-known triad of wealthy merchants and committed polygamists. RI's sister, popularly called "Mgbe" and known for her beauty, similar to RI's good looks, became one of several wives in a rather large family setting.

As a student at Awka College, R.I. Uzoma developed an early respect for women, especially for their right to education. He appreciated the need to treat women with dignity and justice, having met and interacted with female missionary teachers, as they worked side by side with their male counterparts in the CMS education system. Indeed these were among the mentors who took special interest in his career because of his academic strengths, and facilitated his sponsorship through the system. RI frequently made it known to his children that one of his regrets was the fact that he was too young to prevent his elder sister, Mgbe, from being married off so early in life with no schooling.[83] It was a regret that was so strong that he was determined to prevent the same mistake being made with his younger sisters.

At a time when early marriage for female children was the norm, R.I. Uzoma made it a principle that going forward, his sisters and other female relatives would be encouraged to acquire as much formal education as possible before marriage. In addition, he would encourage monogamous Christian marriage for them, preferably to suitors from the emerging class of western-educated teachers, church workers and colonial service staff in that sector known as Oru Bekee (White man's work). This preferred life-choice for RI's sisters and female relatives was not always easy to achieve. From 1931, due to Awka College training, his posting to Ekwulobia and DMGS, followed by departure to Achimota College in 1938, RI found himself living largely away from Nkwerre. Meanwhile his younger siblings were still growing up in Nkwerre with their mothers. RI addressed the problem by instructing that

---

83   Ibid

The Man and his Principles

they remain registered in primary school. Thereafter whenever possible, he took them to live with him at his various stations. This was a strategy that continued even after he married in 1942 and started his own family.

Equal opportunity in education for all children without discrimination became such a core life-principle of R.I. Uzoma that, unlike many of his peers, he set for himself the goal of finding a life-partner who had received the best formal education that was available for the girl-child in his time. R.I. Uzoma's marriage to his very educated wife became one of the early examples of his practice of leading by example. As earlier mentioned, his first daughter, Dr. Adaoha Chibuzo Okwuosa, became the first female University graduate from Nkwerre and subsequently the first female to get a doctorate degree. RI saw education as an important entitlement of every child and did not believe that marriage was the only vocation for women. He frowned at the fact that some communities were still discriminating against the girl-child in education, and believed that Nkwerre community should make a difference in that regard. R.I. Uzoma was in this respect quite ahead of his time. In order not have his sisters marry without formal education, he on occasion refunded the dowry paid by suitors in his absence, insisting that his sisters must be reasonably educated before marriage. As a result, three of his younger sisters Margaret, Sussana and Beatrice, were able to acquire significant formal education before getting married.[84]

Before 1920, primary and secondary education in Nigeria was laregly within the scope of voluntary Christian organisations. Out of a total of twenty-five secondary schools established by 1920 in colonial Nigeria, three were for girls and the remainder was exclusively for boys.[85] In 1920, the colonial government started giving out subventions to voluntary organizations involved in

---
84 Ibid
85 Adentunji Ogunyemi. "A Historical Reconstruction of the Colonial Government Education Expenditure" Historical Research Letter,1940-1957

education. The grant-giving lasted till the early 1950's and at that point, education was placed under the control of the three regions. By 1949, only eight out of a total of fifty-seven secondary schools were exclusively for girls. Among these schools are Methodist Girls' High School, Lagos (1879), St. Anne's School, Molete, Ibadan (1927), Holy Rosary College, Enugu (1935), Anglican Girls' Grammar School, Lagos (1945), Queen Amina College and Alhuda College, Kano. From 1950 up till 1960, six more notable secondary schools were established and by 1960, there were fourteen girls' schools, ten were mixed and sixty-one were for boys' only.[86]

In the 1960's when most African states began to gain their political independence, there was considerable gender-disparity in education in Africa. Girls' enrollment figures were very low throughout the continent. In May 1961, the United Nations Declaration of Human Rights and UNESCO's educational plans for Nigeria were announced in a conference held in Addis Ababa, Ethiopia. A target was set to achieve 100% universal primary education in Nigeria by the year 1980. The implementation in the 1970's of the free and compulsory Universal Primary Education (UPE) was in line with this UN plan.[87] Since then, UNICEF and UNESCO and many other organizations have sponsored research and conferences within Nigeria on the education of girls. Up until the 1970's, considerably more boys than girls participated in education in Nigeria.

Pervading cultural traditions across Nigeria preferred that a woman's place be in the home, and this kept many girls away from education. However over the years, with increasing government intervention and public awakening, parents began to send and keep their girl-children in school. The voluntary agencies which largely include the Missions, also joined in the effort to close the gender-gap in education. Consequently, women's involvement

---

86 *Ibid*
87 UNESCO Report on the Education of Girls in Africa. The Ouagadougou Declaration and Framework for Action 1993

became more visible. It is noteworthy that purposeful plans of action led to an increase in the number of females in schools from 1990. While more boys than girls were enrolled in 1991, by a difference of 138,000, by 1998 the difference was reduced to 69,400.[88] These were developments that made R.I. Uzoma very happy in his later years as a senior citizen.

RI's campaign for women's education and improved access to schooling was one of his lingering legacies. To help parents aspire for more education for their daughters and realize the gain in schooling, he utilized his official roles to promote the ideals of girl-child education whenever he could. The few young women who demonstrated exceptional intelligence in the school system, he quickly employed as teachers when he became a top official of the CMS school system. Those he employed in teaching with only Standard Six certificates, he encouraged to advance into the Teachers' Training Colleges. In several instances he also recommended brilliant students, male or female, for admission to higher institutions within his authority. He did not allow clannish sentiments or ethnic bias to influence his recruitment of teachers, neither did he attach any subjective tags or expect gratification for recruiting any teacher. To him, it was an exercise based purely on merit, and in the service of humanity.

As earlier mentioned, RI equally used his strategic membership of social platforms such as the Nkwerre Aborigines Union, to address the gender gap in education whenever he could. In Nkwerre for instance, he generally encouraged academic scholarship by calling on many Nkwerre businessmen and merchants to sponsor brilliant but indigent male and female students into further education. His own personal career achievement from pupil-teacher to university graduate encouraged the upcoming generation in the 50s and 60s to aspire higher in education. Within his own family he gave his daughters exactly the same encouragement and support for education to the highest level, as he did his sons.

---

[88] *Ibid*

Today, Nkwerre has produced many female University graduates such as Prof. Elsie Obianyo (nee Agugua) the first female medical doctor and first female Professor, Justice Chioma Nwosu-Iheme of the Appeal Court System, first female indigenous judge, and Late Chief (Mrs) Ethel Iheme, who was the first female lawyer in Nkwerre. There have also been two female military officers, namely Major Mary Onyejiaka (Rtd), Nigerian Army, and Lt. Commander Sylvia Nwosu-Iheme (Rtd), Nigerian Navy. In addition, many educated Nkwerre daughters are living in the diaspora as accomplished professionals. The awareness that sprang from R.I. Uzoma's pioneering actions in the field of education placed Nkwerre ahead of many communities in terms of formal education. There is hardly any family in Nkwerre today without a female university graduate and several male university degree holders.

Humane, Impartial, Unassuming

At Ekwulobia Central School (ECS) early in his career, the humane approach which RI brought to his role as a teacher began to manifest. Ekwulobia was his first teaching deployment as a qualified High Elementary teacher after Awka College. It was a short posting, because he soon had to leave for DMGS, and then for Achimota College on CMS Mission scholarship. At ECS, RI made an impact that was still etched in the memory of some of his pupils for several decades. Two of his pupils, the Okpala brothers from the neighboring Ugah community, attracted his special attention. They were attending school daily all the way from Ugah by bicycle, a "luxury" item in those days. It was the responsibility of the older brother to transport the younger brother on the handlebar of the bicycle like a "passenger". The two were good students' inspite of the challenges of lateness and absenteeism. RI interviewed them and learnt of the long

The Man and his Principles

distance they covered each day, with attendant hazards, in order to receive formal schooling. He recalled that this was a plight he had been lucky not to suffer during his school days at Nkwerre Central School. Without hesitation he offered the Okpala brothers free accommodation for the weekdays in his modest teachers' quarters, in order to improve their performance in school.

Almost 40 years later in 1973, the younger Okpala brother, Bertram Ikedinachukwu Okpala had become a Professor, and was Dean of the Faculty of Biological Sciences and Head of the Department of Zoology, at the University of Nigeria, Nsukka. One of the younger daughters of R.I. Uzoma, Mrs. Ugochi Eziaha Onwumere (nee Uzoma), was in the process of registering as a freshman for Zoology studies at UNN. She reported at the office of the Head of Department with some of her mates for his signature. Professor Okpala, looked at the list of new students, and became curious to know which Uzoma this was, and the young lady told him she is R.I. Uzoma's daughter. The professor's early experience of unusual kindness from his Second-Master at Central School Ekwulobia, more than thirty-seven years earlier, was still fresh in his memory. He did not hesitate to excitedly narrate that unique experience to the rather bemused young lady.[89] RI's daughter was not surprised because the family had gradually over the years become aware, that RI's public service career was marked by several such interventions.

Another instance came later in RI's career, while he was serving as a Commissioner in the Public Service Commission of Imo State. In 1979, R.I. Uzoma was on a screening panel for the selection of Boy Scouts from the State, to join a team representing Nigeria at the Boys Scout Convention in Birmingham, United Kingdom. The best candidate from the results of the tests, turned out to be a young student from Government College, Owerri named

---

[89] Report of the Pan African Conference on Education for Girls', Ouagadougou, Burkina Faso, 28th March - 1st April 1993

Ntochukwu Obinna Ilona. His father was Mr. Martin Igwegbe Ilona, the Chief Lands Officer in the State Ministry of Lands. Mr. Ilona, an indigene of Ozubulu in Anambra State, happened to find himself serving in Imo State because he was deployed there in 1976, on the creation of Imo and Anambra States from the erstwhile East Central State. That deployment was necessitated by the fact that there was no Imo State indigene senior enough to start off the Lands Division in the new Imo State civil service. On his deployment to Owerri, Mr. Ilona had to transfer his young son from the College of Immaculate Conception (CIC) in Enugu, to Government College, Owerri. Mr. Ilona was a keen Scout and so was his young son Ntochukwu, hence the latter's excellent performance on the tests administered by the Public Service Commission.

However, the euphoria of creation of new States at the time resulted in some unhealthy politicization of issues. Several members of the Owerri screening panel for the international Boys' Scout event felt that the "successful" candidate should be an indigene of Imo State, considerations of merit notwithstanding. R.I. Uzoma held the contrary view that the matter should not be politicized and merit must always be upheld. He argued that the team to Birmingham was going to represent all of Nigeria and not any one state. To ensure that merit was maintained above politics, RI personally made a written intervention to the next level, which was the then Head of Civil Service in Enugu, Mr Anthony Aniagolu. This was how the best candidate received justice in the end as the final nominee. More than three decades later in 2017, Mr. Ilona of Ozubulu is in a position to narrate this experience to R.I. Uzoma's family.[90]

R.I. Uzoma had an unassuming, and somewhat spartan life-style, which he acquired as a mission-trained teacher. It remained with him when he became a high-profile public officer in powerful government positions, and did not leave him even after retirement.

---

90   Oral Interview with Sir Martin Igwegbe Ilona, retired Chief Lands Officer of Anambra State, in Enugu, Saturday 9th December 2017

The Man and his Principles

It was a life-style that shunned ostentation and the unnecessary display of wealth and status. It dictated his easy style and personal touch with his domestic staff at home, and with junior aides in his office.[91] Invariably he was uncomfortable with any social or cultural role-expectations, and group-memberships that encouraged ostentation.

When the practice of honouring selected lay members of the Anglican Church with investiture into Knighthoods was introduced in Owerri Diocese, RI did not hesitate to voice his concerns about the practice. He had been invited to attend a meeting of the Knights of Saint Christopher in Atta in Owerri Diocese, with a view to becoming a member. RI's concerns were based on his knowledge of medieval history and the violence by knights in the 11th to the 13th Centuries during the spread of Christianity in the period of the crusades. He feared that the Knighthoods in the Anglican Church of Nigeria, would carry a connotation of aggressive, fanatical Christianity. In a 1985 letter to the then Bishop of Owerri, R.I. Uzoma stated that he would rather abide by the baptismal injunction to every Christian "to continue as Christ's faithful soldier and servant unto his life's end" rather than join the Knighthood.[92] It was only after the program had run for some years, and RI was convinced of the progressiveness and symbolism of that innovation, merely as a latter-day recognition of dedicated, selfless service to the Church, that RI was persuaded to accept that honour, but on the condition of an exemption from their tail-coat uniform.

In 1989, R.I. Uzoma accepted to be formally admitted into the rather colourful order of the Knighthood of St. Christopher of the Okigwe/Orlu Anglican Diocese. Sometime before the ceremony, R.I. Uzoma used the opportunity of a sermon that he was invited to give, to reiterate his position on that honour, which

---

91   Oral Interview with Elder Augustine Esonwanne, R.I. Uzoma's personal driver for over 10 years, in Nkwerre (Umukor Village) on 9th June, 2017
92   From R.I. Uzoma's letter to the Bishop of Owerri, Rt Rev B.C. Nwankiti dated 20th February, 1985; R.I. Uzoma's Archives

has since become very much sought after by many. The event was a Dedication Service of the DMGS Old Boys Association, held at St. Michael's Cathedral, Aba on Sunday April 30th 1989. In the address, RI expressed his view that admission into the Knighthood was about humility and serving the people. The investiture should be seen merely as a ceremony aimed at,

> Emphasizing, recapitulating and confirming to you, as an adult Christian the service injunction and charge given to you as an infant when you were baptized......it is pertinent therefore, for me to add that whether you are formally admitted into the church's knighthood or not, once you are baptized you are a knight in spirit, member of the "chosen generation", of the "royal priesthood" who should show forth the praises of Him who hath called us out of darkness into His marvelous light. In the Middle Ages, a title was chosen by a Pope for himself and that title has stuck – "Servus Servorum Dei", literally the "Servant of the servants of God". "Servus" literally means "Slave". A knight should by virtue of his position, be a servant of the church congregation, not their master, expecting special recognition and seat on special occasions.....The code of conduct of a knight involves thinking of others first, the French 'Apres Vous', defending the weaker party." (Uzoma, R.I., 1989)

Another life-time experience that told the story of R.I. Uzoma, the man, was the 1992 celebration of the Golden Jubilee Anniversary of his wedding to his wife, Jemimah. The modest event was arranged by his children on Boxing Day 1992. Many prominent citizens of Nkwerre and Imo State at large were in attendance. At that occasion there were several moving speeches and testimonies on RI's life. Led in particular by Chief Emmanuel Nwogu and Chief Emmanuel Iwuanyanwu, the idea of an R.I. Uzoma Trust Fund was spontaneously floated. Several pledges and cheques donating various amounts of money for the fund were issued on the spot by a number of individuals including Chief Emmanuel Akwiwu, Chief Emmanuel Iwuanyanwu, Ambassador G.A. Onyegbula, Mr. Albert C. Okeke and Sir E.C.O. Uzoukwu.

The Man and his Principles

At the close of the ceremony however, R.I. Uzoma calmly told his children that, although he very much appreciated the spontaneous action of guests at the occasion, the cheques donated by them should not be presented. His reason was that he would not welcome the idea of monies being donated in his name, in his life-time for any philanthropic purpose. He would rather continue to undertake such by himself while he lived. He however directed that it could be misconstrued or even rude to return the cheques because of the sincere good faith in which they were issued. The cheques should simply be allowed to lapse, and this was done. This was a hint from RI to his family, of his private silent philanthropy, especially in the form of financial support to numerous persons in difficulty, which he sustained over the years. It was after his passing, that the family discovered among his papers and files, significant evidence of informal "bursaries" which he had operated in confidence. He never made it public to his family. In many instances, RI requested the recipients to keep his financial assistance confidential.

In the process of looking through RI's archives for this biography, about eighty-four letters of appreciation from recipients of RI's generosity were uncovered. These letters of gratitude were from individuals in need, schools, churches, corporate bodies and various organizations. RI in his life time hardly failed to honour invitations requiring his financial assistance, from diverse organizations. If he was unable to attend, he would make sure he wrote a letter to that effect with a cheque or sent someone with a letter excusing his absence. These were all carefully filed away under the title, "Appeal for Aid". In that file, there were many letters of appeal from Nkwerre sons and daughters asking for assistance for payment of school fees, for WAEC registration fees, help for admission into schools, for employment and other such matters. RI found time to respond to such letters and would often request recipients of his financial assistance not to publicize it because, "Kind deeds are not for broadcast, keep it to yourself."

He also had another file similarly titled, "Giving unto God". In the end, R.I. Uzoma's family made effort to be guided by his brand of silent philanthropy, in taking actions to immortalize his name after his passing.

R.I. Uzoma's family was however fully aware of another level of philanthropy which he could not hide, namely that of informally "adopting" brilliant children from struggling families and sponsoring their education. When R.I. Uzoma returned from Achimota College in 1939, he awarded primary school scholarships to two school children from Nkwerre. One was from St Paul's CMS Central School, the other from the St Thomas' the Roman Catholic Central School, these two primary schools being the only ones existing in Nkwerre at the time. Later on, RI in addition, supported the education and living costs of four boys and girls from his Obinuhu kindred up to the level of tertiary education. Two went to university and two others into teaching. In the 1990s, RI supported another brilliant young man from Nkwerre, who was admitted into university but was struggling against all odds to complete the course. The young man eventually qualified as a lawyer. As Education Secretary living in Umuahia and later at Owerri, R.I. Uzoma at various times equally "adopted" altogether ten boys and girls who resided in his expansive home as part of his family and were educated at his cost. These young people were from Mbano, Ngwa, Etche and Ibeku, and two of them became university lecturers, while others succeeded as teachers and in private business.[93]

A Principled Stand: The Nkwerre Chieftaincy Affair

One other event that provides further insight into the personality and life principles of R.I. Uzoma, was the Nkwerre chieftaincy matter of 1983. This took place during the second three-year tenure of Ambassador Godwin Onyegbula as President-General

---
93   R.I. Uzoma's biographical notes for the NAU Golden Jubilee Celebrations; R.I. Uzoma Archives

of the NAU. The Ambassador's tenure was a period of visionary leadership which lasted from 1979 to 1983, followed by a second term from 1983 to 1986. The incident under reference, put to test the question of whether the traditional title of Nze, which is taken by personal choice, should become a prerequisite to an honourary chieftaincy title conferred on individuals by the Nkwerre community, on the basis of objective personal merit. The *dramatis personae* in that debate were the Eshi Eze J.O. Ugochukwu, R.I. Uzoma, by then recognized as an eminent citizen within and outside Nkwerre community, and the town union (NAU).

There have been a number of different perspectives written and oral, put forward on the matter. The most straightforward, although summarized narrative however, is that contained in the book published in 2005 by Ambassador Godwin A. Onyegbula, himself the President-General of the town union at the time of the incident. It briefly narrates how in 1983, the Nkwerre Town Union (NAU) took a decision to honour several of its own prominent citizens with chieftaincy titles. Prior to this, during the first four-year tenure of Sir Godwin Onyegbula as President-General, a written Constitution of the Union had been adopted which made the award of such honours a joint-mandate of the Union and the Paramount Ruler of Nkwerre, the Eshi of Nkwerre, at the time Eze J.O. Ugochukwu. Persons to be honoured were to emerge through bi-partisan selection by the two pillars of leadership in the town, namely the Eshi and the NAU. Ten (10) nominations for 1983 were apportioned such that the Eshi put forward four names, while six names came from NAU. The nominees from the Eshi for that year were Nze Emmanuel Nwogu, S. Okeigwe, Emmanuel Anumnu and J.O. Ihekwaba. The nominees from the town union were Nze D.I. Ukaegbu, John .R. Anyaehie, Hon R.I. Uzoma, S. Oharka and A.N. Nwakanma (Onyegbula, 2005: 227).

All the candidates were eminent indigenes of Nkwerre town, yet in a strange twist, the Eshi decided to impose a personal selection criterion apart from meritorious service, namely enrolment into the cultural title of Nze. He did so, notwithstanding that such a requirement was not a provision in the NAU Constitution. The Eshi in previous years had conferred Nkwerre chieftaincy titles, purely on merit on other personalities who were non-indigenes of Nkwerre. The Eshi based on his new condition, decided to exclude R.I. Uzoma from the list submitted by the NAU, with the excuse that he had not enrolled into the Nze title. The Eshi's refusal to be persuaded by several visitations from the President-General of the NAU, and other shocked citizens of the town, and from outside, escalated the matter to a chieftaincy dispute. In the end, the controversial nature of the traditional ruler's position was soon to become most evident.

Many could not understand how a man who had put the name of Nkwerre on the map as its first university graduate, and also of old Orlu Division, and as the first Minister of Education in the Eastern Region, could be denied a local chieftaincy honour. Two such personalities were Eze Ibenye Ugballa of Okporo and Eze Ikonne of Aba, who personally visited the Eshi of Nkwerre to persuade him over the matter. The Eshi expected R.I. Uzoma to quickly make arrangements to take the Nze title before the appointed date for the chieftaincy ceremony as some others had agreed to. This was not about to happen as R.I. Uzoma had his reasons based on principle, and he stood his ground. Those principles were borne out of RI's informed understanding and appreciation of the history of the chieftaincy institution and Nze titles in Igbo society.

R.I. Uzoma held on to his knowledge that the concept of chieftaincy and the title "Chief" was used in the colonial period, to describe those appointed by the colonial administration to positions of authority, such as "Warrant Chiefs" and Tax Collectors. It was also ascribed to those recognized as community leaders or spokespersons by the people. In Nkwerre, Chief Anyiam

The Man and his Principles

Emeghara Udo of Umunaga was the last bona fide warrant chief. However in 1957, the Nkwerre community under the aegis of the NAU appointed J.O. Ugochukwu, a successful businessman based in Port Harcourt, as their community chief or Paramount Ruler under the title of Eshi of Nkwerre (Obialor, 2006: 78). As Paramount Ruler and cultural head of the community, the Eshi was required to enroll into the Nze title. In modern times however, the Nze-title in Nkwerre came to be taken as a status symbol by other successful citizens, of their own accord and by individual choice. Being an Nze was never a condition for honourary chieftaincy awards and is not conferred by the community.

The Nze title qualifies the individual to exclusive membership of a society or club, which in Nkwerre, has the Eshi as its fulcrum. It is quite distinct from the modern contemporary chieftaincy title which is purely honourary, and is conferred on individuals based on objective recognition of merit. Such chieftaincy titles do not enrol the individual into any sort of society as does the Nze title. In modern Nkwerre, the Nze title itself had also undergone changes. It has become an accepted status-symbol of materialistic "arrival" or "success" for some, although not for others. It is not culturally a pre-requisite for honourary and meritorious chieftaincy by the community of Nkwerre, although it appears to be so by convention. However, R.I. Uzoma had strong reservations about the materialism and showmanship that accompanies the Nze title.

In the face of the obstinate stand of the Eshi, R.I. Uzoma, true to his pacifist and unassuming nature, was inclined to let sleeping dogs lie. A chieftaincy title was not for him a do or die matter. At the time of the chieftaincy issue, R.I. Uzoma had already received and declined several offers of such a title from other Igbo communities. In 1965 he had been honoured by the Federal Government of Nigeria with the National Honour of Officer of the Order of the Federal Republic of Nigeria (OFR). It was a decoration which followed the equivalent honour of Officer of the

Magnificent Order of the British Empire (OBE), conferred on him by the Queen of England in 1961. R.I. Uzoma was among a small group of Nigerian citizens from the former Eastern Region who sought to renounce their British Empire honours at the Office of the Deputy High Commission in Enugu on 6th September 1967, in protest against the role of Great Britain in the civil war at the time. However it became apparent that the renunciation was not accepted. At R.I. Uzoma's passing on 4th April 2000, the then British High Commissioner in Abuja, Sir Graham Burton, was one of those who sent a written condolence message to the Uzoma family, making reference to the OBE honour. Furthermore in 1989, RI was honoured with the befitting chieftaincy title of "Ochonma-Oha" of Orlu meaning "Promoter of Public Good", from a senior Paramount Ruler, Igwe Patrick Acholonu of Orlu. Indeed, in his lifetime R.I. Uzoma received so many honours, of which the most gratifying for him was the conferment of an Honourary Doctor of Laws (LL.D Honouris Causa) for service to education, by the University of Nigeria, Nsukka in April 1990.

However, regarding the Nkwerre chieftaincy matter, it was the insistence of R.I. Uzoma's family, and kindred, led by his brother Dr. James Uzoma and Nze Emmanuel Nwogu, that persuaded RI to seek justice in a court of law. Dr. James Uzoma was then serving as the vice-president of the NAU, and he was very much in the know of the written constitution of the town union which had spelt out the terms and spirit of honourary chieftaincy titles. The filing of a suit in the Nkwerre High Court seeking declaration that R.I. Uzoma's nomination for an Nkwerre chieftaincy, was valid and constitutional according to NAU Constitution, brought issues to a head. The Eshi as First Defendant finally saw reason and agreed to respect the NAU's position. The High Court recorded judgment along those lines and the chieftaincy ceremony went ahead smoothly in August 1983. R.I. Uzoma was formally conferred the title of Ukeje I Nkwerre, meaning "The One who is Different from his Peers", or "A First among Equals." It was a name that was already a 'salutation-name' for him in traditional circles.

Unfortunately the 1983 chieftaincy dispute, which many considered most unnecessary, marked a sad watershed in the history of the NAU and its relationship with the traditional rulership of Nkwerre. The period before the 1980's saw the glorious days of the NAU, when strong community spirit and visionary leadership, empowered the town union to spearhead many development projects. These included the founding of St. Augustine's Grammar School and the St. Catherine's Girls' Secondary School. The petty debates that accompanied the 1983 chieftaincy matter marked the beginning of a downward-slide in the values of meritocracy and achievement-based leadership. Unhealthy materialism and aggressive individualism gradually took control, as traditional honours and titles came to be largely predicated on wealth.

The R.I. Uzoma Educational Foundation (RIUEF)[94]

In line with the sentiments expressed by R.I. Uzoma to his family, the idea of a foundation in his name was put on hold while he lived. It was not until 2014 that the family incorporated the RIUEF and kick-started it in 2015. The RIUEF came into existence on the foundations laid by a scholarship scheme which the 2nd Anglican Bishop of Orlu Diocese, Rt. Rev. Dr. B.C.I Okoro, had initiated on his own volition. The scheme was designed for financially challenged school children of the Diocese under its education programmes. The RIUEF followed as a registered entity, and transformed the forerunner scholarship scheme into a corporate body with a legal identity. This means that the RIUEF can operate independently of the Diocese within Nigeria, and internationally. The Foundation has as its core objectives, the promotion of quality education for Nigerian youth, irrespective of social background, gender,

---
94 All information in this segment is from R.I. Uzoma Foundation (RIUEF) Offices, Bishops' Court, Nkwerre, Imo State

religion or ethnicity. In addition it seeks to encourage such quality education through the institution of awards, bursaries and prizes for students and educators alike. The foundation also aims to support the provision of educational facilities through networking and collaboration with similar-interest agencies within and outside Nigeria.

The leadership of the Foundation, which was incorporated on 20th June 2014, is by a Board of Trustees, headed by the Bishop of the Anglican Diocese of Orlu in Imo State, Rt. Rev. Dr. B.C.I. Okoro as Founder/Chairman, with nine other members. Those other members of the Board are, Chief Uzoma Nwosu-Iheme KSC, Dr. Adaoha C. Okwuosa OON, KSM, Dame Adeline Uwanaka, Sir Johnson Asinugo, Mrs. Ugochi Onwumere, Barrister Adaku Akwiwu LLM (Legal Adviser), Venerable Francis N. Chukukere JP, Sir Emmanuel Iwuoha, Sir Billy G. Ukwuoma (Manager/Secretary). Barrister Charles C. Uzoma M.A, is Legal Officer for the Board. Presently, for convenience, the administrative headquarters of the Foundation is in the Diocesan offices at the Bishop's Court in Mbara Layout, Nkwerre, Imo State. Specifically, the registered aims and objectives of the Foundation are listed as follows:

- To promote and support quality education for Nigerian youth irrespective of class and gender.

- To promote and encourage equal opportunities for, and equal access to quality education for all Nigerian youth irrespective of class and social background

- To award scholarships and bursaries for challenged, but deserving students for primary, secondary and tertiary education.

- To institute and award prizes for deserving educators, teachers and educational institutions in Nigeria.

- To promote awareness on educational issues and needs in Nigeria and network with similar organizations, in and outside Nigeria for the benefit of education
- To support the provision of modern educational facilities towards the enhancement of learning in Nigeria.

On 3rd December 2015, the Foundation's programmes were kick-started with the award of cash prizes for "Excellence in Adversity" to seventeen (17) deserving students of selected independent secondary schools, and four tertiary institutions in Imo State. The beneficiaries were thoroughly screened by a committee appointed by the Trustees. The successful candidates were selected on a non-denominational and non-partisan basis, with criteria of sustained good academic performance and good character in the face of personal and/or social challenges, such as loss of parents and lack of finances. All efforts were made in the exercise to underscore the national public-service role and personal life philosophy of R.I. Uzoma. The award was also a tribute to R.I. Uzoma's passion for equal access to education for all, rich or poor, male or female, a passion which led him in his life-time, to have sponsored the education of many individuals who were not his children. Although the Foundation's programmes were initiated in Imo State, plans are being made by the Trustees to extend them to the national platform, as more funds become available. The list of the 2015 pioneer beneficiaries with their schools and institutions is documented on attached tables.

AWARD OF 2015 R.I. UZOMA EDUCATIONAL FOUNDATION (RIUEF) CASH PRIZES FOR "EXCELLENCE IN ADVERSITY" TO DESERVING PUPILS AND STUDENTS FROM SELECTED IMO STATE SCHOOLS AND INSTITUTIONS (held at the R.I. Uzoma Memorial Cathedral Hall, Bishops court, Anglican Diocese of Orlu, Nkwerre, Imo State, 11.00 am, Thursday, 3rd December, 2015).

LIST OF BENEFICIARIES

A. *SECONDARY SCHOOLS:*

Name	DOB	Class	School	LGA/State
Nwokorie, Cynthia Chidera	16/08/2005	JSS 2	Fatima Secondary School (Technical)	Umuakagu-Nsu, Ehime-Mbano LGA, Imo State
Ukwuoma, Ugochukwu T.		JSS 3	St. Augustine's Grammar School, Nkwerre	Nkwerre LGA, Imo State
Dickson, Gift	17/11/2001	SS 2	Okpala Secondary School Okpala	Ngor-Okpala, Imo State
Nwokeoma, Chukwuebuka	05/04/2002	JSS 3	Ife Grammar School Ezinihitte	Mbaise LGA, Imo State
Oparaji, Favour	07/01/2001	SS 1	Akabo High School PMB 1064 Akabo	Ikeduru, Imo State
Ibeh, Chigozie Peter	02/02/2000	SS 1	Baptist Model School Obinze	Owerri West LGA, Imo State
Adimmadu, Ugochi Blessing	11/06/1999	SS 1	St Linus Secondary School, Isieke I	Awo-Omamma, Oru East LGA, Imo State
Okehie, Chidinma C.	28/03/2002	JSS 2	St. Catherine's Girls Secondary School, Nkwerre	Nkwerre LGA, Imo State

Name	DOB	Class	School	LGA/State
Ifeanyichukwu, Ogochukwu	01/01/1998	SS 3	Mount Olives Seminary Umuezeala-Nsu	Ehime-Mabno LGA, Imo State
Nwafor, Chidera Gift	04/06/1999	SS 2	Anglican Secondary School, Okigwe	Okigwe, Imo State
Okaparaeke, Lois	18/03/2003	JSS 2	Archishop Nwankiti Missionary Secondary School, Oguta	Oguta, Imo State
Emeh, Chisom Gift	16/03/2004	JSS 2	St. Augustine's Grammar School, Nkwerre	Nkwerre LGA, Imo State
Obinali, Chioma	07/07/2001	JSS 3	Methodist College Ihube	Okigwe, Imo State

B. *TERTIARY INSTITUTIONS:*

Name	DOB	Course of Study	Year	Institution/State
Uche, Majane Nwanyinnaya	27/07/1990	Purchasing and Supply	2nd	Federal Polytechnic, Nkede Owerri, Imo State
Onyedinma, Chizitere Chinanu	14/01/1992	Food Science and Technology	3rd	Federal University of Technology PMB 1526, Owerri, Imo State
Adieme, Ugochukwu Emmanuel	-	Accountancy	2nd	Imo State Polytechnic, Umuagwo, Imo State
Erege, Chukwuebuka Jude	-	Computer/Mathematics	2nd	Alvan Ikoku Federal College of Education, Owerri, Imo State

7

A PARTNER IN SERVICE: JEMIMAH CHINYERE UZOMA

On the tenth day of December 1922, the year ten-year old Reuben Ibekwe started his primary education at the CMS Central School in Nkwerre, a baby girl was born, in the verdant green farming community of Ezeoke-Nsu, in present day Ehime-Mbano Local Government Area of Imo state.[95] She was born the second of a set of twins to the young family of Eze Daniel Nwokocha Nwachukwu and his young wife, Ugo-eze Rebecca Nwanyichukwu Nwachukwu. That baby girl was baptized with the biblical name Jemimah, and the vernacular name of Chinyere, while her twin sister was named Rebecca and Chinuru. Her life as the first daughter of a warrant chief became one of privilege and glamour, and so many 'firsts'. Her marriage in 1942 at the age of nineteen, to the brilliant teacher, Reuben Ibekwe Uzoma, from an average Nkwerre family, positioned her for a life of service to humanity. Her royal background notwithstanding, Jemimah also chose to render that service to women and the church through a career in teaching, and community leadership.

---

95   The Nsu Clan is the largest autonomous community in Ehime-Mbano with the six villages of Ezeoke, Agbaghara, Umuezeala, Umuanunu, Umuopara and Umuakagu.

Family Roots and Antecedents

Jemimah Uzoma's personality and life career are best appreciated against the background of the role of her father, and of her grandfather in the early history of Christianity, in her home community. That history is rooted in the first two decades of the twentieth century. Jemimah's father, Eze Daniel Nwokocha Nwachukwu Nwadigo, was born in 1892, the first son of Eze Nwachukwu Nwadigo, the *Omefo Oburuaku*, and *Ogbabiruogwe of Nsu* in Ehime-Mbano in today's Imo state. His mother was Nwonuhie Nwachukwu Nwadigo (nee Nwoku of Okpoetere of Onicha-Uboma). Daniel Nwokocha's grandfather was Nwadigo Nwelue *the Ekpechuo-Ogu of Nsu*, described as the Natural Ruler of Nsu, who before the arrival of the colonialists unified all the warring clans of Nsu into one autonomous community. (Uzoma, J.C., 1989).

As a teenager around 1910, Daniel Nwokocha's father the Eze, handed him over to the District Commissioner (DC), and allowed him to join the soldiers of the West African Frontier Force (WAFF) on one of their expeditions from Okigwe to Arochukwu. He was one of their support staff. It was a long trek of camping, soldiering and volunteer service, which enabled Daniel Nwokocha acquire familiar knowledge of the Arochukwu–Itu–Calabar route, in the territory of the lower Cross-River and Calabar area. More especially, it brought him into contact with the early missionaries, in particular those of the Presbyterian Church, who operated in that part of Colonial Nigeria. One of them took special note of him as an intelligent and hard working youth. The missionary adopted him as his ward, and enrolled him into the first primary school in the then Eastern Nigeria, the Duke Town School in Calabar. The return of the soldiers of the WAFF back to their Okigwe base after several months, without the teenage Daniel, raised quite some concern and anger with the Warrant Chief Nwachukwu Nwadigo and the entire community of Nsu. The 'Nwa DC' in Okigwe was told in no uncertain terms, that Daniel as the Regent and future successor to the throne of Nsu could not be lost in a strange land ('Okpara anaghefu n'ije') (Uzoma, J.C., 1989). If the DC wanted peace to continue to reign in Nsu, Daniel had to be brought back home. And so he was with the next expedition of soldiers.

A period of youthful adolescent rebellion followed on the part of young Daniel, who sometimes resented his withdrawal from school and the subsequent curfew, which his rather intimidating father imposed on his movements. Young Daniel was convinced that sitting around at home, and listening to conflict-resolution meetings and Native Courts cases, chaired by his father, was not enough for him. The courtiers in the palace, who sometimes did not understand his frustrations, regarded him as a heady young man. They readily assisted in channeling his energies into such physical activities as hunting of game, sawing of timber, wood-work and wrestling in the village square. Daniel being a strong and well-built young man proudly excelled in all these (Uzoma, J.C., 1989). By 1912 at the age of twenty years, Daniel Nwokocha was not only the best wrestler and hunter in Ezeoke-Nsu, he was considered highly qualified for initiation into manhood and preparation for marriage through the customary ceremony of 'Iwa-Akwa'. He subsequently married in 1918. From then on, Daniel focused his sometimes rebellious energies towards bringing much controverted innovations into his still largely-pagan community, particularly under the umbrella of Christianity.

A significant event in the royal palace in Ezeoke-Nsu community during Daniel Nwokocha's turbulent teenage years, was the return from Arochukwu in 1913, of a freed female slave known as Nwangborie (Nzeduru, 2013:1-5; Uzoma, J.C., 1989). It also became an important turning-point in Daniel's relationship with his father. They became partners and team-players in the subsequent events that transformed the Nsu community by leaps and bounds. Nwangborie Iwundu, as she was eventually identified to be, was a native of Umuezeala-Nsu, one of the four communities that make up the Nsu clan. Although slavery had been abolished statutorily since 1807, many slaves in the Colony and Protectorates of Nigeria, either did not know this, or were unable to return to their original home communities, having lost knowledge of the long-routes they had trekked into slavery. Nwangborie's return to Nsu was facilitated by two notable palm oil merchants from Ezeoke, namely Ekeoba Nzeduru and Duruochie Oparaeke, on one of their journeys to Arochukwu. They identified her roots through her dialect, and directed her homeward journey. Her access to the royal palace in Ezeoke, a feat that was not easy at the time, was made possible because she was a younger sister to one of the wives of the Warrant Chief Nwachukwu Nwadigo (Nzeduru, 2013:1-5).

Nwangborie's subsequent summons before the Royal court for official testimony became a historical landmark in the community, and in the lives of its citizens. Her testimony was corroborated by the witness statements of Ekeoba Nzeduru and Duruochie Oparaeke (Nzeduru, 2013:1-5). The substance of Nwangborie's story was of white missionaries, church buildings, schools and teachers, white man's medicines which work, Bibles and books, people living in brick homes with lanterns, and a belief in a new faith and new teachings in the schools. In addition, it was about security and freedom of movement. Eze Nwachukwu Nwadigo by this time had become quite curious and anxious to confirm these stories from third parties. They were reports of new ideas and changes in those distant lands along the Cross River which his heady teenage son had often talked about, and which he had hitherto dismissed as youthful fantasies.

It was Nwangborie who confirmed the positive reports of activities of missionaries, and innovations of the Christian Church in Arochukwu, which she garnered as a freed slave. She was able to convince the Eze Nwadigo that if such ideas were brought into Nsu by the 'Eze' himself, it would not only bring peace and progress, but would enhance his influence and respect as a powerful man of change (Nzeduru, 2013:1-5). After several briefing sessions, the warrant chief was convinced by the good news, and changed his attitude to cross-country movements by his son and heir. He bought the innovative ideas and immediately sought to take possession of their potentials. He decided that his son would lead a royal delegation to Arochukwu, since he was already familiar with the route. The young man, who nine years later became Jemimah's father, was now the right-hand man and full representative of his father, the Eze.

Thus in the same year 1913, Daniel Nwokocha Nwachukwu, Jemimah's father, as a young adult aged about 21 years, found himself leading a delegation of able-bodied young men to Arochukwu, with the mandate of his father Eze Nwachukwu Nwadigo. Their goal was to meet with the white missionaries of Arochukwu for the purpose of bringing their mission to Ezeoke-Nsu. The 12-man delegation led by Daniel Nwokocha Nwachukwu carried a letter, requesting for the establishment of a church in Ezeoke. They also had a cash sum of about twelve pounds, a huge sum of money in those days. The money was for the posting of a church-teacher who would start a school in Ezeoke. Other members of the delegation were James Udechukwu, Apati Onuoha, Wilfred Iwunze, Nwonyeoma Nwopuru, Simon Ekeudo, Michael Nwadigo, Amos Ginigeme, Aaron Ogbonna, Oke Iwuoha, Reuben Durunneji and Luke Nwokorie (Nzeduru, 2013:1-5). It was a journey of several days of trekking by foot, but one which Daniel was more than happy to undertake. One report of that experience is that in Arochukwu the team met with a Reverend Richardson of the Free Church of Scotland. Yet another version is that it was a certain Reverend Octivom of the same Free-Church of Scotland, which today is the Presbyterian Church, whom they met with (Nzeduru, 2013:6).

The members of the delegation were driven solely by their enthusiasm and, energy, based on the riveting stories of Nwangborie, the harbinger of great tales, and by the commanding orders of a powerful warrant chief. They did not have the benefit of knowing that the white missionaries had already 'zoned' the territory of the Southern Protectorate among themselves. The Reverend Richardson had the task of informing Daniel and his men about a gentleman's agreement among the three church missions operating in that part of Nigeria at the time. These were the Free-Church of Scotland, the Anglican Church Missionary Society (CMS) and the Methodist Mission. By that agreement, the Okigwe district or zone from which the Ezeoke-Nsu delegation came, belonged under the purview of the CMS Mission. Daniel and his men needed to take their request for the goodies of Christianity, to the CMS missionary leadership. The Rev. Richardson obliged them by giving them a letter to the leadership of the CMS mission at Egbu-Owerri in the person of Rev A.C. Onyeabor, the priest who later as Bishop became famous for the translation of the Bible into Igbo.

It was only after a tedious return journey from Arochukwu, followed by another long trek to Egbu, that the determination of the Ezeoke delegation began to yield results. The indomitable spirit and energy of Daniel the leader, was such that the mission could not fail in spite of several mishaps on the way. Such incidents included the theft of the twelve pounds cash on them by a local bandit on their way to Egbu-Owerri, while crossing a stream. That first Egbu-trip was aborted and the money had to be replaced on their return to base, before a second successful trip was undertaken. At Egbu, the Rev. Onyeabor informed the exhausted team that the final approval for the establishment of a church station and posting of a teacher, could only come from the CMS head quarters located at Ozalla-Onitsha on the banks of the River Niger in Onitsha (Nzeduru, 2013:7).

The senior CMS official responsible for this was the famous Archdeacon T.J. Dennis, who gave the necessary approval. He also directed the group to Onicha-Olona in present day Delta state, in successful search of the first church teacher to Ezeoke-Nsu, a certain Mr. Joseph Chiejina. The immediate willingness of Mr.

Chiejina, an enthusiastic first-generation Christian, to accept the job and physically go with the delegation, was a crowning glory to the Daniel Nwokocha Nwachukwu missionary journey. Reports have it that Mr. Chiejina was carried all the way into Ezeoke town in Imo state, in a hammock on the shoulders of the able-bodied youth. The date was the 13th day of August 1913. The CMS Church started first as a small station which held services on Sundays and Bible classes on other days. August 13th 1913 has become etched in history as the birth day of the CMS Church in Ezeoke. It was not until May 27th 1926 that the foundation stone of the permanent church building was laid, on land provided by Daniel Nwokocha Nwachukwu, next to his family compound. By then he had taken up the Eze-ship after the death of his father. The church building was dedicated in 1929, two years after the laying of the foundation stone (Uzoma, J.C., 1989).

It was against this backdrop of a family that had become a beacon of radical social change and bold innovation that Jemimah Chinyere Nwachukwu came into the world. The first decades of the twentieth century in the Colony and Protectorates of Nigeria, saw the major political and administrative steps that followed from the 1914 amalgamation of Nigeria. It also saw the sweeping social and normative changes that impacted on the rural communities with the spread of Christianity. These changes included the end of slavery, the stoppage of practices of superstition such as twin infanticide, the rapid institution of schools and churches by the various missionary societies. They constituted important catalysts in the community, and on the lives of the young people born in that period. Yet the persisting undercurrent of negative cultural values in many respects, such as child marriage for girls, male-child preference and some stubborn pagan practices, were still in existence. It is after all, a well-known thesis that normative change, or change in attitudes and values, is always several steps behind change in social artifacts in human society.

From Childhood to Queens College Lagos

By the date that Jemimah Chinyere and her twin sister Rebecca Chinuru were born in the early hours of December 10th 1922, the Anglican CMS Church station already had a humble but proud presence in Ezeoke-Nsu from 1913. The adjunct Ezeoke Central Primary school had also followed a few years thereafter. Both were located within a close distance of the compound of the Nwachukwu Nwadigo family. The two baby-girls became the first set of twins to have been saved and nurtured together in Ezeoke, at a time when the superstitious beliefs that supported twins-infanticide, were still prevalent among many Igbo-speaking communities. For the young Eze Daniel Nwokocha and his even younger wife Rebecca Nwanyichukwu, there was no question that they would keep the two beautiful baby-girls, given the family antecedents, and the Eze's personality within the community. In January 1918, Eze Daniel Nwokocha and his wife Rebecca became the first couple in Ezeoke to be wedded in church. They thereby committed to a monogamous marriage, something quite unusual at that time, especially for such a powerful traditional ruler. The bride, Rebecca, who was then 16 years old, was born in 1902 as the youngest child of Okorie Obasi of Lowa I and Mary Akure Okorie (nee Nwokorie Ebo) of Lowa II in Onicha-Uboma, a neighboring clan to the Nsu communities.

The arrival of the twin daughters on December 10th 1922, for the Eze and his wife Rebecca, was a momentous event because they had waited patiently for a child for four years. That period of waiting was for the handsome Eze Daniel Nwokocha perhaps the first major test of his new Christian faith. In those four years, he was continuously under pressure from his courtiers and community members alike, to marry a second wife. They would constantly remind him that as the Eze, he needed to have a male heir as quickly as possible, and he would ask them if they were God. Indeed it was not unusual for members of the community whom he encountered daily in his duties of presiding over inter-community matters, to make him offers of their daughters as second wife. He was after all the powerful wealthy Chief who worked closely with the DC, and presided over the native courts. Eze Daniel Nwokocha's adoption of Christian values of family-life was however paramount for him, and it was his goal to demonstrate such to his large household of aides.

Jemimah and her twin sister were nursed quietly from birth in a closeted setting. There were several nannies and assistants who kept them away from the prying eyes of the constant stream of visitors to the palace. Unfortunately tragedy struck very soon after, and Rebecca was lost in a cot-death at the age of about three months. The experience merely emboldened the Eze and his wife to want nothing but the best for the surviving twin, Jemimah. She had been baptized and given the biblical name that she grew up with. Jemimah's childhood years saw her being raised with a silver spoon, in an idyllic home-setting, punctuated with a regimented cycle of morning prayers, church going and early schooling. She was the only surviving child of the family for a period of eight years before the arrival of another daughter Joy Nkechinyere. By that time she had already started primary schooling at the CMS Central School Ezeoke, located a shouting distance from her home. Her formal schooling was richly complemented with a home-education. She benefitted from the domestic-science training that her mother had acquired from missionaries at the CMS Women's Home craft Training Centre in Emii, Owerri.[96]

It was the practice in those days, for young women from privileged Christian families to be sent for a home craft training-programme at places like the Emii Centre, for a few months

---

[96] The CMS Women's Home craft Training Centre at Emii in Owerri, at the time graduated many "famous mothers" across south eastern Nigeria, including the mother of Emeritus Professor O.C. Nwana. Prof. Nwana is a Knight of St Christopher (Anglican) and Knight of John Wesley (Methodist). He is also Ugwuaro of Aro-Okeigbo and Omekaibeya of Aro-Ndizuogu a Lt. Col. (CNC) of the Nigerian Legion and one-time Adviser to two respective Ministers of Education, Prof. Jibril Aminu and Prof. A. Babs Fafunwa

before marriage. Attendance at the centre for the young women was like "going to University." A good picture of the importance of this experience for the early Christian families of south-eastern Nigeria is provided by Emeritus Professor O.C. Nwana in his autobiography. He writes,

> My mother, Ucheomumu (christened Selina) was born to the polygamous home of Ichie Obi in Ekwulu-Mmiri town of Nnewi Division of Eastern Nigeria in 1901. Mama had a relatively modest formal education, which consisted of basic literacy as well as an intensive Home Making/Marriage Craft training program run by the Niger Delta Pastorate (now Anglican Church) at Emii in the Owerri Division of Eastern Nigeria in the early 1920s. Such missionary notables from England as Miss Beswick and Miss Humbim operated the Emii Women's Centre where mama had an education available only to very few women of her age. At that point, there was hardly any meaningful formal education for the female gender in the Eastern part of Nigeria. (Nwana, 2012:2-3)

Jemimah Nwachukwu's proud mother, wife of Eze Daniel Nwokocha, was one of the earliest beneficiaries of this programme following her engagement to the Eze at the age of about fifteen years. Jemimah as a school girl therefore, acquired a keen interest in such household skills as knitting, sewing and cooking from her mother, especially since she did not have to do any farm work. It was however Jemimah's natural intelligence in school work at the local primary school in Ezeoke, that impressed her teachers including, a certain pupil-teacher named Reuben Ibekwe Uzoma.[97] After one year as pupil-teacher at Nkwerre Central School in 1928, the young Reuben Uzoma had been moved to Ezeoke-Nsu where he was to have a two-year stint from January 1st 1929 to December 31st 1930. His father, a migrant farmer and trader from Nkwerre, had at some point settled his family in Umuopara-

---

97 Oral Interview with Mama Dinah Erinne, wife of Mr. D. Erinne, former Principal of Bishop Lasbrey College (ITC) Irete, Owerri and for many years a teacher at CMS Central School, Ezeoke and family friend of the Nwachukwu Nwadigo and R.I. Uzoma families. Interview was conducted on October 26th 2016 in Lagos

Nsu, one of the farming communities within Eze Daniel Nwokocha Nwachukwu's domain. The CMS Central School Ezeoke was the only CMS School in the vicinity; hence, it was not a surprise that Reuben Ibekwe Uzoma found himself serving as a pupil-teacher in that school. He easily became close friends with the Nwokocha Nwachukwu family, due to the fact that the Eze was always a welcoming host to all CMS personnel.

Eze Daniel not only considered the new CMS Church at Ezeoke, and the school his pet projects, but also treated the staff of both institutions as his friends and guests. It came naturally to him to intimate to his daughter's teacher of his ambition for her to have the best education that opportunities of that time could offer. That was how the pupil teacher, R.I. Uzoma suggested further secondary education for Jemimah. He let the Eze know that it would be a waste for her not to go any further than primary school, because she was clearly ahead of her class in so many respects.[98] The two men, the youthful Eze and the young adult pupil-teacher found themselves to be kindred spirits in terms of sharing the same progressive ideas on girls education, and thereby being ahead of their times. This was how the ideas were hatched which led to Jemimah's journey to distant Lagos, for secondary education at Queens College, at a time when most girl-children were preferably married off as quickly as possible for a dowry.

At this point which was about 1930, destiny had taken over in an unpredictable turn of events. It was as though Jemimah was destined for a special role of partnership with a future icon of education and public service, in the person of the pupil teacher, Reuben Ibekwe Uzoma. It was as if Jemimah's life was being directed by fate towards working hand in hand with Reuben in making a mark on girls' rights, and the growth of education, as well as on community service in the erstwhile Eastern Region of Nigeria.

---

98   Ibid

An important first step for Jemimah followed when in early 1935, news reached the Eze, and his friend R.I. Uzoma confirmed that some white women were coming to the East from Lagos to conduct the entrance examination into Queens College Lagos, then the premier secondary school for girls which had been opened in 1927. Jemimah was escorted to Aba for the examination at the Government Primary School. She easily passed the test and became one of a select group of female children from the then Eastern Region at the time, to gain admission into Queens College Lagos, in 1935. Before then, the schools admission roll was characterized by a glaring low presence of young girls from the Eastern part of Nigeria. The majority of students were naturally from the Lagos Colony and the Western Protectorate area.

The combination of long distance and the late acceptance of secondary education for girls by most hinterland communities in Eastern Nigeria, limited the number of students from the Eastern Region who were admitted to Queens College in its first years, until the 1930s. Jemimah and her 1935 set of girls were part of the group that shattered the glass-ceiling and began a gender revolution of sorts in Eastern Nigeria. Another factor that restricted the girls from the East was the erroneous belief that young ladies being sent to school in Lagos, was like courting of disaster because, Lagos was considered the wild city. However, by the time this set of girls all successfully completed their studies and were seen to come and go safely, and to become responsible family members, the pessimistic values began to recede. The impact of that gender-revolution, which Jemimah was a part of, came to characterise her life of service all through.

Jemimah often recounted to her children how the journey to and from Lagos for each school term was a tedious one. Her father, the Eze however, always did his best to make it easy for his beloved daughter. The long-legged energetic teenager and her father were determined to prove the many cynics wrong. Secondary education was still at this time a rare privilege for all and even more so, for girls. For each trip to Lagos, Jemimah would be escorted by male and female aides, by a combination of foot-trekking and carriage by hammock, or by back to Umuahia. From Umuahia, it was a slow train journey to Port Harcourt where the rest of the journey to Lagos was undertaken by steamer ship. At Port Harcourt, for the boat journey, Jemimah would meet up with other schoolmates of hers. She spoke particularly of Stella Obi from Onitsha, who became Mrs. Rebecca Nzegwu. But for all the girls, the long journey together and the excitement of feeling specially selected, created a sense of solidarity, which stayed with them all through their lives, and brought together some of their offspring.

The successful attendance at Queens College by these pioneers from today's South-East and South-South states of Nigeria, who became well-groomed educated ladies, and not wild 'Lagos girls', led to an upsurge in the number of girls going to Queens College from south-eastern Nigeria. Firstly, the fact that many of them studied on colonial government scholarship was an incentive. Jemimah was however not one of those lucky ones. Secondly, the curriculum at the Queens College was such that the ladies received an all-round training, which molded them into potential career women as well as efficient housewives and mothers.[99] Many of them left Queens College with special skills such as piano-playing, confectionery-making, embroidery and dress-making. Above all, they were well equipped to become what was then termed 'pivotal teachers'. In those days, to go to teacher training college after secondary education, made one a pivotal teacher, and there was a growing number of teachers' colleges established by the Church missions in those days. Quite a few among Jemimah's mates however, went overseas for further professional training as medical doctors, nurses, pharmacists or lawyers and came home as "firsts" in those careers.[100]

---

99   From Pass on the Torch - A History of Queens College Yaba Lagos; 70 years of Excelling- A publication on the 70 years anniversary of the School, released in 1997.

100   Oral Interview with Chiedu Ofodile, lawyer-poet and writer, in Abuja in September 2016. Mr. Ofodile has researched on Queens College history.

The Queens College curriculum, within the limitations imposed by shortage of teachers, was packaged to strike a good balance between pure academic knowledge and all-round physical and humanities development. Such subjects as Geography, Mathematics, English and History were tailored towards the British Cambridge Certificate, senior and junior. They were combined with classes in Music, Needle-work, House-wifery and Sports such as Hockey, Lawn Tennis and Net-ball.[101] It was at Queens College that Jemimah acquired and perfected her skills on the piano and the organ, along with her friend Rebecca Obi or 'Becky' as she called her, who as Mrs. Nzegwu, later served as organist at the Christ Church Cathedral in Onitsha. Jemimah in addition, took her academic studies at Queens College to the Senior Cambridge Level and emerged in 1939 as the first female Senior Cambridge School Certificate holder in the Old Owerri Province (Uzoma, J.C., 1989). With her tall lanky physique, she equally excelled at Net-ball, even while leading her class in Mathematics and History.

Jemimah often proudly and happily recalled her Queens College days. One highlight for her was that her English and History teacher, whom all the girls regarded as a role model, was Lady Kofoworola Aina Ademola (nee Moore). She was the first African female graduate of Oxford University, born 1914 and graduated in 1935. Another memorable item for her was a caring schoolmate whom she referred to as 'Sister-Antoinette' (Antoinette Bob-Manuel) who took Jemimah under her wings, especially in her first years, and taught her how to plait her dense hair in braids, the Lagos way. She also happily recalled that the loneliness of visiting days was broken once for her in 1937, when her father Eze Daniel Nwokocha Nwachukwu came to visit all the way from Ezeoke-Nsu in the East, by train and by boat. All her friends from the then Eastern Region gathered to meet him. The Eze had undertaken the tedious trip to Queens College to see his daughter after the fire incident at the college in that year, which had affected one of

---

101 From Pass on the Torch - A history of Queens College Yaba, Lagos 1927 - 1997

A Partner in Service: Jemimah Chinyere Uzoma

the buildings and caused much concern among parents especially those in the far away Eastern Region.[102]

A close look at the Queen's College roll call, identifying the girls from the Eastern Region of Nigeria, who were admitted along with Jemimah Nwachukwu from 1935, makes interesting reading. So also does the list of girls that followed a few years thereafter.[103] In Jemimah Nwachukwu's set at Queens College were Margaret Onumonu who is Mrs. Oputa and mother of the notable activist and musical entertainer Charley boy, Margaret Egere who became Mrs. Njemanze and mother of Chief Bobo Njemanze, Retired Chief Justice Benjamin Njemanze, and Mrs. Viola Amuta, among others, Victoria Manumihe who became Mrs. Amadi, and whose first daughter Elelaonu Okoro (nee Amadi), is a retired Director of Admissions, Joint Admissions and Matriculation Board (JAMB).

Among Jemimah's set were also Rebecca Obi who married Dr. Nzegwu the medical doctor/engineer of Onitsha, and is mother of Dr. Nwachuku Nzegwu, Antoinette Bob-Manuel who became Mrs. Ejiwunmi and mother of Gwendoline Ike-Nwachukwu, a retired federal permanent secretary and wife of retired General Ike-Nwachukwu; May Kemmer who was Mrs. Uwechia and mother of Azuka Uwechia and Nwando Edu; Ekanem Ana who became Mrs. Ikpeme, the first female pharmacist from the East and mother of Dr. Iwo Ikpeme. Others among this special group of women from the former Eastern Region of Nigeria were Affiong Ikpeme, Christiana Nnanna, Maggie Wachukwu, Christiana Nwagbo, Cecilia Egbunife, Cecilia Egwuatu, Beatrice Ogbolu, Juliana Odogwu, Mabel Waboso and Constance Wokoma, Violetta Kemmer, Priscilla Irochukwu, Yenna Okagbue and Clarice Spiff.

Coming over a period of about a decade after 1935, to join the first group of early pioneers were a second group of bold and brave young women. They included Priscilla Nzimiro, the first Igbo

---

102 Oral Interview with Dr Adaoha Okwuosa, daughter of R.I. Uzoma and J.C. Uzoma, in Abuja on 9th December 2016
103 Roll Call of Queens College students from 1927-1937 and 1938-1948; taken from Pass on the Torch- A history of Queens College Yaba, Lagos 1927 - 1997

female medical doctor, Eunice Nwozo the second female medical doctor of Igbo extraction, Mercy Abaecheta who became Mrs. T.O.S. Benson, Grace Alele (Professor Alele-Williams) the first female University vice-chancellor in Nigeria, Esther Egere, Felicia Chibogu Asika (Mrs. Emodi), Phillipa Ada Chiedu, Helen Uzoamaka Olisa, Gloretta Bob-Manuel, Faustina Bob-Manuel, Kate Bob-Manuel, Patricia Bob-Manuel, Lilian Egwuatu, Grace Pepple, Cecilia Alozie, Eudora Ibiam, Idah Nkemena, Grace Udom, Mercy Njemanze who became Mrs. Iheanacho and Dorothy Wadibia.

Taking one example, Dorothy Wadibia, became Dorothy Mbanefo and is one of the many Queens College girls of the period, who rose to the peak of their chosen profession in a man's world. After Queen's College, she graduated in Economics from the London School of Economics, after studying in the UK from 1954 to 1959. Mrs. Mbanefo came home to serve in the civil service in Port Harcourt as the first female Assistant District Commissioner in the Eastern Region from 1961 to 1963. She later in the 1980s, worked with the first female federal permanent secretary, Mrs. Francesca Emmanuel on the favourable review of public service rules and regulations, especially as they affect women. She eventually retired from the federal civil service as Director in the Primary Healthcare Programme of Professor Olikoye Ransome-Kuti in the 1996.[104] Her youngest sister and ward, Ambassador Nkem Wadibia-Anyanwu OON, is Nigeria's former Ambassador to Ireland, and a retired federal permanent secretary. She is the first and only female career ambassador to have held the post of permanent secretary in the Ministry of Foreign Affairs.

From School-Mistress to Pivotal Teacher

Soon after Jemimah Nwachukwu completed her studies at Queens College Lagos in early 1940, she returned home and became engaged to Reuben Ibekwe Uzoma. As fate would have it, the latter

---
104 Oral Interview with Ambassador Nkem Wadibia-Anyanwu, OON, in Abuja on 10th February 2017

had also completed his studies in record time at Achimota College in the Gold Coast, and returned to Nigeria by the end of 1939, at the start of the Second World War. The interim period in 1940 and 1941 while waiting for her wedding, was spent by Jemimah as a school-mistress at St. Bartholomew's Primary School in Enugu, where one of her pupils was Beatrice Anyaehie, wife of Sir John Anyaehie, an Nkwerre business tycoon. It was a brief period in which she was happily initiated into her chosen career of teaching in her favourite subjects of Mathematics (Arithmetic at primary school level), Bible Knowledge and History. Following her wedding in Nkwerre on January 7th 1942, Jemimah relocated to Awka with her husband who was then on the staff of the Awka College and principal of the College Practising School. It was in Awka that their first child, a boy, Anele Nwachukwu was born on 9th December, 1942, one day before Jemimah's twentieth birthday.

The periods in Jemimah's working life which she spent as a full-time housewife without any formal teaching job were brief. They covered the three years from 1942 to 1945 in the first instance. Teaching was her passion and she constantly sought to perfect her skills in that profession. In this regard, she always had the full support and cooperation of RI who was himself a strong advocate of the teaching profession. Hence, each time that her husband was transferred to any location where she could not have a formal teaching appointment, Jemimah would either be studying, or offer to help out on a part-time basis, with classes in any nearby primary or secondary school. From 1944 to 1946, she was a full-time housewife while RI served as principal of Okrika Grammar School. It was in this period that Jemimah took the first step to advance herself as a certified teacher. She studied hard and obtained the Teachers Grade II Certificate, also known as the Higher Elementary Certificate, which together with her Senior Cambridge Certificate made her a "pivotal teacher".

From 1946 to 1947 ending, while RI was at the Institute of Education, University of London for a Postgraduate Diploma in

Education, Jemimah found herself deployed to teach in one of her most gratifying formal teaching assignments. She became the first indigenous teacher of Mathematics at the oldest all girls' secondary school established by the CMS Mission in Eastern Nigeria, namely the Girls' Secondary School, Elelenwa in present-day Rivers State. Among her students in that school were Keziah Nwanyidirim Asinobi (nee Nwachukwu), a former federal minister in the civilian regime of President Shehu Shagari, Mrs. Beatrice Ekwueme (nee Nwajagu) teacher and wife of a Former Vice-President of Nigeria, Flora Nwapa (Mrs. Nwakuche) a renowned educationist and Africa's first female novelist, Justice Victoria Ayo Onejeme (nee Ezenwa) and Mrs. Joy Nkechinyere Akwiwu (nee Nwachukwu) wife of Sir Emmanuel Akwiwu, SAN, and younger sister to Jemimah herself.[105]

By 1947, RI had returned from the United Kingdom. From 1948 to 1950 he was redeployed by the CMS Mission as General Manager of schools for the Niger Delta Diocese. After a brief stay in Port Harcourt, he relocated to Old Umuahia where Jemimah briefly took up a teaching assignment at the Women's Training Centre (WTC), Umuahia. This was followed by another brief period of being a full-time housewife from December 1951 to December 1953 while RI went to the Eastern Regional Assembly as the elected representative for Orlu, and was appointed Minister of Education. It was however in the longer period of 1954 to 1962 when her family returned to Old Umuahia after RI's ministerial duties, that Jemimah found time for a second time to take steps towards further enhancing her academic qualifications. She studied for, and obtained the GCE Advanced Level Certificate in three subjects even while being a teacher at the St. Silas Primary School in Old Umuahia. It was also in that same period that Jemimah was one of seven women leaders from Nigeria who were sponsored in 1962, by the USA and Nigerian governments

---

105 Oral Interview with Dr Adaoha Okwuosa, daughter of R.I. Uzoma and J.C. Uzoma, in Abuja on 9th December 2016

to undergo a Diploma Course in Social Psychology (Leadership) at the Columbia University, New York, USA. Other members of the group were Mrs. M.O. Ahamba, Mrs. Mercy Eluwa, Mrs. Dinah Ihezue, Chief Mrs. Shodeinde, Mrs. Elizabeth Pam and Mrs. Comfort Dikko. This team of young educated mothers all excelled in the programme and became friends across the country for many years.[106]

From 1963 to 1967, R.I. Uzoma resided in Owerri with his family and continued duties as Education Secretary for the newly created Owerri Diocese. In that period, Jemimah again took up teaching at the Uzii Lay-out Primary School located within the immediate environs of the Diocesan Education Offices in which her husband worked. However, with her pivotal teacher status, and recently acquired "A" Level qualifications, as well as so much cumulative teaching experience, Jemimah now stood at a much greater advantage for higher positions in any future teaching deployments by the authorities. In the Nigerian education system of those days, pivotal teachers were more likely to be considered for headship of a school. This was a qualification that was very much sought after by the army of teachers in the mission education system, who did not have the benefit of a secondary education. They made up the majority of teachers who had gone straight into Teacher Training Colleges (TTCs) from Standard Six. They had to address the gap towards pivotal teacher status, by sitting for GCE "Ordinary" level examinations on an extra-curricular basis. Pivotal teachers remained the stars of the teaching profession before the gradual influx of many university graduates from the 1960s. However, most of the young men and women whom the CMS and government subsequently sent to university on scholarship, were first pivotal teachers.[107]

---

106 Oral Interview with Mrs. Ugochi Onwumere, daughter of R.I. Uzoma and J.C. Uzoma, in Enugu on 9th December 2016
107 Oral Interview with Chiedu Ofodile, lawyer-poet and writer, in Abuja in September 2016

From 1967 to 1970, the R.I. Uzoma family sat out the civil war in Nkwerre. With the end of the civil war in 1970 and the dire need for qualified teachers to rebuild the secondary school system in the former Eastern Region, Jemimah Uzoma was appointed Vice-Principal of the St. Catherine's Girls' Secondary School, Nkwerre in 1970. This was another cherished appointment for her, because St. Catherine's was the school in whose establishment in the 1950s she was very much involved, as will be subsequently demonstrated. In addition to administration, her main teaching subjects were Mathematics, Religious Studies and History. From St. Catherine's Girls' School, Jemimah was transferred to the neighbouring Owerri-Nkworji Girls' Secondary School in 1975 as Principal. At that school, she had the huge task of rehabilitating and reorganising the school in order to bring it back to standard. Owerri-Nkworji Girls School had served as a military camp during the civil war and was not immediately revived as a school at the end of the war. It was from Owerri-Nkworji Girls School that Jemimah retired in 1977, from the Imo State Schools system. She thereafter had more time on her hands for the many women's development programmes and other NGO activities in which she had developed a keen interest during her years as a teacher.

Service to Women

Nkwerre Aborigines Union/Women's Section (NAU/WS)

A hallmark of Jemimah Uzoma's adult life was the extensive demands made on her skills as a pioneer female teacher, by the many non-governmental social movements of her time. In January 1942, Jemimah joined the community associations of Nkwerre women by virtue of her marriage to R.I. Uzoma. She was aged nineteen years but within a short period of time, she was to become a noticeable force in the socio-economic and other activities of women of that community, through her active role in community church programmes. The wedding of Jemimah to R.I. Uzoma, which took place at the St. Paul's CMS Church, Nkwerre on 7th January 1942, made them the first couple to marry in church in Nkwerre.[108] In that regard, Reuben once again showed himself to be a pacesetter in Nkwerre. With time, it became clear to him that he had acquired in Jemimah, a wife as well as a kindred spirit and an "executive partner" in the pursuit of his most important social ideals.

Quite early in her marriage, Jemimah endeared herself to her new Nkwerre family and community, and was quickly integrated into its networks. In those days, it was unusual for young Nkwerre men to marry wives from outside their home communities and its immediate environs. Any such wives were treated with some measure of curiosity and they were not easily accepted into positions in the local women's groups. This was not the case with Jemimah, who soon mastered the local Nkwerre dialect and customs. In addition, the fact that she came to Nkwerre as a Queen's College educated teacher, at a time when Nkwerre people were hungry for education, stood her in good stead in the aspiring leadership of the nascent women's wing of the Nkwerre Aborigines Union (NAU).

In 1949 at the age of twenty-seven years, and already a mother of three young children, Jemimah Uzoma was elected to serve Nkwerre women as the first Secretary of the NAU/Women's Section (NAU/WS). The women's wing of the NAU came into existence just one year earlier in 1948, nine years after the main umbrella body had been formed by the men in 1939. Jemimah was one of the founding mothers at the time and was well-positioned to assume duties in which the basic skills she had acquired from a secondary school education could be applied. Other foundation mothers included Sarah Akaose, Eunice Eriaba Ihegboro, Catherine

---

[108] Another couple who were among the first to have a church wedding at the St. Paul's Church in Nkwerre, were Mr. Silas Ihiekwe and his wife, Jane Ihiekwe, who became close friends with Jemimah Uzoma all through their lives

Nwanu Uju, Felicia Nwaigbe Uzoechi, Mabel Egwueke, Christiana Onwuzuruigbo, Jane Ijeuru Agbawo, Christiana Nwakwa Ukegbu, Grace Uzoamaka, Angelina Ugochukwu, Florence Nwachi Nworisa, Grace Nnadi, Rose Ohayagha and others (Obialor, 2006: 96).

Jemimah was easily elected as secretary (Ode Akwukwo), and she served the women in that capacity for all of 22 years from 1949 to 1961. In that period, she worked hand-in-glove with presidents who were highly reputable Amazons of commerce and business in Nkwerre, in spite of their having little or no formal education. Jemimah gave them all due respect and full cooperation. These titans of female emancipation included Da Sarah Akaose who was president of the NAU/WS from inception in 1948 to 1954. She was followed by Madam Eunice Eriaba Ihegboro ("Da Eriaba") who served from 1955 to 1972, and Madam Felicia Nwaigbe Uzoechi (Da Nwaigbe) who held forth from 1973 to 1978. These women were forerunners of women's rights in Nkwerre, they were charismatic personalities and were wealthy. Naturally, they found themselves enamoured with the talented young school-mistress Jemimah Uzoma, from the Eze Nwachukwu family of distant Ezeoke, in Mbano, whom Reuben Uzoma had brought into their fold. They were impressed with her ease with paper-work, record-keeping and other organisational demands of their new association, which soon became a powerful development organ of the community. It was not long before the young Jemimah became known as "Da Jemimah" as a sign of respect among the people of Nkwerre.

The period of Jemimah's service as Secretary of the NAU/Women's Section, saw the golden years of community development, driven by strong solidarity and group mobilisation among the citizens of Nkwerre, male and female. This was the period in which the St. Catherine's Girls' Secondary School was built entirely by the women of Nkwerre. It is reported that Jemimah's role was so effective that Nkwerre women, through her, saw for themselves, the advantage of secondary school education for girls, and decided to send more of their daughters for higher education. According to Obialor,

> Though Sarah (President of NAU/Women's Section) was an illiterate, she was very intelligent. So she was helped in organising the women by Mrs Jemimah C. Uzoma, the first certified Nkwerre female teacher, who became the first Secretary to the union. Jemimah compiled the names of the women and arranged them according to their places of abode. This arrangement made their collection of five shillings annual levy, so perfect and water-tight, that in three years, the women were able to raise more than thirty thousand (30,000) pounds which initially enabled them start off the project. The school was opened in 1955. Like the men's wing, the women handed over the school to the CMS Mission, to ensure an efficient management" (Obialor, 2006: 92).

Following the successful commissioning of the girls' secondary school in January 1955, Nkwerre women were energised and motivated into being major contributors to other similar infrastructural projects. They worked in tandem with the NAU main umbrella body, controlled by the men. The General Hospital project followed, as did also the Civic Centre in the 1980's and 1990's. By then, the NAU had grown into a nation-wide organisation with branches in all major cities of Nigeria where Nkwerre men and women could be found pursuing their business and their careers (Obialor, 2006:147). In 1961, Jemimah handed over the books to Abigail E. Achigbu who served in that capacity till 1973 before being succeeded by Mrs. Stella Chigbu, another professional teacher who had been mentored by "Da Jemimah." Abigail Chigbu was herself the second female high elementary teacher in Nkwerre after Jemimah, although the first who was an indigene.

In 1979, at the age of fifty-seven years, Jemimah was elected president of the NAU Women's Section. She held that position for another rather lengthy term of office (19 years). In 1998, she finally handed over leadership to her protégée, Mrs. Stella Chigbu who had been a dedicated and effective secretary in the period of Jemimah's leadership. The remarkable impact of Jemimah's period of leadership of Nkwerre women was evident following her passing on 2nd January, 2003. At "Da Jemimah's" interment in Nkwerre on 18th February 2003, the incumbent Executive Committee of the NAU/WS gave directives for a "mass return" of Nkwerre women from all the branches nationwide, to give her the final honour. It was a momentous event and Jemimah's family could barely cope with huge numbers of brave Nkwerre women who turned up.

"Nzuko Ekeukwu" and Mothers Union

Over the years, it became clear that Jemimah Uzoma's keen interest and natural aptitude in organising and mobilising women had merely found training ground in the NAU/WS. By the 1950's following her husband's appointment to the government as Eastern Regional minister, Jemimah began to extend her interest and energies to the service of women on other non-governmental platforms, apart from the local community union. She started first with the Church, a natural move for her, given her upbringing and missionary roots in her home community of Ezeoke.

In 1952, Jemimah Uzoma was elected as the foundation president of an association of women of the St. Paul's Church in Nkwerre which she helped to initiate. That body came to be known as the Nzuko Ekeukwu, a meeting of all women members of the St. Paul's Church at home and "abroad" (living outside of Nkwerre). The annual meeting date of the body was fixed for Eke-days only, within the native weekly calendar, hence the name "Ekeukwu". The core objective of this body was the promotion of the CMS church through practical deeds, such as provision of lay services in church and domestic support for church projects. Mrs. Uzoma became more-or-less a "life-president" of this body because the women would not let her vacate the position of president until almost forty (40) years later in 1990. The only breathing space which enabled Jemimah to handle this role in addition to her other commitments, was the fact that meetings were usually held only on the festive holiday periods in the year. Those were the times of the year when Nkwerre citizens, as a habit, would return en-masse to their home community with their families, for a break from their businesses.

A related area of Jemimah's long-term service to women through the Church was the Mothers' Union of the Anglican Church of Nigeria. This organisation is affiliated to the global Mothers' Union which is an international Christian charity that "seeks to support families worldwide." Founded by Mary Sumner in the United Kingdom in 1876, the world wide body today has over seventy (70) branches in different countries of the world. The Mothers' Union (MU) of the Anglican Church of Nigeria has as its core objective, the ideal "to uphold Christ's teaching on the nature of marriage and promote its wider understanding (and) to encourage parents to bring up their children in the faith and life of the Church."[109] These ideals have led the Mothers' Union of Nigeria to make marriage and baptism, according to the Anglican Church Order, requirements for formal enrollment into its membership.

The above requirement was one reason which motivated Jemimah to mobilise the alternative platform of Nzuko Ekeukwu for all women who were dedicated members of the Nkwerre CMS St. Paul's Church, irrespective of their mode of marriage. The majority of Nkwerre women were in polygamous marriages. As a committed leader of the NAU/WS, Jemimah felt a need to provide a sense of inclusiveness for the hard-working women of diverse backgrounds, with whom she worked side-by-side in the town union. This did not stop her from finding time through her membership of the Mother's Union to serve both church and community. From 1963 to 1966 and 1976 to 1984, she

---

[109] See R.I. Uzoma Archives for files of Mrs. J.C. Uzoma; Also Mothers Union Worldwide at www.themothersunion.org.worldwideand Mothers Union-Church of Nigeria at https://anglican-nig.org

was a leading member of the Mothers' Union Women's Work of Owerri Diocese. In 1976, Jemimah Uzoma was installed as a "Lay Canon" of the Diocese of Owerri by the then Bishop, the Rt. Rev. Benjamin Nwankiti. She was the only female among the six leading lay members of the Diocese who were so appointed into this innovative role. This unique recognition was the result of her tireless work in the Mother's Union, as well as in other arms of the church such as the choir at Christ Church Parish, Owerri. Following the relocation of her family to Owerri from Old Umuahia in 1963, Jemimah had served as an organist at Christ Church, Owerri. Like the biblical Dorcas, and with the help of her second daughter Ugochi, she made all the robes for the English language choir, and generally worked tirelessly to improve their music skills.

Subsequently, on the creation of the Okigwe/Orlu Diocese in 1984, the need arose, for organising the Mother's Union in the new diocese. Jemimah Uzoma was officially appointed Leader of Women's Work, by the Mary Sumner House in London. One of her legacies in the new diocese is the establishment of the first chapter in Nigeria, of the Girls' Friendly Society of England, a group dedicated to the mobilisation of young girls for church work, side-by-side with the Mother's Union. She continued in these capacities in the new diocese for a few more years before her retirement.

The Young Women's Christian Association (YWCA)

Another chosen platform of long service and leadership for Jemimah was the Young Women's Christian Association (YWCA) of Nigeria. With the spread of CMS schools and other institutions in the 1960s, the YWCA was growing rapidly in membership across the country. It was an association which gave further opportunity for expression of Jemimah's keen interests in women's empowerment in all of the locations in which she found herself residing with her family. Hence in 1963, she became the foundation chairman of the Owerri branch and later pioneer president of the Imo State YWCA Chapter from 1976 to 1980. In this capacity, she also functioned as a national vice-chairman. This was a period in which the National YWCA was a vibrant non-governmental organisation operating from its self-owned offices at 8, Moloney Street, on Lagos Island. The office buildings on three floors also housed a decent hostel accommodation for young girls and women who needed urgent accommodation in Lagos. Sadly, during the field research for this book, these national YWCA facilities were found to be run down and in desperate need of rehabilitation.

The YWCA of Nigeria, as a non-denominational Christian organisation was founded in 1906, and serves as a bridge between women of all denominations who come together with the aim of promoting the rights of women and girls. This is done through such activities as vocational training, provision of Christian counselling and welfare support such as child-care services. The World YWCA is a multi-faith organisation founded in 1855. It is described as "a movement working for the empowerment, leadership and rights of women, young women and girls in more than 120 countries. The membership and supporters include women from different faiths, ages, backgrounds, beliefs and cultures." The YWCA of Nigeria was founded in 1906 and is affiliated to the world body. Today, the Nigerian body defines its mission as uniting "young women in groups for fellowship, service, and activities which will promote their spiritual, mental, social and physical welfare."[110]

In the 1970's, the leadership coincided largely with some of the first educated women of Lagos and its environs, along with a few of their sisters from the former Eastern Region. In 1978, the national executive officers of YWCA were listed as follows: Mrs T. Oguntayo as President, Mrs. J.C. Uzoma, Mrs. V.N. Amadi and Mrs.

---

110 See R.I. Uzoma Archives for files of Mrs. J.C. Uzoma; also World YWCA Website at www.worldywca.org and YWCA Nigeria at https://ywcanigeria.org

W.I. Shonekan as Vice-Presidents. The National Secretary was Mrs. A.A. Oladipo while a former founding National President, Lady O.M. Abayomi, was listed as consultant. The organisation had its responsibilities structured for action under committees. While Mrs. Jemimah Uzoma chaired the committee for Finance, other committee chairpersons were listed as Mrs. W.I. Shonekan (Programmes), Mrs S.M. Baptiste (Membership), Mrs. T. John (Building), Mrs. V.N. Amadi (Personnel and Training), and Mrs. O.O. Onagbesan (Publicity). The National Treasurer was Miss C.O.K. Olaiya, while the Recording Secretary was Mrs. S.U. Osagie, and the Auditor was Mr. M. Oluwa. It is worthy of note that the YWCA of Nigeria in the 1970s, included into its executive ranks, representatives of the World Council of Churches in the persons of Mrs. A. Mbanefo and Mrs. J. Fajemisin.[111]

In the 1970s and 1980s, the National Executive was established impressively in head offices located at No. 8, Moloney Street, Lagos Island in Lagos. The national offices, apart from providing hostel accommodation with cafeteria and other services, also supported vocational training and rehabilitation programmes for young women especially in the aftermath of the Nigerian civil war. These were all projects which Jemimah Uzoma's tenure in Owerri, did well to replicate from 1971. With the dedicated support of such leaders as Esther Onuoha, Mrs. Joy Ononuju, Mrs. Christie Onyekuru, Elfrida Aguta and Clara Ajoku, the Owerri sector of the YWCA of Nigeria opened and operated a hostel or dormitory for girls. They also had a daycare facility as well as a vocational training centre which they gave the grand name of Career Development Centre. The aim was to empower women through small-scale entrepreneurship in order to alleviate financial poverty

---
111   *Ibid*

and hardship within their households. These projects were all executed on the basis of volunteer work and private donations, with a modest yearly subvention from the state government which was painstakingly accounted for each year.[112]

As at the time of producing this book, the dormitory for girls as well as the daycare facility, were still operating although on a much reduced scale. In the face of the current economic recession, neglect and NGO-fatigue have afflicted the YWCA both locally and at the national level. A hallmark of Jemimah Uzoma's leadership as president of the Imo State chapter, from 1976 to 1990, was her determined efforts to take the YWCA into rural locations. She personally championed the opening of rural branches in Nkwerre and Amaigbo in order to change the image of the organisation as an urban-based body. Before her efforts, all known branches of the YWCA had been located in the state capitals and major cities only, such as Lagos, Ibadan, Enugu, Owerri and Port Harcourt. Unfortunately, Jemimah's efforts have not been followed through by the subsequent leadership of the YWCA. The rural branches have not thrived and many of the urban branches have undergone changes due to the many contemporary forces that have affected orthodox churches in Nigeria. One such factor is considered to be the rapid spread of the pentecostal movement and its new-fangled methods of mobilisation of and leadership.

The National Council of Women's Societies (NCWS)

The National Council of Women's Societies (NCWS) of Nigeria provided another platform on which Jemimah Uzoma extended many years of leadership and women-mobilisation skills in her lifetime. In 1958, she participated as a founding member in the

---

[112] YWCA Owerri File Records from 1971 to 1988 show documentation on the YWCA projects namely: Nursery/Daycare Centre, Career Development projects and a Dormitory/Hostel facility. Also on State government subvention and other transactions. As at the time of interview for this book in early 2017, all are in the dedicated care of a loyal long service YWCA Owerri member, Madam Josephine Ezue, who was originally appointed Matron of the dormitory.

creation of the Eastern Region National Council of Women's Societies. In this regard, she joined hands with other Amazons of women's emancipation such as Mrs. Oyibo Ekwulo Odinamadu, Lady Kofo Ademola (the First National President), Lady Abayomi (First National Vice-President), Mrs. M.O. Eluwa, and Mrs. Titi Shodeinde among others, who gave support from the nascent national body in Lagos (Nwakanma, O., 2007).

The NCWS Nigeria was conceived as an umbrella organisation of all women's associations in Nigeria with voluntary membership, non-governmental and non-political in nature, it works with government to the benefit of all women of Nigeria. As a national body, the NCWS came into existence following a 1958 seminar organised for women leaders by UNESCO in Ibadan. The theme of that seminar was the "African Woman Designs Her Future".[113] At that forum, the international nature of attendance and presentations opened the eyes of the small educated class of Nigerian women, who were participants, to the existence of a sophisticated structure of women's organisations in other parts of the world. They took note of their affiliation to the International Alliance of Women and the International Council of Women. The Nigerian delegates there and then at the seminar formed their own equivalence.[114]

The Eastern Regional NCWS was formed in the same year with Mrs. Oyibo Odinamadu as President and Mrs. Jemimah Uzoma as Vice-President while Mrs. Mercy Eluwa was the Secretary. Other notable founding members are recorded as Mrs. Mary Nzimiro, Mrs. M.O. Ahamba, Mrs. .U. Onyeador, Madam Okoye of Enugu, Mrs. Felicia Obua of Oguta, Mrs. Margaret Ikokwu, Mrs Ada Chinwuba Udogu, Miss U. Wachukwu. The operations of the Eastern Regional NCWS were subsequently disrupted by the civil war between 1967 and 1970. Nonetheless, during the civil war, Mrs. Jemimah, as a founding member of the NCWS was member of a team of four

---

113 From YWCA Owerri File Records, Report of the 1958 Ibadan Conference, by Mrs. Mercy Eluwa.
114 *Ibid*

leaders from the former Eastern Region who were sent overseas to solicit for a peaceful end to the civil war, due to the increasing human toil and suffering in the then "Biafra." That team was led by Chief Mrs. Janet Mokelu and included Mrs. Oyibo Odinamadu and Chief Mary Ededem (Nwakanma, O., 2007).

Following the creation of new states after the civil war, the East Central State NCWS was formed in 1970 with offices in Enugu under the leadership of two of the founding members, namely Oyibo Odinamadu as President and Jemimah Uzoma as Vice-President. From 1976 when the state structure of the federation was further devolved, Jemimah Uzoma continued as president in Imo State. It was a position she tirelessly served in until 1984, assisted by such executive members as Dr. Rose Ekeleme, Mrs. M.O. Ahamba, Joy Ononuju, M.O. Eluwa, Chief Virginia Egwim, Rachel Chukueke and others. Jemimah Uzoma's dedicated leadership of the NCWS in her state, unavoidably resulted in her exposure to other ad-hoc appointments to public service roles. For instance, she was appointed by the Imo State Government as a Supervisory Councillor on the Caretaker Local Government Council of Nkwerre from 1986 to 1988. She was also a Trustee in the Imo State Endowment Fund Committee under the Military Administration of the state about the same period.

A unique project of the Imo State NCWS under the leadership of Mrs. Uzoma was the compilation in 1981 of a compendium titled "The Voice of Women" (Uzoma, J.C., 1981) The book which was put together by Mrs. Uzoma entirely at her own cost, documents numerous conference and seminar reports, addresses at special NCWS occasions, presentations and academic papers by women, on the platform of NCWS programmes. The production of this book by Jemimah Uzoma at a time she was involved with so much work in so many NGOs, was a feat that did not fail to amaze her close family. In particular, this was in a period in which she was also serving as a member of the Governing Council of the University of

Ibadan for three terms from 1972 to 1984, and hardly missed any meetings of council.

The "Voice of Women" mirrors the growth of the NCWS at national and state levels from 1958 to 1980. Jemimah's goal was to sensitice future generations and other critical groups in society who might be inclined to misconstrue the work of the NCWS as mere feminist agitation. Hence, she ensured that the publication was painstakingly sent out to all post-primary institutions at no cost. Since those glorious days of the women's movement, the NCWS like many other NGOs has sadly also become afflicted with politicisation and commercialism.

In her twelve years at the service of the University of Ibadan as a member of the Governing Council, Jemimah Uzoma became similarly known for her motherly interventions in disciplinary issues that affected students and junior staff, especially as she was assigned to the committee on junior staff matters. At the end of her last tenure, she was only too happy to institute a Jemimah Uzoma prize for best graduating student in Community Medicine.

R.I. Uzoma as Minister of Education 1951-1953

R.I. Uzoma after his return from University of London, 1947

Mr. and Mrs. R.I. Uzoma in Enugu, 1952

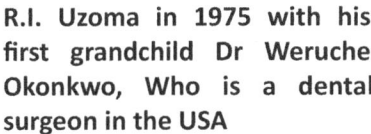

R.I. Uzoma in 1975 with his first grandchild Dr Weruche Okonkwo, Who is a dental surgeon in the USA

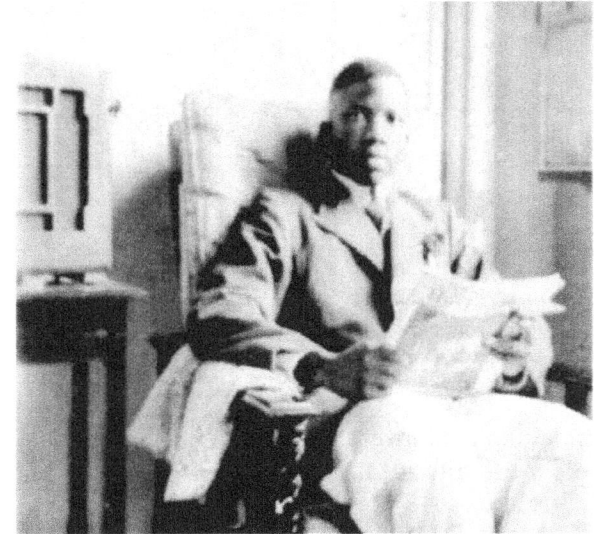

R.I. Uzoma at Achimota, Ghana "Achimota College University House Reception Room Achimota 1938"

Mrs. Jemimah Chinyere Uzoma
8th July 1961

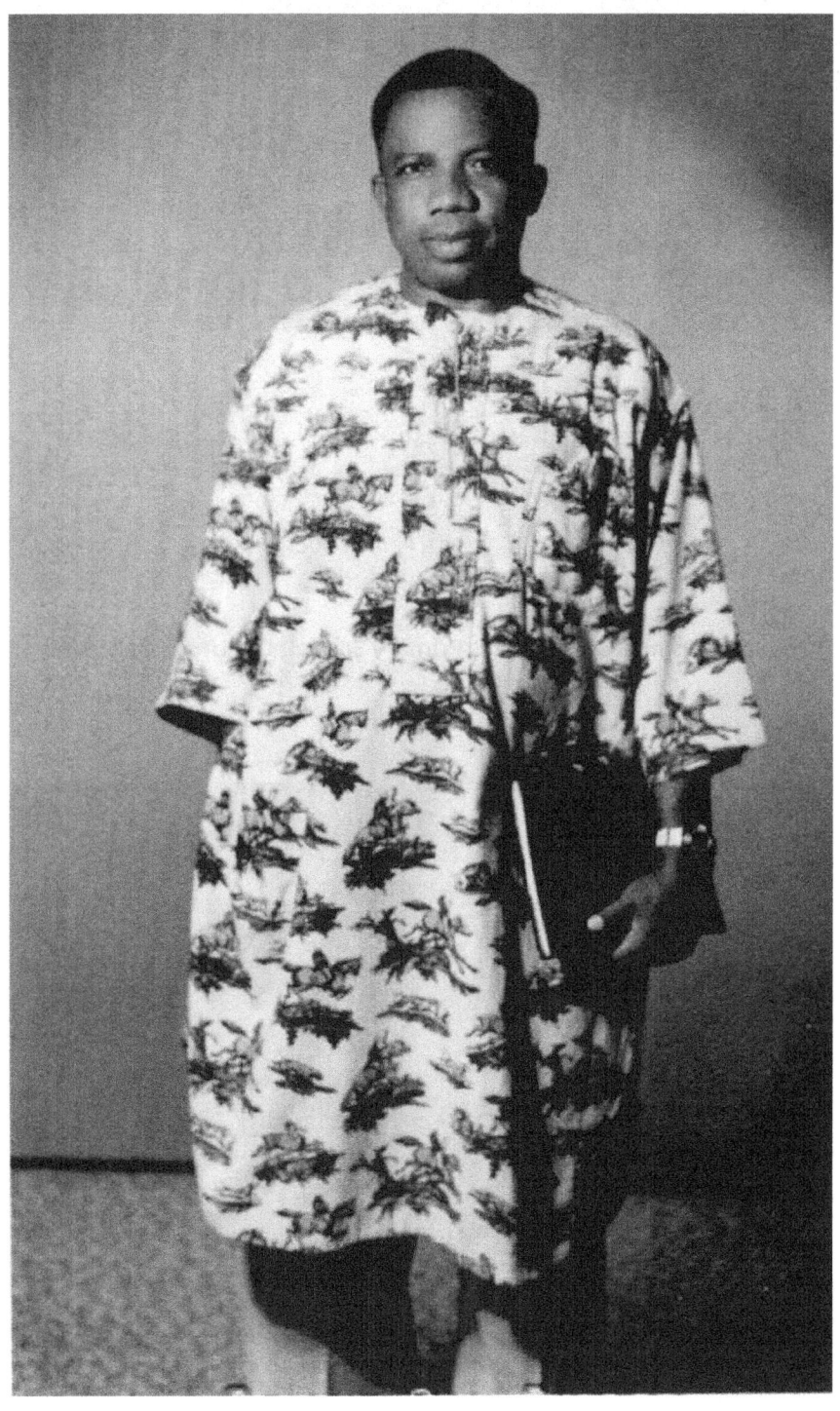

R.I. Uzoma as Education Secretary, and Supervisor of Schools, about 1960

Jemimah as a teacher at Silas Primary School, Old Umuahia, 1949

Mr. & Mrs. R.I. Uzoma with the Oxford Members, a society in the Awka College Practising School, 1943

Mr. & Mrs. R.I. Uzoma with Okigwe District Students, Awka College, 1943

Okrika Grammar School, 1944
The Principal and his senior boys

"Crowther House, CMS College Awka, 1940"
R.I. Uzoma as a Tutor

Awka College, R.I. Uzoma as a Tutor with Bishop A.C. Onyeabo, and a Confirmation class

Okrika Grammar School R.I. Uzoma (sitting fourth from the right) with the Vice-Principal, T.N.P Birabi (sitting fourth from the left) and a class of senior students Chief E.C. Akwiwu SAN, is first on the back row, Right.

Okrika Grammar School
R.I. Uzoma with his Vice and the school football team
(RI is sitting 4th from the left)

Awka College, R.I. Uzoma with his friend, Mr. S.I. Okediadi and a class of sudents (R.I. Uzoma sitting 4th from left S.I. Okediadi sitting 3rd from right)

Queens College, Lagos, Jemimah and friends "Class VI girls in Yoruba attire in memory of their leaving" 1940.
Jemimah is 2nd from the right.

Cambridge Conference, Sept. 1952

"Delegates to the Cambridge Conference on African education hold a Conference of their own before serious business begins. The Hon. S.H.O. Awokoya, Minister for Education, Western Nigeria makes a point. Left to right: Mr. E.E. Esua, General Secretary, Nigerian Union of Teachers; Paramount Chief, Kai Samba of Sierra Leone; Mr. F.O. Awosika, M.H.R from Western Nigeria; Mr. U.U. Okure, Assistant Vice-Principal, Methodist Boys' High School, from Ikot-Ekpene, Eastern Nigeria; The Hon. R.I. Uzoma, Minister for Education, Eastern Region, Nigeria; The Hon. A.M. Margai, Member of Executive Council responsible for education, Sierra Leone; The Hon. Shettima Kashim, M.H.R. Minister for Social Services, Nigeria; The Hon. aliyu, M.H.R, Makaman Bida, Minister for social Services, Northern Region, Nigeria; Miss M. gyimah, Head Teacher, Kumasi, Gold Coast; Mallam Ahmadu Coomasie, Provincial Education Officer, Northern Nigeria; Mr. Awokoya; M.H.D. Alghali, Muslim Teacher, Sierra Leone."

(Official 1952 Caption)

Sir. & Lady R.I. Uzoma 50th Wedding Anniversary 1992

R.I. Uzoma as Provincial Administrator during the Civil War, 1967-1970. RI is standing sandwiched between two uniformed officers

Cambridge Conference, Sept 1952 "There were no set places at mealtimes in the old hall of King's College, so that a Nigerian who at lunchtime sat next to a Somali might at dinner find his neighbour to be a Chief Education Officer of an English County Council. The Hall also provided an excellent setting for speeches of welcome and of farewell. The cheerful atmosphere of the whole conference is well shown in this photograph of some of the delegates and conference staff at lunch."
RI is in the middle of 2nd Row from right.
(Official 1952 Caption)

R.I. Uzoma and his extended family in Nkwerre, 2nd January 1950
The author is third from the left on the floor
RI is standing (in suit) first from the right

Jemimah in her last year at Queen's College, Lagos, 1940

Jemimah Chinyere Uzoma (Nee Nwachukwu) As a teacher in Owerri in the 1960s

RI's mother, Janet Nwannediya at the age of about 90 years

Okrika Grammar School, Mr. & Mrs. R.I. Uzoma with a mixed group of juniors and seniors to mark RI's departure to the UK
The author is arrowed in front of Mrs. Uzoma

R.I. Uzoma being sworn in as Teacher's Service Commissioner 1974 by the East Central State Administrator, Ukpabi Asika

Queens College, Lagos, 1939, Jemimah and friends "Becca, Mary, Bola, Efuns, Maggie, Jem" (Jemimah)

Queens College, Lagos, Jemimah and friends "Sitting: Jem, Maggie Kneeling: Mary, Becca, Efuns, Bola"

R.I. Uzoma with colleagues at Awka college, Mr. S.I. Okediadi, first from the right, Mr. Reuben Ekpunobi, first from the left

Queens College, Lagos, 1940, Jemimah and friends
"**Standing:** Elsie Spiff, Phillipa Chiedu, Christianan Nwagbo, Patricia Bob-Manuel, Priscilla Nzimiro, Ada Chinwuba, Kate Bob-Manuel, Faustina Bob-Manuel
Sitting: Jem (Jemimah) **Laying Down:** Dora Jaja
(Caption by Mrs J.C. Uzoma)

Mr. & Mrs. R.I. Uzoma Wedding Day, 7th January 1942

Mr. & Mrs. R.I. Uzoma with children, on their 10th Wedding Anniversary in 1952, RI as Minister in Enugu

Jemimah (wearing a helmet) fresh from Queens College, as teacher at St. Barth's Primary School, Enugu, 1941

R.I. Uzoma and his nuclear family in 1960
(The author is standing in a floral dress)

R.I. Uzoma with his fellow Commissioners of the Imo State Public Service Commission, 1976-1980 (RI is seated 3rd from the left)

December 3rd 2015, The Chairman and Trustees of the R.I. Uzoma Educational Foundation with some of the pioneer beneficiaries of the RIUEF Bursary Award for "Excellence in Adversity"
Bishop's Court, Nkwerre.

**The famous Awka College Chapel
(Photo by RI)**

**The famous Clock Tower at Achimota College
(Photo by RI)**

Sir & Lady R.I Uzoma 50th Wedding Anniversary 1992

Mr. & Mrs. R.I. Uzoma with Children, In-Laws and Grandchildren, At their 50 years Wedding Anniversary, 1992

APPENDIXES: FROM THE R.I. UZOMA PAPERS

APPENDIXES: FROM THE R.I. UZOMA PAPERS

Documents from a man's life can often speak better about the man than any narrative that is written on him by others. This chapter presents a set of Appendices consisting of such documents from the life of Reuben Ibekwe Uzoma. These are documents that have either been generated by him, or are the product of his education and growth, and his actual career and life of service. They represent only a small selection out of the vast material available and are in the form of policy proposals and memoranda by R.I Uzoma, addresses and lectures, interviews that he granted, and some private and official correspondence.

The appendices also include letters of appointment and certificates, honours, and awards received by RI in his lifetime, as well as congratulatory messages from colleagues and friends. All these serve to complete the portrait of a unique individual, which has been painted in this biography. The appendices are also expected to provide a deeper insight into an interesting generation in Nigeria's history.

APPENDIXES: FROM THE
P.W. OTOMO PAPERS

Appendix 1

A. PUBLICATIONS, PAPERS, MEMORANDA, ADDRESSES

The 1952 UPE Proposals of R.I. Uzoma as Minister of Education titled Education Policy for the Eastern Region, December 4th 1952.

4th December, 1952.

Education Policy for the Eastern Region

Sessional Paper No.20 of 1947 entitled "Memorandum on Educational Policy in Nigeria" which was drawn up by Mr. R.A.McL. Davidson, C.M.G., at that time Director and now Inspector-General of Education, opened by stating :-

> "It may be taken as axiomatic that education policy must aim at assisting the fulfilment of the ultimate purpose of the Imperial Government. The general policy of the latter is the administration of the Colonial Dependencies with the object of guiding and helping peoples, not yet able to stand by themselves, to achieve self-government."

Nobody will quarrel with this, but what the average Nigerian questions is the extent to which not only teachers but all those engaged in educational work in Nigeria realise this aim of our education. There is no doubt that a great deal of our education has been dull and mechanical and has neither helped us to create what we need nor to realise to their full the resources of the country. It is the aim of Government in the Eastern Region within the next few years to direct education towards the fulfilment of the aim stated above, and at the same time to relate it to the needs of the country.

2. *Primary Education.* Our aim is to provide universal primary education in the shortest possible time. By universal primary education we mean that all children in the Region should receive a basic primary education. We prefer the use of the term "universal" rather than the commonly-used "compulsory and free". The reason for this is that it is idle to pretend that education on such a large scale will not in fact cost a great deal of money while compulsion should be left to the various local government bodies to introduce as and when they feel they are ready to do so. At the same time it is our aim to encourage Local Government bodies to introduce compulsory schemes of primary education as soon as they can provide their share of the necessary funds. We aim at giving the best possible education to the largest possible number at the least possible cost.

It is the present aim of Government that 55% of the cost of primary education should be borne by the grant-in-aid votes placed at the disposal of the Regional Governments; the remaining 45% should be found by the local communities. Already Local Government bodies are levying education rates in order that communities should bear a share of the cost of primary education and it is our intention to encourage that these rating systems be spread wider so that the whole of the share of the local communities will fall on rates and that school fees in the basic primary schools will be abolished.

The present system of primary and secondary education in the Region is popularly known as the 4/4/4 system, by which is meant a four-year junior primary course, followed by a four-year senior primary course, followed by a four-year secondary course. The four-year secondary course is, in fact, not yet widely achieved and the five-year course is much more common, although in practice in the better senior primary and secondary schools the last two years of the senior primary course overlap to some extent with the first two years of secondary schooling.

167

- 2 -

It is our intention that this scheme should continue unchanged for the present. As soon as rating schemes are properly established and Local Government bodies are prepared to levy the increased rates which will be necessary, the primary course of four years basic junior primary plus four years senior primary should be changed to a basic primary course of six years; during the waiting period the standard of teaching should improve sufficiently to enable a course which now takes eight years to be achieved in fact in six. It will be a duty of the Department of Education in the Region to keep a close watch on the progress of primary education, and to devise means for meeting any shortcomings in a six-year basic system by the provision of post-primary courses. Such courses may be additional to the secondary course of six years which would normally follow a primary course of six years. To put it shortly, the intention is that the 4/4/4 system should evolve into a 6/6 system. At all times great care will be taken not merely to maintain standards but to improve them.

In recent years the demand for education has been such that the degree of dilution of the teaching Staff by unqualified teachers has been excessive. As will be seen later in this paper, it is our aim immediately to introduce measures to change this position.

While we shall encourage local communities to continue the practice of providing Primary School buildings we propose to introduce a system of building grants for such schools. Grants will also be given for Primary School equipment though in this connection it must be remembered that a great deal of teaching apparatus should be made by the teachers themselves.

It may be necessary in areas which are now regarded as educationally backward to relax the regulations regarding the numbers and classes assigned to any one teacher; where this is found to be necessary it is our aim to provide safeguards to ensure that standards do not fall as a result.

3. **Secondary Education.** Appendix A to this paper shows the situation and nature of secondary schools existing at present. It is clear from this schedule that many areas have no secondary schools. It is our aim that there should be an adequate distribution of secondary schools throughout the Region and with the expansion of primary education which we envisage, the demands for secondary schools will, it is expected, increase rapidly.

Where new Secondary Schools are needed and local communities show that they are prepared to contribute towards their establishment we intend to provide funds to assist in the construction of buildings and the provision of the necessary equipment. We attach particular importance to all Secondary Schools being under responsible ownership, whether of long-standing Voluntary Agencies or of recently-formed Boards of Governors. Boards of Governors, in fact, should take over the control of all Secondary Schools and we regard it as of the utmost importance that there should be the fullest representation of the local communities on such Boards of Governors.

../3.

Appendix

In the expansion of secondary education our first concern will be the provision of adequate qualified staff and of good equipment. Buildings need not be expensive so long as they are serviceable and weatherproof. Boarding facilities must comply with the requirements of the Medical Department but again need not be of an expensive type. The provision of adequate playing fields is a matter of importance and is unfortunately one which has been somewhat neglected in the past, particularly in townships.

It will be our policy to encourage African-owned Secondary Schools which have not reached the standard for approval to attain this standard as soon as possible, and in this respect emphasis will be laid on vesting property rights of such schools in registered Boards of Governors, with Trustees. Further, Local Government bodies or communities will be encouraged and assisted to formulate sound proposals for the establishment of new Secondary Schools in their area with due regard to the overall expansion plan of the Region.

Existing Secondary Schools are of the Grammar School type and there is no doubt that many children in such schools are not fitted in aptitude and intellect to do Grammar School type of work. It will be our policy, therefore, to encourage the growth of Secondary Modern Schools and of Secondary Schools with a technical or rural bias.

4. **Teacher Training.** It is our intention to embark immediately on schemes for the expansion of teacher training. In the immediate future the enrolment at our Teacher Training Colleges will be brought up to the maximum possible with the buildings and staff at the disposal of the agencies owning the colleges, while greater provision than exists at present will be made for the training of teachers employed by Voluntary Agencies which do not possess their own facilities for such training. In particular the training of women teachers, especially for work in the lower classes of Primary Schools, will receive our urgent attention. Advantage will also be taken of every possible means of training teachers for Secondary School work and the Regional Scholarship Scheme will be used for the training of staff for work in Secondary Schools and Teacher Training Colleges. In this connection it must be admitted that up to the present the conditions of service for graduate teachers have not been sufficiently attractive so that the requisite numbers of qualified Africans have not been forthcoming. It is our belief that these conditions will be improved in the very near future and it will be our aim to employ an ever-increasing number of Africans in Secondary School work; encouragement will be given to Voluntary Agencies to employ increasing numbers of Africans and we see no reason why within a very few years the recruitment of expatriates for such work should not cease except in exceptional circumstances.

The potential annual output of trained teachers is at present about 1,300. We aim at increasing this to some 2,500 per year in the next few years in order to provide the staff which will be necessary for universal education. Our plans for this expansion are already in hand and much can be brought about by increasing the accommodation in existing Teacher Training Colleges and by converting Preliminary Training Centres into Training Colleges. In addition the erection of one or two new Training Colleges will probably prove necessary.

../4.

5. **Girls' Education.** Efforts will be made to increase the number of girls at school to equal those of boys. It will not be the general policy to provide separate schools for girls before the Secondary School stage though where a system of girls Schools has already been provided it will of course continue. As the quality of Primary Education improves the Primary School leaving age should not in general exceed twelve years, before children begin to be conscious of their sex.

The increase in the number of women teachers which we envisage should accelerate the increase in the number of girls at school. The training of women teachers, as has been already mentioned, must therefore receive special attention and training facilities will be expanded to keep pace with those for men.

The main obstacles to the sending of girls to school are sociological and only a change of attitude on the part of parents can help to remove such obstacles. For example the weighing of bride-price against the cost of sending a girl to school, and the custom of keeping girls at home to act as nursemaids, are practical problems which can only be solved with the co-operation of parents.

6. **Adult Education.** More attention will be paid to Adult Education, and more money will be voted for all aspects of adult education, especially literacy campaigns. Anybody who has seen the good work being done amongst women in the Uyo Division will inevitably press that this type of work be extended to other parts of the Region.

When an adult realises that it is possible for him to change from illiteracy to literacy within a short time his whole outlook on life changes and he begins to desire changes in other directions. Community development and village improvement then follow. The consequent changes in environment and tradition will help gradually to determine the results of formal education given to children at school.

It is the intention to hold from time to time a "Mass Literacy Month". The slogan during such months will be "Each one teach another". Leading members of the community including members of the House of Assembly will, it is hoped, lead the campaigns in their areas, and the object of these campaigns will be that every literate person is expected to make another person literate.

7. **Administration and Control.** Our policy will be that the control of Primary Education will become the responsibility of Local Government bodies. The actual responsible body will be termed "The Local Education Authority" and it will work through a Local Education Committee. It is our intention that the Local Education Authority will become responsible for the establishment of new schools and the financing of Primary Education and will be the body which disburses not only the rates provided by the local communities but also grants-in-aid from Government. It is not in any way our intention that the transfer of the control and management of Primary Schools to Local authorities will result in making education purely secular.

../5.

It is not intended, however, that this system will be introduced precipitately. We appreciate that we owe the long-established Voluntary Agencies a debt of gratitude for the wonderful educational work which they have done and are doing and it is our intention that the control of Primary Education by Local Education Authorities will be brought about by the exercise of goodwill on the part of all concerned. It is our aim, however, that local communities will think of all the schools in their areas as "our schools" and not differentiate between schools owned by Voluntary Agencies and by Government or Native Authorities. We shall seek the co-operation of Voluntary Agencies and hope that their representatives on Educational Boards and Committees will give their assistance in the interests of education in the Region as a whole regardless of denominational interests.

At all levels it will be our policy that the personnel engaged in educational activities will be African. We realise that the process of Africanisation of staff will be slower in Secondary Schools and Teacher Training Colleges than in Primary Education and slower still in Technical Education, but we shall do all we can to expedite the training of Africans for work at all levels. In Primary Education the process must be rapid though in the Inspectorate, for some time to come the assistance of expatriate experts may be sought.

8. **Religion.** It is our intention that the religious and moral aspects of education will continue in the hands of the Missions which at present form the greatest proportion of the Voluntary Agencies. At the same time we shall insist on the enforcement of the regulations made under the Education Ordinance which are aimed at preventing religious discrimination. We shall, if we deem it necessary, introduce legislation to ensure that no child is penalised in any way on religious grounds, and that the religious atmosphere of all assisted schools is free and comfortable to all.

In Secondary Schools religious knowledge will not be a subject for entrance examinations.

9. **Finance.** This subject has already been mentioned in various parts of this paper but we must add here that provision will be made for special grants to encourage practical subjects such as Domestic Science, Woodwork and other crafts and Rural Science in order to encourage aspects of education which, we consider, have received insufficient attention in the past.

Scholarships will be awarded not only for University and Technical Education but also for Secondary Education. University and Technical scholarships are intended to supply the trained personnel and experts necessary for the development of the Region. Secondary School Scholarships are intended to raise the general educational standard of the Region and to spread Secondary Education in areas which are educationally undeveloped; in particular we shall encourage the education of girls by the award of scholarships at all levels.

We have already mentioned that Scholarships will be awarded in order to train teachers for Secondary Schools and Teacher Training Colleges.

../6.

10. **The Education Department.** The Education Department should be re-organised so that the Administrative staff is separated from the Inspectorate. The latter should be relieved of administrative duties and to ensure that there should be uniformity of standards in all Regions should be closely associated with an Inspectorate appointed and paid by the Central Government.

It will be necessary to increase the number of Branches or Sections of the Education Department which at the moment are divided into:-

(a) Administration

(b) Inspectorate
  i. Primary
  ii. Secondary
  iii. Teacher-Training

(c) Finance

(d) Women's Education

(e) Technical Education

(f) Adult Education

though at present the Inspectorate, particularly at the provincial level, has much administrative work. Additional Sections which appear to be necessary are :-

(g) Examinations and Syllabuses

(h) Scholarships

(i) Buildings and Architecture

(j) Research.

_____
Director of Education,
Eastern Region.

_____
Minister of Education,
Eastern Region.

APPENDIX 2

Publication titled "Universal Schooling in Ngwa Clan of Aba Division, Nigeria" by R.I. Uzoma, General manager and supervisor, Anglican Schools. Reprinted from Overseas Education Vol. XXIII, No. 2 of January 1952, pp 234-236

Reprinted from "Oversea Education", Volume XXIII, No. 2, January 1952 pp. 234-236.

UNIVERSAL SCHOOLING IN NGWA CLAN OF ABA DIVISION, NIGERIA*

by R. I. Uzoma, General Manager and Supervisor, Anglican Schools

ABA DIVISION is made up of the four clans of Ngwa, Ndoki, Asa, and Omuma; Ngwa being the largest. In all these clans there is a growing movement towards universal schooling for all children, and only those who are in direct contact with the people know of it. The practice of the whole village, rather than individual parents, paying the school fees of all its children, is not a new thing in Ngwaland, and so people do not proclaim it in the Press as is done in other parts of the Eastern Provinces. But the Ngwa system which obtains in about six-sevenths of all Anglican schools in the Division has special peculiarities of its own which make it interesting. It is rooted in the soil. The fees are not just paid from money contributed by wealthy young men. They are paid from money realised from the cutting of palm nuts from communal palm groves owned by old and young, rich and poor alike. The palm harvest is reaped in the schools.

There does not seem to be a definite history of this system of self-help. The first villages to try the experiment with Anglican schools did so about 1940 when they realised that the mission would not consider raising the status of a school from the Standard 2 grade (third grade) to the Standard 4 grade unless there was a definite number of children in the school. Once the scheme started in one village as a means of increasing enrolment, it spread all over Ngwa, and the neighbouring clans. Now the realisation of the fact that "social usefulness", as reflected in enrolment and village support, is a criterion for Government assistance has given the system double impetus. Consider the following figures from some Anglican schools in the Division.

School	Enrolment 1948	Enrolment 1950 1st term
Abayi Umuocham	354	618
Umuobasi Amavo	358	535
Ohanze Isiahia	243	397
Oza Umuebuku	196	306
Uratta	299	327
Akwete	333	447
Azumini	269	443
Oza (Asa)	240	409
Obokwe	non-existent	206
Aro 11 (Anglican)	non-existent	182
All N.D.P. Schools in Aba Division	11,934	15,252

Net increase since 1948 . . . 3,318

The significance of these figures will be appreciated when it is realised that in many parts of the country enrolment is decreasing now. Of the number of children at school, one-third are girls. The disparity between the numbers of boys and girls is due not to the unwillingness of parents to send girls to school, but to early marriage and the keeping behind of young girls by mothers to act as nursemaids.

* Reprinted from *The Nigerian Schoolmaster* by courtesy of the editor and of the author.

2 UNIVERSAL SCHOOLING IN NGWA CLAN OF ABA DIVISION

Side by side with the increase in enrolment there is also the growth in the number of good permanent school buildings, most of them erected from the same source—the harvest of palm nuts. Schools that would elsewhere probably possess temporary mud buildings are in this area erecting classrooms of concrete and pan. The following Anglican rural schools have completed or are about to complete permanent school buildings: Obegu, Obokwe, Asa-Umunka, Ohanze-Isiahia, Abainchokoro, Ogwe, Ovom 1, Ukpakiri, Oza Umuebuku, Abayi-Umuocham, Omoba, Eberi Omuma, Umuobasi-Amavo, Okpu Umobo, Umuojima-Ogbu, Akpa 1, Itungwa, Ndiolumbe, Aro-Amano, Umuakpara, Akwete, Ohuru, Ohanku, Umuomainta, Osusu, Umuosu, Amapu-Ntigha, Umualeghele, Ihie, Agburuke, Amaoji, Owerrinta, Uratta, Mgbedeala, and Ohambele.

Now how does the scheme work in an individual town or village? I give below a description of its operation at Ohanze-Isiahia given by a prominent member of the town whose name, for some reasons, I shall not mention. In other villages or towns there are variations in the details of the operation of the scheme, but the essence is the same. Says Mr. X of Ohanze:

"There are eight villages in our town, Ohanze-Isiahia, the elders of all of which decided to support St. Chrysostom's Anglican School, Ohanze, by the wealth of our palm trees.

"At the beginning of the scheme we gave each village one week during the palm season (March–May) to cut the palm-nuts from their grove. When the palm-produce was sold, the money from each village was put into the village box. After doing this two or three times the elders were able to determine the relative value of the palm wealth of each village and to establish a kind of proportion on the basis of which the villages are now assessed. Today we assess the villages twice a year at say £25, £20, £18, etc. according to the value of their palm grove. When this is done the villages go back and assess their young men at say 5s. or 10s. each and give them a day or two to cut palm nuts. A strong young man may be able to cut nuts worth about £2 on those days. He pays in his assessment to the village elders and pockets the balance. Because of this every young man is anxious to go out and cut palm nuts on the days declared open for him. On the night previous to the day when the villages are expected to pay in their assessment we beat our big drum called 'Ikoro' to warn the villages. When the day dawns we gather in the school premises and pay in the money which is kept in the village box. We have our Treasurer, Secretary, and Financial Secretary. The village box and its key are kept by village elders in rotation. If an elder from one village keeps the box, we give the key to an elder from another village. We use this money to pay the school fees of all our children, male and female, and to erect buildings. In cases of emergency, if there is no money in our box, we raise loans from eight young men from the eight villages and pay them back when we cut our palm nuts. If a father, for no just cause, refuses to send his son to school we sue him in the Native Court for breach of contract. If he withdraws the child after fees have been paid he must pay back the fees to us. If a father wishes his daughter at school to stop in order to marry, we may give him a loan of £25 in lieu of bride-price, so that the girl may finish her course. The amount is refundable when the girl has passed Standard 6. I cannot think of any child in our town now who does not go to school."

It should not be imagined, however, that the scheme runs smoothly in every village. There have been cases where the enthusiasm of villagers has been damped by the contractor bolting away with their money without finishing his contract. There have been cases where, owing to the weakness of elders or the

UNIVERSAL SCHOOLING IN NGWA CLAN OF ABA DIVISION

intrigue of young men who have an axe to grind, a rival school has been built belonging to another organisation and its sponsors claim support from the palm harvest, even though they were party to the original agreement to support one school, and even though it is quite certain that the town is not large enough to maintain two or more schools. This often leads to litigation and dissipation of energy and, in my opinion, this is where a strong neutral local education committee would be most useful. But these difficulties and others arising from administration can, in my opinion, be surmounted gradually in future and are at present more than compensated by the keen interest of the villagers in education, irrespective of age or creed, and by the deep feeling among them that the village school is theirs, not just something put there by the Government or Church.

The greatest problem of the general manager or supervisor in this area is to meet the demands of the various villages for certificated teachers. Villages are reluctant to allow their children to attend a school in another village, no matter how near. The reason for this is that the parents of the children will be asked to pay fees by that other village, whereas if the children remain in their own village the fees are paid communally. It is true that there are one or two villages who are generous enough to pay for every child, no matter where he comes from; but these are exceptional cases. Every village wants its school to develop into a full primary school as soon as possible. Since many of these villages are large enough to have a full primary school, the only obstacle in their way is a dearth of certificated teachers, and it is an obstacle that can only be removed as soon as training colleges turn out more and more trained teachers.

Printed by Jarrold & Sons, Ltd., Norwich

APPENDIX 3

"Short Memorandum on Future Political Arrangements for Nigeria" by R.I. Uzoma, OFR, OBE Undated

SHORT MEMORANDUM ON THE FUTURE
POLITICAL ARRANGEMENTS FOR NIGERIA

by Chief R. I. Uzoma, O.F.R.

Anybody who lived through the First Republic 1960-66 and also through the Second Republic 1976 - 79 could write a large volume on the weaknesses and deficiencies that led to the fall of these Republics. Because of the shortness of the time at my disposal and in order to reduce the volume of documents the Political Bureau will wade through I shall deal with a few aspects of the political arrangements, point out what I feel are the holes and defects that need to be plugged up; and what aspects need to be completely scrapped and changed.

1. FAILURE OF THE FIRST AND SECOND REPUBLICS:
   The main causes of the failure of the First Republic are:
   a) the centrifugal forces set in motion by our politics of ethnicity and by the geopolitics of regionalism which made the Regional Governments almost more powerful than the Federal Government.
   b) Corruption generated by the greed to grab everything for self and Region.

   With the creation of 19 States out of the 3 or 4 large Regions the centrifugal forces mentioned above became less violent and one can safely say that the Second Republic collapsed mainly because of grab, corruption and in fact, bare-faced looting of the Treasury.

2. SYSTEM OF GOVERNMENT - PRESIDENTIAL OR PARLIAMENTARY
   Many people have said that there is nothing wrong with the Presidential System or the Parliamentary System of Government. The fault is with the people who operate the system. This statement is true to the extent that human nature has not been taken into account. In our context here in Nigeria where an election candidate spends fortunes before he is elected, where it is alleged a youngman has to pay heavily to the Party

Appendix

-2-

leadership before he is nominated Commissioner and also pay a huge ransom to the Party members of the House before his nomination is approved, it will be a miracle if such a youngman, initiated into politics with corruption, fails to try to recoup himself when he is appointed Commissioner under the Presidential system and told that his decision in his Ministry is final in everything including finance - in short that he is Commissioner,

Chief Executive and the Chief Accounting Officer of his Ministry authorising and, at the same time, disbursing payment and not liable to answer an audit querry.

With the Parliamentary system there can be corruption but the door is restricted because of the in-built checks and balances. With the Presidential System the door for corruption is thrown wide - open. Corruption thrives unabated and there is nobody to expose it, because of an emasculated press, because of the fact that almost everybody is lobbying for contract award or Board appointment and because there is a conspiracy within the corrupt gang of rulers, a conspiracy on "quid pro quo" basis, and because there is an organised thuggery to silence opposition and/or exposure of evil, a conspiracy about which partisan police officers appear powerless.

Because of the above-mentioned weaknesses of the Presidential system in the Nigerian context I would prefer a return to the Parliamentary System in 1990.

3. Other features of the Presidential System

There are other featurws of the Presidential System which, though not bad in themselves, are in my opinion luxury to a country like Nigeria, which owing to economic recession is unable at present to provide universal free education even at the primary level (not to talk of the secondary and tertiary levels) at this time.

a) **Payment of allowance to legislators for staffing and furnishing the Constituency Offices.**

This innovation, which we copied from the American Presidential System, is an unnecessary item of expenditure which we cannot afford at this time. This novel allowance also appears to increase the temptation on the part of the legislator to be fraudulent. He declares one room in his house as his constituency office, and appropriates the rent for it. His wife or his sister is declared overnight to be his Secretary and his jobless brother or cousin, his messenger, and so all the vote from poor tax-payer's money, for the staffing, furnishing and rent of his constituency office, goes into his family kitty.

b) **Payment of huge sums of money to Political Parties as re-imbursement for election expenses.**

The idea of re-imbursing political parties all or part of their election expenses is not in itself bad. The main complaint now is that in most cases, the money gets into wrong hands. It goes to National leaders of the Party in Lagos who do whatever they like with it. It hardly reaches the States to help to relieve the financial burden of the struggling candidates. The ease with which that money is misappropriated on one pretext or the other e.g. rent payment, offers some people another wrong motivation for engaging in politics. Can we really afford this payment with our meagre resources at the present stage of our economic development especially as the knowledge that Government will re-imburse makes parties very extravagant?

c) **Tax dodgers and politics:** In the Presidential System ministers and Commissioners are appointed from outside the legislature. This in itself is not bad but it can

Appendix

be abused in our lust for power and money. It is possible (and it did happen during the last civilian regime) for a tax dodger who is disqualified by FEDECO from standing for an election because of non-payment of his tax, to be appointed a minister or Commissioner simply because he has wormed his way into the mind of the Governor or the party hierarchy through a handsome donation. This situation is, in my opinion, morally indefensible and makes for irresponsible citizenship as well as for corruption.

d) Impeachment: The Presidential System phenomenon called <u>impeachment</u>, which we understand has been effectively used in U.S.A., has as usual been abused here in Nigeria and used not only as an instrument of distablising and wrecking a government but also as a "sword of Damocles" over the heads of Governors with which money can be shamelessly and corruptly extorted from him from the Security Vote. With this sort of thing happening openly before young school leavers, are we surprised at the wave of armed robbery in the country?

e) <u>Corruption and embezzlement of Public Funds</u>
These are much easier in the Presidential system since the Chief Executive controls money any way he likes and a Minister or Commissioner appears not to be bound to accept the advice of his permanent secretary. He is Commissioner, Accounting Officer and everything is done in his name and under his seal – NO checks and balances.

<u>The Westminster type of Parliamentary Government</u>
I have earlier advocated a return to the parliamentary government of the Westminster type in 1990 with two or three national parties. What we need is an extensive <u>political education or our people to look upon opposition as inevitable</u>

in life and regard politics as a game. After all our lawyers mix up freely, eat and dine together after opposing themselves in the courtroom. Why does opposition in politics lead to fighting and the breaking of one another's head? The answer is mainly

i) lust for power and all that goes with it, and
ii) lust for ill-gotten wealth.

Recommendations:

i) I recommend therefore that the remuneration of the members of the State and National legislatures be NOT made very attractive. It is by so doing that we shall get in the legislatures people motivated by the desire to serve and not by the lust for wealth; men who are satisfied with what they already have and wish to serve their people, and not hungry or insatiable people itching for looting and people unwilling to quit even when they know they are voted out.

ii) The general assessment of the performance of the last State legislatures was that they had not enough work to do to justify payment for full-time job. Very often one found that they were either discussing administrative matters within the competence of the various Government Ministers, statutory bodies or Commissions; for example, debating the termination or dismissal of a civil servant or teacher or, if they were not doing this, they would be debating the damage to a school roof by tornado in a remote corner of the State, a matter that the headmaster and the local committee can take up with the appropriate State authorities or parastatal. In view of what has been said above I recommend that the State legislators be placed on a "per diem" allowance and paid only for the days they sit, and not on a full annual salary.

Appendix

I understand this is done in some American States and a lot of Savings are affected.

iii) Legislators' Overseas tour should be cut down to a minimum. The present system whereby legislators and their wives go on a "jamboree" overseas should be stopped. It is during these disgraceful tours that they perfect the technique for siphoning money out of the country to overseas banks and commit other acts that tend to wreck our economy.

iv) One important aspect of the Parliamentary System is that the permanent secretary of a ministry is the Accounting Officer. He curbs the financial excesses of Commissioner and vice versa, and on the national level the presence of a President (even though he be merely ceremonial) acts as a check on the Prime Minister. In addition although a Minister or Commissioner can be removed from his post by the Prime Minister or Premier, he cannot be removed from the legislature by the latter and he can expose irregularities on the floor of the House, if he resigns his ministerial appointment.

v) Audit: The Federal and State Audit Departments should be so enlarged and strengthened that all accounts are audited the same year the income come in and expenses made and not after the "dramatis personae" has left. The law should be amended to make an audit query have the force of a court fiat or order so that it is not flouted.

Election Campaigns: I feel like many others, that the period for election campaigns should be shortened. The longer the campaign period the more the various methods of rigging and the incidence of thuggery. These evils of our political system are planned and perfected during election periods.

Polling:

There were wide-spread rumours and allegations of party polling agents in some booths colluding among themselves to close their eyes to various acts of rigging provided the top

-7-

brass of the various political parties grease their palms. The takings for the day are said to be shared by the party agents among themselves irrespective of party affiliation. If these allegations are true, as many believe they are, it seems the only solution is to make sure that FEDECO appoints honest responsible polling officers capable of checking these party agents in each booth. FEDECO Polling Officers should be deployed in L.G.A.s other than their own to ensure strict supervision of party agents. It is alleged that party agents regard election time as their opportunity to collect their "ten percent."

APPENDIX 4

"A Second Memorandum to the Political Bureau" by Chief R.I. Uzoma, OFR, 21/6/86

A SECOND MEMORANDUM TO THE POLITICAL
BUREAU BY CHIEF R.I. UZOMA, O.F.R.

1. THE UNITY OF THE COUNTRY

The Constitution of the Federal Republic of Nigeria States categorically in Section 15 (1) that "the motto of the Federal Republic of Nigeria shall be Unity and Faith, Peace and Progress" and every effort was made to incorporate in the said Constitution everything to ensure the existence of that "Unity and Faith, Peace and Progress", which is our motto. For example, we have such pious and moving provisions as:

(i) "Every citizen shall have equality of rights, obligations, and opportunities before the law. "Section 17 (2a).

(ii) "A citizen of Nigeria of a particular community, ethnic group, place of origin, Sex, religion or political opinion shall not, by reason only that he is such a person, be subjected either expressly, or in the practical application of any law or any executive or administrative action of the government, to disabilities or restrictions to which citizens of Nigeria of other communities, ethnic groups, places of origin, sex, religions or political opinions are not made subject" Section 39 (1 (a)).

The spirit and letter of these two and other provisions of the Constitutions have often been violated to the extent that at times doubt has been raised in people's minds as to the realisation of our goal of Unity.

2. " STATISM "

Some of those at the helm of our affairs at different times are victims of the myopia which makes them see their state as being larger or more important to them than the Federal Republic of Nigeria. Some politicians have termed this myopia "Statism".

There are several ways in which "States has manifested itself in the affairs of the various states. These include

(a) Differential scales of fees for "indigenes" and "non-indigenes"all of whom are citizens of the Federal Republic of Nigeria which professes, "One country, One destiny".

../2

- 2 -

(b) Offering <u>contract</u> appointment to "non-indigenes" of the state and permanent appointment to "indigenes".

(c) In some cases, employing "non-indigenes" when "indigenes" are not available and laying them off as soon as "indignes" are available.

(d) Refusal of scholarships to "non-indigenes" who are pupils in their States even where the parents of the pupil reside and pay their tax in the particular state, and the pupil is selected to represent the state in inter-state sports competition and wins a medal or trophy, the glory and credit for which the state accepts.

(e) Refusal to allocate plots of land to "non-indigenes" even though restrictive conditions are not stated in the advertisment for the plots.

(f) Sections 23 to 29 of the Constitution define Nigerian Citizenship. It is quite clear that a citizen of the Federal Republic of Nigeria by the Constitution automatically becomes a citizen of all the states of the Federation. Is this true infact? Some of our governors appear to be re-writing the Constitution to create "state citizenship" as distinct from the citizenship of the Federal Republic of Nigeria.

3. FEDERAL ACTIONS WHICH TEND TO SUPPORT "STATISM" AND MILITATE AGAINST UNITY

The Federal Government itself tends to lend support to "Statism" through some of its administrative directives - Viz

(a) Differential cut-off points in examinations for Federal institutions and J.A.M.B. This single act alone tends to place a premium on mediocrity and discourage hard-work.

(b) Reserving the Junior posts in Federal industries and institutions to applicants from the State where the institution or industry is situated. The Federal Government knows that Federal industries and parastatals are <u>not evenly spread out</u>. In fact some <u>States have not a single Federal industry</u>. The Federal Government also knows that only four states of the Federation have any office or branch of the Nigerian Ports' Authority as a parastal.

../3

Appendix

- 3 -

(c) <u>The Quota System</u> - of the Federal Government for admission into the Federal Educational institutions, the Armed Forces and the Police in my opinion will not be faulted if only

   (i) There is one reasonable <u>cut-off point</u> for everybody which will be set bearing in mind the need to maintain high standards.

   (ii) The quota for each state is in proportion to the population of the state. Large States like Kano, Oyo, Imo and Anambra should not be allotted the same number of intake as the smaller states.

(d) ABANDONED PROPERTY: The earlier the abandoned property issue is settled the better for the peace and unity of this country. It is sad that a citizen of the Federal Republic of Nigeria has had his property seized for years <u>without rent or compensation</u> when he is anxious to take back possesion of the property. To such a citizen all talk of Unity is a hoax.

4. EDUCATION:

The classification of the states of the Federation into "educationally advantaged" and "educationally disadvantaged" cannot be explained on the grounds of history or on that of logic. Some of the states classified as "educationally disadvantaged" are the very states whose sons and daughters brought the light of education to the hinterland states like Imo and Anambra. <u>One would like to see the epithets</u> scrapped as misnomer. The states that appear "disadvantaged" can be grouped into two:

(i) Those, like the Rivers State, whose people know, as well as anybody else, the value of Western Education but who are placed at a disadvantage because of the geography of their land space. Such <u>"geographically disadvantaged"</u> states need no incentive or coercion to send their children to school, <u>but they need extra financial aid to help in</u> solving their more difficult <u>logistic</u> problems, for it is much more difficult to administer schools in the area of the Niger Delta than in the hinterland states.

(ii) Those states, mostly in the Northern part of the country, where in <u>some Local Government Areas</u> (not all)

../4

there is apathy towards Western education. In these
areas, the measures being adopted now by the military
governors, of incentives, persuasion and gentle
coercion on parents coupled with incorporation of
Islamic teaching in the school curriculum will, we
hope, yield some fruit. These States need <u>specially
trained</u> teachers who will be able to win the confidence
of parents and attract the children to schools. In
my opinion, they also need extra financial aid for
this, especially as some of the states are also
"geographically disadvantaged" owing to drought, long
distances between settlements, and in the more remote
northern areas, the nomadic nature and inaccessibility
of the inhabitants. In all these cases it is not in
my opinion psychologically advisable to use the phrase
"disadvantaged States" as this phrase gives the impression
of discrimination to some poeple and to the "disadvantaged
States" themselves the feeling of complacence and resignation to fate, which militates against hard-work and
determination to ameliorate the harshness of physical
and climatic environment.

5. SUMMARY:

For the sustained unity of the country the Governments
of the Federation should in addition to other efforts
being made, for example the NYSC scheme and Unity Schools:

(a) Endeavour to keep both the letter and the spirit of
the Constitution.

(b) Think more of the Federal Republic of Nigeria and
less of their individual states.

(c) Abolish differential scale of school fees for
"indigenes" and "non-indigenes" in a state.

(d) Stop offering contract appointmet to any Nigerian
below the age of 45.

(e) Offer scholarships to deserving pupils in their
areas, irrespective of "State origin".

(f) Allocate plots of land to qualified applicants
irrespective of "state of origin".

(g) Accept that the citizenship of the Federal Republic
of Nigeria makes every Nigerian the citizen of every
State in Nigeria.

../5

Appendix

h) Abolish the policy of reserving Junior posts in Federal industries and parastatals exclusively for "indigenes" of the state where the industry or parastatal is sited.

(i) Review the quota system so that the quota for a state is proportional to the population of the state.

(j) Abolish the system of differential cut-off point for different groups of states both for entrance examinations into Universities and Federal colleges and for entry into the Armed Forces and the Police Force.

(k) Endeavour to complete solving expeditiously the problem of "Abandoned Property" and bury it so that it may not rise again in the history of the nation.

(l) Continue to give special assistance to solve the problems of education in geographically and sociologically difficult areas without necessarily dividing the states into "educational - advantaged" and "educationally disadvantaged".

(m) Taboo the words "indigene" and "non-indigene" and remove "state of origin" from all application forms etc.

By so doing we shall have laid to rest the ghost of mini-apartheid existing in our beloved country.

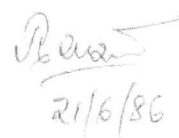
21/6/86

APPENDIX 5

"The Church Missionary Society in Eastern Nigeria" by Chief R.I. Uzoma, OFR, OBE, LL.D (Hons), dated 14/9/91

"THE CHURCH MISSIONARY SOCIETY IN EASTERN NIGERIA"
BY CHIEF R.I. UZOMA, O.F.R., O.B.E., LL.D (HOn).

1. INTRODUCTION:

The word "mission" is derived from a Latin word meaning "to send". The word is used to include not only a body of persons sent to a foreign country to conduct negotiations or to convert the heathen, but also the field of activity of those sent, and the objective for which they are sent.

The Church Missionary Society is a virile body of dedicated Christians of the Anglican Church whose main aim is to raise funds to sponsor missionary work of the Anglican Church outside Great Britain. Most, if not all, of our bishops and a few of us laymen in Nigeria, are "honorary" members of the Society. It was this society that sponsored the mission led by the Rev. Adjai Crowther in 1857 which founded what we call the "C.M.S. Niger Mission", with headquarters at Onitsha. From there the "good news" of the Mission spread to the hinterland. Previous missions led by Europeans had failed because of the havoc of malaria in West Africa.

In 1864 the Rev. Adjai Crowther was consecrated Bishop and missionary work began in Bonny in 1865 even before it was possible for the early pioneers to penetrate through thick forests and hostile villagers to Owerri area. Bishop Crowther and his team travelled to Bonny by launch through rivers and creeks. It was this "mustard seed" of the Gospel sown in 1857 and 1865 that has grown to become the present giant "tree" of eleven dioceses (if you include Asaba and Warri Dioceses and the two new "missionary" dioceses of Calabar and Uyo). As important as the growth in numbers is the fact that with the inauguration of the Province of West Africa in 1951 and of the Province of Nigeria in 1979, the Church in Nigeria became autonomous without being separatist. The filial link of love and gratitude to the Mother Church of England and her Missionary Society shall not be severed; one of the important links binding all Provinces of the Church together being the Lambeth Conference. The significance of the autonomy of the Church in Nigeria is that our bishops are now elected and approved in Nigeria and consecrated in Nigeria by our own Archbishop. The Archbishop of Canterbury in relation to the other bishops of the Anglican Communion, serves only as "primus inter pares" - first among equals.

The Rt. Rev. E.T. Dimieari enthroned Diocesan Bishop of the newly created Niger Delta Diocese in 1952, was the first Nigerian Diocesan Bishop on this side of the Niger after Crowther just as the Rt. Rev. S. Odutole, enthroned Diocesan Bishop of Ondo-Benin 1951 in the area West of the Niger, was the first Nigerian Diocesan Bishop after Crowther.

A faithful and dedicated missionary, past and present, is not just a mere adventurer looking for members of other religions to capture. In their job of preaching, the Gospel, missionaries come up against the stark reality of poverty, disease, ignorance malnutrition etc and they are compelled by their conscience to do some thing about these. Says David Livingstone in his "Missionary Travels and Researches in South Africa" and I quote: "In the glow of love which Christianity inspires, I resolved to devote my life to the alleviation of human suffering". The early missionary found himself as preacher, teacher, doctor, agriculturist rolled up in one individual, if he was to make any impact at all, as it is only a healthy, well-fed

../2.

Appendix

individual who will listen attentively to a sermon. Let us point out that the dichotomy in the level of education between the Southern States of Nigeria and some of the Northern States is traceable to the banning of early missionary activity from the Northern Emirates by the Lugard Regime. The missionary should not be suspected of proselytization.

2. SOME ACHIEVEMENTS OF THE C.M.S. IN EASTERN NIGERIA

(a) FORMAL AND INFORMAL EDUCATION:

The Church Missionary Society started its educational activity with the establishment of primary schools, in most cases with the support of the various Church Communities. Awka College, established about the first decade of this century, the D.M.G.S. Onitsha, St. Monica's girls school Ogbunike, Elelenwa girls' secondary school are all, so to speak, "gifts" to us from the Missionary Society. Church - inspired community effort in the building of secondary schools started with Okrika Grammar School 1940. St. Augustine's Nkwerre 1948, St. Catherine's Nkwerre 1955, and Ogidi girls secondary school, before the flood gate was swung open from the fifties of this century.

Awka College established for the training of school - masters, catechists and Divinity students was, up to the Government take-over of educational institutions in 1970, regarded as the "power-house" of the Niger group of Dioceses because of its impact on the educational, spiritual, moral and evangelistic life of the Church. As recently as the thirties of this century, boarding and tuition at Awka were free. In addition, all categories of students received a small monthly allowance, and two sets of round-neck jumpers called "Otogbo" in Igbo (blue for ordinary days and white for sunday). In the days when there was stark poverty - no oil boom, these things were real bonanza showered on us by "Father Christmas" called the C.M.S.

When we talk glibly about technical and practical education, we should remember that the C.M.S. Niger Mission was the first to introduce and emphasise the technical aspect of education through the establishment of the "Onitsha Industrial Mission" where our first set of carpenters, masons etc were trained in the early decades of this century. A similar practical course was established in Hope Waddell, Calabar, about the same time famous for printing and other trades. It was run by the Church of Scotland Mission. Perhaps many of us do not know that it was a C.M.S. missionary (from Canada) the Rev. Kenneth Prior, based at Awka College, who went round in the forties preaching the gospel of "Grass all Church and School Compounds", "Don't leave any part of your compound bare" "Make contour ridges on your farms, not mounds", "Prepare your compost now for the next planting season". Before the arrival of the Rev. K. Prior all Church and school compounds used to be scraped and swept bare every saturday. He was the most vocal of the campaigners against erosion. He and his Government counterparts brought about the awareness of the importance of Rural Science in the curriculum of our schools and made it possible for Rural Science /Agric. Science to be introduced into our school time-table.

(b) TRAINING HOMES FOR MOTHER CRAFT ETC.:

The C.M.S. Niger Churches established marriage training homes where women engaged to be married to Christians in the Church were compulsorily sent to learn to read and write in Igbo and also to learn Home Management, Personal Hygiene, Sewing, Cookery, Baby-care etc. There is no doubt today, looking back on this regulation, which to us appears strange today, that it was necessary in the circumstances of the early decades of this century when most people were stark illiterate. Women trained in these homes returned to their villages and the running of their homes became an example for the illiterate neighbours to copy. Thus the general standard of living continually improved.

(c) **EFFECTIVE DISTRIBUTION OF CHURCH AND SCHOOL BOOKS:**
The C.M.S. Niger Mission, Eastern Nigeria, was to my knowledge, the first organisation to run an effective chain of bookshops with its counterpart the C.M.S. Yoruba Mission. The C.M.S. Bookshops (now renamed C.S.S. Bookshops, meaning Church and Schools Supplies Ltd) was a pace-setter in the printing and distribution of religious and educational books in Nigeria - the first of its kind. It had branches in Portharcourt, Aba, Owerri, Nkwerre, Onitsha, Awka and Enugu. It has also a printing press in Portharcourt, and has similar net-work in other parts of Nigeria. Through the C.S.S bookshops books of all types have for years, been made available to people. The first missionary to over here to engage in the distribution of the Bible was Mr. F.E. Welcock who was later ordained and rose to be the Archdeacon and Diocesan Secretary at Onitsha. He was succeeded by Mr. A.T.F. Roberts.

(d) **TRANSFER OF EXPERTISE TO COUNCILS:**
The Church in Eastern Nigeria led the way in transferring expertise in the management of secondary educational institutions to county councils without any ulterior motive of taking over the proprietorship of the institutions from them. The job was regarded as part of the legitimate educational "mission" of the Church. The following institutions were built by various County Councils under the supervision of the Church and were managed by the Niger Delta Diocese, the Diocese appointing the staff and Manager of the Institutions and the Councils appointing about three-quarters of the members of the Board of Governors who were educated on the functions of the Board of Governors and those of the Principal and Staff:

i. Ngwa High School, Aba - for Aba Ngwa County Council.

ii. W. Ahoada County Grammar School - for W. Ahoada County Council.

iii. Ikwerre-Etche Gram School, Igrita - for Ikwerre - Etche County Council.

iv. Birabi Memorial Gram. School Bori - for Khana (Ogoni) County Council.

✱ v. Nsulu Teachers' Training College Nbawsi - for Northern Ngwa County Council.

✱ This college was after the civil war converted to "Nsulu Games village" by the Imo Government.)

(e) **EFFECTIVE TACKLING OF THE PROBLEMS OF THE RIVERINE AREAS:**
The physical nature of the area covered by the delta of the Niger river has always posed a serious problem. Churches have been established as far back as the days of Bishop Crowther and also primary schools; but it was only in the last forty years that the problem of secondary education was addressed especially in the Southern part bordering the Atlantic ocean. A secondary school was established in Yenagoa in 1956 after a survey by Bishop Dimieari and the writer in July 1955. Other secondary schools in Abonnema and Bonny followed and Teacher training institutions were established in Oporoma and Okordia - Zarama in the fifties too to solve the problem of staff from the mainland refusing

to go deep down into the creeks.

(f) TRANSLATION OF THE BIBLE INTO IGBO LANGUAGE:
The fashioning out of Igbo orthography and translation of the Bible into Union Igbo by a team drawn from various dialect areas of Iboland under the leadership of Archdeacon Dennis and the Rev. (later Bishop) A.C. Onyeabo is one of the most important contributions of the C.M.S. Niger Mission to the development of the Country. It has great political, religious, economic and educational significance uniting the Ibos together, facilitating communication, and education in the mother tongue. The fashioning out of a union dialect acceptable to all and sundry "was the Lord's doing and it is marvellous in our eyes".

Efforts have also been made and continue to be made by prominent members of the Church in the Delta area like Mr. Peters of Okrika, to translate the bible and hymns into various dialects of Ijaw language, all to the credit of the Church East of the Niger. With the translation of the Bible and hymns into the various Nigerian languages and the age-long insistence of the Church that young converts must learn to read (and write) the holy scriptures before baptism, we can safely tell the Minister of Education that the Church has now achieved almost 100% literacy in the vernacular among her membership.

(g) HEALTH CARE DELIVERY:
Some years after the establishment of the "Niger Mission" in Onitsha the Iyienu hospital was established by the C.M.S. to cater for the health of the masses all over the huge area. Iyi-enu became a house-hold word not only because of the medical treatment given at the hospital but also because of the net-work of supervised maternity homes and clinics established all over the then Mission area. In the thirties and forties teachers and Catechists trained at Awka, were made to spend one month at Iyi-enu learning first-aid to help them to cope with emergency cases in the remote schools and villages where they would work.

The Oji River Settlement, also founded by the C.M.S., was second only in age to the Uzuakoli Methodist Centre in fighting the scourge of leprosy rampant in our society then. Leprosy camps were also built all over the area for the treatment of less serious cases by itinerant doctors from Oji/Uzuakoli. The Church was the first to tackle the problem of leprosy.

(h) NIGERIANISATION AND HIGHER EDUCATION:
A proper appraisal of history will credit the C.M.S. with setting the pace in Nigerianisation starting with the sending out of the Rev. Adjai Crowther to head the Mission that founded the C.M.S. Niger Mission 1857 and consecrating Crowther the first Diocesan Bishop 1864. I have earlier mentioned the enthronement of the Rt. Rev. S Odutola as the Diocesan Bishop of Ondo – Benin 1951, the Rt. Rev. E.T. Dimieari, the Diocesan Bishop of Niger Delta 1952 and the Rt. Rev. A.B. Akinyele the Diocesan Bishop of Ibadan both in 1952, eight years before Nigeria became Independent.

By 1932 there was only one Nigerian University graduate on the entire staff of the Niger Mission. He was the late Rev. A.W. Howells (jnr) (later Bishop). The late Dr. A Ikoku had just left the staff of Awka College to found his own Secondary School. The late Dr. Oli, then senior tutor at D.M.G.S. Onitsha who obtained his degree in 1935 was senior tutor at D.M.G.S.

The architect of the Higher Education Scheme of the then Niger Diocese was, in my opinion, the then Principal of Awka College, the late Rev. A.M. Gelsthorpe (later Diocesan Bishop of Sudan.) At a time when the D.M.G.S. had not grown up to the school Certificate class, the Rev. A.M. Gelsthorpe in 1931 arranged for some of the students (all standard six holders) at Awka to be prepared and entered for the Junior Cambridge Certificate examination. He also arranged for a selected few of us to be coached privately in Latin and Mathematics. Not satisfied with this, on his way back to Nigeria from leave he called at Achimota College, Gold Coast (now Ghana) and arranged with the Principal to offer the Niger Diocese one or two places a year in his College for a serving teacher to come and do the School Certificate and London Intermediate degree exam in 2½ years - a period the Gold Coast school certificate holder spent on Intermediate degree course alone. The first Niger Diocesan scholar was sent in 1935 and others followed in the succeeding years.

The committee to select these scholars was the foundation of our Higher Education committee which later, after 1954 when the Delta Diocese was created, became the Joint Higher Education Committee whose business was to select serving workers for higher education. The Clergy of the Diocese also instituted a fund for training a young Clergyman with the necessary qualification to obtain a University degree.

With the creation of Owerri Diocese the Joint Higher Education Committee faded out and Diocesan Higher Education Committees took its place. It is gratifying to note that some of our Church leaders today, some university dons and vice-chancellors, some retired and serving civil servants are products of the generous scholarship scheme of the Niger group of dioceses. It is also worthy of note that when the crisis of 1967 - 70 led to the exodus of expatriate missionaries, we were able to staff our secondary institutions properly till they were taken over by Government. In fact the women trained under our scholarship scheme sustain secondary education even up till today and are among the women leaders in this part of the country.

Our own late Dr. E. Oli was the second Nigerian to be Principal of an approved, grant-aided secondary school in the Eastern part of Nigeria (1940) the first being the late Dr. Alvan Ikoku who was proprietor and Principal of Aggrey Memorial Secondary School, Arochuku - a private institution, and a former senior tutor at Awka College.

The first Chief Executive of the Education services of a Diocese is Dr. R.I. Uzoma who is also the first Nigerian to represent the Christian Council group of Churches at the Board of Education.

The record of the Niger group of dioceses has been that of upholding and pushing forward the faith, trying to show immense gratitude to our benefactors while at the same time trying to improve on the solid foundations they have laid.

> "Teach us, Good Lord, to serve Thee as Thou deservest,
> To give and not count the cost,
> To fight and not heed the wounds,
> To toil and not seek for rest,
> To labour and not ask for any reward,
> Save that of knowing that we do Thy will".

Ignatius Loyola.

APPENDIX 6

Sermon Preached at the 1989 Annual Thanksgiving and Dedication Service of DMGS Old Boys Association, at St. Micheal's Cathedral, Aba, on Sunday April 30th 1989, by Chief R.I. Uzoma, OFR, OBE

SERMON PREACHED AT THE 1989 ANNUAL THANKSGIVING AND DEDICATION SERVICE OF THE D.M.G.S. OLD BOYS ASSOCIATION AT ST. MICHAERL'S CATHEDRAL, ABA ON SUNDAY 30TH APRIL, 1989.

BY CHIEF R.I. UZOMA, O.F.R: O.B.E

INTRODUCTION:

I am grateful to the President, Officers and all members of the D.M.G.S. Old Boys' Association for inviting me to share in the fellowship of your thanksgiving and dedication service, for this year, and particularly for asking me to preach on this occasion, in spite of my inadequacies and inspite of the fact that my connection with D.M.G.S. was for only one year 1936. *1936 an epoch-making year [1st Set of School Cert boys]*

This is a thanksgiving service and naturally *[1st Year of introduction of Sema]* my first reaction is to thank God for the services of the early *Sema the fact* missionaries and our benefactors, those who contributed towards creating the famous image and tone of the school. We think of the late Rt. Rev. B. Lasbrey, the first Bishop on the Niger, who was *enthroned* in 1922 and who, through his efforts, got the C.M.S. to start the school in 1925. We think of the famous linguist and translator, the Ven Archdeacon Dennis after whom the school was named. He was drowned during the first World War while going home on leave. It was he, Dennis, the late Rev. A.C. Onyeabo (Later Bishop) our father-in-God, who with a few other people translated the Bible into Union Igbo for us - a translation which has not only made the word of God available to the common man but has also helped to unify all the Igbo - speaking people of Nigeria. We think of the first principal, the late Rev. Taylor, and others who followed him, the late Rev. Charles Fowler, *Later Abp of W Africa* the Rev. Cecil Patterson, the Rev. Eric Clark - the longest *RevpJBoss* serving principal, Mr S. J. Cookey, the first Nigerian Principal, Mr. S. Ogoazi, the first old student to head the school. We thank God particularly for the inspiration of the life and services of the late Dr. E.I. Oli to whom goes the pride of place as our mentor and inspirer. We salute the pioneer Nigerian teachers who, so to speak, made bricks without straw. The late Dr. E.I. Oli, it is said, was D.M.G.S. and D.M.G.S. was Dr. Oli. He was the longest serving member of staff, and was Vice - Principal for most of the time ensuring that even though Principals might change, the tone, discipline, moral and academic standards did not drop. The late Dr. Oli and the late Dr. Alvan Ikoku were the first gentlemen from this part of the country to obtain a London University external degree without going into any tertiary institution.

TEXTS:

Having made these introductory remarks, I would like you to look at the following passages in the Bible for my message: 1st Peter 2: 9 "But ye are <u>a chosen generation, a royal priesthood, an holy nation, a peculiar people</u> that ye should show forth the praises of Him,, who hath called you out of darkness into His marvellous light".

AT YOUR BAPTISM: The Priest said "We receive this child (or this man or woman) into the congregation of Christ's flock, and do sign him with the sign of the cross, in token that hereafter, <u>he shall not be ashamed to confess the faith of Christ crucified, and manfully to fight under His banner against Sin, the world and the devil and to continue Christ's faithful soldier and servant unto his life's end"!</u>

MOTIVATION:

As I was, some time ago, trying to find out the motivating force that drove the early missionaries from their comparatively comfortable homes in Europe to the relatively

../3

Appendix

undeveloped continent of Africa, I stumbled upon this very striking sentence from Dr. David Livingtone's book. In the country "Missionary Travels and Researches in South Africa". Quote "In the glow of love which Christianity inspires, I resolved to devote my life to the alleviation of human suffering." Unquote. That motivating force it was, which led to the establishment in this part of our country of not only Churches, Dioceses, and districts, but also to the founding of Iyi-Enu Hospital, Awka College and D. M.G.S. in the late 19th Century and early part of this century. Elelenwa, Okirika and St. Augustine's came some decades later. The motivating force generated a momentum resulting in the development of local manpower, mainly priests and teachers, who were recruited into the task of the development and growth of indigenous dioceses of the Anglican Communion replacing the former Missionary Dioceses. You and I are the products of that growth. We are the products of the momentum, and it is our duty to see that that mocmentum continues and that our Church in Nigeria grows from strength to strength.

There is a famous saying by an English writer, Coleridge, which goes thus: "The dwarf sees farther than the giant when he has the giant's shoulder to mount on". We dwarfs of today, so to speak, if we see farther than men like Anyaegbunam Onyeabo, Dimieari, Spiff, Ibeneme, Oli and other pioneer, priests and teachers, it is because we are standing on the shoulders of these giants.

We are a chosen generation, a lucky generation, a royal priesthood, a holy nation, a peculiar people, and so we should show forth the praises of Him who has called us out of the darkness into His marvellous light. I know the deprivation

../4

that some of these early pioneers suffered. Several, for lack of medical facilities and drugs died of simple complaints like malaria, Pneumonia or Pleurisy, which today we get rid of with one or two tablets or injections.

THE PRIESTHOOD OF ALL BELIEVERS:

We are indeed a chosen, lucky generation and being that we are a chosen generation, a royal lucky what do we do? How do we show priesthood? In several places in the Bible the baptised, dedicated christian is referred to as a "Priest". The teaching of our church on "The priesthood of all believers" should attract your attention. It implies that since the harvest is plentiful and the labourers are few, since the work of evangelisation is so extensive and enormous we, lay christians, should not abandon it to the ordained Clergy and Bishops of our church. All hands must be on deck. If you are a lawyer or a doctor, an architect or an engineer, a teacher or a quantity Surveyor, a Contractor or a businessman, you have to try and give part of your time to the service of the church wherever you may find yourself, and of course you won't forget your home church. The church needs the advice, services and help of experts in various fields of learning and various fields of human endeavour. You will even derive joy and satisfaction by serving God in a field in which you are no specialist.

Secondly, and this is very important, wherever you may be, in the office, or in your home, in your place of work or in the Club or recreation hall, remember to show by your action, by your words and general behaviour that you are a witness for Christ - not just witness on sundays and witness for some other master on other days. You should be Christ's own witness every hour of the day.

../5

Appendix

- 5 -

CHRISTIAN COUNCIL PROJECT IN PORTHARCOURT:

It is this idea of projecting Christ not only in our homes and neighbourhood but also in our place of work that prompted the Christian Council of Nigeria, Eastern Wing, to set up the Christian Council Project in the Industrial town of Portharcourt - the aim being to teach practising christians to project Christ in their place of work and to exhibit good, and acceptable christian personal relationship with fellow workers, and good work ethics avoiding malingering, dishonesty, partisanship, jealousy, greed etc, etc.

KNIGHTS OF ST. CHRISTOPHER:

Some of us have recently been conferred with the knighthood of St. Christopher by our Diocesan Bishops. We congratulate those so honoured and thank our Bishops for their action. May I remind those so honoured that the religious investiture ceremony is, in our opinion, aimed at emphasising, recapitulating and confirming to you, as an adult christian, the serious injunction and charge given to you as an infant when you were baptised - that you shall not be ashamed to confess the faith of Christ crucified, and manfully to fight under His banner against sin, the world and the devil, and to continue Christ's faithful soldier and servant unto your life's end!

It is pertinent, therefore, for me to add that whether you are formally admitted into the church's knighthood or not, once you are baptised you are a knight in spirit, a member of the "chosen generation," of "the royal priesthood" who should show forth the praises of Him who hath called us out of darkness into His marvellous light. In the Middle Ages a title was chosen by a Pope for himself and that title has stuck - "Servus Servorum Dei" literally the "servant of the servants of God" - "Servus" literally means "slave". A knight should be the servant of the church congregation, by virtue of his position. /6

- 6 -

not their master expecting special recognition and seat on
special occasions. I know of some of our bishops and church
leaders who after church meetings do not sit down for
refreshment till everybody else has been seated. *The code of conduct of a knight involves thinking of others (called chivalry) first, the French "Apres vous", defending the weaker party – all christian teaching*

LIFTING OF THE BANN ON POLITICS: *Talking of fighting under its banner against sin, the world and the devil and the battle front will be active against sin, the world and the devil*
In a few months from now the ban on partisan politics
will be lifted and we, christians, should not shy away from
it simply because politics in this country has acquired
some measure of notoriety on account of the corruption and
violence very often involved. Unless God-fearing men and
women, like you, go into politics, always bearing in mind that
you are Christ's "faithful soldier and servant" it will
continue to be a rotten exercise. We urge you to go in *to clean the Augean stable* staff
untainted and aim at coming out untainted. When *nocturnal*
meetings are being held to arrange some compromise with evil,
when contract papers are being overloaded with a view to
extracting ten percent, when money is being dangled before you
with a view to buying your conscience, *remember*, remember that
you are there as an ambassador of Christ through His Church.
Remember you are there as the product of a famous school
whose motto is "Lux Fiat" - "Let there be light". Imagine
Jesus standing in front of you asking you the same question
He asked of Peter: "Simon, Son of Jonas, lovest thou me more
than these?" "Okeke son of Eze, of X Constituency, lovest
thou me more than the huge sum dangled before you?". Your
answer, as the servant and soldier of Christ, should be "Yes,
Lord, Thou knowest that I love Thee more than filthy lucre'
The Church is repeating to you the words of St. Paul to the
Corinthians, words *perhaps* drummed into your ears during your commissioning service when you left school some years ago: "Ye are
our epistle written in our own hearts, known and read of all
men" "Let there be light" "Lux Fiat".

29/4/89

APPENDIX 7

"Education in Nkwerre Town" Undated handwritten address by R.I. Uzoma

Education in Nkwerre Town

History: The Anglican Church was established in Nkwerre in 1918 with the arrival of Mr Moses Ibelu of Nenu as the evangelist sent by the Rev J. Ibeneme to establish the Church in the town. Education was then a very strong instrument of evangelisation and the village school was regarded as the hand-maid of the village church. It was, therefore, Mr Moses Ibelu who started the first vernacular school where boys and girls were taught to read and write in 1960.

The Rev J Ibeneme, the priest who brought the light of the gospel to Nkwerre moved from Ndizuogu to Nkwerre in 1921 and with his coming a formal primary school was established in 1922 with the appointment of the late Mr Andrew Onubogu (later the Rev) as the headmaster of Nkwerre Central School. Mr Onubogu was a trained certificated schoolmaster. The Central School Nkwerre situated at the site of the present Church hall in the present St Pauls' Pro-Cathedral compound, was moved to the present site of Nkwerre Central School in Obinocha Umuduruagu in 1926/27 and was the first and only standard six school in the whole of the then Okigwe D...

which embraced the present Okigwe and Orlu zones. The result was that there were boys from places like Ezeoke, Anara, Uli, Ubulu, Ndimoga residing at Nkwerre. They attended school from Monday to Friday and usually trekked home after school on Friday to bring raw food for the following week. It would have been impossible for small boys like me to be attending school in those days if the school had been far from my home and I had had to do the long trekking to and fro.

The first set boys to pass the Govt standard six examination from the school did so in 1927 and the Nkwerre boys among them were Nze Daniel Nwosu Onuoha (middle of 1927) and Chief Reuben Uzoma December 1927.

While the primary school at Nkwerre was being nursed in the early twenties, there were some notable Nkwerre gentry who had heard of Hope Waddell Training Institute, Calabar, Methodist Uzuakoli Govt school and had sent their sons to these schools. Later others sent their sons to Government schools in Aba or Azumini. Thus even before Nze Daniel Nwosu Onuoha and Chief Reuben Uzoma passed standard six at the Nkwerre Central School men like the present Nze Ezekiel Asugha, late Thompson Chagwa, Nze Silas Nwekwe,

Appendix

the late Thompson Chagwa, the late Timothy Orurukwe, and others, had passed standard six in institutions outside Nkwerre. Later Chief Fred Anyiam and the late Barrister U. U. Anyiam passed the same examination from Good Schools in Aba or Azumini; and went from there to Government College, Umuahia.

It should be emphasised that in those early boys from Umuko & Ebe-asa attended the C.M.S Central School. The Catholic Secondary Education Primary school was established later.

The D.M.G.S. Onitsha was opened in 1925. One of the foundation students was an Nkwerre boy called Ezekiel Enseanuru, younger brother of the late Mr Uzoukwu Enseanuru who was his guardian, and sponsor died the same year. From the story told of the illness there was sufficient evidence to believe that he was struck down by malaria — a terrible disease in those days when little or no cure was known. But the relations and many others from this paper attributed his death to foul play and so the ugly story spread and was stamped in the minds of people. The result was that for some years after no parent allowed his son to take the entrance examination to D.M.G.S Onitsha or to any other secondary school for that matter. The first to break this taboo in this area entering a secondary school was the late Mr Nathaniel Chiaen of Abba

The normal thing in those days for a boy who passed standard six was either to take up a job with the Government, a firm or to apply to be appointed a pupil teacher by the church. Both Chief R.I. Uzoma and Nze D.I. Onuoha started as pupil teachers after passing standard six and entered the famous St Paul's College in 1931 to train as teachers. They were thus the first to obtain any approved qualification higher than standard six. That was in 1934 when they passed the Teachers' Higher Elementary Certificate exam. From then the flood-gate for Nkwerre boys and girls to obtain higher qualifications.

St Augustine's Grammar School Nkwerre. Started in 1948. The oldest secondary school in Orlu Zone and the second in the former Eastern Region to be built by a community. It was handed over to the Anglican Church to manage. The first principal (in acting capacity) was Mr Mark Anyiam of Umunachi Nkwerre

St Catherines Girls' Sec School. Founded 1955. The first exclusively girls' secondary school in Imo State, also the first to be built entirely by the effort of women (in this case the Women's wing of Nkwerre Aborigines Union. It was also handed over to the Anglican Church to manage. First Principal (in acting capacity) was Miss Paulina Ezenwoye (now Mrs Eme)

Appendix

First Nkwerre University graduate is Chief R.I. Uzoma, OFR; OBE; ER Dip Ed; F.R.G.S; B.A (Hons) Lond of Umudumaji.

First Nkwerre Medical Doctor was the late Dr Augustine Onyejiaka of Umuko.

First Nkwerre lawyer was the late Barrister U.U. Anyiam of Ukwuinyi.

First Nkwerre women university graduates are (1) Dr (MB) Ada Okwuosa (neé Uzoma) (a Sociologist)
(2) Mrs Miriam Nwuocent (neé Akaose) (a lecturer)
(3) Dr (MB) Elsie ?? (neé Agugua) (A consultant surgeon)

Professors:
(1) Professor J. Osondu Eze-Uzomaka (Prof of Engineering) UNN
(2) Professor Azubuike (Prof of Paediatrics UNTH)

APPENDIX 8

R.I. Uzoma's written Response to a questionnaire interview by the Orlu Zonal Students Association, University of Ibadan, dated November 17th 1988

From Chief R.I. Uzoma,
P. O. Box 99,
Nkwerre,
Imo State.

17th November, 1988

Orlu Zonal Students Association,
University of Ibadan Branch.

<u>Q 1</u>: The answer is contained in the curriculum vitae enclosed.

<u>Q 2</u>: I did not have the benefit of a secondary school education. I went to Awka Teacher-training College after serving as a pupil teacher. I entered the college in 1931. The Selection Committee of the then Diocese on the Niger selected me. I was told, because I was top on the entrance examination list;and even though many thought I was too young the expatriate principal of the college, the Rev. A.M. Gelsthorpe and a few others convinced the committee that it was the younger people like me that the college then wanted because we were going to start the four-year course instead of the former three-year course.

The encouragement given to brilliant and hard-working students of the college by the Rev. A.M. Gelsthorpe was responsible for my looking beyond the Higher Elementary Teachers' Certificate examination which was the goal of the four-year course. For example, the Principal (the Rev. A.M. Gelsthorpe) entered some of us in 1932 for the Cambridge Junior School Certificate examination, which I passed, and also arranged private lessons in Latin and Mathematics for us. In those days there was no University in Nigeria and the only graduate from this part of the country was the Late Dr. Alvan Ikoku. One could obtain a degree in Nigeria only by working for the London external degree examination and English, Mathematics and either Latin or Greek are compulsory for obtaining exemption from the London Matriculatin examination for an Arts Degree

To answer your question precisely I would say that the desire not to disappoint those who reposed great confidence in me, the desire to show that finance for overseas education should not be an obstacle, the desire to serve in a higher capacity were the motivating force.

../2.

Appendix

- 2 -

It is not easy to compare the administration of education under the church (missionaries) and that under the Government. Take for example this. Between 1963 and 1967, I was in charge of education in the Owerri Diocese of the Anglican church. That Diocese then covered the present Owerri, Okigwe and Orlu zones. The number of post-primary institutions I was managing in these three zones was only about 5 per cent of the number of secondary schools I managed in Orlu zone (excluding Oguta-Ohaji-Egbema) <u>alone</u> in 1980—83 as Chairman of Orlu Zonal Education Board. Under the voluntary agencies the Management was much closer to the schools and teachers. One problem *facing* the with state management of schools is the problem posed by <u>enormous explosion in school population</u>. In the voluntary agency system there was no sharp division between staff and management as they worked like a family team. The boss knew his teachers by name and posted people where they would give of their best. On the other hand the staff are <u>materially better-off</u> under the State Management because of improved conditions of service and regular promotions. Under the old voluntary agency dispensation there was one salary scale for a higher elementary teacher, one for a senior certificate holder and one for a graduate, and once you got to your scale of salary, you could only move to another if you passed a higher examination, and if you became a graduate you could remain on the maximum of the graduate salary scale for 20 or more years and retire there. Fringe benefits like <u>leave allowance</u>, <u>transport</u> and <u>housing allowance</u> etc. were unknown. There was nothing like Promotion from, say, scale 5 to scale 6 for a grade two teacher or from scale 8 to scale 9 etc for a graduate teacher. Every teacher went into a straight-jacket scale for his grade and could only wriggle out of it by passing a higher examination till he became a graduate and the straight-jacket graduate scale for the graduate was the end of the road for him.

By the Government take-over of schools the State lost the invaluable "free" service of various church personnel (priests) in the management, especially of primary schools, and also lost the careful screening of applicants for employment as teachers. Under the State school system "wolves" and some unsuitable characters have infiltrated into the teaching fold, especially during the "Crash Programme" era and are now being weeded out by the State Schools Management Board and Teachers' Disciplinary Committee. On the other hand I think that on the whole genuine teachers are happier because of enhanced prospects of training and advancement and the fact that they are now welded into <u>one united professional body</u> with the State as their employer instead of the situation existing

../3.

in the old Voluntary Agency days when they thought of themselves as "Roman Catholic teachers" "Anglican teachers" "Methodists teachers" etc. This is a very important point from the point of view of the Unity of the Country. The days of compartmentalisation of teachers are over and any teacher can be posted to any school irrespective of his denomination.

Q 4: There is no doubt that the quality of graduates being produced has been affected by the rapid increase in the number of universities in the country but we should not be worried by this, in my opinion. You will find that those who advocate that no more universities should be approved by the Federal Government are those who already have a university in their own State. In our days, before the founding of Ibadan University in 1948, no one could be admitted into the London University Matriculation for an Arts course without passing with credit in English, Mathematics, Latin or Greek. Now Latin or Greek is no longer compulsory because not only that they are "dead" languages (though useful), English is a second language to us. Up to a few years ago we were discriminating against American degrees. But it is not so now. Even now some institutions in the country discriminate against Indian degrees. Our people are thirsty for education and Government is justified in building several institutions of higher education to satisfy the need. My advice to all of you is to work hard in your chosen field. If possible try and obtain a good honours degree and a second degree. Today people are judged mainly by their job performance and not on how many degrees and where obtained.

Q 5: It is not fair to compare education in my days with what obtains today. In the first place I was the youngest in my class when I started my primary school education but I am sure I was not less than six years old. My own children started their primary school education at the age of four after about 2 years in the kindergarten. In our days, the length of primary education course was 8 years— Infant one, Infant two, Standard one to Standard six. Now the primary education course has been shortened to six years. In our days many finished the primary education course at the age of 25 years or more. Now most pupils finish at the age of 12 years. The syllabus for the 8-year primary education course being

../4.

Appendix

— 4 —

undergone by adolescents who might be up to 20 — 25 years is telescoped into six years to be undergone by "babies" under 12 years. When you compare the performance of the pupil in our days with the pupil today and say that the Elementary six boy of today cannot write a good letter or do "simple proportion" in Arithmetic, have you compared their ages and their Intelligence Quotient which grows with age? It is just like me expecting you to speak in proverbs for over 30 minutes like your old grandfather at home.

The only thing I would say is that the State School Board can help to still improve the conditions in the present-day primary schools by (a) minimising mid-year transfers of teachers so that there will be stability in schools. (b) Ensuring that all schools have their full complement of staff. Because of Financial constraints there are many vacancies on the staffs not filled. (c) That unqualified teachers in secondary schools are down-loaded to primary schools. (d) That headmasters and principals exercise their powers to check absenteeism, lateness and malingering so that pupils do not remain idle during the period for any particular subject.

Let me give this as privileged information, having been Chairman of Orlu Zonal Education Board for 3 years. The students who give the most trouble and the worst law-breakers in any of the secondary schools are mostly the children from the village owning the school.

Q 6: Yes. The problem here as with many Government proposals is that the proposal of a policy is one thing, the planning and **implementation** is another.

In your Zone (Orlu) most communities have provided the technical workshop and the equipment has been delivered but the machines have not been installed and the staff to teach Introductory technology is not yet available. In fact in some communities it has been reported that some of the expensive equipment has been stolen. This applies to several other States in the Federation. But efforts are being made to train the technical teachers. This type of school is what in some countries they call "multi-lateral" school. Children who have no strong aptitude for academic work can concentrate on technical or Business Education after their Junior secondary course and finish up with some useful practical knowledge which will enable them to earn a living.

../5.

Q 7: The answer is that Imo State is one of the few large states that have no "pockets" of backwardness in education. All the zones are evenly developed and have the same zeal for education. If you allow me to compare Imo State with Anambra State, there is not as much zeal for education in Abakiliki and Nsukka zones of Anambra as there is in Onitsha, Enugu and Awka. Statistics will show this.

(PLEASE NOTE THAT THIS ANSWER IS for your own consumption not for publication please).

Q 8: The answer is implied in the answer to Question 7. Imo State spends a greater per-centage of its revenue on Education than any other state. Lagos offers free education but it derives immense revenue from taxes and property rates etc. Imo derives no revenue from any big Federal Industry as there is none.

Q 9: I believe strongly in the admission of students young into our higher Institutions. I am not very conversant with many of the universities but I served once on the Governing Council of Lagos University and on the first Governing Council of the Federal University of Technology Owerri. The young students know what they are in the university for they know the advice and wishes of their parents and guardian.

Many of us feel (and we may be wrong) that a good number of those who cause trouble in the universities are the older students who want to ride on to power on the shoulders of the innocent younger ones. Some of them, we hear, are frustrated students who have failed their exams several times. We hear some are not even ready to attend classes or are not students in the real sense but they register and plant themselves in the Campus ready to capitalise on any eventuality to cause trouble. Parents would like such people to be flushed out of the universities. Those of us who studied overseas are ashamed of the constant eruption of trouble in our compuses which we did not witness overseas. We give the impression of being a nation of unruly, indisciplined people.

../6.

Appendix

Q 10: When the economy improves and fees are reduced or entirely removed from our <u>Secondary</u> schools the vocational schools will die a natural death. They are patronised now because they charge <u>lower</u> fees than the State schools and they pay anything they like to the teachers most of whom are not really qualified. In any case a good number of their students are <u>not</u> secondary school material at all in the real sense.

Q 11: Please see answer to question 9.

Q 12: This question is not easy. When you talk of the present-day students do you mean secondary school or university students? About 70 per cent of the present day secondary school students would not have been admitted at all in the forties and fifties because admission in the forties and fifties was highly competitive. One important difference I have emphasised is the large numbers involved today. In the forties when I was principal of Okrika Grammar School, I was the only graduate teacher on the staff, teaching — English, English Literature, Latin, Geography, Bible Knowledge and Mathematics in class 5. After the close of school at 2.00 p.m. I went back by 4.00 p.m with the same class 5 having a break by 6.30 p.m and going back by 8.00 p.m to continue teaching till 9.30 p.m. In those days, if a student failed in English Language, he would fail in the whole Cambridge School Certificate Examination. I was able to do this because <u>the students were very keen</u> and their parents used to come and ask me to flog them if they misbehaved or if they went to Port Harcourt without permission. The expected reward then was the fame and reputation of scoring 100% success in the Cambridge exam. My salary then was only £120 per annum. We worked for <u>prestige</u> and recognition not for money. Most of the present day teachers work hard to inspire their students but they have not the prestige and recognition accorded us by parents and the public in our days. Many students themselves work very hard inspite of the fact that they are relatively younger, and we are very impressed by the way some of them tackle the present day innovation of giving a university student <u>a project</u> to tackle and produce result before the end of his course. The way they approach those in a position to help them in their

../7.

project and the incisive questions they ask show the great development in the spirit of enquiry and method of collection and arrangement of data which is an essential part of university education.

Q 13: This is true of certain parts of Orlu Zone. I am not at all opposed to this because education is not free at all levels in the State at present. I think that it is because of the fact that we are a Zone of business men, that we can boast of at least one secondary school in every autonomous community built by community effort. At Urualla, Nkwerre, Oguta, Ndizuogu, Amaigbo, Ihioma, Okporo, Awo-Omama, Ubulu, Amiri etc there are several scholarships awarded by walthy indigines of these towns to children of indigent parents. After all, we cannot all be academicians. Orlu Zone has one of the largest proportion of pupils at school. There is nothing wrong with this trend provided we do not go to be apprentice traders. The course is changing with the formation of limited liability companies and the demand for graduates in Economics, Business Management, Accountancy, Law and Engineering to run these companies.

(to the extreme of withdrawing first-class brains)

Q 14 and Q 15:

These two questions are too personal for my liking. I wish to state that first and foremost, I am a christian and believe in christian doctrines and **Ethics**. I do not accept the politicians' doctrine that in Politics there is no permanent friendship, no permanent enmity. This doctrine, in my opinion, tends to support compromise with evil for immediate gain. It is Machiavellian and in my opinion unchrstian. I will not dump a friend unless I prove him to be unreliable and dishonest and no longer worthy of the trust I reposed in him. I believe strongly in honesty and integrity and my interpretation of "service to God" is rendering selfless service to my fellow men while at the same time worshipping God and believing in Christ's redemption of mankind.

To you, young men and women, I would advise: Remember your God and parents, avoid fast and false life, keep your hands clean, avoid cigarettes and heavy drinking.

../8.

Appendix

- 8 -

Finally ponder over these quotations from which I have drawn inspiration:

(a) "Better than costly urns of sculptured marble are the monuments we build for ourselves in the hearts of our fellow men; and these memorials will endure when we are crumbled into dust; for Love is stronger than death, and the good deeds contain within themselves and in themselves the germs of immortality" —— (the author's name forgotten)

(b) "Teach us Good Lord to serve Thee as Thou deserveth,

To give and not to count the cost.

To fight and not to heed the wounds;

To toil and not to seek for rest,

To labour and not to ask for any reward

except that of knowing that we do Thy will". Amen.

Prayer of St. Ignatius Loyola.

APPENDIX 9

Interview with Chief R.I. Uzoma, Former Chairman Zonal Education Board, Orlu, conducted by Messrs I. Umezurike, P.N. Abamara, Ifeanyi and Anene Ogidi of the Orlu Zonal Educator, Editorial Board

14/4/80

INTERVIEW WITH CHIEF R. I. UZOMA

FORMER CHAIRMAN, ZONAL EDUCATION BOARD, ORLU, CONDUCTED BY MESSRS I. UMEZURIKE, P. N. ABAMARA, AND IFEANYI IHEJIASI & ANENE OF THE ORLU ZONAL EDUCATOR EDITORIAL BOARD:

Below are the educative, penetrating, rewarding and inspiring answers to the questions put to Chief R. I. Uzoma by the members of the Editorial Board.

Question:

Chief Uzoma, one would rightly call you one of the pioneers of Western education not only in the old Orlu Province, but also in the former Eastern Region of Nigeria. Besides your natural endowments, in what other ways did your family background and immediate environment motivate you to pursue education relentlessly?

Answer:

It would be wrong to say that I pursued education 'relentlessly' in the twenties when I was in the Primary School. The C.M.S. Central School Nkwerre, the oldest "Standard Six" School in Orlu Zone, happens to have been situated in my village at Nkwerre - a pole or two from my compound. My father sent me to school at a tender age; if I had to trek six or more kilometres before getting to school, I don't think I would have gone to school at all. Probably, I would have been a trader like other Nkwerre people. My father was a busy tobacco trader. He rather left me with my grandmother who so pampered me that today, I wonder how I managed to do well at School. My grandmother at any given time had two or three of her nieces to live with her and serve her. As my father was her only son, and I, her first grandson, I was not allowed to do any serious work.

I was admired by my teachers for being particularly good in Arithmetic and I had a relatively good retentive memory.

In fact, I did little or no home work nor any private study after School. It was only when I went to Awka College in 1931 did that I developed the habit of reading.

From the above, I can say that at the Primary School stage, I pursued education by the sheer accident of being born in a village that had a Central School planted in it as far back as 1922, and the next motivation was the interest my Headmaster and my teacher had in me for my good memory and ability in figures. I think I was the "darling" of the teacher.

Question:

Chief, you chose teaching as a career and remained in it even when you had options of more lucrative opportunities in the Government Service or the Commercial Houses of the early days, or even to take to business. Why did you chose teaching in particular? Any regrets so far?

Appendix

Answer:

I must tell you, there was in fact no other avenue of furthering ones education beyond Standard Six in Orlu area at that time. The only Nkwerre boy who was a foundation student of D.M.G.S Onitsha in 1925 died there that same year and this tragic event so scarred people over here that nobody sat for D.M.G.S. entrance examination again till about 1928 or 1929. Moreover C.K.C. Onitsha and Government College Umuahia had not then been established.

I passed the Government Standard Six examination (the first to do so in Nkwerre at the first attempt) in 1927 and it was believed that a brilliant young man or lady could more easily become a graduate if he or she were a teacher than if he were a Civil Servant or clerk in one of the Commercial Houses. Most of the people who sat for the London Matriculation in those days were mainly teachers.

Finally, I have no regrets whatsoever because even in the days of expatriate missionaries, I was appointed Principal of Okrika Grammar School (succeeding the late Dr. E. Oli) and given free hand to plan my own work and execute it without interference from any quarters. Really derived great job satisfaction from the results achieved. Nigerianization in the Anglican Voluntary Agency was real and complete.

Question:

You were once the Minister of Education in the former Eastern Region of Nigeria. What were the major achievements of the Ministry under your leadership?

Answer:

Yes, I was the Minister of Education of the former Eastern Region between January 1952 and December 1953. During this period some achievements were made by the Ministry.

First, the planning of the Universal Primary education was laid out. The idea was to make the first two classes free in the first year, and in the second year extend to the third class. This plan was carefully drawn up taking into consideration the financial resources of the Region which were not as immense as those of the Western Region which made a lot of revenue out of Cocoa and tobacco under the principle of drivation in the Revenue Allocatic In 1955 OR 1956 after the House had been dissolved the N.C.N.C. Government introduced free education in all the classes at once and by 1957 the financial burden nearly caused the collapse of the Government.

Secondly, we introduced a Scholarship Scheme by which a good number of youngmen and women with requisite qualification were helped to obtain high academic qualifications. This enabled them fill places in the Government service left by expatriates when indepandence came in 1960 and the expatriates left after taking their lump sum gratuity.

Thirdly we ~~entrenched~~ *entrenched* the principle of probity and accountability, we shunned bribery and corruption. It was during our time that the area of Enugu called Uwani was laid out and demarcated into plots. We, the Ministers, decided that no Minister should apply for any piece of land or benefit directly from the scholarship scheme. Consequently none of us had a plot, or a scholarship for his son or daughter. We believed in serving the electorate first and not ourselves. In fact one of the main causes of the 1953 crisis was our firm stand against corruption, political jobbery, nepotism etc. We tried to uphold the Christian ethics of integrity and honest service. I remember a contractor *reporting* ~~relating~~ to another that we, the Ministers, did not know 'how to do business' because we refused to accept bribes to offer Scholarships or award contracts at inflated prices to incompetent people who might be wearing party badges.

Finally, I personally sponsored a bill banning nudity in the old Abakiliki Province.

Question:

Sir, you rather had a brief spell in Politics first as an elected representative and Minister, and again as a Provincial Administrator during the Civil war. It appears you had no real interest in active politics, probably you were more of a reluctant politician.

Any comments Chief?

Answer:

If you are a convinced Christian and care about your reputation, going into party politics as it is played today would be like going into a pig sty. I am sure you have read the stinking exposures made before the various tribunals and panels.

Question:

It would appear there was a tendency on the part of our capable mission trained pioneers to shy away from active politics, thus giving people of less competence and doubtful integrity all the opportunity; what would you say caused this apparent indifference?

Answer:

The first reason is the answer I give in the last question. The second reason is the fact that a good mission trained teacher would not............ (Continued on Page 4).

Appendix

be prepared to bribe his way to the House of Assembly or Representatives and if he would, he might not be able to afford the money.

QUESTION:
You were once the Education Secretary for the Anglican Mission and ipso-facto the manager, administrator and a teacher of teachers. Can you please identify some of the management and administrative techniques and skills that made the mission work in education a tremendous success?

ANSWER:
In the first instance, integrity and accountability were practised and not merely preached.

Secondly, all workers were regarded as members of one family in the christian spirit of being one in Christ. There was no division into 'Senior' and 'Junior' staff and no jostling for position as the post one held depended on ones certificate, year of certification and experience. If you by sheer blackmail or intrigue pushed out your immediate superior officer the chances of your replacing him were remote, and even if you did, you would not be given the salary he earned.

Thirdly, there was proper devolution of authority from the Diocese to the Parish level. The administrative set up was fool-proof and even the smallest pupil-teacher in a remote village was known. The devolution of power was such that teachers were free to appeal on any matter to the Diocesan Board.

Finally, it should be remembered however that an Anglican or Catholic Education Secretary before the war, rather managed fewer institutions than there are in one local Government area today not to talk of one Zone.

The growth of number of pupils, students and institutions since after the Nigeria Civil war has been quite phenominal.

QUESTION:

Looking back at the period you were the Chairman of the Zonal Education Board Orlu, what would you say were the principal achievements of your administration. And having to work with Board members of differing backgrounds and political persuasions, what problems did you encounter?

We succeeded in extablishing the Zonal Board office in Orlu. Secondly, we showed Owerri, by example, that a lot of money could be saved by avoiding the use of (direct) contract~labr. By permission of Owerri we did the partitioning and wiring of buildings in our Holy Rosary Umuna temporary site by using the students and staff of Umuowa Technical Secondary school and theydid an excellent piece of work at such a small cost that we earned the praise of the Commissioner for Education and the gratitude of the staff and students for offering them the opportunity of pratical work outside. The girls in their jeans doing wiring told me "What a man does, a woman can do as well".

Thirdly, I put down my foot against corruption. Orlu was the only Zone that removed a Board member for corrupt practices. Several teachers were surcharged or removed as a result of bad audit reports on their class or school.

Fourthly we treated all teachers and schools alike irrespective of clan, political leaving or religious affilation.

As for Board members who might regard their appointment as an opportunity to share party "cake" or to reward themselves for their efforts for the party, the early removal of an erring member showed them that I was not going to tolerate political jobbery and corruption.

Above all, after the coup that overthrew the Shagari regime, Orlu Zone had no query to answer, and there was no rioting in any of our schools during my tenure of office, no illegal levies etc.

QUESTION:

Chief, we have been discussing issues of the past, now I wish we could look at the present and future issues, the new National Education Policy aptly called the 6-3-3-4 system while being acclaimed as the key to our technological break-through, is also seen by some critics as having a curriculum too superficial and occupation oriented and lacking in academic content. You may express some views Chief:

ANSWER:

I don't know what people mean by lacking in "academic content". If you know the History of the whole world, and can quote all the works of Shakes-peare and other literary giants, but have no job, your education is valueless to your family in our Nigerian context. For long the Western countries have talked of "Education for leisure" or "Education for the development of the whole man". The Eastern Block countries on the otherhand have emphasized the utilitarian

Appendix

aspect of Education, the education that will help you earn your daily bread without waiting for somebody to employ you. This, in my opinion is what the new 6-3-3-4 education system aims at and what Nigeria needs today to check unemployment and the resultant wave of armed robbery, without of-course sacrificing the other aims of Education as emphasised by the Western countries.

QUESTION:

One other criticism of the new National Policy on Education is that the students are made to choose their subjects of specialisation or career at a rather early stage, at the end of the Junior Secondary School course. The critics argue that it does not take ample cognisance of late developers. Do you see this as a major defect?

ANSWER:

NO! I took time to study the British multi-lateral school system, though this was many years ago. I believe the principle will be applied in our case. There will be a method of moving children from the Technical section to the Grammar or Commercial section and vice-versa. The division in my own opinion should not be water-tight.

But I must warn that many young people including brilliant ones get frustrated in life by being unable to make up their mind in time as to what they want. They try their hand in this, leave it and jump to another, and also abandon it. In the end they finish a frustrated lot.

QUESTION:

Some have argued that the proliferation of post Primary schools in the recent past in our State has dangerously sacrificed high quality education for quantity. What is your assessment of the situation, Sir?

ANSWER:

What the proliferation of Secondary schools has done is that it has enabled the son of the labourer or farm worker to have the opportunity of Secondary School education which was formerly available to the children of the middle and upper classes. Just as the number of poor school certificate holders have increased, so also has the number of the very good ones. The trouble is that the poor results attract more attention. At this point, I better remind you that Imo State still leads in the number that pass JAMB examination.

If anything has affected the quality of Education it is: first, irregular payment of teachers' salaries, especially in the last civilian regime, resulting in strike action, work-to-rule etc, secondly, the delay of posting qualified teachers from Universities and colleges of Education at the beginning of the school session, and thirdly, constant transfer of teachers in the middle of term. These problems are problems created by our poor financial resources.

QUESTION:
It has been pointed out that whereas it takes a relatively shorter time to procure and instal equipment for the technical workshops, it takes a much longer time to train the teachers. What is your advice on staff recruitment and training to ameliorate this problem?

ANSWER:
This is not an easy question, because teachers are now afraid of going on in-service training since they are not sure of automatic posting on the completion of their course. But I think the present arrangements whereby some technical teachers are trained overseas and others trained locally is a good one. I do hope that technical teachers will be posted as soon as they report at Owerri.

QUESTION:
The Boarding system in our Post Primary institutions has faced serious criticisms. In view of our neighbourhood school system, do you consider the full introduction of the system relevant in our context?

ANSWER:
The Boarding system has never been phased out in this State as far as I know. What has happened is that older schools that were formerly exclusively boarding eg. Bishop Shanahan, Ihioma Girls, St. Augustine's, St. Catherine's have thrown their doors open to day-students and Government has rightly decided that boarding account in each school should no longer be subsidised. It should be self-balancing. In view of the explanation above, the question of "full introduction of the Boarding System" does not at all arise. Any body who wants his child to be a boarder can easily arrange for him or her to go to a school that has boarding facilities. In Sta Catherine's and Ihioma Girls, you have daughters of people in Lagos, Portharcourt, Owerri, Onitsha etc. We have even children from other States and Ethnic groups

QUESTION:
Some people strongly believe that Nigeria needs more tertiary institutions like Colleges of Technology, Poly- technics, Colleges of Education etc which in reality offer

...../8.

Appendix

students the pre-requisite knowledge and skills for technological development instead of more of the conventional universities.

Do you share these views Sir?

ANSWER:

I would not advise more Polytechnics or Colleges of Technology in this country at present till there are enough facilities for students in the existing institutions to have sufficient practical training experience during their period of attachment. At present they don't have sufficient practical experience.

QUESTION:

We see Education today at this cross roads. Parents are now more inclined to prefer "business" which they believe assures money, big name and respectability to Education for which they are no longer sure of the returns. It is now a known fact that an increasing number of boys drop out from school these days to look for quick money at a rather tender age. What advice do you have for parents and our young people?

ANSWER:

There is nothing wrong with some boys going out to be apprentice traders. I would rather advise that they do so after completing their Junior Secondary course. In fact, it will fit in very well into your 6-3-3-4 system. After the junior secondary course, the boy who wants to be a trader will switch over to "practical Commercial Education" instead of the Grammar school or Technical type of Education, after receiving proper counselling from the Guidance and Counselling officer of the school, based on the boy's performance in the school, his interest and aptitude. An apprentice trader is after all under-going the practical course of his commercial secondary education. You can have education in Onitsha or Aba market as well as in the class room.

QUESTION:

Chief, looking at your career and your person, one can say without any fear of contradiction that you have a successful and rewarding life in spite of your modest material possessions, and one would say that you have kept wonderful looks and good health that perhaps make you look younger

...../9

APPENDIX 10

"The Relevance of Continued Education" An Address delivered to the Clergy of Okigwe/Orlu Diocese at Ezihe on November 25th 1986 by Chief R.I. Uzoma, OFR, OBE, BA.(Hons), Dip.Ed. FRGS

Bertrand Russell

"THE RELEVANCE OF CONTINUED EDUCATION"

An address delivered to the Clergy of Okigwe-Orlu Diocese at Ezihe on the 25th of November, 1986

by

Chief R I Uzoma, O.F.R., O.B.E.
B.A.(Hons) Dip.Ed., F.R.G.S.

Thanks

Introduction

A complete man is made up of body, mind and soul. All the three components need to be constantly fed for the man to remain complete. When the body is not fed, kwashiokor steps in, and the mind ceases to work effectively. When the mind is not fed, the man becomes a walking log of wood, a moron. A man starved of spiritual food becomes a lawless beast, roaming aimlessly the streets of his environment, oblivious of his Creator and the purpose of his creation. The Latin tag "Mens sana in corpore sano" - a sound mind dwells in a sound body - expresses a good aim of education, in an era when many doubted the existence of the soul. Today we would emphasise that a sound training (or feeding) of the body, of the mind and of the soul go side by side in a well-planned christian educational system. It is only in an environment of a sound mind in a sound body that man's spirit easily finds a right sense of direction towards the Creator. The process of creating this healthy body and healthy mind for a healthy soul is Education; and it is a continuous process, A PROCESS which stresses the inter-relationship of the body mind and soul - the component parts of a normal living human being.

Aims of Education:

Whether we view the aim of education as training an individual to acquire knowledge purely for its own sake, for the enjoyment of his leisure and full integration into the citizenship of his city State, or like the totalitarian countries of the Communist bloc who view education as a process of shaping an individual virtually into a veritable human machine - tool for production, the fact still remains that the process of education is continuous. Education does not end even when formal schooling STOPS, and this is the message I wish to leave with you today.

From the day a child is born, he begins to learn under the eyes of the mother. He learns to suck the breast, to kick his legs, to lift his hand and, by waving her hand across his face, the mother helps him to focus his eyes correctly and see. He is even, by rubbing, coaxed to empty his bowels. He is helped to crawl, to walk, to learn to talk, and later to bathe himself. This process of home or informal education continues even after the child has started school. The only difference then is that he has two sets of teachers - those at school and the parents at home.

Education continues with adults even when formal college and University education has ended. Education is like feeding. It is an exercise that should continue till we go to the grave. The word "Education" is derived from two Latin words "ex" meaning "out" and "ducere" meaning "to lead". It means 'leading" out the best traits and qualities in an individual and developing and polishing them and at the same time "leading" out the bad traits in the individual and by a process called sublimation in Psychology, replacing them with more acceptable traits, and this operation is performed by teaching and example in the case of children and adolescents, and by reading, lectures, symposia etc. in the case of adults.

explain

--/2

Appendix

A famous teacher, once said, the education in an individual is what remains after he will have forgotten all that he crammed for purposes of passing an examination. For you, as a Clergyman, if we may use the above yard-stick, your education now is made up of your life style as taught and learnt at home and the Colleges you attended.

(b) What you remember now of the subjects taught you at College;

(c) The desire for or habit of reading you acquired at College which pushes you to refresh your memory of past lessons and to break new ground'

(d) The urge to update your knowledge and life-style and keep abreast of the time so that you may not become what in common parlance we call 'dead-wood", remembering that life is not static. Our Education is for service to God and Society, and Society is not static.

SOME REASONS FOR CONTINUED EDUCATION THROUGH WIDE READING:

i) Reading carefully selected books, pamphlets, magazines, etc. is a means of further improving one's education and better equipping oneself for the challenges of one's job in particular and of life in general. Late Sir Winston Churchil was not a holder of University degrees, but he was one of the most knowledgeable, imaginative and eloquent men of his days, and the unforgettable Prime Minister of Britain during the second world war. Surely "the cowl does not make a monk."

ii) Reading is a means of joyfully spending your leisure and avoiding tension and high-blood pressure. In the, bus, train or tube (underground train) in Europe you find everybody reading. The only time you hear some loud voices is when African or West Indian students come in; otherwise everybody is quiet reading.

iii) Wide reading is specially necessary for the priest who, like the doctor and the teacher, has to deal with human beings — God's own children. Committing an error in these professions through ignorance, could be "fatal" in one way or the other. No matter what you think or say, interesting and intelligent sermons, coupled with good singing and class-teaching are among the aspects of our worship that draw the people to it. The injunction of Jesus Christ, "Feed my Lamb", implies feeding them with nourishing food and not with chaff; and your stock of nourishing food can only be replenished by reading, thinking and, of course, devotion. Our church members have often passed through the ordeal of listening to 45 minutes' sermons (usually from untrained Catechists) where the Preacher rambled through unrelated passages from all the books of the Bible from Genesis to Revelations with the usual, "Onye natara ya gue", and in the end went home not remembering any concrete point or lesson from the sermon.

iv) Wide reading is more important today than ever before with the increased number of educated members among our congregations. Even in the remotest villages, we have not only retired educated members but also younger ones working in our large towns who come home into the village at week-ends to attend development meetings and worship in their home Church. We, as a rural Diocese

.../3

have to do all we can to sustain their interest in the village, for we depend very much on their support. Reading helps a Priest by making his addresses more interesting, more appealing, less monotonous and humdrum. Let me say that the Lay members of the congregation do easily spot out those priests who read widely and those who do not.

v) Theology and philosophy which is related to it, are dry subjects because they deal with abstract ideas. Our sermons of course deal with theology/philosophy. In order, therefore, to make our sermons interesting to the ordinary man and woman, we need to add spice into them in the form of stories, anecdotes and illustrations from topical events and you can get this spice to dress your sermons and make them more appealing, through wide reading.

vi) The priest in a remote rural parish is seen not only as a spiritual leader but also as the "Information Officer" of both the Local, State and Federal Government. Members come to him to ask for information and advice on such topics as the 6:3:3:4 system of education on S.F.E.M., on Foreign Exchange, on O.I.C. on Health matters, etc. You cannot help them with useful information on such topics if you, yourself, have no idea what these topical issues mean and how they affect your church - members. If you accept the above thesis, it follows, therefore, that you should read not only religious and theological books, you should read local papers, good magazines and periodicals, simple books on Economics, Government and Sociology. You should, in fact, try, through newspaper articles, to have some idea of such high-technology subjects as "Missile", "Rockets," "nuclear re-actor."

What all these mean is that spheres of knowledge are inter-related and it is only for purposes of teaching and convenience that we try to compartmentalise them into "subjects". An educated man knows a little about every subject.

vii) Wide reading improves your level of general knowledge, and knowledgeability inspires confidence wherever you go and banishes complex. After all, the sort of training you received in Trinity College is not inferior to that offered in Bigard Seminary, or any other Institution of its class.

PLANNING OUR TIME-TABLE

It is not enough for you to make up your mind that you will from today try and read much more widely than you have done in the past. I want to offer one or two pieces of advice.

i) You should draw your own personal time-table. In the time-table, after making provision for the compulsory functions you must perform e.g. Morning and Evening prayers, Visiting, Period for office work when you deal with official matters and receive official visitors, you should try and set aside at least one hour two or three times a week for reading.

ii) You should let it be known to members of your congregation the time set aside for them to bring up reports and complaints that do not come under "emergency".

--/4

Appendix

iii) It is advisable that your period for private study and reading should be spent in your study room or Chapel, if you have any, to avoid disturbance.

iv) You should dress up early by 8.00 a.m. and try, as much as possible without being rude, to prevent a stream of visitors from upsetting your time-table to a large extent.

SUGGESTIONS ON READING MATERIAL:

I am not competent to advise on theological books but I find the books of William Barclay e.g. "Ethics in a permissive Society" and those of C.S. Lewis e.g. "The problem of pain" and "Miracles" useful.

Each parish priest ought to take one local paper daily to know what is happening in the country.

For detailed investigative journalism on major events in Nigeria and the outside world one should read magazines like "Newswatch", and "Times International." You can also often get useful insight into what is happening in other Churches and read educative essays in "American Times" and "Readers' Digest" which are foreign papers not printed in Nigeria.

For books on secular subjects, if you can get copies of "Teach yourself" series they will help you, for they are written in simple non-technical language.

Don't be taken in by the title of a book, glance through the catalogue of contents and read one or two paragraphs to ensure that the language is such as will not scare you off.

Finally, I do hope you can arrange among yourselves a system of book lending and borrowing. Thank you.

APPENDIX 11

"Education in a Changing Africa: Concepts and Practice" by Mr. R.I. Uzoma, OFR (Undated)

Education in a Changing Africa
Concepts and Practice. Mr R.I. Uzoma OFR.,

Introduction: I want to start off straight away by thanking the Principal and his staff for inviting me to speak on the subject of "Education in a Changing Africa" The subject is a very vast one and I don't think I consider myself to be an authority on the subject and even if I were I would require much more time than what I had at my disposal to prepare what could be considered an academic lecture. Considering the time at my disposal, however, and the mixed nature of my audience I propose to point out a few trends in our educational policy in the forties and fifties and make some comparisons with the policies in the French African countries where our fellow Africans and brothers live. I shall point out some of the major changes and improvements in policy and practice since 1960 when we became independent and took over fully control of our own affairs and leave you to judge whether we have succeeded or failed.

Aim: The Spens Report puts down the aim of education in this simple language. It is "the training of the pupil first as a person with a body, a mind and a spirit second as a future citizen of, a <u>Democratic</u> country and third as one who will have work of some kind or other to do for a livelihood." There are not three aims expressed in this statement. There is only a single aim; that is in the words of the great educationist, Sir Percy Nunn - "<u>the highest degree of individual development</u>" An individual whose education cannot help him to do work of some kind or other is not fully developed, nor can the highest degree of individual development be achieved in a vaccum. Man is a social being. Your way of thinking and your behaviour pattern, all those things that make up an individual called "James" or "John" are the heritage of our society. They are to a large extent conditioned by society. Take for example the right claimed by a man in our society of taking a girl of his choice for a life partner. The man does so because it is part of the cultural pattern of our society. There is at least one society where the cultural pattern is different in this respect - the Tchambuli describe by Dr Mead in her book "<u>Sex and temperament in 3 primitive societies.</u>" Among these people a man waits and prays that a woman may choose her for a partner and they think that our custom is odd just as we think theirs is. What you think are your private beliefs and convictions are not, most of them, really yours but those of the whole or part of your social environment. Most of us are R.C. or Protestant, not by choice because our parents or relative belong to that denomination or because the particular church is the first to exist in your village. Plato and the Greeks (sed Thucydides 1.70) said quite rightly <u>that the individual developed most fully as he took his rightful place in his society.</u> You started to wear clothes not because you thought it was reasonable but because sentiment made you do what others around you do; and then reason came in to confirm what started with sentiment. Ten years ago you thought that a long frock for girls was very beautiful. Today your society thinks it is not good and you an adult have also changed your view and some of us even feel that a "mini" or French pair of shorts is the best for a young lady.

Appendix

I have given these illustrations to show that full individual development, physical moral and spiritual can only be attained in society, and the society has a magical educational influence on the individual. Sir Percy Nunn quoting Lord Balfour talks of those "who feel that they are never more themselves, never more masters of their own fate, than when they recognise that they are parts of a greater whole from which they can draw inspiration and strength, and to which they can give inspiration and strength". We are more truly ourselves with our society. The disire of an individual for freedom need not clash with the limitations set by society in order that it may maintain its cohesion. Individual freedom should not mean individual licence. It is the ordered freedom necessary for the achievement of any end, the ordered freedom that distinguishes us from the lower animals. On the other hand no democratic society can truly be free and happy with an orderliness that is tantamount to regimentation, an orderliness that is not the result of decisions made by individuals under conditions of real choice. Ordered freedom should mean a synthesis, a welding together and preservation of the values of society and those of the individual. Professor Tsuji of Hiroshima (Japan) has defined education as "an effort to eternalise values" and mark you these values of society even the changes are brought about through the perseverance of talented individuals.

The African society: Having seen the ralation of the individual to Society each wielding a mighty influence on the other we shall now examine our African society and the policies of education pursued in different parts. Our present society is in a state of flux. Owing to acculturisation it is a rapidly changing society. Here in Nigeria, for example, we are not only grappling with the problem of the mixing of the cultures of the various ethnic groups but we are also facing the problem of the cultures of all the ethnic groups together mixing with the white-man's culture. Our society is no longer the simple isolated indigeneous, tribal society nor is it a European society. The question our Education policy makers, have been trying for years to answer is this: "Is it advisable for all the time-honoured African culture to be swept away so that we may be "black Europeans" or is it better to pick out the good in African culture and tradition and the best in European culture and build up a culture which though hybrid will will accord with our changed society?" In short the question is "what degree of change is best suited for us."

It can safely be said that the French policy of Assimiliation in their colonies aimed at wiping out all traces of African culture. On the other hand the British policy is that of grafting the new on to the old stock, that is that of adaptation to African needs. It is the policy which in administration is responsible for the theory of Indirect Rule. In education it expresses itself in the encouragement of the vernacular, of African art, music and literature of African dress and social organisation. Mr Mayhew a well-known British Administrator said that British intention was not to make Africans bad Europeans but to make them good Africans. The French, on the other hand could be said to want to increase the stature of France by absorbing the Africans culturally and politically into France. The vernacular was discouraged in their schools on the pretext that it has no literature and does n't open the door to ancient pholosophy and literature which are missionaries who came along with the Colonial masters and who as a matter of fact spear headed the move to educate the African stuck faithfully to the policy. It was they who first reduced the African languages into writing translated the Bible into the vernacular, produced other vernacular books. They and a few missionary-minded colonial civil servants first saw the need to adapt education to our needs and culture encouraged the study of our history and geography. They first introduced school for carpentry and farming in the belief that we would all starve if we became a nation of pen - pushers alone. The introduction of Rural Science into schools and the covering of school and church compounds with grass to prevent erosion were preached all over by people like Herrington and Prior. The teaching of Science was introduced for the first time in our Secondary Schools by missionaries in D.M.G.S. & C.K.C. and in Government College Umuahia by Clergy-man civil servant, Rev. Robert Fisher - the first Principal.

You will see ladies and gentlemen that our educational policy is that of taking what is good in European culture and grafting it in the best in our own culture. We have rejected the French policy of "Assimulation" of the Africans in the former French territories since we fear it tends to lead to what psychologists call "split mentality". Nor do we think that the policy of "Dualism which the Dutch calimed to have perfected in the East Indies is realistic - that is to say, the policy of keeping the indigineous culture intact and separate from the European Dutch culture, none absorbing the other. We aim at educating our people for purposeful change. Our education aims at creating in the African a frame of mind which preserves what is good in African culture and rejects what is bad and purposeless in European culture. It is wrong to think that everything European is ideal. Our strong family relationships rather than the rugged European individualism our yam rather than the European potato, our dress if need be adapted, etc. etc. - these are to be preferred. Our education, should moreover equip us with the knowledge that will help to make our lives healthier and richer, to discover the beauty in our music, at and folk-lore, to tap our natural resources and get more yield from our soil. Our education aims at stirring us up to think and giving us subjects to think about so that we may make our contribution to world discoveries. The real education in you says a famous philosopher, is what is left in you after you will have forgotten all the stuff you crammed to pass an examination.

Since 1960 when we became independent and took control of the planning of our education we have not made much change in our aimsand policy but we have <u>made a significant change in emphasis and, therefore, in the structure of our curriculum</u>. For example in our schools now Nigerian and African history and geography have taken precedence over British and Empire history and geography. Research goes on into our music and musical instruments. On the Secondary School level our languages have been emphasised and Science and French have pushed out dead Latin and Greek. French has become as popular as English in view of the fact that we are surrounded by French-speaking countries. If I had spent the 8 years I spent on Latin in learning French, Yoruba or Hausa, I would have felt much better - educated today. This shift in emphasis is all to our good and will continue unabated.

It is quite obvious that for education to be of the greatest benefit it should influence the largest number and not just a few. This leads to the big problem of mass and adult education. Our education is not confined to the four walls of the class-room. The use of mass communication media like the radio the cenima, the television etc. is very important for reaching the masses; so are adult education classes, extra-mural lectures, literacy classes etc. We are already doing very well in these various fields. We aim at filling all available places in our schools. We no longer expel children because they have no uniform so long as they look clean and neat. Children are not expelled because they fail an examination. It was Oscar Wilde who says "In examinations the foolish ask questions that the wise cannot answer."

-2-

Appendix

- 3 -

only accessible through the medium of the French language. The culture of France was the only culture worth preserving and Africans must renounce theirs and embrane it. African institutions ere discouraged and the Africans were made to take pride in being French citizens and to be represented in the French Parliament etc, and to hold important offices in Government. The French colonies are regarded as " la France d'Outre - Mtr" - France beyond the seas. This policy was started after the French Revolution to regain the strengyh lost during the Napoleonic wars. Let me quote a few sentences from the declaration of policy by the Minister for France beyond the Seas "<u>Education must be given exclusively through the medum of the F French language M. Rene Pleven has said that we should gradually transform the French African ix into an African Frenchman. That is our end; Our new educational policy is the means.</u>" (see Colonial Review Sept. 1946.)

Some of us Africans criticize the encouragement of African institutions and culture as an attempt to keep down the African. There is a certain amount of truth in this especially if we remember that some of the colonial masters felt that to give education to the African was "to educate themselves out of job." It is my view, however, that the various Christian

APPENDIX 12

Report of the Committee on Higher Education presented to the Joint Council of the Dioceses, East of the Niger (Undated)

REPORT OF THE COMMITTEE ON HIGHER EDUCATION
PRESENTED TO THE JOINT COUNCIL OF THE
DIOCESES, EAST OF THE NIGER.
****

APPOINTMENT: At the Joint Council Meeting of the Dioceses, East of the Niger, held at Christ Church Owerri on 21st September, 1989, a Committee was set up to advise the Joint Council on the need for the Joint Council to establish a Higher Institution.

MEMBERS OF THE COMMITTEE:-

1. Chief R. I. Uzoma — Chairman.
2. Prof. B. Ukeje
3. Prof. C. Chiagu
4. Sir Jonah Wachuku
5. Rev. Canon A. M. Onuaguluchi
6. Rev. Canon A. E. D. Mgbemena
7. Ven. G. C. Echefu:
8. Dr. Felix Ndu
9. Mr. G. A. Ugwuegede
10. Chief C.K.G. Nwobike ✓
11. Sir Sidney B.C. Anyanwu. — Secretary.

TERMS OF REFERENCE:

No specific terms of reference were given to the Committee. The Committee was however asked to use as a Working Paper two memos on Higher Education submitted to the bishops by Prof. B. Ukeje and Sir Sidney B.C. Anyanwu respectively. Those two memos were available to the Committee and the Committee made use of them.

NEED FOR A HIGHER INSTITUTION:

This issue was discussed in detail. The present role of the Union Theological College Umuahia was considered. It was agreed that this Institution though serving a useful purpose, does not satisfy the need for a Higher Theological Institution.

/2...

Appendix

- 2 -

Nigeria has aptly been characterized as a nation in which nothing works. And nothing really seems to work in Nigeria today largely because, unfortunately, indiscipline is fast gaining the upper hand among the social ills of the Nigerian Society.

Social ills associated with indiscipline are increasing, multiplying and being intensified. It is doubtful if the existing traditional and conventional higher educational systems and institutions are paying or even capable of paying sufficient attention to attitudinal development of their products. Thus Nigeria seriously needs a change in the orientation of her programmes of manpower development and production - an orientation towards the development and inculcation of proper and wholesome attitudes. And this can be achieved through the establishment of a Pilot Higher Educational Institutions - an institution that will focus largely on the production of good citizens who could become effective catalysts for the re-construction of The Nigerian Society.

The Committee unanimously agreed to recommend to the Joint Council the establishment of a Degree Awarding Theological Institution for the following needs among others.

a) The present dearth of graduate priests.
b) The level of education of the congregation is rising fast. The pulpit should continue to be higher than the pew.
c) The dearth of graduate priests as principals of institutions even up to schools.
d) The need for people with moral orientation to give sense of direction to our youths.
e) The need for Christian schools.
f) A good number of school certificate holders including products of our Seminaries who are seeking employment as Catechists, are potential University material.
g) The Institution will produce staff that will man our Seminaries, Theological Colleges, and even serve in the State Schools and Civil Service.

/ 3...

- 3 -

Further to the above, the Nigeria of today beset with myriad of national problems centred on indiscipline, it is necessary and desirable to establish a higher educational institution that can and will propound, inculcate and internalize in the products the needed cardinal virtues for national survival, of discipline, honesty, integrity, intelligence, self-reliance, industry and patrotism.

It is therefore believed that the proposed Anglican Institute can and will provide the needed atmosphere for the production of well educated, properly motivated, disciplined, honest, responsible, intelligent, morally upright, industrious, self-reliant and patriotic Nigerian citizens for the future progress and survival of the Nigerian Nation.

PURPOSE:
Therefore the purpose of the Institute shall be the production of Christian Scolars,-scolars who are liberally educated, morally upright, ethically sound, discipline and productive.

The Institute shall therefore uphold the classical tradition of liberal education namely:

        To Seek the Truth
        To Teach the Truth and
        To Preserve the Truth.

The Institute shall also be religious and functional. Religious in the sense that it shall always and at all times uphold the tenets of Anglican Christian Ethics and Morality. And it shall be functional in the sense that it shall always be sensitive to the needs and problems of the time and age. Above all, the Institute shall always recognize and uphold the fact that higher educational institutions exist not only to breed scholars but also to produce useful citizens.

/ 4...

Appendix

- 4 -

Therefore, the Institute shall endeavour to produce knowledgeable, disciplined, and productive citizens for the needed reconstruction of the Nigerian Society.

Specifically, the objectives of the Institute shall include:-

1. To hold forth to all classes and communities whatsoever an encouragement for pursuing a regular, but religious Christian and liberal course of education.

2. To promote research and the advancement of science and learning.

3. To organize, improve and extend education of post-secondary standard.

NAME OF THE INSTITUTE:
After discussing several options, the Committee recommended the name of the proposed Institution to be "Anglican Theological College" (or Institute).

PROPRIETORSHIP:
The Committee felt that the Joint Council that set up this Committee should be the Proprietor because, it felt the need for setting up the institution. It was however seen that the Joint Council is not a registered body. The alternative is for the Proprietor to be the Christian Council which already has other Institutions like the Union Theological College. Ideally the Joint Council should be the Proprietor. The matter is left for the Bishops to decide.

SITE/LOCATION/PREMISES:
At the Joint Council meeting, the Committee was asked to consider the premises of the former Awka College. The Joint Council was informed that the Institution had been returned to the Diocese of Awka.

/ 5...

The Committee held one of its meetings at Awka College, in order to inspect the facilities and assess the suitability of the site. The Committee recommends that in view of the existing infrastructure, the historical role, the position of Awka College, the College be the location of the proposed Institute. Based on the number of existing buildings, the Institute may not require any new buildings for classrooms, hostels etc. for some years.

(See Appendix for facilities existing)

CURRICULUM:

The Committee recommends 3 Units in the first instance - viz:

i) School of Theology: (a) Old Testament Theology
                      (b) New Testament Theology
                      (c) Philosophy of Religion
                      (d) African Traditional Religion
                      (e) Doctrine Dogma etc.
                      (f) Comparative Religion

ii) School of Humanities: (a) English Language & Literature
                      (b) History
                      (c) French Language & Culture
                      (d) Music
                      (e) Fine & Applied Arts
                      (f) African Language and Culture.

iii) School of Social Studies: (a) Sociology and Anthropology
                      (b) Geography
                      (c) Economics
                      (d) Government
                      (e) Business Studies.

Within these three schools it should be possible for the Provost and his staff to arrange a one-year Ordination Course for graduates in other disciplines who wish to enter the ordained Ministry for example a course in Pastoralia.

Appendix

- 6 -

At the appropriate time, other schools like school of Natural and Applied Sciences, and School of Education will be added. Further details will be worked out by the Heads of Divisions and /& Affiliate Universities

AFFILIATION:

Since the Federal Government has prohibited the opening of private Universities, the option open to the Joint Council is to seek affiliation to a recognized University. The Committee considered two alternatives.

(a) Affiliation to a Nigerian University.
(b) Affiliation to an Overseas University.

The Committee recommends affiliation to a local (Nigerian) University preferably University of Nigeria, Nsukka. The Committee also recommends that help be sought from our sister Churches abroad overseas, in particular in Britain.

FUNDING:

The Committee recommends that adequate education of this nature of the Anglican Diocese be critical but it would it be feasible. The Committee believes that with proper organisation, healthy members and the reasonable financial assistance. The following sources of funding were identified:-

(a) Grants by each participating Diocese; to be filled in by annual monetary provision according to agreed formula.

(b) Endowments: A list of names will be compiled. They will be requested to endow chairs. High dignitaries be visited and the need explained to them.

(c) Fees: Students will be required to pay fees.

/7...

(d) **General Appeal:** College Development; Various organizations of the Church, eg. the Laity Councils, the Knights, the Youth, the Women Organizations will be contacted to make financial contributions.

(e) **General Launching By each Diocese:** It is suggested that if the Bishops can spare the time, launching for endowment and donations should be undertaken by the Bishops and Laity starting with Onitsha, the mother Diocese then to Niger Delta and ending with Awka, the youngest Diocese.
The psychology of our people is that the presence of the Bishop draws out money, and this is as it should be.

(f) **Aid from outside:** Possible assistance will be sought from our "Link" Dioceses.

STAFFING:
The recruitment of Tutorial and non-tutorial Staff will be undertaken after the details of the curriculum might have been worked out. An Implementation Committee when set up will ensure that the recruitment reflects the interest of the various participating Dioceses.
If we are to be self-sufficient in the matter of staff, we recommend to the Bishops and their Diocesan Boards to release now any graduate clergymen who wants to return to the University to do a doctorate degree in one or two of the chosen fields. Such a clergyman must have obtained a second class (preferably upper) division certificate.

STUDENT INTAKE: The Committee recommends that the basic entry requirements be as applicable to other higher Institutions. An initial intake of 200 is recommended, rising to an optimum size of 1,000.

/ 8...

Appendix

– 8 –

DATE OF OPENING:
Considering the fact that the basic infrastructure is available in Awka College, the Committee recommends that the target date for reopening be sometime in 1991.

IMPLEMENTATION COMMITTEE:
The Committee recommends that the Joint Council should appoint an Implementation Committee to work towards the take-off of the Institution in 1991, provided we can assemble enough qualified staff and funds before then.

INTERIM GOVERNING COUNCIL:
The Joint Council is also advised to set up an Interim Governing Council to work out broad policies, draw requisite Constitution etc. The Committee recommends that the composition should reflect the interest of the various Dioceses.

APPRECIATION:
The Committee expresses its appreciation to the Joint Council for finding the members suitable for this assignment. The Committee assures the Joint Council that it (Committee) is committed to the successful take-off of this Institution and will be prepared to serve in any capacity called upon to do so.

SIDNEY H.C. ANYAMBU (SIR)
(Secretary)

CHIEF A. E. OZIGA
(Chairman).

APPENDIX 13

"Information Leaflet" Undated handwritten document by R.I. Uzoma, on the work of the Committee on Higher Education of the Joint Council of the Niger Group (Anglican) Dioceses (Undated)

Page 1

Information Leaflet

1. The famous St Paul's College Awka, where most of the older clergy and schoolmasters of the Anglican Dioceses East of the Niger were trained, was taken over by the Government, like other educational institutions, after the civil war. It was converted into a College of Education for training teachers for the N.C.E examination. This institution, with its imposing Chapel, which every member of the Anglican Communion regards as the "Spiritual Power House" of the Niger group of Dioceses was returned to the Diocese of Awka this year and the Diocese has magnanimously placed it at the disposal of the Niger group of Dioceses.

2. The Joint Council of the Niger group of Dioceses (7 in number) has decided that, considering the important place Awka College occupies in our hearts and in the growth of the Church in this part of the country, and also considering the existing infrastructure the campus should be converted into a Degree-awarding Theological Institute which will be affiliated to one of our Universities. Nothing less than this will satisfy the aspiration of our people. The existence of such a degree-awarding Institute will be without prejudice to the existence of Trinity, Umuahia.

3. It should be pointed out that in the Western part of the country the protestant dioceses have

P.T.O

Emmanuel College Ibadan as a degree-awarding College affiliated to Ibadan University. In the North there is one affiliated to Ahmadu ~~College~~ University, Zaria. Our Roman Catholic brothers have the Bigard Seminary in Enugu and one in Ikot-Ekpene affiliated to Rome and ~~also~~ have one for the whole of West Africa in Patharcourt and a new one in Onitsha.

(4) The decision of the Joint Council on the conversion of Awka College into a ~~~~ degree-awarding Institute is a venture of hope. We have absolute hope that the decision ~~at~~ is in accordance with the wish and aspirations of our people. The Institute when fully operational will ~~offer a school of~~ Theology, (2) Humanities and ~~(c)~~ Social studies. ~~It~~ will also offer a shorter course for lawyers, engineers, doctors accountants and other professionals who want to get ordained into the Holy Ministry

(5) In order to realise the dream of creating this degree-awarding institute our Church members, we hope, will be prepared to donate generously, since Government grant will not be available. The Implementation Committee will go round the Diocese with the Bishops or their representatives, asking for Donations and Endowments, starting from the Niger and the Niger Delta dioceses, and ending in ~~Awka Diocese~~ the youngest Diocese, Awka.

(6) We shall be asking for (a) Donations:
All church members male and female are expected to give even their widow's mite for this grand proposal and every old student of our church institutions and his children will be expected to do something to promote the work of the Church by planning for the lecture.

(b) Endowments: We shall also ask for endowment of Chairs of professors/lecturers in the proposed Institute. The endowment should be a donation of not less than ₦250,000.00 and the aim is that the interest on the amount every year will at least cover the annual expenditure of the chair endowed. We hope that we shall get at least 5 men or women of "timber and calibre" in each diocese to endow chairs. Two or more people can endow one chair. They may recommend to the authorities the name they wish to give to the chair eg "Bishop X Chair of New Testament" or "Archdeacon X Chair of English" or "Chief X Chair of African Traditional Religion" "Sir X chair of Economics or Doctrine" The donor may ask for the chair to be named after himself. All donations and endowments will be properly documented and placed in the library or Archives of the Institute. The object of the endowments is to reduce the financial burden which the running of the Institute will impose on the Dioceses if they are to be asked to

PTO

Appendix

~~asked~~ to pay very heavy ~~subuse~~ subvention or grant annually to the Institute.

The Committee will go round and will be prepared to answer questions.

R.I. Uzoma
Chairman

APPENDIX 14

The New Okigwe/Orlu Diocese by Chief R.I. Uzoma, OFR. 20/11/84, prepared on the inauguration of the new Diocese

THE NEW OKIGWE/ORLU (ANGLICAN) DIOCESE

BY CHIEF R.I. UZOMA, O.F.R.

1. HISTORICAL BACKGROUND

Christianity was introduced into the present Okigwe and Orlu Archdeaconries from two directions in the first decade of this century. From Onitsha evangelists and teachers of the Church Missionary Society trekked into the Orlu section and established small churches and schools here and there. No serious organised and co-ordinated evangelistic work was done till the late Rev. J.E. Ibeneme, having moved from Ndizuogu, settled down and established his headquarters at Nkwerre in 1921 as the first pastor and Superintendent of what was then known politically as Okigwe Division and ecclesiastically as Okigwe District. His counterpart for the Owerri District was the Rev. (later Bishop) A.C. Onyeabo. Orlu political Division was carved out of Okigwe Division in April 1947. In 1967 Orlu Division was constituted into a Province made up of Nkwerre and Mgbidi Divisions, and after the civil war the Province was split into four Local Government Areas Nkwerre/Isu, Orlu, Ideato and Oru. As far as the Anglican Church is concerned the part of the then Okigwe Division lying to the north of the Imo River was not touched, as, by agreement between the early missionaries, this northern section of Okigwe (i.e. Isuikwuato-Okigwe Local Govt. Area) was, in those days left for the Methodist Missionary Society. For this reason, Okigwe town, after which the area is named had no Anglican Church till 1977.

While the Church Missionary Society workers under the Rev. J.E. Ibeneme at Nkwerre, with curates at Ndizuogu and Ezeoke, were pushing into the present Mbano and Etiti areas of Okigwe Division establishing churches and schools, the Niger Delta pastorate (N.D.P.) Mission about the same time had crossed the Imo River from the Eastern bank along Umuahia. N.D.P. Churches and schools were established side by side with the C.M.S. in the area now known as Mbano and Etiti, within the then Okigwe District under the Rev. J.E. Ibeneme and also in the present Mbaise area of the then Owerri District under the Rev. A.C. Onyeabo.

In March 1931 the Niger Mission (C.M.S.) and the Niger Delta pastorate Mission (N.D.P.) were merged to form the Diocese on the Niger, the N.D.P. area from Umuahia down to Brass being constituted into the Delta Archdeaconry of the Diocese.

../2.

Appendix

- 2 -

In 1952 the Delta Archdeaconry was carved out of the Niger Diocese and constituted into the Niger Delta Diocese. With the creation of the Niger Delta Diocese, the area of the Owerri Province within the Niger Diocese (i.e. Owerri, Okigwe and Orlu zones) was constituted into the Owerri Archdeaconry of the Niger Diocese.

This Archdeaconry developed so rapidly that in 1959 (i.e. seven years after the creation of the Delta Diocese) it became a separate Diocese and was divided into two Archdeaconries:-

(a) Owerri with the headquarters at Owerri and
(b) Okigwe/Orlu with headquarters at Nkwerre.

2. Extent

The Owerri Diocese by 1983 was one of the largest numerically (not spatially) in the church of Nigeria (Anglican Communion). It had about 57 parishes 29 of which are in the new Okigwe/Orlu Diocese. In terms of the senatorial zones of the era of party politics the new diocese embraces the whole of the Okigwe senatorial zone and the whole of the Orlu senatorial zone except the Oguta-Egbema-Ohaji Local Government Area. At present the diocese is made up of two large archdeaconries namely: Okigwe, with headquarters at Ezeoke-Nsu in Mbano Local Govt. Area, and Orlu, with headquarters at Nkwerre in Nkwerre/Isu Local Govt. Area. By some accident of history the Anglican Communion for many years had only one church in Orlu Urban and none in Okigwe Urban before 1977. Since then, Okigwe has become the headquarters of a new virile parish which includes not only churches on the southern side of the Imo River but also churches in Okigwe Urban, Isuochi and Isuikwuato on the northern side of the Imo river.

3. Motivating Force

As far back as 1971 at the Owerri Diocesan Synod held at Obizi, Mbaise we had "prophesied" that, with the improvement in the economy of the country, and the consequent recovery of the churches from the ravages of the civil war the archdeaconries of Owerri Diocese would develop into full-fledged autonomous dioceses. It was not, however, till 1977, during the funeral of the late Dr. Aaron Ogbonna in the same Obizi that the stark reality of the enormity of numbers stared us in the face. The crowd from the Owerri Diocese was so great that both the church building and compound could not take them - men and women,

../3.

big and small, rich and poor, young and old, school children e.t.c. Two of us, Eze J. Ovuike of Umuihi in Etiti Local Govt. Area and I, after a short discussion decided to call a meeting in my house to feel the pulse of the Okigwe/Orlu christians as to the desirability to ask for a separate Okigwe/Orlu diocese. The proposal having been unanimously supported by leading delegates and Chiefs, we formed the Okigwe/Orlu Christian Association whose main objective is to mobilise human and material resources in the two Archdeaconries for the purpose of realising our dream of a new diocese. The first approach was made to the Bishop of Owerri on 30th September, 1977 to discuss the matter.

The motivating force for the creation of the new Okigwe/Orlu Diocese out of Owerri Diocese was, therefore two-fold:

(a) the need to seize time by the fore-lock in respect of what appeared to us to be a call to supplement and strengthen the work of evangelisation in that part of Okigwe zone lying to the north of the Imo River.

(b) the need to have smaller dioceses, in place of a single large one, so as to make for greater ease of administration, greater supervision and to bring the centre nearer to the grass-root.

It is true that the more administrative units you create the higher the overhead administrative costs. But it is also true that the closer the supervision, in this case, the more intensive the teaching. The resultant greater spiritual growth will manifest itself in greater sacrifice on the part of the people and a more readiness to give freely what one has for God's work. In the end, the extra over-head costs are more than compensated for and better results and greater satisfaction and greater sense of belonging are achieved.

4. Conclusion

It is my sincere hope that more dioceses will be created out of our dioceses in the Eastern part of Nigeria provided, of-course, that a careful study of visbility is made in each case, as we did in the case of the new Okigwe/Orlu diocese. When dioceses or any other administrative units are created without any consideration for viability then the exercise generates balkanisation. Viability, of-course, is determined by statistics which is given special consideration in the boards and synods of Anglican dioceses.

26/11/84

APPENDIX 15

Memorandum Submitted by the Nkwerre Community to the Imo State Local Government, Agada Panel Visiting Nkwerre on July 20th 1976, prepared by Chief R.I. Uzoma OFR, OBE

MEMORANDUM SUBMITTED BY THE
NKWERRE COMMUNITY TO THE IMO

STATE LOCAL GOVERNMENT AGADA
PANEL VISITING NKWERRE

ON 20TH JULY, 1976

This memorandum was prepared and written by Chief R. I. Uzoma, O.F.R; O.B.E., No part of it shall be quoted or reproduced without the written consent of Chief R.I. Uzoma or the Nkwerre Aborigines Union.

MEMORANDUM SUBMITTED BY THE NKWERRE
COMMUNITY TO THE IMO STATE LOCAL
GOVERNMENT AGADA PANEL VISITING
NKWERRE ON 20TH JULY, 1976.

Gentlemen,

We the undersigned on behalf of ourselves and the entire people of Nkwerre in Nkwerre in Nkwerre Division of Imo State wish to congratulate you on your appointment to the State Local Government Panel and pray that God may guide you and give you the wisdom to sift truth from falsehood so that your recommendations may lead to decisions that will bring lasting peace to our State by upholding what is just and fair and by silencing agitators and pseudo-politicians who, looking forward to 1979, now deliberately trouble the calm waters in various Divisions in order to fish therein.

We have read the terms of reference given to your panel by the State Government and in this memorandum we wish to deal mainly with the first of them, namely – the Name of the Division or Local Government Authority and we rest our case on:-

(a) History: (b) Present Performance:

After these two sections we shall summarise under section (c) General. When you will have gone through the memorandum, you will have seen the argument of the agitators for a change (if they have any) demolished and their inconsistency and irrationality laid bare.

SECTION A.   HISTORICAL:

1. Long before the advent of the British the Nkwerre people had been the link between the other communities of the division and indeed of Owerri Province and the rest of the outside world particularly in matters of trade and industry. They were reputed as skilled blacksmiths and traders and as such settled in villages and hamlets far away from their homes. The people from the neighbouring villages imitated the Nkwerre people and went out with them and claimed everywhere they went that they were Nkwerre people. This fact is borne out by the Intelligence Report of 1936 prepared by Mr. G.I. Jones A.D.O., Orlu which reads inter alia:-

"25. In the past the wealth and reputation of the Nkwerre as blacksmiths and traders was so great that other Isu traders from the district usually called themselves Nkwerre and the name Nkwerre is still the only Orlu village area - name universally known throughout the Province. 'However wealthy an Isu may be he is still the slave of the Nkwerre' is a local Proverb which is still current".

2. The intrepid spirit of adventure, the wealth and military strength of the Nkwerre people as a result of their being traders and makers of guns (Nkwerre Ogia-egbe) certainly earned them the undisputed position of leadership which the present generation has kept up through investment in higher education, trade, and industry and through avoiding communal strife and litigation.

3. To prove further that the name "Nkwerre" is generic - applicable to communities within a radius of about 20 miles let us remind you that the Nkwerre traders and money-lenders came under fire by the women during the Aba Women's riot of 1929 and Capt. Cook the A.D.O. then at Orlu submitted a report on the term "Nkwerre people" to the Commission of Enquiry that looked into the riot. On page 324 of the Report paragraph 7 Capt. Cook explains as follows:-

"7. It is clear, therefore, that the term 'Nkwerri people' cannot be exclusively and correctly applied to the inhabitants of Nkwerre town proper, for such a term in the mind of the woman NWAIYURUWA an inhabitant of Oloko in Bende division and possibly in the minds of other persons, pictures inhabitants of NKWERRI, inhabitants of ISHIGWENESI, inhabitants of ISU-NJABA, inhabitants of INYISHI and AMAIMO (in Owerri Division) in short inhabitants of all towns of the Isu sub-tribe. The term "Nkwerre" people" (Umunkwerri) is applied loosely by the inhabitants of Bende and Aba divisions to all members of the

Isu sub-tribe and cannot truly be said to apply exclusively to the inhabitants of Nkwerri town proper. The true term to designate inhabitants of Nkwerri town proper is "UMUNKWERRI KPONKWEM".

4. The famous King Jaja of Opobo has always been referred to as "Jaja nwa Nkwerre" even though his ancestral home is in Amaigbo and his descendants will tell you that they are of Nkwerre origin.

5. A few weeks ago when Dr. Anozie, the Commissioner came to Nkwerre division with his Permanent Secretary to investigate the agitation, the Eshi of Nkwerre asked one of the spokesmen of the agitators Mr. Odunze of Amucha whether it was not true that he was an enrolled and financial member of the Nkwerre Family Meeting a few years ago while he was resident in Portharcourt. He did not deny this.

6. Nkwerre Division was created in 1966 by Edict, along with other Divisions like Nnewi, Ihiala, Oguta, Arochukwu, Ohafia etc, by the then legal Government of Eastern Nigeria. It was one of the two Divisions carved out of Orlu Province; and remained so throughout the war and, with some minor adjustments, throughout the regimes of Mr. Asika, Colonel Ochefu and Colonel Kpera - a period of ten years now. It was the intention of the Ojukwu administration to try and encourage villages that and clusters of population to develop into urban centres so that our people might have more facilities for investment and so that exodus from the then Eastern Region might be reduced to a minimum and the chances of mass massacre of Ibos outside the Region might also be minimised.

7. With the abolition of the Provincial System, incorporating the then Orlu Province, by the Asika Regime, Orlu lost its place as a Provincial or Divisional unit. The Chiefs and people of Nkwerre Division, incorporating Orlu, in a welcome address to Ex-Administrator Asika on his visit in 1970, pleaded for an amendment of the Edict to allow Orlu and its environ to be up-graded to an Urban Divisional Status, whilst the rest of of the Division retained its name, with its headquarters still

..../4

Appendix

at Nkwerre. This address (copy of which is attached) was voluntarily subscribed to by Chiefs J. A. Nwosu of Amaigbo, C. C. Osuala of Isu-Njaba, Nnadi Duru of Isiekenesi, P. I. Acholonu of Orlu, S.N. Okoli of Akokwa, A. A. Duru of Okwudor, E. O. Imo of Ndizuogu and the Eshi of Nkwerre amongst others - for themselves and on behalf of their people. No one then called for the abrogation of the name Nkwerre, for the Division, nor for any other substitute fancy name. This happened at a time when political demagogy had not been introduced into the arena. This address was tendered before the Commissioner Dr. Anozie and was admitted by Chief Nwosu of Amaigbo who with chiefs A. Duru of Okwudor and C.C. Osuala of Isu-Njaba have now been driven by fear of pseudo-politicians to agitate against a decision they took in 1970 in the interest of peace and unity. Such is the character of some so-called chiefs and such their fate!

8. Soon, however, professional agitators reared their heads, and demanded drastic changes in the status quo, and the substitution of Isu, for Nkwerre, as the name of the Division. The Asika Government set up a high-powered Commission of Enquiry comprising two former Permanent Secretaries - Messrs Anyaegbunam and Ogbuah, in 1971. The Commission's recommendation, approved by the Government, was largely in accord with the earlier immediate post-war unanimous proposal by the Chiefs that Orlu be given Divisional status, along with Nkwerre. The lame demand for a change of the name of Nkwerre Division was not entertained. Instead the former Orlu Province was reconstituted into Nkwerre, Orlu and Oru Divisions.

9. Those who want Isu to be substituted for Nkwerre as the name of the Division claim that Isu was earlier the name of the Native Authority establishment for the area. The fact is that in 1936, the then Colonial administration, arbitrarily and without consultation, created an Isu Council comprising 41 villages in the then Orlu District of Okigwe Division.

Several Chiefs in the area were imprisoned for refusing to accept "Isu" tax receipt for their people. Orlu town itself was part of this imposed "Isu" Council but, when the area was raised to full Divisional status, independent of Okigwe, it was given the name "ORLU" Division. In any case, the so-called Isu Council soon disintegrated because of inherent contradictions and opposition to it. First the 13 Nwabosi towns - many of whom are close neighbours of, and sharing a common ancestry with Nkwerre - broke away in protest and joined the Orlu North-East County Council which is now part of Orlu Division from where some now seek to rejoin their kith and kin in Nkwerre, following the demise of the unacceptable Isu nomenclature. Nine others, including Orlu town, of the remaining 28 towns in the ill-fated Isu set-up were recently carved out by the Anyaegbunam Commission to join with Nwabosi towns in the resuscitated Orlu division whilst only 19 towns remain in Nkwerre Division. Isu Council thus ceased to exist when its components regrouped themselves under Nkwerre, Orlu, and Nwabosi. It is interesting to note that of the two communities still going by the "Isu" name, the senior section of one of them Umuozu is challenging the pretensions of the other Isu towns, and is seeking its own identity with facts and figures as a separate Community Council under Nkwerre Division, even renouncing the name "Isu".

10. Evidence was led unchallenged in 1956 during the Jones Commission of Enquiry into the status of Chiefs to the fact that the following chiefs in the old Orlu Division were appointed and received their cap and staff of office on the recommendation of late Chief Anyiam of Nkwerre:

    (i) Ndiribe Okwarojiaku of Isu-Njaba.
    (ii) Nwosu Ugoho of Amaigbo (father of present chief)
    (iii) Orisakwe Ahanonu of Owerri-Nkwoji
    (iv) Ihenacho Ogbunigbara of Amucha.
    (v) Ezeihekaibeya of Umuma-Isiaku.
    (vi) Ezeanyika of Urualla.
    (vii) Onuoha of Eziama.

Appendix

  (viii) Mgbemena of Umudi
  (ix) Ndoo of Eziachi
  (x) Obiareri of Orsu-Ihiteukwa.
  (xi) Exerioha of Ihite-Owerri
  (xii) Okem of Amokpara.
  (xiii) Akano of Isu (father of present chief)
  (xiv) Duru Ojinnaka of Orlu (father of Chief P.Acholonu)

11. Nkwerre people on the death of Chief Anyizm installed the present incumbent, Chief J. O. Ugochuku II the Eshi of Nkwerre on July 5 1958 and he has ruled since then without any hitch or complaint.

SECTION B. PRESENT PERFORMANCE

1. Every Permanent Secretary in Enugu in 1970 at the end of the Civil War will tell you that most of the files and equipment used to re-open offices were those saved by the Eshi and people of Nkwerre – who took steps to prevent looting. Equipment and drugs saved by Nkwerre people were handed over to Amaigbo hospital (which was looted by the Amaigbo people. Also equipment and drugs were handed over to Queen Elizabeth hospital Umuahia and Borromeo hospital, Onitsha. On the other hand, at Isu-Njaba Primary School, the home school of Chief agitator Mr. Ikemezie, the vehicles and stores of the Owerri Ministry of Works housed there were looted completely and at Isu Grammar School where Mr. Ikemezie was Principal before and after the war, and the home town of Barrister Ahaneku, another agitator, all the vehicles and stores of the Army Headquarters were completely looted.

   Moreover, since after the war the iron pipe-line, laid during the war to lead water from Eziama reservoir through Isu-Njaba to Amandugba has long been cut and stolen and nobody, not even Mr. Ikemezie, who was a Councillor, reported to the authorities.

2. The Nkwerre Community was responsible for the pipe-borne water supply which most of the towns in the division now enjoy. Official receipts for the lump sum of £3,000 (three thousand pounds) deposited by Nkwerre community alone in 1963/64 which forced the hands of Government were tendered before the Anyaegbunam Commission and were not challenged.

..../7

The Nkwerre people own all the land offered free to Government for the Divisional Headquarters. You are aware of the consequence of the injustice of siting a station on Mr. A's land and calling the station B, for example Umuahia to which the name Ibeku (the owners of the land) was later appended to mitigate the injustice of the past.

3. Since the end of the war the Nkwerre people have supplied the following needs free of charge:-

   i. Furniture for the D.O's house and Magistrate Courts at Orlu and later at Nkwerre.
   ii. Accommodation for the Police Station at Nkwerre.
   iii. Accommodation for the Mobile Police to cover Nkwerre, Orlu, Oru and Mbano divisions.
   iv. Accommodation for Motor Licensing Office at Nkwerre.
   v. Accommodation for the Magistrate Court at Nkwerre.
   vi. Accommodation for the Divisional School Management Board.
   vii. Accommodation for the Ministry of Education at Nkwerre.
   viii. Accommodation for the Ministry of Agriculture including Veterinary Services.
   ix. Accommodation for the Ministry of Information.
   x. Accommodation for Sports Commission.

4. In addition to the usual development projects like roads, markets undertaken by Nkwerre, Abba, Owerri-Nkwoji, Atta, Umuaka, Amokpara Umudi, Amandugba and other serious minded towns, the Nkwerre Community is building a N200,000.00 Court Complex, the foundation of which was laid by Justice Balonwu.

5. The Eshi of Nkwerre and a few gentlemen represented the division in the Chief Onukogu Committee for the creation of the Imo State. The financial contribution expected from the division for the work of the committee was paid by Nkwerre town alone for the division.

Comparisons are odious but we are sorry to say that we are driven by circumstances to make them. In the few towns the agitators have their stronghold eg. Amaigbo, Isu-njaba and Isu Ofe-iyi there is no development project worth the

..../8

Appendix

name since 1970 except that in Isu Ofe-iyi there are about <u>five</u> cases now in the Magistrate and High Courts, in which Chief agitator, Barrister Ahaneku, and his people are involved. That is his idea of "Development". The agitators continue to misdirect development efforts and funds in their areas in order to foster their own selfish interests. Even your appointment and visit is used as an excuse for imposing a levy on their supporters for "fighting" Nkwerre and the Government.

SECTION C. GENERAL

1. Since the agitation for a change of the Divisional name "Nkwerre" is borne out of malice, spite, and opportunism, the protagonists of change will peddle anything as a neutral name just to spite Nkwerre. They have now dropped their demand for "Isu", and have suggested all types of names to confuse the unwary. In one breath, they propose the name of an Amaigbo dried-up stream "Nwangele"; or the Isu ancestral god "Njaba"; or "Mgbabo-ano" (meaning a crossing of four roads) and even "Nwicheku" (the name of a tree in Nkwerre); the last two being landmarks on Nkwerre soil. Such is their mentality and inconsistency that they will rather go by a juju name, or any other ludicrous name thus making the whole Division a laughing stock. Though hundred percent of the land occupied by the divisional headquarters is owned by Nkwerre who are willing to give more land if needed, these confusionists try to incite our neighbours to claim the land, but have been rebuffed. That these confused people will abhor the name "Nkwerre" but be enamoured of the name "Nwicheku" or "Mgbabo-ano" which are land-marks in Nkwerre shows their irrationality.

2. These confused agitators told the Commissioner, Dr. Anozie, that they wanted a neutral name (that is, a name that is not the name of a town) and yet towards the end of the Commissioner's investigation, they said that if they did not get their request they would like to be in Orlu division and "Orlu" is the name of a town much smaller than Nkwerre <u>both</u> quantitatively and qualitatively.

..../9

This one statement alone shows their inconsistency, and the fact that the agitation is motivated purely by jealousy and malice. It also shows that these people want, through the back-door, to re-open a case already investigated by the Anyaegbulam Commission and on which Government had taken a decision - namely the case as to whether "Nkwerre" or "Orlu".

3. We maintain that the retention of Nkwerre as the name of the division is the fairest thing to do and a decision most conducive to stable administration. One can forsee what a chain reaction of agitations and events in places like Oguta that will follow any change in the name of a division that has been in existence for over ten years. We affirm the equality of all communities in the division and their inalienable right to equal treatment by all arms of Government and the respect for each other's culture and history which has helped the various communities to work harmoniously together for years. We have talked of our own history and achievements in self defence and not as an excuse, for claiming any special privileges or the rights of others. Nor shall we feel happy if others attempt to take away what is due to us. We are convinced that a <u>firm</u> confirmation of Nkwerre from Government will stop the agitation which erupts with every change of Government.

There is no doubt that you will receive many memoranda from Nkwerre and Orlu divisions. We wish to emphasise that those communities - in the division who do not want the name Nkwerre should be allowed to join a division of their choice and, as we believe some of our kith and kin now in Nwabosi area of Orlu division may wish to rejoin us, we hope you will give any requests from them a favourable consideration.

4. Finally, we end by repeating that our case rests on <u>history</u> and on our <u>present performance</u>; and that the case of the agitators fails woefully because it is based <u>on jealousy</u> and <u>malice</u> and is continually nursed by <u>illegal collection</u> of funds from innocent village folks. Moreover, the case is ruined by <u>irrationality</u>, <u>illogicality</u> and <u>inconsistency</u>.

We remain,

Your compatriots,
for and on behalf of Nkwerre Community,
(Sgd).
S. N. Ohanka,
Ag. President-General
Nkwerre Aborigines Union.

(Sgd.)
J. O. Ugochuku II
Eshi of Nkwerre.

Date 14th July, 1976.

Appendix

A WELCOME ADDRESS PRESENTED BY THE CHIEF'S AND PEOPLE OF NKWERRE DIVISION TO HIS EXCELLENCY MR. UKPABI ASIKA, THE ADMINISTRATOR OF THE EAST CENTRAL STATE OF NIGERIA ON THE OCCASION OF HIS FIRST OFFICIAL VISIT TO NKWERRE DIV.

Your Excellency,

We the Chiefs and people of Nkwerre Division wish to express our profound gratitude to your Excellency for finding time, amidst your arduous and onerous duties, to visit us here today. You are welcome.

2. We have been extremely delighted by your great concern for the sufferings of the ordinary man in the East Central State which is implicit in the tremendous efforts made and urgent steps taken by you, soon after the end of the civil war, to send food through the Rehabilitation Commission to the various Divisions in the East Central State. The food has in varying quantities continued to come to us. We cannot help mentioning, in this connection, that we are not in any way surprised by the urgency with which you addressed yourself to this task; for a study of your speeches and utterances during the civil war shows to what extent and in what depth you were conversant with the problems of the East Central State. For what you have so far done we are deeply grateful and happy. We are happier when we reflect that your performances and magnanimity on the morrow of Nigeria's victory over chaos and disintegration have given you out as the one man to repair the enormous physical and spiritual damage caused by the war. It will stand to your credit and that of the Federal Government that the end of the war had not been identified with mass destruction of lives and property. This, you will recall Sir, formed the most poignant propaganda weapon of the former rebel Government against the Federal Government. That you and the Federal Government have admirably lived up to your promises in this regard will for ever ingratiate you with the people of this State-nay the country and the thinking population of the world.

3. Another example of the Government's efforts to rehabilitate the people of this State is the current payment of £20 to each depositor of the old Nigerian and Biafran currency notes. While appreciating the fine gesture of Government about this matter we would wish to place on record, Your Excellency, that it was not possible for all our people to deposit the old currency notes. The slow process of the machinery for making the deposits

..../2

made it impossible for close on three quarters of our people to deposit their money. The result is that these people are unable to receive the £20. It is our hope that Government would examine this question to see what could be done to the people who were unable, through no fault of theirs, to deposit their old notes.

4. The people of this Division are a commercial people- resourceful, enterprising and hardworking. As it is well known, the baneful destruction of their economic life during the civil war rendered a hitherto prosperous people very poor. As part of your post-war reconstruction programme we would earnestly pray Your Excellency to initiate, through the Rehabilitation Commission, a loan scheme whereby money could be made available to our people to re-activate their business. We would also request in addition that your Excellency take steps to see to the defreezing of our Bank assets including our enormous assets in the Rivers State for purposes of realising Bank credits as this will go a long way in restoring our business into its pre-war level.

5. In addition to the existing Police post in Nkwerre Division we would request that three more Police posts be established at Isu, Umuaka and Arondizuogu in view of the great distance of existing Police posts from these areas.

6. We are encouraged and cheered by the cordial relationship existing between the Army, the Police and the Administration on the one hand and the people of this Division on the other. These arms of Government in this Division have always approached our problems with sysmpathy and understanding. It is our view that the prevailing peaceful atmosphere augurs well for the post-war development and reconstruction programme.

7. Nkwerre Division was created along with others in 1966. Nkwerre had since then been the headquarters of the Division. In view of recent Government decision that Orlu should be the Administrative Headquarters of Nkwerre Division, it is the humble prayer of the people of this Division that your Government finds money to develop and upgrade Orlu to an Urban status in the earliest possible time in order that Nkwerre, which is one

..../3

Appendix

of the most developed towns in the Division, could resume the position of being the Administrative Headquarters of Nkwerre Division.

8. Finally Sir, we would wish to request that in the post-war reconstruction programme this Division be remembered regarding the establishment of more hospitals. The only major hospital in the Division – the St. Mary's Joint Hospital, Amaigbo, was looted following the confusion at the end of the civil war. All the hospital equipment was removed or destroyed. We ask that Government comes to the aid of this hospital in assisting to re-equip it to reach its pre-war position.

9. Your Excellency, it requires a man of courage to face the enormous post-war reconstruction programme with which your Government will grapple. We pray that God gives you the strenth to discharge your responsibilities to this State and the nation.

Sir, as a mark of our appreciation of this your august visit we humbly present this token gift. We wish you a happy stay in this Division.

We are,
Your Excellency
for and on behalf of the Chiefs & the
People of Nkwerre Division

1. (Sgd) Chief P.I. Acholonu M.B.E.
   The Igwe of Orlu.

2. (Sgd) Chief A.A. Duru
   The Eze Duru Obi of Okwudor.

3. (Sgd) Chief J.A. Nwosu M.B.S.
   The Igbo of Amaigbo

4. (Sgd) Chief R. Ojinaka
   The Obi of Mbano Umuaka.

5. (Sgd) Chief C. C. Osuala
   The Okwara Eze Obi of
   Isu Njaba.

6. (Sgd) Chief Nnadi Duru
   The Eze Oha II of Umuezala,
   Isiekenesi.

7. (Sgd) Ven. Archdeacon S.N. Okoli
   The Okwara of Akokwa

8. (Sgd) Chief E.O. Imo II
   The Eze of Ndizuogu

(sgd.) Chief J.O. Ugochukwu
The Eshi of Nkwerre.

APPENDIX 16

Memorandum Submitted to the Anyaegbunam Local Government, Re-organisation Committee by the Nkwerre Community, Nkwerre Division, 21/7/71, prepared by Chief R.I. Uzoma OFR, OBE

Gentlemen,

We wish to start off by welcoming you to Nkwerre Division and expressing our implicit confidence in the composition of the Committee. We believe that your impartiality and sense of justice will lead to recommendations that will bring peace and harmony to the various towns of this large Division.

We wish also to express through you, our loyalty to and confidence in His Excellency, the Administrator of East Central State, Mr. Ukpabi Asika and his administration.

In making our submissions, we are sticking to your terms of reference and assume that the "Divisional Administration Edict" referred to by the Senior Divisional Officer in his Public Notice NWD/1/12 of 6th July, 1971 has not been published and is in fact not an Edict yet. It is at present, we imagine in the "bill" stage not yet promulgated and, therefore, the Provincial Administration Edict No.33 of 8th December, 1966 has not been abrogated.

This 1966 Edict of the legitimate Government of the former Eastern Region specifically created Nkwerre division <u>with headquarters at Nkwerre.</u> From 1966 up to a few weeks ago the <u>D.O. lived at Nkwerre and had his office at Nkwerre.</u> The Public Notice quoted above is, in our opinion, misleading in section (b) of its first paragraph when it talks of "the need to maintain the status quo, namely to retain Nkwerre Division with the Administrative headquarters at Orlu". Our contention is that <u>the status quo has been Nkwerre Division with the headquarters</u> at Nkwerre; and this is what is in the 1966 Edict.

1. The creation of the divisions by the legitimate Military Governor of the then Eastern Region was not made in a hurry. It was made after an exhaustive enquiry by top Administrative Officers led by Mr. Leach who, as an expatriate, would be impartial and neutral. Various towns and communities were given an opportunity, even after the enquiry, to make representations to Enugu and it was after careful consideration of the report of the Leach Committee and the representations made by communities that the divisions were finally created. We attach herewith as <u>appendix A</u> a copy of a letter dated 31st Jan. 1967 from Mr. J. A. Nwachuku, then acting Divisional Officer for both Nkwerre and Mgbidi Division, accepting buildings offered by the Nkwerre community for the temporary use of the Divisional office and staff.

..../2

Appendix

No other town could have met such a heavy demand for suitable accomodation, not even Orlu town plus the Government station.

It is significant to emphasize that Mr. R. Odinkemelu who is now head of the Administration Division of the Chief Secretary's office was a member of the Leach Committee which unanimously recommended the creation of Nkwerre Division with headquarters at Nkwerre after being satisfied with the spacious accomodation provided and the large acreage of suitable land offered by Nkwerre community. The same Administration Division of the Chief Secretary's Office under Mr. R. Odinkemelu has moved the headquarters from Nkwerre to Orlu. Mr. Odinkemelu comes from Mgbidi our neighbouring division!

2. When His Excellency, Mr. Ukpabi Asika, paid an official visit to this division last year the chiefs and representatives of the division presented him with a welcome address in which they said inter alia: "Nkwerre division was created along with others in 1966. Nkwerre had since been the headquarters of the Division. In view of recent Government decision that Orlu should be the Administrative headquarters of Nkwerre division, it is the humble prayer of the people of this Division that your Government finds money to develop and upgrade Orlu to an Urban status in the earliest possible time in order that Nkwerre, which is one of the most developed towns in the division, could resume the position of being the Administrative Headquarters of Nkwerre Division". We attach a copy of this welcome address as appendix B.

We request you to attach special importance to the views expressed in this welcome address because they were made in an atmosphere free from political campaigning, lobbying, blackmail and undue influence, factors which made the days of political parties notorious and which have reared their heads since the Divisional Officer's public notice about your visit went out to the towns in this division. We would humbly ask you to examine the tone of the request in the welcome address and note the innuendo that had the government consulted the people before moving the headquarters to Orlu they would have advised against it. This welcome address was signed, among others, by Chief J. Ugochuku of Nkwerre, Chief E. O. Imo of Ndizuogu, and Chief P. Acholonu of Orlu. Copies of this welcome address were cyclostyled and sent to all towns in this division and since it was presented, no town has dissociated itself from any paragraph or the whole of it. We therefore ask you to regard any views expressed by any town now, contary to those in the welcome address, as "influenced".

..../3

3. Our case for an Nkwerre division with headquarters at Nkwerre hangs on a third peg-namely the <u>historical importance of Nkwerre town</u>. To substantiate this we enclose herewith as <u>Appendix C</u> the Memorandum we submitted in 1956 to the Jones Commission enquiring into the status of chiefs and ask you to note the quotations from Intelligence reports and archives which we have marked in the memorandum.

4. Our final point is the fact that, in relation to the division as a whole, Nkwerre is the most centrally situated town. If the Provincial system of Administration were still in existence nobody would argue against Orlu station being suitable for the administration of the Province i.e the present Nkwerre and Mgbidi division.

But with the abolition of the provinces by Government (and not by Nkwerre people) Orlu has become most unsuitable for administering Nkwerre division a division which is the second largest in the State and the largest in school population.

We humbly request you to ask the S.D.O. and a neutral chief like Chief Ben Obi, of Mgbidi division, who was the chairman of the former Orlu County Council, to take you round the Orlu Government Station and show you the boundary between Nkwerre divisional land and Mgbidi divisional land and you will be shocked to know that this huge division is being administered from Mgbidi land because the Divisional office, the Stadium, E.N.D.C. premises, the Police barracks, the Treasury, the Post Office even the huge storeyed building used by the Magistrate Court and the A.C.B., are all on Amaifeke land in Mgbidi division. How would people in the East Central State feel if their headquarters were to be in Asaba in the Mid-West State? Any offence committed in Nkwerre Divisional Office must go to Mgbidi Magisterial Court if Orlu were to be the headquarters.

The fact is that Orlu town is on the periphery of Nkwerre division. Over 75 per cent of the Government station is on Mgbidi land outside the division. Of the rest, Umuna village in Nkwerre division owns more than two thirds. The station itself is cramped, having no room for expansion and there is bound to be litigation and agitation if one division continues to be administered from the land belonging to another division.

With regard to the position of Nkwerre town, the centrality of its position comes into sharp focus if you examine this map which we attach as <u>Appendix D.</u>

..../4

Appendix

Nkwerre is roughly 12 miles from Ndizuogu on the northern border, and 12 miles from Umuaka - Amazano on the southern border. It is six miles from Orlu station on the western border and six miles from Isu and Agbajah on the eastern border. It is the focal point of the division on which all roads converge.

We wish to warn the committee against the red-herring of a comparison with Owerri division. The geographical and sociological factors are not the same. Owerri town is surrounded entirely by villages of the Oratta clan and is their focal point. It is not like Orlu station which is owned by villages in two distinct divisions, belonging to two distinct clans, speaking different dialects having different customs and almost encircled by Amaifeke in Mgbidi Division.

We thank the committee for the patience they have exercised in reading through our memorandum. We ask that Nkwerre division should stand with headquarters at Nkwerre. The Senior Divisional Officer and all those offices intended to serve Nkwerre division alone should move to Nkwerre where there is ample accomodation for all - in fact better than what they have in Orlu station. Those offices intended to serve both Nkwerre and Mgbidi divisions may remain in Orlu station, for example that of the Senior Agric Officer (and the Chief Magistrate or Judge when appointed).

We wish to emphasize that we are not opposed to the creation of Orlu into an Urban area even if it means slicing out one or two towns from Mgbidi division and one or two from Nkwerre division provided that any such creation does not do damage to the existence of Nkwerre division with headquarters at Nkwerre. We assure you that we shall get our young businessmen and professionals to co-operate in making any proposal for an urban status, if made, to materialise. Already a young Nkwerre doctor has given Orlu station its only clinic. We are also not opposed to Ndizuogu and/or Mbanasa being created a separate division if statistics show that it will be viable. All we are asking for is that what Government has given to us on merit, namely Divisional Headquarters, should not be taken away from us simply because man is a jealous animal. We say this because we believe that jealousy is the motive force behind the agitation that led to this enquiry. When there was an Orlu Province, a Provincial Secretary at Orlu and a Divisional Officer at Nkwerre, there were no petitions to Enugu, no agitation.

Pray, we ask, were the provinces abolished by Nkwerre? Both in our own country's history and in the history of the world as a whole there is plenty of evidence that a more-developed town or country has never been the darling of her less-developed neighbours. If jealousy were not blind, as we say, a more rational attitude for the less-developed neighbour to take would be to befriend the more-developed neighbour in order to learn the secrets of her success.

It is a fact that Nkwerre town produced the <u>first</u> graduate in the division in 1943. It is also true that, with the possible exception of Ndizuogu, Nkwerre has produced more university graduates and professionals than all the other towns in the division put together. It is on record that the <u>first</u> boys' Secondary School in the division, St. Augustine's Grammar School, Nkwerre was planned and executed by Nkwerre in 1945-48. It is also on record that the <u>first</u> girls' Secondary School in the division, St. Catherine's Girls' School, Nkwerre was planned and excuted by Nkwerre women in 1952-55. It is on record that the pipe-borne water scheme for the area was initiated by Nkwerre who paid the <u>first</u> deposit of £2,000 to the Government treasury in 1963 and a further £1,000 in 1966.

It is a fact that soon after the last civil war three young Nkwerre doctors - Dr. J. C. Uzoma; Dr. E. Ojinma and Dr. S. Emezie, quickly moved into the Amaigbo hospital and started the work of saving the lives of people in Nkwerre and neighbouring divisions. It was thus the first hospital in the State to start functioning. If other people choose to spend more on title-taking and wearing long feathers and we prefer to invest more on town development and the production of high-level man-power is that a sufficient reason for Nkwerre to be obliterated from the map of the East Central State?

We pray God to continue to give us the vision, tact and energy to offer leadership to this division so that our contribution to the State, which is second to none, may continue to grow. We pray Him also to make our neighbours less jealous. We believe

..../6

Appendix

that our prayers will be answered through your Committee.

For and on behalf of the Nkwerre Community.

Sgd _____
His Highness J. O. Ugochuku II
The Eshi of Nkwerre.

Sgd _____
Mr. S. E. Ihema
Chairman Nkwerre Community Council

Sgd _____
Mr. R. I. Uzoma, OFR., OBE

Sgd _____
Chief F. U. Anyiam.

Sgd _____
Chief J. S. Asomugha.

Sgd _____
Mr. A. A. Onyejiaka.

The facts in this document were collected, collated and presented by Mr. R. I. Uzoma. The document may only be quoted in part or whole by the written consent of Mr. Uzoma or the Nkwerre Aborigines Union.

APPENDIX A

GOVERNMENT OF EASTERN NIGERIA

Telegrams: EXECUTIVE
Telephone: ORLU 2

DIVISIONAL OFFICE
P. M. B. 4
ORLU.

Your Ref ....
Our Ref. 480/......................
(All replies to be addressed to the
Divisional Officer).

31st January, 1967.

Chief J. O. Ugochukwu,
The Eshi of Nkwerre.

Quarters and Office Accommodation:
Nkwerre Division

I write to inform you that the Divisional Officer in-charge Nkwerre Division, the Assistant Divisional Officer and staff will move down to Nkwerre on or before the 6th of February, 1967. I shall be grateful if the following buildings offered rent free to Government now required for immediate occupation are made available for occupation by the Officers and Staff concerned:-

(i)	Egbebelu Hall	–	Office Accommodation
(ii)	Mr. C. I. Azodo's Storeyed building (top floor)	–	Divisional Officer's Quarters.
(iii)	Mr. John Anyaehie's Storeyed building (top floor)	–	Asst. Divisional Officer's Quarters.
(iv)	Mr. Paul Aguchu's Storeyed building (ground floor)	–	Staff Quarters
(v)	Mr. Nathan Anene's (Bungalow)	–	Staff Quarters
(vi)	Late Dick Anuebunwa's Storeyed building (top floor)	–	Staff Quarters.
(vii)	Dr. A. Onyejiaka's Storeyed building (ground floor)	–	Staff Quarters.
(viii)	Inspector Onyejiaka's Storeyed building (ground floor)	–	Staff Quarters.
(ix)	Mr. F. U. Ihekwoaba's Storeyed building (Top & Ground floors)	–	Staff Quarters and Office Accommodation.

...../2

Appendix

- 2 -

You will be informed when other buildings shall be occupied.

2. I saize this opportunity to inform you that the Provicial Administration Committee will visit Nkwerre on Tuesday 7th February at about 10 a.m. to inspect the site for the proposed Divisional Headquarters Nkwerre. Will you and <u>few representatives</u> of Nkwerre community please meet the Committee at the Egbebelu Hall at the time stated above, to accompany the Committee to the site.

                                              Sgd. (J.A. Nwachukwu)
                                              Ag. Divisional Officer,
                                              Mgbidi & Nkwerre Divisions.

APPENDIX B

A WELCOME ADDRESS PRESENTED BY THE CHIEFS AND PEOPLE OF NKWERRE DIVISION TO HIS EXCELLENCY MR. UKPABI ASIKA, THE ADMINISTRATOR OF THE EAST CENTRAL STATE OF NIGERIA ON THE OCCASION OF HIS FIRST OFFICIAL VISIT TO NKWERRE DIVISION

Your Excellency,

We the chiefs and people of Nkwerre Division wish to express our profound gratitude to Your Excellency for finding time, amidst your arduous and onerous duties, to visit us here today. You are welcome.

2. We have been extremely delighted by your great concern for the sufferings of the ordinary man in the East Central State which is implicit in the tremendous efforts made and urgent steps taken by you, soon after the end of the civil war, to send food through the Rehabilitation Commission to the various Divisions in the East Central State. The food has in varying quantities continued to come to us. We cannot help mentioning, in this connection, that we are not in any way surprised by the urgency with which you addressed yourself to this task for a study of your speeches and utterances during the civil war shows to what extent and in what depth you were conversant with the problems of the East Central State. For what you have so far done we are deeply grateful and happy. We are happier when we reflect that your performances and magnanimity on the morrow of Nigeria's victory over chaos and disintegration have given you out as the one man to repair the enormous physical and spiritual damage caused by the war. It will stand to your credit and that of the Federal Government that the end of the war had not been identified with mass destruction of lives and property. This, you will recall Sir, formed the most poignant propaganda weapon of the former rebel Government against the Federal Government. That you and the Federal Government have admirably lived up to your promises in this regard will for ever ingratiate you with the people of this State-nay the country and the thinking population of the world.

3. Another example of the Government's efforts to rehabilitate the people of this State is the current payment of £20 to each depositor of the Old Nigerian and Biafran currency notes. While appreciating the fine gesture of Government about this matter we would wish to place on record, Your Excellency, that it was not possible for all our people to deposit the Old currency notes. The slow process of the machinery for making the deposits made it impossible for close on three-quarters of our people to deposit their money. The result is that these people are unable to receive the £20. It is our hope that Government would examine this question to see what could be done to the people who were unable, through no faults of theirs, to deposit their old notes.

4. The people of this Division are a commercial people-resourceful, enterprising and hardworking. As it is well known the baneful destruction of their economic life during the civil war rendered a hitherto prosperous people very poor. As part of your post-war reconstruction programme we would earnestly pray Your Excellency to initiate, through the Rehabilitation Commission, a loan scheme whereby money could be made available to our people to re-activate their business. We would also request in addition that Your Excellency take steps to see to the defreezing of our Bank assets including our enormous assets in the Rivers State for purposes of realising Bank credits as this will go a long way in restoring our business into its pre-war level.

5. In addition to the existing police post in Nkwerre Division we would request that three more police posts be established at Isu, Umuaka and Arondizuogu in view of the great distance of existing police posts from these areas.

6. We are encouraged and cheered by the cordial relationship existing between the Army, the Police and the Administration on the one hand and the people of this Division on the other. These arms of Government in this have always approached our problems with sympathy and understanding. It is our view that the prevailing peaceful atmosphere augurs well for the post-war development and reconstruction programme.

7. Nkwerre Division was created along with others in 1966. Nkwerre had since then been the headquarters of the Division. In view of recent Government decision that Orlu should be the Administrative Headquarters of Nkwerre Division, it is the humble prayer of the people of this Division that your Government finds money to develop and upgrade Orlu to an urban status in the earliest possible time in order that Nkwerre which is one of the most developed towns in the Division could resume the position of being the Administrative Headquarters of Nkwerre Division.

8. Finally Sir, we would wish to request that in the post-war reconstruction programme this Division be remembered regarding the establishment of more hospitals. The only major hospital in the Division - the St. Mary's Joint Hospital, Amaigbo, was looted following the confusion at the end of the civil war. All the hospital equipment was removed or destroyed. We ask that Government comes to the aid of this hospital in assisting to re-equip it to reach its pre-war position.

9. Your Excellency, it requires a man of courage to face the enormous post-war reconstruction programme with which your Government will grapple. We pray that God gives you the strength to discharge your responsibilities to this State and the nation.

Sir, as a mark of our appreciation of this your august visit we humbly present this token gift. We wish you a happy stay in this Division.

We are,
Your Excellency
for and on behalf of the Chiefs & the
th people of Nkwerre Division

1. (Sgd.) Chief P.I. Acholonu MBE
   Igwe of Orlu

2. (Sgd.) Chief J.A. Nwosu MBE
   The Igbo of Amaigbo

3. (Sgd.) Chief A. A. Duru
   The Eze Duru Obi of Okwudor.

4. (Sgd.) Chief R. Ojinmaka
   The Obi of Mbano Umuaka

5. (Sgd.) C. C. Osuala
   The Okwara Eze Obi of Isu Njaba

6. (Sgd.) Chief Nnadi Duru
   The Eze Oha II of Umuezeala, Isiekenesi

7. (Sgd.) Ven. Archdeacon S.N. Okoli
   The Okwara of Akokwa

8. (Sgd.) Chief S.O. Imo II
   The Eze of Ndizuogu.

(Sgd.) Chief J. O. Ugochukwu
The Eshi of Nkwerre.

APPENDIX 17

Memo on Financing Imo State University, by Chief R.I. Uzoma OFR, OBE, to the Secretary, Task Force on Financing Imo State University, Cabinet Office, Economic Department, Owerri, dated 21/01/85

>
> Chief R.I. Uzoma, O.F.R., OBE,
> P.O. Box 99,
> Nkwerre,
> 25/1/85.

The Secretary/Member,
Task Force on Financing of Imo State University,
Cabinet Office,
Economic Department,
Owerri.

Sir,

<u>Financing Imo State University</u>

I have read your call for memoranda on the above subject published in the "Nigerian Statesman" of 24th January 1985 and send the following suggestions for what they are worth.

I. <u>Tapping the resources and zeal of our women</u>

In most villages women play a prominent role in Community development and you get the best out of them <u>when you assign a specific project</u> to them to accomplish, not when you ask them to be mere tributary to men's venture. If we mobilise our women and speak to them in the usual pleasant language, and assign to them the building of ~~the~~ say, The School of Liberal Arts, I believe we shall receive some positive response. If the women in Imo State pay, say, two Naira each (₦2.00) they will raise over ₦3,000,000.00 (Three million Naira) for the project.

/2..

Appendix

- 2 -

The Churches fall back on their women members when they find things difficult, and I believe that the women of the State will rise up to the occasion. It might well be that the women would prefer to build a "Women's Hostel" inside the Campus for the accommodation of women students. Although Government has directed that the question of Hostels be left to private entrepreneurs, it is the <u>wish of the majority of Parents</u> that young female students be accommodated in hostels <u>within the Campus</u>, run and/or supervised by the University authorities. If our women choose to build a Women's Hostel in the Campus they should be allowed to do so.

If an honest and dynamic lady who has never dabbled in partisan politics, eg Mrs Bridget Nwankwo, could be available for some months to tour round and organise the women they would be galvanised to achieve the goal they have set for themselves.

2. <u>Persuading our businessmen and autonomous Communities to immortalise their names or those of their ancestors by donating Research, Teaching or Faculty Blocks</u>

/3...

- 3 -

In recent years we have had a series of launching for this or that project and nauseam. I suggest that, if we are going to have any launching at all for the Imo State University, it should not be at this initial stage. Separate meetings of our traditional rulers and prominent "milionaire" businessmen should be arranged at which the Military Governor, assisted by selected individuals, will appeal to them on the need for them to donate subject or faculty blocks which will be named after them or their parents, if they so wish. It should be emphasised that this is a more realistic, more lasting way of using their wealth to help the State and the common man. Their attention should be drawn to the examples of wealthy people in other countries - like Lord Nuffield in Britain, Carnegie in U.S.A., or even Sir Bank Anthony in Lagos, who recently donated an expensive block to the Igbobi Orthopaedic Hospital. We would like to have, for example, an "Nnanna Kalu School of Natural Sciences", an "Anyaehie School of Economics and Political Science," an "Emman Iwuanyanwu School of Engineering" etc etc.

For the traditional rulers we should mobilise them to put up a block to be named after their community. We shall be happy for example, to have an "Abiriba Agricultural Science

../4

Block" an "Ndimuogu Auditorium" etc etc. The traditional rulers might even agree to undertake one block each Zone. We have five zones in the State and this will mean five blocks. If they agree on this, they will go back and share the money among the various L.G.A's and autonomous Communities in their zone.

3. <u>Help from the big Business Combines and multi-national Companies</u>.

This is the time for us to ask for assistance from big firms like U.A.C., S.C.O.A., Ash-land Coy, Agip Shell Coy, Mobil etc. The ordinary man in Imo State feels that big donations from these Companies have for long eluded Imo State. This is the time for these companies to wipe off this impression by helping us in any way they think fit. An appeal should be made to them.

4. <u>General Remarks</u>: (a) If we agree to name blocks after their donors we shall be getting away from the old practice of naming University buildings after living politicians.

(b) If wealthy individuals and/or Communities and zones agree to put up some teaching

/5.....

blocks, it may be advisable for experts to work out an average amount which they are expected to raise and leave the actual construction to the University authorities or the construction Task Force to be appointed by Government, in which the Army, the Police and the donor will be represented. For example we may ask for ₦1,500,000.00 or ₦2,000,000.00 from each individual, Community or Zone. This suggestion is made to ensure that a uniform high standard of construction is maintained.

(c) All consultancy services (eg services of architects, quantity Surveyors, structural and electrical engineers) should be provided by Government. The charges for these services make the cost of building in Nigeria prohibitive. These charges should not, therefore, be included in the calculation of the amount each donor will be expected to pay as contained in 4(b) above. Where Government consultants are not available to render these services Government should appeal to the older Universities and/or private consultants for Free service as their contribution.

(d) Individual donors may, if they request, be granted some tax relief and/or automatic admission for at least two of their children/wards (not necessarily in the same session), provided they satisfy the conditions of JAMB.

APPENDIX 18

Paper titled "State-Management of Schools" prepared by Mr. R.I. Uzoma OFR, in response to the request of the Bishop of Owerri for the 1970 Synod, dated 27/6/70

STATE-MANAGEMENT OF SCHOOLS:
(Mr. R.I.Uzoma, O.F.R.)

In his first broadcast speech at the end of the civil war His Excellency, the Administrator of the East Central State, Mr. Ukpabi Asika announced that Government would be taking over the management of all schools and colleges in the state. Coming as it did at a time when things were not settled and when there was general confusion and uncertainty all over, the announcement set people wondering what the future had in store for them in respect of education.

It is hoped that with the recent appointment of the Commissioner for Education, government will spell out in a white paper the detailed implications of the new policy. Until this is done it will be premature to express an opinion on it. With the re-opening of schools at the end of the civil war, inspectors of schools were appointed for all the divisions in the state and they relieved our education secretary, general manager of schools and parish priests of the onerous duty of posting teachers and paying their salaries. Government has also taken over the responsibility for the collection of fees, a responsibility which in the working of the former system proved a nightmare to voluntary agencies in certain areas, and caused delay in the payment of teachers' salaries where it did not stop payment completely.

One can see at once that by this decision to take over the management of all schools and colleges the new government has abolished the old colonial dichotomy between "Government" and "Non-Government" schools, a classification which caused much injustice since about ten times more money was spent on a government school than on a non-government school of comparable standard. The decision has also abolished the much-criticised division of schools into "Grant-aided" and "Non-grant-aided" since government will now assume responsibility for every school it allows to open. For years financial consideration had led government to the unreasonable practice of refusing assistance to a new school after granting the proprietor approval to open. This illogicality was mainly responsible for the abuses the general public complained of in several unassisted secondary schools. These will all now be things of the past, we hope. The tax-payer will now expect that he will not be unduly fleeced through the the payment of all sorts of fees and that his child will have a fair share of the states revenue spent on him, no matter which school he attends.

The instinct of acquisition, of possession is very strong in man, and the church is made up of men and women. I know that it will not be easy for most of us to stop thinking and talking in terms of "our schools" and "our teachers". It should be emphasised that so far the school in the village is very much "ours" – as much "ours" as it was in 1967. It has not ceased to be "ours" because the pastor has stopped acting as paymaster. He is still free to go into the school to minister to the religious and spiritual needs of the children. The children themselves and the majority of the teachers are still, and will continue to be members of the church. The curriculum of the schools has not been changed and religion still occupies an important place in it. We do not subscribe to the view that the criterion for determining whether an institution should be labelled "christian" or not is whether the management is church-appointed or state-appointed. The quality and character of the teaching staff and the contents of the education given are very important factors to reckon with.

The Government take-over of the management of schools has created an entirely new situation which throws a challenge to the church that wants to remain very much alive. We believe that in the changed situation and changed relationships the church, without being possessive, can still be very much alive in the schools and colleges of the state and in the various boards and committees that will be set up to superintend and finance them.

271

Our wealth of experience in the field of teacher-education, our expertise in school management and supervision, our methods of economy in building and management, etc. can be placed at the disposal of the state, not with a patronising air but in a spirit of humble service and co-operation which this period calls for.

The new situation calls for a rapid expansion of the church's chaplaincy service so that she may be able to cope with the task of ministering to the spiritual needs of the schools and colleges now that they are no longer under her direct management and supervision. It challenges the church to a re-examination of her role in education, and to the application of her pioneering spirit to discover neglected fields and uncharted areas calling for exploitation by dedicated pioneers. The church's energy and resources can now very well be directed towards such fields as adult education including adult literacy and community development. They can be directed towards specialised fields like the education of the handicapped and the deformed — the less fortunate members of the community who are likely to be neglected in the rush to catch up at a time when resources are limited. May God grant us the vision to see the wide vista before us!

27. 6. 70

APPENDIX 19

B. HONOURS, AWARDS AND CONGRATULATORY MESSAGES

Postgraduate Diploma Certificate issued to R.I. Uzoma B.A by the University of London, Institute for Education, in 1947

UNIVERSITY OF LONDON
INSTITUTE OF EDUCATION

THIS IS TO CERTIFY THAT

REUBEN UZOMA

took, during the Session 1946-1947, a Course of Training in the THEORY AND PRACTICE OF EDUCATION, with special reference to conditions in Colonial Dependencies.

The COURSE included :—

The General Principles of Education.
Elementary Educational Psychology.
English Educational System.
Problems of Education in Tropical Areas
Comparative Education in Tropical Areas.
The Study of Society, an introduction to Social Anthropology.
Phonetics.
Tropical Hygiene.

The Principles of Teaching, with special attention to the methods of teaching the following subjects :—

English as a Foreign Language; Geography; New Media; Mathematics(S); Teaching the Three R's in the Primary School; Special Method for Tropical Areas

Teaching under Supervision ; Observation and Discussion of Lessons, and visits to specially selected schools and other centres of education.

Optional Practical Subjects :—

Arts and Crafts

PROFESSIONAL EXAMINATION (Theoretical and Practical) :—
Either The Examination for the Teacher's Diploma of the University of London
Result :—

PASSED

Or The Alternative Professional Examination conducted by the Institute of Education Board of Examiners.
Result :—

Appendix

REMARKS :—

Mr Uzoma is a good teacher, possessing a pleasant disposition, exhibiting consistency of effort in preparation, and a thoughtful attitude towards his exposition of material. He gets on well with pupils and staff and is constructive in his attitude towards criticism.

His participation in discussion is shrewd, timely and reasonable. His written work is marked by clarity of expression, carefulness of selection of facts and a sound exercise of powers of judgement.

Mr Uzoma has made excellent use of his opportunities and should carry back to Nigeria a widened experience and increased capacity for the successful direction of his school.

DIRECTOR

APPENDIX 20

Certificate of Election of R.I. Uzoma as a Fellow of the Royal Geographical Society (FRGS) dated November 25th 1946

Royal Geographical Society,
Kensington Gore,
London, S.W. 7.

25 November 1946

Sir,

I have the honour to inform you that the Council have this day elected you a Fellow of the Royal Geographical Society subject to the conditions governing the completion of such Election as provided in the Bye-Laws.

I have the honour to be

Sir,

your obedient Servant

Honorary Secretary.

R. I. Uzoma, B.A.

APPENDIX 21

Letter from the Secretary to the Government of the Federation to Reuben Ibekwe Uzoma conveying Appreciation and the Award of Nigeria National Honour of Officer of the Order of the Federal Republic (OFR), Ref: Gazette Notice No. 75, Vol. 52 of 1965

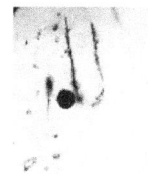

EXECUTIVE OFFICE OF THE PRESIDENT
POLITICAL DEPARTMENT
TAFAWA BALEWA SQUARE
LAGOS.

P.M.B. 12571, LAGOS

Telegrams.....SGF.......... Ref. No. 58358/S.5/XI/148.

Telephone ...630442........ Date: ...26th June, 1980...

REUBEN IBEKWE UZOMA
c/o Civil Service Commission,
OWERRI.

SECRET

LETTER OF APPRECIATION NIGERIA HONOURS AND AWARDS FOR NATIONAL DAYS 1ST OCTOBER 1965

NAME	HONOUR
REUBEN IBEKWE UZOMA	OFFICER OF THE ORDER OF THE FEDERAL REPUBLIC (O.F.R.)

I am directed by the President of the Federal Republic of Nigeria and Commander-In-Chief of the Armed Forces to write this letter of appreciation and to present to you the Honour and Award indicated in the gazette notices No. 75 Vol.52 of 1965 made to you in absentia.

2. I am to express our very best wishes to you and your continued service to this great nation.

S. A. MUSA.
Secretary to the Government
of Federation.

SECRET

APPENDIX 22

Copy of the Eastern Nigeria Gazette No. 39 Vol. 10 of June 10th 1961 listing the 1961 Queen's Birthday Honours, with Reuben Ibekwe Uzoma as Officer of the Most Excellent Order of the British Empire

Extraordinary

Eastern  Nigeria Gazette

Published by Authority

No. 39   ENUGU – 10th June, 1961   Vol. 10

CONTENT	Page
Birthday Honours	341-2

EASTERN NIGERIA NOTICE No. 632

BIRTHDAY HONOURS, 1961
Eastern Nigeria List

Her Majesty the Queen has been graciously pleased to make the following appointments:—

To be a Companion of the Most Distinguished Order of Saint Michael and Saint George:—

CHIEF NYONG ESSIEN

To be a Commander of the Most Excellent Order of the British Empire:—

PETER FORBES GRANT

To be Officers of the Most Excellent Order of the British Empire:—

RICHARD WHITFIELD HARDING
REUBEN IBEKWE UZOMA

To be a Companion of the Imperial Service Order:

PETER EGBO EYO ARCHIBONG

To be Members of the Most Excellent Order of the British Empire:—

JEREMIAH AMADI ENYEAZU
JOHN STANLEY BLANKSON IKPE
LILIAN MURPHY
MARGARET LILIAN OGLE
KALU CHIMA OKORIE
JANET MATAGU OKOYE

By His Excellency's Command,
R. J. GRAHAM
Secretary to the Governor

Enugu,
10th June, 1961.

(341)

Appendix

EASTERN NIGERIA NOTICE No. 633

His Excellency the Governor has been pleased to award Certificates of Honour to the following persons:—

PIUS ANIOKE, Chairman, Grade I, Ministry of Town Planning.
DENNIS IKWUEGBU EGELAMBA, Assistant Produce Officer, Ministry of Agriculture.
IBUNGHA EKERE of Obubra Division.
ARINZE EZEBULE of Obinofia, Udi Division.
GEORGE AMOS HORSFALL, Senior Interpreter, Grade II.
JOHNSON EGWU IDUMA of Afikpo Division.
EMMANUEL KOFI MARSHALL, Senior Staff Officer, Ministry of Finance.
EMMANUEL MGBOJIKWE, Assistant Nursing Superintendent, Ministry of Health.
EGBERT OKEKE NDOZI, Forest Ranger, Ministry of Agriculture.
MAURICE NWAOHU NNOROM of Abakaliki.
ARET ESSIEN OKOKON, Assistant Nursing Sister, Ministry of Health.
PHILIP OKONJI, Head Messenger, Ministry of Commerce.
CHIEF ISU EGWU ORIE of Afikpo Division.

By His Excellency's Command,

R. J. GRAHAM
Secretary to the Governor

Enugu,
10th June, 1961.

APPENDIX 23

Warrant of Appointment under the Queen's Sign Manual, for Reuben Ibekwe Uzoma Esq. OBE

CENTRAL CHANCERY OF THE ORDERS OF KNIGHTHOOD
ST JAMES'S PALACE
OFFICES – 8, BUCKINGHAM GATE, S.W.1.
TELEPHONE – VICTORIA 2837 & 2838

The Secretary has the honour to transmit a Warrant of Appointment, under the Queen's Sign Manual, to the Most Excellent Order of the British Empire, and to request that the receipt of this Warrant may be acknowledged on the attached form.

The Secretary would be glad to receive notification of any change of permanent address, and in the event of the decease of persons holding such Warrants Executors are earnestly requested to notify the Secretary.

Reuben Ibekwe Uzoma, Esq.,
O.B.E.

APPENDIX 24

Letter of Recognition and Declaration of a Philanthropist from H.R.H. Eze P.I. Acholonu MBE, KSM, PM, Duru VIII, Igwe X of Orlu, to Chief R.I. Uzoma, on September 5th 1989

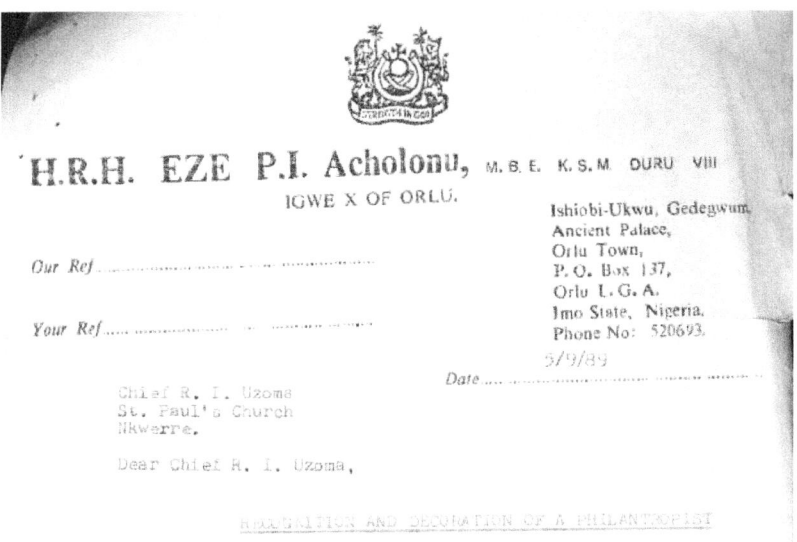

H.R.H. EZE P.I. Acholonu, M.B.E. K.S.M. DURU VIII
IGWE X OF ORLU.

Ishiobi-Ukwu, Gedegwum,
Ancient Palace,
Orlu Town,
P. O. Box 137,
Orlu L. G. A.
Imo State, Nigeria.
Phone No: 520693.

Our Ref ....

Your Ref ....

Date: 5/9/89

Chief R. I. Uzoma
St. Paul's Church
Nkwerre.

Dear Chief R. I. Uzoma,

RECOGNITION AND DECORATION OF A PHILANTROPIST

I have the pleasure to inform you that the Anniversary of my 90th years Birth-Day coincides with my 44th Annual New Yam Festival of 24th September, 1989.

In an occasion of this nature, something historic has to be done to mark the celebration. This year, you quickly came into the picture considering the testimonies of both friends and foes, Colleagues, Business Associates, Customers and sub-ordinates in all the firms, companies and industries you contributed immensely to establish and develop, one is compelled to think of what to do to reciprocate, not only your selfless services but your wonderful human relationship also. You have been described as industrious, hard-working, dependable, tolerant, humble, gentle and good natured.

In recognition and acknowledgement of your services and qualities, an architect of peace, philantropism, people's friend, generousity to all-and-sundry without limitation and integration which earned you a co-ordinator, are experienced every-where in Nigeria, especially your contributions and donations in the Church, and in Imo State with impunity, I have to project you before the distinguished guests.

Having considered the degree of the above qualities and others unmentioned, as one of the elderly fathers of this country I have to show my own appreciation of your ingenuity by according you with An Ancient Traditional Symbol of Honour to whom the Honour is due which will be performed during the occasion day before the Natural Traditional Rulers of this Country.

I would like you to indicate your consent and acceptance of the above unequivocal honour which in my humble opinion you deserve, before two weeks from the date of this letter to enable me seek permission that your noble Dic for approval and any and disposal.

Thanks and God bless. Congratulations.

Yours Always,

HRH ....
M.B.E., K.S.M. P.M.
Duru VIII, Igwe X of Orlu.

APPENDIX 25

Letter of Conferment of Honourary Degree, dated 6th February 1990, to Chief R.I. Uzoma OBE, OFR, from the Registrar and Secretary to Council, University of Nigeria, Nsukka

UNIVERSITY OF NIGERIA

Telegrams: NIGERSITY
Telephones: 042-771911, 771920, 771939
771941, 771951

Ext. ....
OUR REF: UN/RC.205

NSUKKA
ANAMBRA STATE

OFFICE OF THE REGISTRAR

DATE February 26, 19

Chief Sir R.I. Uzoma (OBE, OFR)
Ukeje I
P.O. Box 9
Nkwerre
Imo State

Dear Chief Uzoma,

CONFERMENT OF HONORARY DEGREE

I am pleased to inform you that, following a recommendation of the Senate of the University, the Governing Council, has approved that an Honorary Degree of Doctor of Laws (LL.D.) be conferred on you at the next Convocation ceremony of the University which is scheduled for 7th April, 1990. This is in recognition of your selfless, honest, and distinguished service, particularly in the field of education, to humanity and to the nation.

Officials of the University will be calling on you, soon, to take measurements for the sewing of your academic regalia and to collect necessary information for preparing a citation on you.

Please, accept my congratulations.

Yours sincerely,

U. C. Umeh
REGISTRAR & SECRETARY TO COUNCIL

APPENDIX 26

Congratulatory telegram from the Rt. Honourable Nnamdi Azikwe, Governor-General of Nigeria, to R.I. Uzoma, on the conferment of the OBE on him ber Her Majesty in 1961

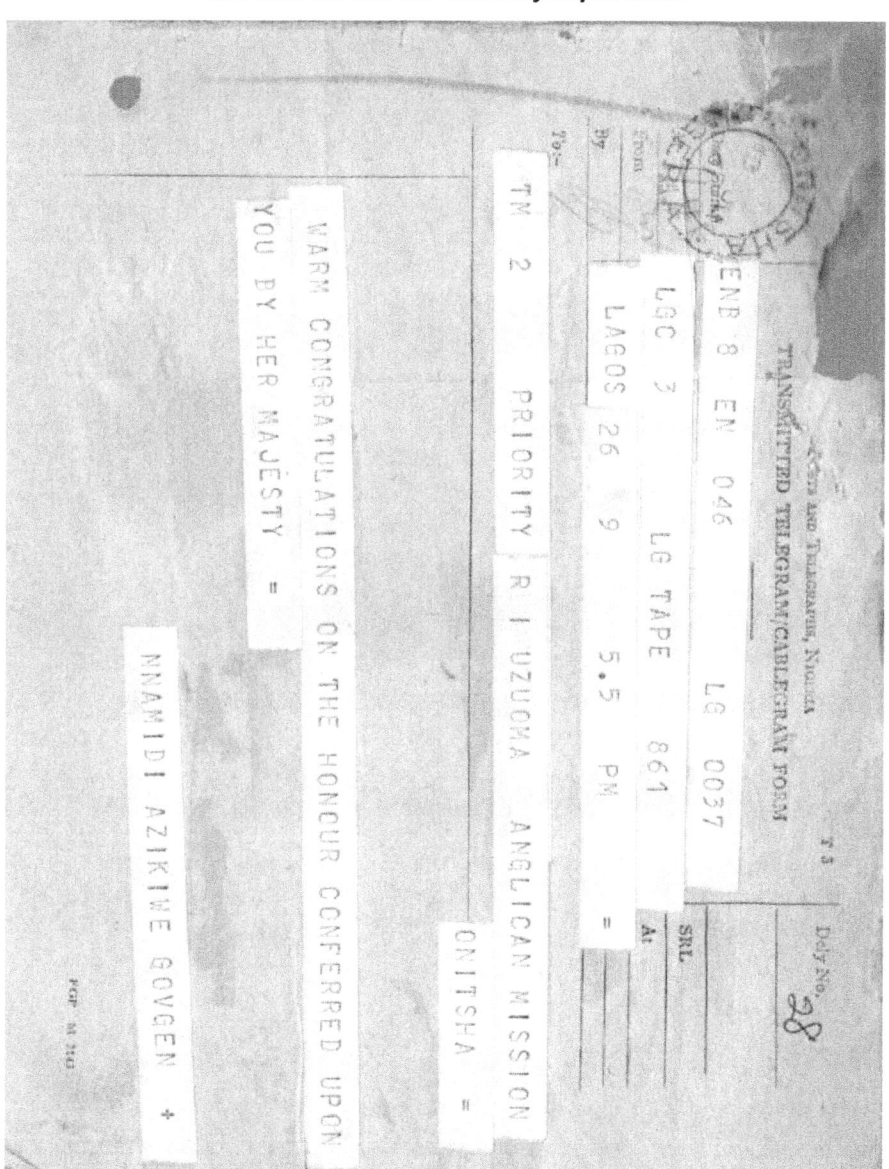

APPENDIX 27

Congratulatory letter dated June 10th 1961, from Rt. Hon. Francis Akanu Ibiam, Governor of the then Eastern Region, to R.I. Uzoma, on his conferment of the OBE

A.6310/34.

GOVERNMENT HOUSE
ENUGU.
NIGERIA

10th June, 1961.

R. I. Uzoma, Esq., O.B.E.,
c/o Trinity College,
Old Umuahia,
Umuahia-Ibeku.

Dear Mr. Uzoma,

    I am very pleased that your sterling work over the years for education in Nigeria has been recognised by your O.B.E.

    This is an honour well earned and I offer you my warmest congratulations and best wishes for the future.

Yours sincerely,

Francis Akanu Ibiam

APPENDIX 28

Letter from the Chief Justice of Eastern Nigeria, Sir Louis Mbanefo, dated June 19th 1961, to R.I. Uzoma, on his conferment with the OBE

The High Court of the Eastern Region
of the Federation of Nigeria

No......................

Chief Justice's Chambers
The High Court
Enugu
19 June, 1961

My dear Uzoma,

I write though belatedly to offer you my warmest congratulations on your appointment as officer of the most Excellent order of the British Empire. It is a fitting recognition of your services of Education in the Region.

With all good wishes

APPENDIX 29

Letter from the Rev. W.J. Wood, Education Adviser to the Protestant Missions, dated June 23rd 1961, to Mr. R.I. Uzoma OBE, on the latter's award of the OBE

THE EDUCATIONAL ADVISER
(PROTESTANT MISSIONS, NIGERIA)

Revd. W. J. WOOD.
Telephone: LAGOS 21682
Telegrams: "METHODIST LAGOS."

Ref: E.A./M.1

22, MARINA,
P.O. BOX 161,
LAGOS, NIGERIA.

23rd, June, 1961.

Mr. R.I. Uzoma, O.B.E.,
Anglican Education Office,
Old Umuahia,
Eastern Region.

Dear Mr. Uzoma,

This comes to offer you sincere congratulations on the recognition of your sterling work in education by the award of the O.B.E.

Those of us who have worked with you know something of the quiet and efficient way in which you have served, not only your own diocese, but a wider field in educational development. This recognition will bring satisfaction to a wide circle of friends within and outside your own church, and to the many congratulations that I know will have reached you I would add my own, belated I fear, but not any the less sincere.

With every good wish.

Yours sincerely,

(Rev. W.J. Wood)
EDUCATIONAL ADVISER.

EAW/WJW:-

APPENDIX 30

Letter from Mr. J.B. Davies, Chairman UAC (United Africa Company) of Nigeria Ltd, to Reuben Ibekwe Uzoma Esq. OBE, on the latter's award of the OBE

THE UNITED AFRICA COMPANY OF NIGERIA LIMITED.
(Incorporated in Nigeria)

HEAD OFFICE
NIGER HOUSE.
LAGOS

OUR REF.

CHAIRMAN,
P. O. BOX 9. LAGOS.
NIGERIA.

14th June, 1961.

Reuben Ibekwe Uzoma, Esq., O.B.E.,
The Education Secretary,
Anglican Niger Delta Diocese,
c/o Bishopcourts Court,
ABA.

Dear Mr. Uzoma,

    On behalf of the Board of Directors and Staff of The United Africa Company of Nigeria Limited, I send you our most sincere congratulations on your award in Her Majesty's Birthday Honours list.

Yours sincerely,

J.B. Davies.

DIRECTORS: JACK BRACHER DAVIES, O.B.E. (CHAIRMAN)
HAROLD GAVIN DAWSON (CHAIRMAN).   CHRISTOPHER EHMODAGHE ABESE.
JACK BRACHER DAVIES, WILLIAM HARDY, RAYMOND RICHARD STRICKLAND MORE.
FREDERICK SPENCER PARDOE
GORDON HENRY WILSON

APPENDIX 31

Congratulatory letter from N.U. Akpan, Ministry of Education, Eastern Region, dated October 4th 1965, to R.I. Uzoma, on the latter's award of the National Honour of OFR

GOVERNMENT OF EASTERN NIGERIA

Telegrams: PERMED ENUGU
Telephone: ENUGU 3041
Your ref................
Our ref................
(All replies to be addressed to the Permanent Secretary).

MINISTRY OF EDUCATION
ADMINISTRATION DIVISION
P.M.B. 1020
ENUGU
4 October, 19 65

Dear Mr Uzoma,

I write to offer you my heartiest congratulations for the honour conveyed on you during the last celebrations of the National day. Your appointment as an Officer of the Federal Republic, (O.F.R.) is a well-merited honour which must gladden the hearts of all your friends. Congratulations and best wishes.

Yours Very Sincerely,

(N. U. Akpan)

APPENDIX 32

Congratulatory Telegram from Dr. Alvan Ikoku to R.I. Uzoma, on the latter's award of the OFR

Mr Uzoma Education Secretary Owerri

Hearty congratulations national day honour

Ikoku

APPENDIX 33

Congratulatory Telegram from the Dimiearis (Bishop Dimieari) to R.I. Uzoma on his award of the OFR

HEARTIEST AMBLY DESERVED NATIONAL HONOUR PRAYERS

R. UZOMA TESTIMONY OWERRI

CR54 BONNY 12 5 1515

DIMIEARIS

APPENDIX 34

Congratulatory Telegram from the Ezekwesilis to R.I. Uzoma on his award of the OFR

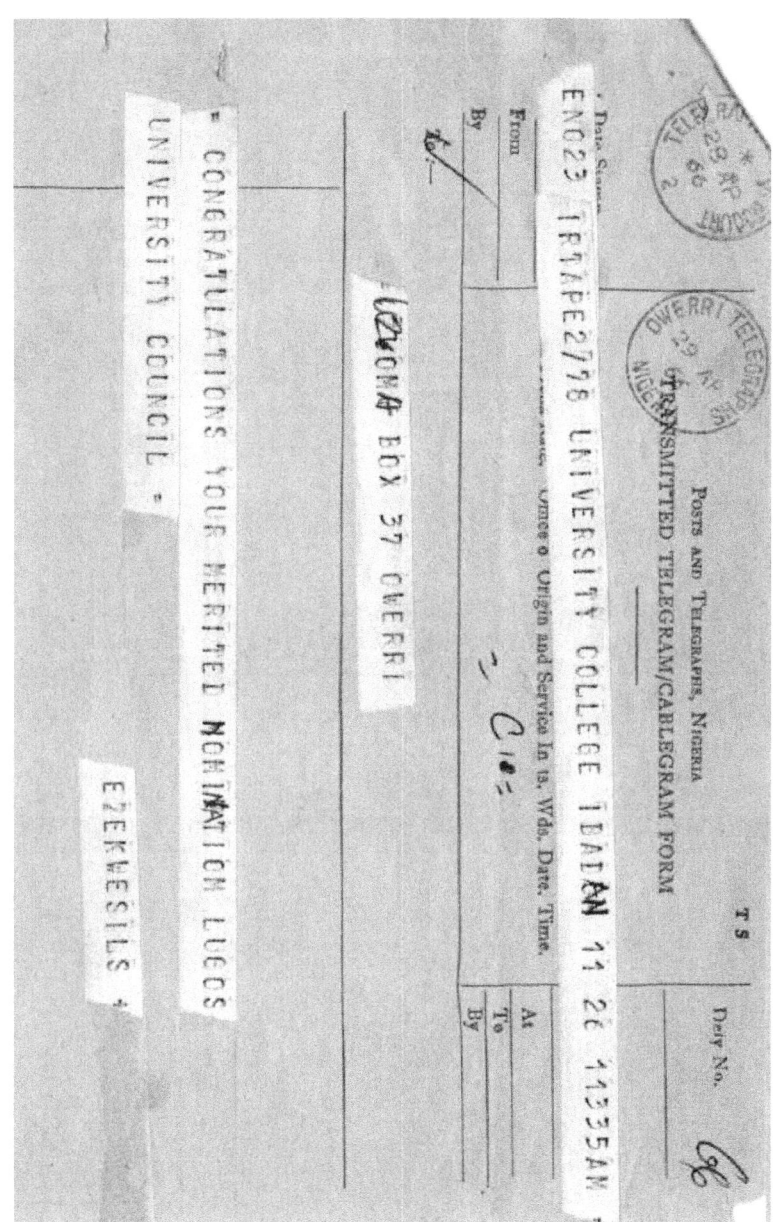

APPENDIX 35

Congratulatory Telegram from Chief Ikechi Nwadinobi to R.I. Uzoma on the latter's award of the OFR

R. I. Uzome Owerri

Congratulation honours award OFR

Chief Ikechi Nwadinobi

APPENDIX 36

Letter of Congratulations, dated April 10th 1990, from Lt. Commander Amadi Ikwechegh, Military Governor of Imo State, to Chief R.I. Uzoma on the latter's conferment with the LL.D Honoris Causa by the University of Nigeria

OFFICE OF THE MILITARY GOVERNOR

Telegrams: MILGOVOWERRI

GOVERNMENT HOUSE
OWERRI

Your ref:
Our ref: GH/MG/S.69/S.1/T/11/775
IMO STATE

10 April, 19 90

Chief R I Uzoma
P O Box 99
NKWERRE
Nkwerre Local Government

Dear Chief Uzoma,

CONGRATULATIONS

1. I have received news of the great honour which you received recently. I am informed that the University of Nigeria, Nsukka, has decided to confer on you the degree of Doctorate of Laws (LL.D) Honoraris Causa. On behalf of my family and myself, I send you warm congratulations.

2. It must be in recognition of your outstanding achievements that the University of Nigeria has given you this rare honour. I therefore urge you to see this as an encouragement to do even more. It is my prayer that God continues to guide you and to use you to do His will among people.

3. Once more, I congratulate you and wish you well.

Yours sincerely,

A. IKWECHEGH
Commander
Military Governor

APPENDIX 37

Letter of Appreciation from Etim O. Inyang NPM, Inspector-General of the Nigeria Police dated January 2nd 1985, to Chief R.I. Uzoma, for the latter's role on the Police Community Relations Committee in Imo State

The Inspector-General of Police
Force Headquarters,
Kam Selem House,
Moloney Street,
Lagos.
2nd January, 1985.

CHIEF R.I. UZOMA,
OBINUHU MKWERRE,
IMO STATE.

DEAR CHIEF,

Appreciation

It is my pleasure and priviledge to write and thank you for the invaluable role you have played in the last twelve months, in the fight against the social maladies that have pervaded our society. Your role in this noble crusade is in your acceptance to become a member of the Police Community Relations Committee. In the annals of the history of policing in this country, the Police Community Relations Committee has proved to be the best forum where personalities of different callings and experience have met to put heads together and make meaningful contributions towards a better Police performance.

2. The sacrifice you have made in your time, mental and physical resources in embracing the problems of the Nigeria Police Force, has, I am sure, placed you in a better position to appreciate the numerous hazards and constraints which militate against better policing. It is only with this inside knowledge that the problem of positive policing of our communities may be intelligently and objectively tackled.

I am particularly happy that your participation in your local Police Community Relations Committee has immensely contributed to the total effort towards better policing and has been acknowledged by the community. I am confident that the spirit of altruism which inspired you to join the Police Community Relations Committee will further spur you to continue to work faithfully in the committee for the pursuit of the noble societal cause of ensuring peace and tranquility and the protection of life and property in your community now and in the years to come.

Finally, may I seize the opportunity of this medium to assure you of my personal sincerity and the co-operation of the Force at all times.

I have the honour to be,
Sir,
Your Obedient Servant.

(ETIM O. INYANG) NPM,
Inspector-General of Police.

APPENDIX 38

C. LETTERS OF APPOINTMENT AND OF RECOGNITION

Letter of Appointment dated April 28th 1966, from the Ag. Permanent Secretary, Federal Ministry of Education, to Mr. R.I. Uzoma, conveying his appointment as a Member of the Provisional Council of the University of Lagos

FEDERAL MINISTRY OF EDUCATION . LAGOS . NIGERIA
Telegrams and Cablegrams: SECEDUCATE   *Telephone:*

Ref. CED/H.127/S.22/45   28th April, 19 66

Sir,   CONFIDENTIAL

    I am directed to inform you that His Excellency the Head of the Federal Military Government and Supreme Commander of the Nigerian Armed Forces has approved your appointment as a member of the Provisional Council of the University of Lagos with effect from the 23rd April, 1966 and until further notice. A notice to this effect was published in the Supplement to Official Gazette Extraordinary No. 43, Volume 53, of 25th April, 1966 under the title "The University of Lagos Act (Amendment) Decree 1966."

2.   I am to request you to be kind enough to signify your acceptance or otherwise of this appointment.

                  I am, Sir,
                  Your obedient servant,

                  (S. S. Waniko),
                Ag. Permanent Secretary.

Mr. R. I. Uzoma,

CONFIDENTIAL

APPENDIX 39

Letter in respect of appointment as Provincial Administrator for Orlu, dated June 6th 1967, to Mr. R.I. Uzoma, from the Chief Secretary to the Military Government of 'Republic of Biafra'

REPUBLIC OF BIAFRA
GOVERNMENT OF ~~EASTERN NIGERIA~~

Telegrams: SECMILGOV
Telephone:
Your ref..........
Our ref. PG/0383/12/16
(All replies to be addressed to the Secretary to the Military Government.)

OFFICE OF THE MILITARY GOVERNOR
(POLITICAL AND ADMINISTRATION DIVISION)
P.M.B. 1060
ENUGU

6th June, 1967

Dear Mr. Uzoma,

I am directed by His Excellency the Military Governor to thank you for accepting to serve as Provincial Administrator for Orlu Province, and to confirm the belief that you will bring to bear on your new office those qualities of impartiality, public spiritedness and devotion to duty for which you have become well known.

2. His Excellency has instructed that the terms and conditions of your appointment as Provincial Administrator will be as follows:-

Term of Office:	Three years with effect from 28th May 1967 when your appointment was first notified to you.
Salary:	This will be at the rate of £2,700 per annum.
Entertainment Allowance:	£300 will be paid to you annually to enable you to give official entertainments.
Housing:	Government quarters will not be provided as you are expected to find your own accommodation in your provincial area. Government will, however, pay a uniform housing allowance at a rate to be determined later.
Leave:	You will be entitled to annual leave of 30 days.
Gratuity:	A gratuity of £150 per annum has been approved for every completed year of service or £37 10/- for every three months service.
Medical Treatment:	This will be available to you on the same terms as for civil servants.
Telephone Bills:	Bills incurred in respect of telephones will be defrayed by Government.

Appendix

Mr. Uzoma — 2 — 6th June, 1967.

<u>Motor Vehicle</u>: You will be entitled to motor vehicle advance to buy your own car under Government guarantee, subject to a maximum advance of £1,200, refundable in three years.
When you use your car for official journeys, you will be paid mileage allowance at the following rates:-

10d per mile for the first 500 miles
8d "   "   "   "   next 500 "
6d "   "   thereafter.

<u>Travelling Allowance</u>: While on tour outside your station, you will be entitled to £2 2/- per night or refund of hotel expenses less the cost of drinks and laundry. If travelling outside the country, you will be entitled to £5 5/- in the United Kingdom, and up to £8 8/- per night elsewhere, plus bed and breakfast.

3. May I add my very best wishes for a happy and successful tenure of office.

Very sincerely yours,

N. U. AKPAN
CHIEF SECRETARY TO THE MILITARY GOVERNMENT

R. I. Uzoma, Esq.,
Provincial Administrator,
Orlu Province,
ORLU.

APPENDIX 40

Letter of Appointment dated June 9th 1971, from the Secretary to the Military Government of East Central State (ECS), to Mr. R.I. Uzoma, conveying his appointment as Chairman, Nkwerre Divisional School Board

GOVERNMENT OF THE EAST CENTRAL STATE OF NIGERIA

CABINET OFFICE,
POLICY DIVISION,
ENUGU.

Ref:80/S.0004/Vol.II/6

9th June, 1971

Dear Mr. Uzoma,

APPOINTMENT OF MEMBERS OF DIVISIONAL SCHOOL BOARD

I am directed to inform you that His Excellency the Administrator, in exercise of his powers under Section 8(4) of the Public Education Edict, 1970, No. 2 of 1971, has appointed you ...... CHAIRMAN ...... of the ... NKWERRE .... Divisional School Board.

2. An allowance of £1,200 per annum is payable to you as ... CHAIRMAN .... of the ... NKWERRE ...... Divisional School Board.

3. I should be grateful if you would signify in writing, as a matter of extreme urgency, your acceptance of this appointment.

Yours faithfully,

(J. O. IBE IAKO),
SECRETARY TO THE MILITARY GOVERNMENT.

MR. R. I. UZOMA
c/o DIVISIONAL OFFICER
NKWERRE DIVISION.

APPENDIX 41

Letter of Appointment dated September 7th 1974, from the Secretary to the Military Government of East Central State, to Mr. R.I. Uzoma, conveying his appointment as a Member of the Teacher's Service Commission

Telegrams: SEMILGOV ENUGU
Telephone:
Your ref:
Our ref: SG/S.0237/2

OFFICE OF THE SECRETARY TO THE
MILITARY GOVERNMENT
CABINET OFFICE
ENUGU

7th September, 1974

Mr. R. I. Uzoma,
c/o Divisional Officer,
NKWERRE.

SECRET

Dear Sir/Madam,

Appointment of Members of the Teachers Service Commission

I am directed to inform you that His Excellency the Administrator in exercise of his powers under Section 3(2) of the Teachers Service Commission Edict No. 25 of 1974, has appointed you a Member of the Teachers Service Commission.

The terms and conditions of your appointment are as follows:-

(i) **Salary:** ₦6,360 per annum

(ii) **Quarters:** Free

(iii) **Leave:** 45 days per annum

(iv) **Transport:** If official transport is not provided, motor basic allowance of ₦50 per month and 10 kobo mileage allowance will be paid

(v) **Travelling:**
   (Local) Refund of cost of accommodation less drinks and laundry
   (Abroad) ESTACODE Rates

(vi) **Medical Facilities:** Free for self and family only

(vii) **Entertainment Allowance:** Nil

- 2 -

(viii) **Upkeep of House and Grounds:** Not more than one labourer will be provided

(ix) **Electricity and Gas:** Free

(x) **Private Telephone Calls:** Maximum of ₦35.00 per quarter will be borne by Government.

It would be appreciated if you would signify in writing your acceptance of the appointment.

Yours faithfully,

(J. O. IBEZIAKO),
SECRETARY TO THE MILITARY GOVERNMENT.

APPENDIX 42

Letter of Appointment dated August 27th 1975, from the Secretary to the Military Government of East Central State, to Mr. R.I. Uzoma, conveying his appointment as an interim member of the East Central State Public Service Commission

GOVERNMENT OF EAST-CENTRAL STATE OF NIGERIA

Telegrams: SEMILGOV ENUGU

Telephone:

Your ref:

Our ref: SS/S107/11/202

OFFICE OF THE SECRETARY TO THE MILITARY GOVERNMENT
CABINET OFFICE
ENUGU

27th August, 1975

Mr. R.I. Uzoma,
Member,
Teachers Service Commission,
Enugu.

Mrs. N.K. Asinobi,
Member,
Teachers Service Commission,
Enugu.

Dear Mr. Uzoma,

I am directed to inform you that His Excellency the Military Governor of East Central State has appointed you a Member of the Public Service Commission for a period of three months with effect from the 27th of August, 1975.

2. You will wish to note however that this is an interim arrangement and is only necessitated by the need to meet urgent decisions which have to be taken by the Public Service Commission.

3. It is to be stated therefore that this appointment is without prejudice to your position as a Member of the Teachers' Service Commission or to any future appointments which His Excellency may wish to make with regard to the Public Service Commission.

Yours Sincerely,

(J. O. IBEZIAKO)
SECRETARY TO THE MILITARY GOVERNMENT

APPENDIX 43

Letter of Appointment dated January 30th 1975, from the Secretary to the Military Government of East Central State, to Mr. R.I. Uzoma, conveying his appointment as a permanent Member of the East Central State Public Service Commission

---

GOVERNMENT OF EAST-CENTRAL STATE OF NIGERIA

Telegrams: SEMILGOV ENUGU
Telephone:
Your ref..........
Our ref. SG/Q.0107/11/227

SECRET

OFFICE OF THE SECRETARY TO THE
MILITARY GOVERNMENT
CABINET OFFICE
ENUGU

30th January, 1976

Dear Sir, **IMMEDIATE**

<u>Appointment of Permanent Member of the Public
Service Commission - East Central State</u>

I am directed to inform you that His Excellency the Military Governor has, in accordance with the provisions of the Constitution of the East Central State of Nigeria, and in exercise of the provisions of Section 6 Sub-section (2) of Central Eastern State (Administration) Decree 1969 (Decree No. 46 of 1969) as amended by East Central State (Administration) (Amendment) Decree No. 34 of 1970, appointed you Member of the East Central State Public Service Commission with effect from 1st February, 1976.

2. A copy of the terms and conditions of your appointment is attached.

3. The swearing-in ceremony by His Excellency will take place at Government Lodge, Enugu, <u>at 10 a.m. prompt</u> on Monday, 2nd February, 1976 and I will be grateful if you arrive at Government Lodge not later than 9.30 a.m. that day.

Yours faithfully,

(signature)

(M. E. P. ODEBIOWA)
SECRETARY TO THE MILITARY GOVERNMENT

Mr. R. I. Uzoma,
Teachers Service Commission,
Enugu.

SECRET

APPENDIX 44

Letter of Appointment dated March 12th 1976, from the Secretary to the Military Government of Imo State, to Mr. R.I. Uzoma, conveying his appointment to the Public Service Commission of Imo State

IMO STATE GOVERNMENT

Telegrams: SECMILGOV OWERRI
Telephone:
Your ref....
Our ref....

OFFICE OF THE SECRETARY TO THE MILITARY GOVERNMENT
CABINET OFFICE
OWERRI

12th March, 1976

Mr. R.I. Uzoma
c/o Public Service Commission,
Owerri.

Dear Sir,

His Excellency the Military Governor of Imo State, Lt.-Colonel S.... Anunu, has appointed you ..... of the Imo State Public Service Commission, with effect from 10th March, 1976. A copy of the terms and conditions of appointment is attached.

2. The swearing-in ceremony of the Chairman and Members of the Commission will take place at 10.00 a.m. on Tuesday, 16th March, 1976, at the Executive Council Chambers in Owerri. It will therefore be very highly appreciated if you arrive Owerri in sufficient time for the swearing-in ceremony.

Yours faithfully,

....
Secretary to the Military Government

APPENDIX 45

Letter of Appointment dated March 12th 1976, from the Secretary to the Military Government of Imo State, to Mr. R.I. Uzoma, conveying his appointment as a member of the State Educational Board (SEB)

IMO STATE GOVERNMENT

CABINET OFFICE
OWERRI.

REF. NO. SGI/S.0140/II/508   1st September, 1980

Sir/Madam,

Appointment of Members of the State Education Board

I am pleased to inform you that His Excellency the Governor of Imo State, Chief Samuel Onunaka Mbakwe, has appointed you a Member of the State Education Board, with effect from Monday, 1st September, 1980. The Board is constituted as follows:

1. Dr. C. A. Duruji,
   Hon. Commissioner for Education — Chairman
2. Mr. S.M.O. Nwosu — Secretary
3. Mr. J. W. Wogu — Member
4. Mr. John Kafor — Member
5. Mr. R. I. Uzoma — Member
6. Mr. W. K. Anuforo — Member
7. Mrs. B. C. Nwankwo — Member
8. Mr. S. B. Ogbonna
   Director,
   Policy & Planning — Ex-Officio Member
9. Dr. C. E. Ebagbulem
   Director,
   Inspectorate & Examination — Ex-Officio Member
10. Mr. A. A. Iwe
    Director,
    School Management — Ex-Officio Member
11. Dr. I. S. Nwokorie
    Director,
    Higher Education — Ex-Officio Member.

2. Your remunerations and other conditions of appointment will be communicated to you in due course by your controlling Ministry.

3. Please accept my very sincere congratulations on your appointment.

Yours faithfully,

Prof. E. A. Anyanwu
Secretary to the Government.

Mr. R. I. Uzoma,
c/o Hon. Commissioner for Education,
Owerri.

APPENDIX 46

Letter of Appointment dated September 1st 1980, from the Secretary to the Military Government of Imo State, to Mr. R.I. Uzoma, conveying his appointment as Chairman of the Orlu Zonal Education Board

Secret

IMO STATE GOVERNMENT

CABINET OFFICE,
OWERRI.

REF. NO. SGI/S.0140/II/511

1st September, 1980.

Sir/Madam,

Appointment of Members of the Orlu Zonal Education Board

I am pleased to inform you that His Excellency the Governor of Imo State, Chief Samuel Onunaka Mbakwe, has appointed you a Member of the Orlu Zonal Education Board, with effect from Monday, 1st September, 1980. The Board is constituted as follows:

1. R. I. Uzoma, Esq.   -   Chairman
2. B. C. Okorofor, Esq.   -   Member
3. G. C. Iwuaba, Esq.   -   Member
4. Ben Nkwo-Meziri, Esq. -   Member
5. Titus C. Ngimah, Esq. -   Member
6. J. O. Nuosu, Esq.   -   Secretary.

2. Your remunerations and other conditions of appointment will be communicated to you in due course by your controlling Ministry.

3. Please accept my very sincere congratulations on your appointment.

Yours faithfully,

Prof. E. A. Anyanwu
Secretary to the Government

R.I. Uzoma, Esq.,
c/o Hon. Commissioner for Education,
Owerri

APPENDIX 47

Letter of Appointment dated July 1st 1982, from the Permanent Secretary, Federal Ministry of Education, to Mr. R.I. Uzoma, conveying his appointment as a Member of the Council of the Federal University of Technology, Owerri, Imo State

REF: No. FME/S/165/T/11

Federal Ministry of Education,
Higher Education Division,
Universities Section,
Lagos.

1st July, 1982

Mr. R.I. Uzoma Ofe, OBE.,
P.O. Box 9,
Nkwerre Via Orlu,
Imo State.

APPOINTMENT OF UNIVERSITY COUNCIL

I am directed to inform you that Mr. President, Alhaji Shehu Shagari, is pleased to appoint you as ......Member.................. of the Council of the Federal University of Technology Owerri, Imo State.

2. The appointment which will be at the pleasure of Mr. President, is for a period of two years and it takes effect from 1st August, 1982.

3. Please accept my congratulations on this honour which I have no doubt is well deserved.

Yetunde Holloway (Mrs)
for Permanent Secretary
Federal Ministry of Education.

APPENDIX 48

Letter of Appointment dated July 19th 1982, from the Secretary to the Military Government and Head of Service of Imo State, to Mr. R.I. Uzoma, conveying his appointment as Chairman, Imo State Teachers Disciplinary Committee

GOVERNMENT OF IMO STATE OF NIGERIA

Telegrams: SECNILGOV

Telephone:

Your ref.

Our ref. SGI/S.0091/83

OFFICE OF THE SECRETARY TO THE MILITARY
GOVERNMENT AND HEAD OF SERVICE
CABINET OFFICE
...........DEPARTMENT
OWERRI

19th July, 19__

Chief R. I. Uzoma,
c/o The Permanent Secretary,
Ministry of Education,
Owerri.

Sir/Madam,

APPOINTMENT OF MEMBERS OF THE TEACHERS DISCIPLINARY COMMITTEE

I have the pleasure to inform you that the Military Governor of Imo State, Brigadier Ike Nwachukwu has appointed you Chairman/Member of the Imo State Teachers Disciplinary Committee with effect from 8th July, 1984.

2. The Committee is composed of the following:

  (1) Chief R. I. Uzoma — Chairman
  (2) Barrister B... Onwubu — Member
  (3) Mrs. D. ... Ibezue — "
  (4) Mr. C.N. Okorafor, Chief Supt. of Schools (in-charge Science), State Education Board, Owerri. — "
  (5) Dr. C.C. Nwigwe, Chief Education Officer, Ministry of Education, Owerri. — "

3. Your remuneration and other conditions of this appointment will be communicated to you by the Permanent Secretary, Ministry of Education in due course.

4. Please accept my congratulations for this well-deserved appointment.

(CHIEF J.O.K. NWOSA)
SECRETARY TO THE MILITARY GOVERNMENT
AND HEAD OF SERVICE.

APPENDIX 49

Letter from the Chairman, Nkwerre Local Government Council, dated October 19th 1995, to Chief R.I. Uzoma conveying approval for the naming of the Local Government Library as R.I. Uzoma Library

IMO STATE OF NIGERIA
NKWERRE LOCAL GOVERNMENT

Telegram ....
Telephone ....
Our Ref: NKLG/CHLOG/130/2
Your Ref: ....

LOCAL GOVERNMENT HEADQUARTERS
Chairman's Office DEPARTMENT
P.M.B. 3005, NKWERRE
19th October, 1995

All replies to be addressed to the Chairman
Nkwerre Local Government

Chief Sir Dr. R.I. Uzoma
St. Paul's Pro-Cathedral
Nkwerre.

Dear Sir,

HANDOVER AND NAMING CEREMONY OF NKWERRE LOCAL GOVERNMENT, LIBRARY

We are glad to write and inform you that the Caretaker Committee and the Advisory Council of Traditional rulers of Nkwerre Local Government have each given their unanimous approval for the naming of the Local Government Library after your goodself.

This gesture is both in honour to you as the first Minister of Education for Eastern Nigeria and in recognition of your unrelenting service to our people in the field of Education.

May we also inform you that the Imo State Library Board is agreeable to this decision. Please note that the tentative date for both the handover of the Local Government Library to the State and the naming ceremony is Thursday 7th December, 1995.

We would appreciate your early confirmation of acceptance of this honour as it would enable us have enough time to plan a successful ceremony.

Congratulations.

Yours faithfully,

Arc. Madubuike Anyanwu Ohiaeri
Chairman
Nkwerre Local Government.

APPENDIX 50

Letter from Principal, St Augustine's Grammar School, Nkwerre, dated August 5th 1982, to Chief R.I. Uzoma, OFR, OBE conveying the naming of a Reuben Uzoma House at the School

ST. AUGUSTINE'S GRAMMAR SCHOOL
NKWERRE, IMO STATE NIGERIA

Our Ref...... SAGS/18/144
Date... 5th August, 1982

Your Ref............

MR. R.I. Uzoma, O.F.R.; O.B.E.
Chairman,
Zonal Education Board,
Orlu.

Dear Sir,

"REUBEN UZOMA HOUSE"
St. Augustine's Grammar School, Nkwerre

Right from the first term of the present School year (1981/82) the tutorial staff of this school expressed the need to revive the two School Houses which were dropped at the end of the Nigerian Civil War in order to bring the number of Houses to eight as was the case before the civil war, and also review the names of the Houses that lack relevance and any meaning to the School.

Not long ago, the staff carried out the exercise at which it was unanimously decided to name one House after you, to be known and called "REUBEN UZOMA HOUSE" with immediate effect.

This is in recognition of the laudable and enduring role which you have continued to play towards the development of the institution as well as the enhancement of its status.

The decision of the staff was unanimously ratified by the Board of Governors of the School at its recent meeting.

It is with great pleasure, therefore, that I convey the information to you through this medium, and send you my warm congratulations on this well-deserved emblem of honour. It is our earnest prayer that God may grant you many more years of useful service to this premier institution.

Yours Faithfully,

(E.I.A. OHAGWA)
PRINCIPAL.

[Stamp: PRINCIPAL, ST. AUGUSTINE'S GRAM SCH. *NKWERRE* IMO STATE.]

APPENDIX 51

D. SELECTED CORRESPONDENCES

Letter from the Librarian of the Royal Empire Society
Northumberland Avenue, London WC2, dated November 1st 1946,
to R.I. Uzoma Esq, in response to his request for library access,
during his year at the Institute for Education, University of London

THE ROYAL EMPIRE SOCIETY

FORMERLY THE ROYAL COLONIAL INSTITUTE
FOUNDED 1868

TELEPHONE:
WHITEHALL 5733 (15 LINES)
PRIVATE BRANCH EXCHANGE

CABLES:
RECITAL, LONDON
INLAND TELEGRAMS:
RECITAL, RAND, LONDON

NORTHUMBERLAND AVENUE
LONDON, W.C. 2

R.I. Uzoma, Esq.,
London. S.W.5.

1st November, 1946.

Dear Sir,

    In reply to your request this Library is open to all bona fide students of Empire affairs providing that they can let us have some suitable reference. I enclose a record card which I would ask you to complete. If you wish to make use of the Library you should either return this or hand it to an assistant when on your first visit to the Library, and if your application is accepted a students card of admission will be issued. Since this is a private Library maintained by the Society, this card of admission is for the sole purpose of reading in the Library and does not entitle students to borrow books or to use other facilities of the building apart from the reading room.

    I would suggest that for your purpose you refer to sections of 'Colonial Population' by Professor Kuczynski, 1937; and 'Labour Problems of Africa' by Noon, 1944. We have in addition a great many periodicals and official reports and whilst I cannot at the moment think of any specific book dealing with population distribution in Nigeria I have no doubt that a more thorough examination of our material by you will find a number of references, mainly in the form of chapters in works such as Lord Hailey's 'African Survey.'

    Pamphlets published by the Society can be purchased here though many are now out of print. We can show you what are available when you call.

Yours faithfully,
James Packman
Librarian.

APPENDIX 52

Letter from the World Association for Adult Education, dated June 19th 1947, to R.I. Uzoma Esq, of 5 Lidlington Place, London, NW1, in response to his request for education-related research materials on other countries, during his year at the Institute for Education, Univesity of London

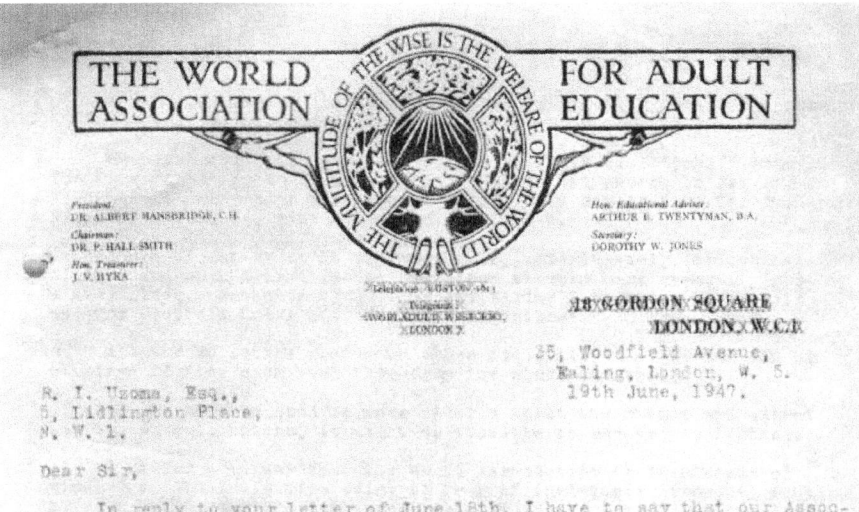

THE WORLD ASSOCIATION FOR ADULT EDUCATION

President:
DR. ALBERT MANSBRIDGE, C.H.
Chairman:
DR. P. HALL-SMITH
Hon. Treasurer:
J. V. BYRA

Hon. Educational Adviser:
ARTHUR E. TWENTYMAN, D.A.
Secretary:
DOROTHY W. JONES

18 GORDON SQUARE
LONDON, W.C.1

35, Woodfield Avenue,
Ealing, London, W. 5.
19th June, 1947.

R. I. Uzoma, Esq.,
5, Lidlington Place,
N. W. 1.

Dear Sir,

In reply to your letter of June 18th, I have to say that our Association has published in its quarterly Bulletins, issued between 1919 and 1946, articles dealing with adult education in its various aspects in a large number of countries.

With regard to the countries you mention, the work in China, which was confined almost entirely to the Eastern part of the country, was brought to ruin under the Japanese occupation. Some of the leaders moved West with the armies and carried on work in the eradication of illiteracy, training for citizenship, etc. An article on "Adult Education and the Chinese Village" (Series 2, No. III) might be useful to you, as also a general survey written some years earlier.

In the case of India, we would suggest the following Bulletins in the Second Series: No V. "Bombay Experiments in the Education of Illiterate Workers"; No. XII, "Problems of Adult Education in India"; No. XXI "Experiments in Literacy" and "Indian Adult Education Handbook"; No. XXII, "Adult Education in South India". Adult Education in India was able to make steady progress during the war and after. If you wish to make a thorough study of the movement in India, it would be advisable to get some of the literature published in India if you can wait for it to reach you. If you will let me know what you think about this, I can put you in touch with Indians who can advise you.

Very little recent material is available with regard to U. S. S. R. The movement made some progress between the wars and great progress was made in the elimination of illiteracy, but the war brought almost everything to a standstill. An article in Bulletin XXXIX (Second Series), "Adult Education in the Soviet Union", supplied from official sources in Russia, gives an outline of the work still being carried on. Two other articles which might interest you are "Adult Education in Russia and the U. S. S. R." (Bulletin XXIII - Second Series) and "Some Tendencies in Modern Russia" (Bulletin XXIV - Second Series). Some articles

- 2 -

on the work carried on in the earlier post-Revolution period are published in the First Series of Bulletins.

We have never published an article on adult education in Turkey. The movement is in an elementary stage there but you could get information about the recent development of People's Houses from The Turkish People's House, 14, Fitzhardinge Street, W. 1.

Adult Education in Latin America is, unfortunately, almost negligible and such activities as have been started have generally had a short life. Bulletin XXVII - Second Series - contains an article on "The People's Universities in the Argentine".

All the Bulletins mentioned above are still in print and can be obtained for 1s. each post free from the above address.

If you care to send me more details about the nature and extent of your investigations, it might be possible to advise you further.

I am sorry to say that the World Association is in process of winding up its activities owing to lack of inadequate financial support arising largely from the continued restrictions governing the international circulation of currency. But we are glad to do what we can to help any inquirers.

Yours truly,

Dorothy Jones

Secretary.

APPENDIX 53

Letter from the Director of Education of the West Sussex County Council, dated May 10th 1947, to R.I. Uzoma Esq, in response to the latter's letter of appreciation after a tour of schools in West Sussex County, United Kingdom

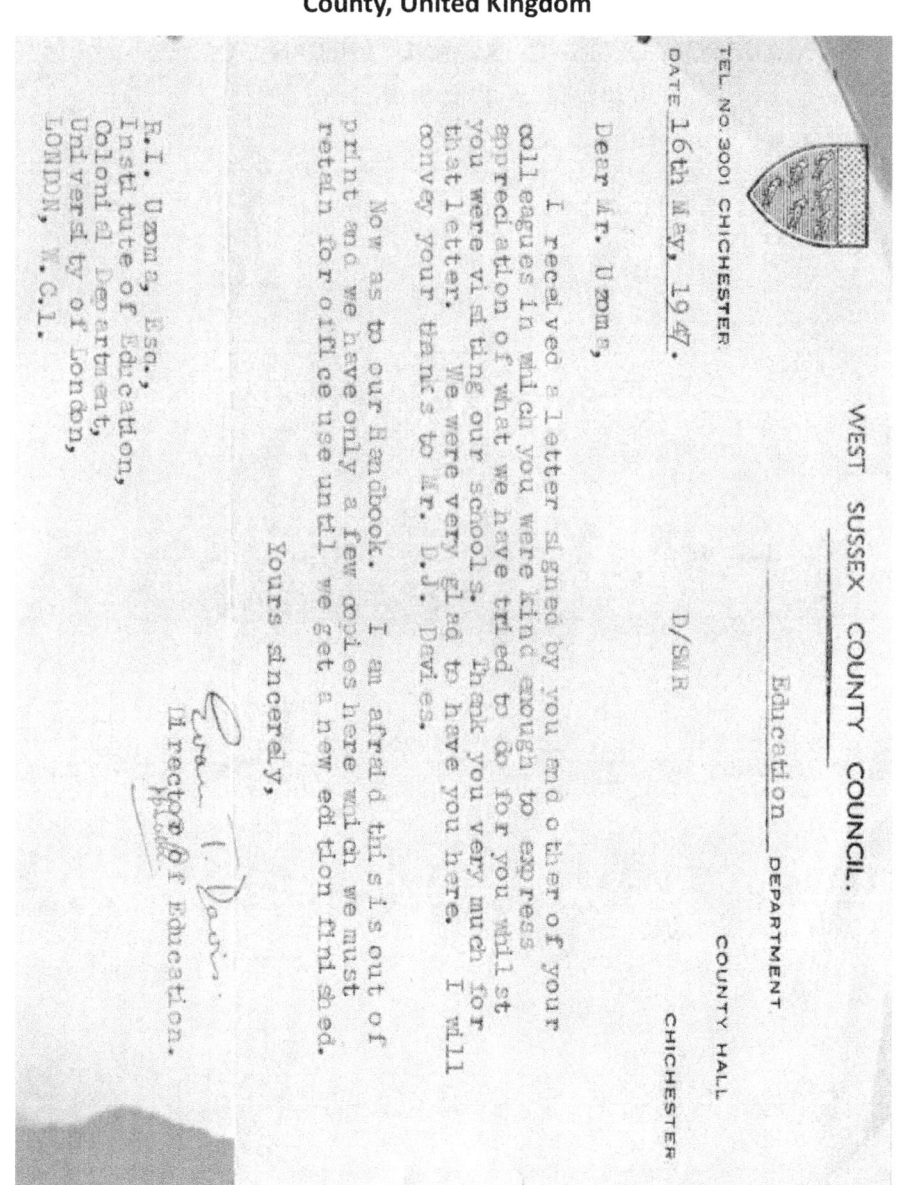

APPENDIX 54

Letter from the School of Oriental and African Studies, dated September 11th 1947, to Mr. R.I. Uzoma enclosing payment for his assistance in checking examination papers in Igbo language, shortly before his return from the University of London

SCHOOL OF ORIENTAL AND AFRICAN STUDIES

UNIVERSITY OF LONDON, W.C.1

Telephone Number: MUSEUM 1023/4
Telegrams: SOASUL, PHONE, LONDON

11th September 1947

Dear Mr. Uzoma,

    Miss Green has asked me to send to you the enclosed amount of £1. for your kind help in checking the Igbo Examination papers a short time ago. She is so sorry there has been the delay in forwarding the amount to you, due to delays at the University.

    Will you please let me know that you receive it safely.

Yours very truly,

Elizabeth Wright

APPENDIX 55

Handwritten Letter from L.J. Lewis, R.I. Uzoma's Tutor at the University of London, Institute of Education, dated September 17th 1947, to R.I. Uzoma, acknowledging receipt of a manuscript from the latter, submitted for publication in *Overseas Education*

87 Whitton Road,
Twickenham
17th September 1947

Dear Uzoma,

Thank you for the mss, which I hope to place for you, with Overseas Education. If it is not accepted by them, I will seek its publication in some other journal.

I am glad you enjoyed your Danish tour. In case I don't see you before you sail, may I extend to you my good wishes for a pleasant return journey and happy opportunities for your future career.

If there is anything we can do to help you in your future work do not hesitate to write us. And please remember, we will be glad to hear of anything you may be doing.

With all good wishes,
Yours sincerely
L J Lewis

APPENDIX 56

Letter from L.J. Lewis, R.I. Uzoma's Tutor, recommending him for a field study in Denmark for August 15th to 27th 1947 as part of a study in social survey at the Institute of Sociology, University of London

UNIVERSITY OF LONDON INSTITUTE OF EDUCATION

MALET STREET, W.C.1
Telephone - MUSeum 5525

COLONIAL DEPARTMENT

Mr. R. I. Uzoma has carried out a period of study in social survey work under the direction of the Institute of Sociology which should be completed by participation in a Field Study in Denmark, August 15-27. It is recommended that Mr. Uzoma be given permission and assistance to carry out the field study in Denmark.

pp. L. J. LEWIS
Tutor.

APPENDIX 57

Letter from the Director, American Library, United Stated Information Service, dated July 18th 1947, to R.I. Uzoma Esq, sending him requested material and books on life in America

UNITED STATES INFORMATION SERVICE

AMERICAN EMBASSY . LONDON

33, Davies Street,

London, W. 1.

July 18th, 1947.

R. I. Uzoma, Esq.,
5, Lidlington Place,
London, N. W. 1.

Dear Mr. Uzoma,

In reply to your letter of July 9th we are sending you a small selection of spare material on life in America and we hope these few pamphlets will be of use to your classes.

To supplement this material, we can offer you text-books and pictures on loan for one or two weeks and we shall be glad to help you further if you can let us know in what subjects you are specifically interested.

Sincerely yours,

Sargent B Child

Sargent B. Child,
Director, American Library.

APPENDIX 58

Letter from the University of London, Senate House, WC1, dated September 23rd 1947, to Reuben Ibekwe Uzoma Esq B.A, conveying his admission and registration for an M.A. Degree in Geography, as an External Student

UNIVERSITY OF LONDON,
SENATE HOUSE,
W.C.1.

Telegrams: University, London.
Telephone: Museum 8000.

23 September, 1947.

1295.2/H

DEAR SIR,

I beg to refer to your application for Registration as an External Student for the Examination for the M.A. Degree in Geography.

I have now to inform you that your application has been considered and approved, and that your name has been registered for the Examination in 1950.*

Your attention is drawn to the fact that Registration does not constitute entry. You should therefore apply in due course for an Entry Form, and make your entry in accordance with the Regulations.

This letter should be sent in with your entry as evidence of registration.

Your attention is further drawn to the following extracts from the Regulations relating to Registration of External Students:—

Modification of Registration.—Any modification of a student's registration must be made in writing at least one calendar month before the last date of entry to the examination, and, on one occasion, may be made without payment of an additional fee.

Transference of Registration.—Registration for any examination does not commit the student to enter for that examination at the date chosen or at all; he may have his registration transferred to a subsequent date without payment of an additional fee, provided that he applies for such transference not later than one month after the last date of entry to the examination for which he is registered. For a second transference of registration the normal fee is payable.

Re-registration.—Any student who enters for the examination for which he has been registered and withdraws, fails, or is referred, will be allowed to re-register for a subsequent examination without payment of an additional fee, provided that such re-registration is effected within one month of the publication of the Pass List. For a second re-registration the normal fee is payable.

Lapsed Registration.—Students who do not transfer or re-register by the appropriate date will be deemed to have allowed their registration to lapse, and should they propose subsequently to proceed to an External Examination they will be required to register afresh as though they had not previously been registered.

Any application for modification or transference of your registration must be accompanied by this letter.

Regulations for External Students.—The Regulations for External Students are revised in September of each year. In cases of important change two years' notice will be given, but registered students will be informed of any changes which will affect them.

Yours faithfully,

T. S. J. ANDERSON,
External Registrar.

* Examination with thesis.
Your thesis subject and syllabus are approved as set out overleaf. No alteration may be made in them without the written permission of the Council for External Students, previously obtained.

Subject for written examination:— The Geography of West Africa.

Reuben Ibekwe Uzoma, Esq., B.A.,
5, Hospital Road,
Portharcourt,
Nigeria,
West Africa.

P.S. You are registered on the understanding that you will be required to attend in England for the examination

Thesis.-   Rural Settlement in the Ibo Country, Southern
                              Nigeria.

   I shall take representative community-areas from different
parts of the country and analyse them, noting:
    (a) The relationship of groups of dwellings to one
        another and to the available cultivable land.
    (b) The relation of a group of dwellings to environment,
        e.g. in building material.
    (c) The effects, so far, of factors like roads which
        have been super-imposed on the traditional village
        pattern by the white man's coming.

   Reference will be made to patterns of settlement in other
parts of Nigeria, e.g. the Delta, to bring about the distinctiveness
the Ibo pattern.

   The effect of the pattern on the economic activities of the
peasant will be discussed.

APPENDIX 59

Letter to R.I. Uzoma dated June 22nd 1970, from the Bishop of Owerri, Rt. Rev. B.C. Nwankiti, requesting his input on state-controlled education system for the 1970 synod of the Owerri Diocese

"URGENT"

DIOCESE OF OWERRI

The Rt. Rev. B. C. Nwankiti,
Bishopscourt, Egbu,
P.O. Box 31,
Owerri, Nigeria.
June 22, 1970.

Our Ref: CD/BS/74/Vol.I

Mr. R. I. Uzoma,
Nnwerre.

My dear Reuben,

In preparing a summary report on the recent Synod, we shall naturally include a chapter on education and this will begin with a summary of the reports delivered to Synod by the Education Secretary and the General Manager of Schools. It would seem however that these reports are a little 'negative' and that we need to sound a note of hope and encouragement and to help the Diocese to understand the important part which the church must play in a State-controlled Education System. I should be very grateful if you would kindly prepare a short article of about 1,000 words which would sound this note and give some guidance and help to christians in what is for most of us an entirely new situation.

Will you please treat this matter as Urgent as The Rev. Canon J. Stephens, who is the Editor, is keen on sending the finished product to the printers in Ibadan early in July.

With prayerful good wishes.

Yours very sincerely,

+ B. C. Nwankiti
Bishop of Owerri

"URGENT"

APPENDIX 60

Circular Notice, dated September 12th 1944 by R.I. Uzoma informing the public about an Adult Education Center started by him in Okrika while he was Principal of Okrika Grammar School

OKRIKA
12/9/44.

An adult education centre was started here at the beginning of this month by Mr. R.I. Uzoma B.A. Principal, Okrika Grammar School The number has in just over a week grown to well over 300 men and women whose ages range between 12 and 45. In some cases husband and wife are both students and the wife seems to make more rapid improvement.

Mr. Uzoma made one important rule, and that is that any student who comes in drunk should not be admitted that day.

The staff is made up of volunteers from the Okrika Grammar School and Central School staffs and the Grammar School boys. One member of staff is a lady, and four are Certificated masters.

Classes are held three times a week and each teacher is on duty once a week. The subjects include Reading, Writing, Spoken English, Hygiene and Figures.

R.I. Uzoma

APPENDIX 61

Some Ministerial notes by R.I. Uzoma on the Eastern Regional Scholarship Awards for 1952

Miss Ada Nwankwo — Onitsha
Miss F. Mbamali — Onitsha
Mrs. K. Nwachukwu — Benin
Miss A. Okeke — Onitsha
Miss. Oti — Enyong
Miss Ikpeme — Calabar

6 job recommended for Onitsha award 1952

Nwankwo.

Appendix

Division	1	2	3	Total	
ABAK	1		1	3	4
ABAKALIKI	1		1	1	2
AFIKPO		1	1	3	4
ABAKPA	1		1	6	7
AWKA	5	1	6	10	16
AWGU				3	3
BAMENDA		1	1	5	6
BENDE	2	5	7	4	11
BRASS	1		1	3	4
CALABAR	3	8	11		11
DEGEMA	3	2	5		5
EKET	1	2	3	2	5
ENYONG	3	4	7		7
IKOM				3	3
IKOT EKPENE	1		1	6	7
KUMBA				2	2
MAMFE				1	1
NKAMBE		1	1		1
NSUKKA		1	1	5	6
ABUDU				1	1
ODUKPA				1	1
OGOJA	1		1		1
OGONI	2		2	2	4
OKIGWI	1		1	9	10
ONITSHA	8	13	21		2
OPOBO	1	3	4	3	7
ORLU	3	1	4	8	12
OWERRI	3	8	11	12	2
PORT HARCOURT	1		1	1	2
UDI	3		3	10	13
UYO	1	3	4	3	7
WUM					
VICTORIA		1	1	3	4
W.I.	2	1	3	1	4
Other Eligibles	1		1		
	50	58	108		

323

In addition to the awards listed above, the Eastern
Regional Scholarship Board have awarded 108 Scholarships.
These are :-

Aba Division	3
Abak "	1
Abakaliki "	1
Afikpo "	1
Ahoada "	1
Awka "	6
Bamenda "	1
Bende "	7
Brass "	1
Calabar "	11
Degema "	5
Eket "	3
Enyong "	7
Ikot Ekpene Div.	1
Nkambe "	1
Nsukka "	1
Ogoja "	1
Ogoni "	2
Okigwi "	1
Onitsha "	21
Opobo "	4
Orlu "	4
Owerri "	11
Port Harcourt "	1
Udi "	3
Uyo "	4
Victoria "	1
Western Ibo	3
Other Eligibles	1
	108

Thus there is a total of 229 Scholarships awarded by
the Eastern Regional Board to date.

Yet further awards.

The Eastern Board will be meeting again in the near future
to consider further awards, this time for Technical Courses.

BIBLIOGRAPHY

I. **Published Works**

Abernethy, D.B. (1969) "The Political Dilemma of Popular Education: An African Case". Stanford University Press.

Adiele, S.N. (2014) "The Contributions of Christian Education to the Development of Southern Igboland",*Perspectives in Religious Studies* Vol III (3), 75

Amucheazi, E.C. (1986) "Church and Politics in Eastern Nigeria, 1945-66: A Study in Pressure Group Politics". Lagos: Macmillan Publishers Nigeria.

Anero, N.I. (2011) "Experiences of Government Politicization in Participating Over Policies and Programmes of Primary Education in Nigeria". *Journal of Educational and Social Research* Vol I (2) 95

Animalu, A.O.E., Onwurah, B.A.C.(1997) Biography of Sir, Dr E. Chukuka Ezekwesili. Nsukka: Ucheakonam Foundation, Nigeria Ltd.

Basden, G. T. (1966) Among the Ibos of Nigeria. Barnes & Noble

Daniel, G.F. (1996) "The Universities in Ghana" Commonwealth Universities Year Book, 1997-98 Vol I, 649-656

Dike, K. O. (1962) Origins of the Niger Mission 1841-1891. Ibadan: University Press.

Ekechi, F. K. (1972) Missionary Enterprise and Rivalry in Igboland 1857–1914. London: Frank Cass & Co. Ltd.

Fafunwa, A. Babs (1995) "History of Education in Nigeria". Ibadan: NPS Educational Publishers Ltd.

Isichei, E. (1976) "A History of the Igbo People" London & Basingstoke: Palgrave Macmillan.

Nduka, O. (1973) Towards a National Policy on Education in Nigeria. *Prospects* Vol III (4), 438-450

Nduka, O. (1976) Background to the Foundation of Dennis Memorial Grammar School, Onitsha. *Journal of the Historical Society of Nigeria* Vol VIII (3), 69-92.

Nwadialor, K.L. & Umeanolue, I.L. (2012) "Missionary Factor in the Making of a Modern Igbo Nation, 1841-1940: A Historical Discourse." *Journal of Religion and Human Relations* Vol I (4), 112-127

Nwakanma, O. (2007) "Oyibo Ekwulo Odinamadu: A Woman of History" *Journal of Culture and African Women Studies,* No. 10

Nwana, O.C. (2012) "Emeritus Professor O.C. Nwana, an Autobiography". Owerri: Peacewise Systems and Prints.

Nwankiti, B. C. (1998) "The Growth and Development of the Church in Nigeria" (2nd Edition) Owerri: Ihem Davis Press.

Nwauwa, A. O., Korieh, C. J. (Eds.) (2011) "Against All Odds: The Igbo Experience in Post-colonial Nigeria". Glassboro, New Jersey: Goldline & Jacobs Publishers Co.

Obialor, S. (2006) "History, People and Culture of Nkwerre Town" (2nd Edition) Lagos: Teamwork Communications.

Obialor, S. (2007) "Nkwerre in Christ" Lagos: Teamwork Communications.

Oni, J.O. (2008) "Universality of Primary Education in Nigeria: Trends and Issues" *International Journal of African Education in American Studies* Vol. II (1)

Onyegbula, G. A. (2005) "The Nigerian-Biafran Bureaucrat" Ibadan: Spectrum Books.

Udoma, E.U. (1994) "History and the Law of the Constitution of Nigeria" Malthouse Press.

Usman, Y.B., & Abba, A. (2000) "The Misrepresentation of Nigeria: The Facts and Figures" *Centre for Democratic Development Research and Training* Vol I (2000)

Uzoma, A.C., (1971) "The Changing Position of Married Women of one Ibo Community (Nkwerre) in Township and Village" Vierteljahresberichte: Probleme der Entwicklungslander: No.44, 113-150. (The Vierteljahresberichte is a Quarterly *Journal of the Friedrich-Ebert-Foundation*, Bad Godesberg, Germany, which publishes articles on Developing societies).

Uzoma, R.I. (1948) "Adult Literacy Work at Okrika in the Delta of the Niger" *Overseas Education* Vol 19(4), 737-741

Uzoma, R.I. (1952) "Universal Schooling in Ngwa Clan of Aba Division" *Overseas Education* Vol. XXIII (2), 234-236

Williams, K. (1962) "Achimota: The Early Years, 1924-1948". Accra, Ghana: Longmans of Ghana Limited.

II. Unpublished Works

Amadi, S.I. (1964) Unpublished Speech at Ngwa High School Prize-Giving Day of 24th September, 1964

Nnamezie, N.I. (2006) "Christianity and the People of Nkwerre Opiaegbe" MA Project, University of Lagos, Akoka, Yaba, Lagos

Nzeduru, H. C. (2013) "A History on the Advent of Christianity in Ezeoke-Nsu (1913-2013)" Unpublished booklet by the Centenary History Committee of the Diocese of Okigwe-South (Anglican Communion)

Onyedum, N. I. (2000) "Nkwerre People and Culture" Unpublished BA Project, University of Lagos, Akoka, Yaba, Lagos

Uzoma, J. C. (Ed) (1981) "The Voice of Women" a Compendium on the NCWS released on behalf of the NCWS, Imo State, Nigeria. Owerri: Diocesan Press, February 1981; R.I. Uzoma Archives

Uzoma, J. C. (1989) Unpublished Biography of Eze Daniel Nwokocha Nwachukwu Nwadigo; R.I. Uzoma Archives

Uzoma, R. I. (1984) "The New Okigwe/Orlu (Anglican) Diocese" Unpublished Paper presented at the Inauguration of the new Okigwe/Orlu Diocese on 20th November, 1984; R.I. Uzoma Archives

Uzoma, R. I. (1988) Unpublished written interview granted to the Orlu Zonal Students, University of Ibadan on 17th November 1988

Uzoma, R. I. (1989) Sermon preached at the Annual Thanksgiving and Dedication Service of the DMGS Old Boys Association at St. Michael's Cathedral, Aba on 30th April, 1989; R.I. Uzoma Archives

Uzoma, R. I. (1991) "The Church Missionary Society in Eastern Nigeria" Unpublished Paper, 14th November 1991; R.I. Uzoma Archives

Uzoma, R. I. "Education in Nkwerre" Undated, handwritten address from R.I. Uzoma's Archives

GLOSSARY

1. Acha-Ama — The fair beauty, a pet name
2. Ala... — Land of... (A prefix to a location)
3. Ama... — Family compound or family lineage of... (a prefix to a location)
4. Amachie — Blocking the lineage: Name of church that opposed polygamy
5. Ama-Enyi — A haunt for elephants, a place name
6. Chochi-Ama-ghere-oghe — Church for lineage-growth or name of church that welcomed polygamy
7. Chochi-Dick-na-Ugoagwu — The Dick-and-Ugoagwu-Church, named after its founders
8. Ebe... — Place of..... (Prefix to a location)
9. Ekpechuo-Ogu — Protector of the People's Totem, title of a powerful ruler
10. Eshi — The founder of Nkwerre
11. Isi... — The root... or source of... (Location name)
12. Iyi-Bekee — The white sandy stream, a body of water in Nkwerre
13. Iyi-Enyi — An elephant stream or watering hole
14. Iwa-Akwa — Tying of a loin cloth, a traditional coming of age ceremony for boys in the Mbano area

15. Mbara-Nwankpa	Nwankpa's grounds, a location name
16. Ndi...	The people of... (A prefix to a village name)
17. Ndi-Nze	The Nze traditional title holders
18. Nguma Festival	A festival of Umunyem village in Nkwerre named after a traditional religious totem
19. Nna...	Father of... or founder of... (Prefix for a clan name)
20. Nwannediya	Husband's sibling, a pet name for a wife
21. Nwa-DC	The young district commissioner
22. Nwanwa	Child of our child, a pet name used by maternal kindred for their daughter's children
23. Nwanwa-Ukwu	A Nwanwa of distinction
24. Nwonuhie	The fair-lipped beauty, a pet name
25. Nzuko-Ekeukwu	The major Eke-day meeting – Eke being one of the four days in the Igbo calendar week)
26. Ochonma-Oha	Promoter of Public Good, a chieftaincy title
27. Ode-Akwukwo	The one who writes, secretary
28. Ofo	A symbol of authority in Igbo culture
29. Ogbabiruogwe	The breaker of obstacles, title of a powerful traditional ruler

Glossary

30.	Ogbunechendo	The mighty oak that shelters, a chieftaincy title
31.	Ohia-Ofoma	The Ofoma forest, a location
32.	Opia-Egbe	The Gun-makers or gunsmiths
33.	Okoro...	The kindred of... (A prefix to a village name)
34.	Okoro-Efo	The kindred of Efo
35.	Okpara-anaghefu-n'ije	The first son or heir does not get lost in foreign lands
36.	Okpuolu	A stand-alone child, an only child
37.	Okwara-Eshi	The first son of Eshi
38.	Omefo-Oburuaku	The winner of trophies, title of a traditional ruler
39.	Onye-Nkuzi	Teacher, also used as a salutation or greeting of respect.
40.	Orashi River	A river in Nkwerre
41.	Oru-Bekee	White man's work, a white-collar job
42.	Oyibo/Bekee	Colloquial/Igbo term for white people and associated things
43.	Ufo/Uhu-Duruaji	The homestead or compound of Duruaji
44.	Uhu...	The homestead of..., a location name
45.	Uke-eje/Ukeje	A person who is different from his peers or a first among equals- a chieftaincy title
46.	Ukwu-Inyi	The base or roots of Inyi, a village in Nkwerre

47.	Umu...	Children of... (Prefix to a village name)
48.	Upo	A traditional thick sauce eaten with yam during the New Yam Festival

INDEX

A

Aba-Ngwa
- County Councils, 73
- District County Council Rate, 76

Abaecheta, Mercy (Mrs. T.O.S. Benson), 146
Abayomi, Lady 160
Abayomi, O.M. 158
Aborigines Rights Protection Society, 32
Achebe, Samuel 41
Achebe, Chinua 28
Achigbu, Abigail E. 153
Achimota College, 33
Acholonu, Igwe Patrick of Orlu 124
Achonu, Chief, 110
Action Group government, 69
Ademola, Kofoworola Aina (nee Moore) 144, 160
African
- Education, 62
- Gospel Mission (AGM – Chochiamaghereoghe, 12

Agada Local Government Panel 100
Agbawo, Jane Ijeuru 152
Aggrey, James Emman Kwegyir 32
Agugua, B.C.U. 100
Agugua, Benneth 94
Aguta, Elfrida 158
Ahamba, M.O. 149, 160, 161
Ajasin, Michael Adekunle, 61
Ajoku, Clara 158
Ajoku, Susan 16
Akaose, Sarah Da Sarah, 98, 151-152
Akpabio UPE programme, 65
Akpabio, I.U. 66, 68, 69
Akufo-Addo, Edward, 33
Akuneme, D. 104
Akwiwu, Adaku, Barrister 126
Akwiwu, Emmanuel 49, 95, 118, 148
Akwiwu, Joy Nchechinyere (nee Nwachukwu), 148
Alhuda College, Kano 112
Aliyu, Hon 62
Alele, Grace (Professor Alele-Williams), 146
Alozie, Cecilia 146
Amadi, V.N. 157-158
Amaechi, Isaiah 94
Amanano, 10
Amorji indigenes, 11
Amuta, Viola 145
Ana, Ekanem (Mrs. Ikpeme) 145
Anchor, Marcus Nwankwo, 12
Anadu, S.C. 43

Anglican
- Church, 2
- Mission, 70-71, 79-90, 102-103
- Education
  - department, 72
  - Secretary's Office of the Niger- Delta Diocese, 73
- system, 73
- Missionary Society (CMS), 136
- Schools System, 71
- Girls Grammar School, Lagos, 112
- Teachers Training College, 29

Aniagolu, Anthony 116
Anierobi, Harford 41
Anionwu, Walter 43
Anti slave-trade activities, 3
Anumnu, Emmanuel 96, 121
Anyaegbu, Matthew 11
Anyaegbuna, Mark 41
Anyaegbunam
- Enquiry, 7
- Local Government Re-Organisation Committee, 100

Anyaehie, Beatrice 147
Anyaehie, John 147
Anyaehie, R. 121
Anyiam, Chief 11
Anyiam, Fred U. 21,94
Anyiam, Mark 97
Anyiam, U.U. 21
"Appeal for Aid" 119
Archdeacon Crowder Girl's Secondary School (ACMGS), Elelenwa, 77
Aro-Ozo Obinuhu 15
Ashby Commission, 25
Asika, Felicia Chibogu (Mrs. Emodi) 146
Asika, Loius 43
Asinobi, Keziah Nwanyidirim (nee Nwachukwu), 148
Asinugo, Johnson Sir 126
Assemblies of God Mission a.k.a. Chochi-Dick-Na-Ugoagwu, 12
Asugha, Christoper 49, 95
Asugha, Ezekiel Ihedioha 17, 20
Asugha, Harold 96
Awgu, M.C. 53
Awokoya, S.H.O. 62-63, 65, 67
Awoshika, F.O. 62
Azikiwe, Nnamdi, 53-54, 66-67
Azodeh, Udeze 96

Index

B

Babangida, Ibrahim 8
Baptist Training College, Ogbomosho, 26
Baptiste, S.M. 158
Barewa College, 58-59
Basic Primary Education, 2
Biafra Police Charge Office, Nkwerre 101
Bida, Makaman 62
Biographical
- construction, 1-2
- theoretical research, 1

Birabi, Bennett N. 77
Birabi Memorial Grammar School (BMGS) Bori-Ogoni Example, 77-80
Birabi, Timothy Naaku Paul 47, 77-78
Bob-Manuel, Antoinette (Sister-Antoinette) (Mrs. Ejiwunmi), 144-145
Bob-Manuel, Faushina 146
Bob-Manuel, Gloretta 146
Bob-Manuel, Kate 146
Bob-Manuel, Patricia 146
Bonny Government School, 20
Bovi, Alfred 44
Boys Scout Convention, Birmingham, United Kingdom, 115
British
- parliamentary system, 52
- Rule, 7

Burton, Graham 124
Busia, Kofi Abrefa 33

C

C.M.S. St. Paul's College, Awka 59
Cambridge
- Conference, 62-63
- (Overseas) School Certificate Examination, 44
- School Certificate Examination, 60

Campaign for women's education, 113
Centres of education, 2
Certificate of Election as a fellow of Royal Geographical Society (FRGS) 1946, 276
Chelds, S.H, 43
Chiedu, Phillipa Ada 146
Chiejina, Joseph 136-137
Chigbu, Stella 153
Chinaka, Geoffrey 49, 96
Chinaka, Samuel 93- 94
Christian Missionary Society (CMS), 48
Christianity in Nigeria, 2

Chukueke, Rachel 161
Chukukere, Francis N. (JP) 126
Church
- Missionary Society (CMS), 10, 26, 40-41
  - Awka College, 53
  - education system, 110
  - in Eastern Nigeria, 188-192
  - Mission, Nkwerre 20
  - missionaries, 346
  - Niger Mission Authorities, 93
  - school system, 113
  - Women's Home Craft Training Centre, Emii Owerri 139
- of Nigeria (Anglican Communion), 26

Circular Notice about Adult Education Center Started in Okrika 321
Civil war, 150
Clifford, Hugh 58
Cockin, Rev. 75
College Rate levy, 76
Collingwoods, P.G 79
Colonial
- civil service, 58
- government, 4
  - scholarship, 143

Colonialism, 4
Community
- independence, 64
- service, 141

Congratulatory
- letter from N.U. Akpan on award of National Honour of OFR , 1965 288
- letter 1961, from Rt. Hon. Francies Akanu Ibiam , 1961 284
- Telegram from
  - Bishop Dimieari on award of OFR 290
  - Chief Ikechi Nwadinobi on award of OFR, 292
  - Dr. Alvan Ikoku on award of OFR 289
  - Ezekwesilis on award of OFR, 291
  - Rt. Hon. Nnamdi Azikiwe, 1961 283

Constituent Assembly 1966, 7
Coomasie, Ahmadu 62
Crowther, Bishop 40

D

Dennis Memorial Grammar School (DMGS), Onitsha 39-40, 53, 95

- Old Boys Association, 118
Dennis, T. J. 136
de Souza, Nwadinafor Chinyelu, 30
Dike, Kenneth O. 44-45, 69
Dikko, Comfort 141
Dimierari, E. T. 75
Diocesan Scholarship Scheme 93
Diocese of Owerri/Owerri Diocese, 87-89
Drinkwater, F.E. 44
Duckworth, E.H. 44
Duke Town School, Calabar 132
Durunneji, Reuben 135

E

Early
- Campaign for Girl-Child Education, 109-114
- missionary education, 105

Eastern
- Nigeria Gazettee listing the 1961 Queen's Birthday Honours as Officer of the Most Excellent Order of the British Empire, 278-279
- Regional Government Scholarships for Tertiary Education, 56

Ededem, Mary 161
Edmonds, Leonard 12
Edu, Nwando 145
Education
- Day, 69
- in a changing Africa: concepts and practice, 224-227
- in Nkwerre Town 199-203
- Law, 1956 68

Egbuchu, Paul Enwereobi 94
Egbunife, Cecilia 145
Egere, Esther 146
Egere, Margaret (Mrs. Njemanze) 145
Egwin, Virginia 161
Egwuatu, Cecilia 145
Egwuatu, Lilian 146
Egwueke, Mabel 152
Egwuekwe, Rufus 94
Ekeleme, Rose 161
Ekeocha, Jonathan Uwakwe 30, 41, 43
Ekeudo, Simon 135
Ekwueme, Beatrice (nee Nwajagu), 148
Ekwulugo, Edmund 44
Elitist Secondary Schools and institution, 58
Elliot Commission, 1943, 25

Eluwa, M.O. 160-161
Eluwa, Mercy 149, 160
Emeanuru, Ezekiel 41, 95
Emeanuru, Uzoukwu 41
Emeghara, Anyiam 12
Emenike, M.C. 94
Emeniko, Jonathan A. 94
Emeto, Ezekiel Uzoma 12
Emmanuel, Francesca 146
Emutchay, D.W. 104
Enemuo, E.O. 31
English education, 41
Erinne, D.C. 44
Eronini, Ijeoma Adaoha (nee Ekeocha), 30
Eshi stool (the traditional ruler of Nkweme), 8
Esua, E.E. 62
Experimental electoral process, 523
Eyo-Ita, 52, 53, 66
Ezeilo, James Okoye Chukwuka 39, 45
Ezekwesili, E.C. 31, 87, 97

F

Fafunwa, 66-67
Fajemisin, J. 158
Fingesi, Promise 49
First African Church Mission, 11
Formal
- Education, 2, 13, 16, 18-19, 22, 40, 48, 56, 83, 95, 105, 107, 110-111, 114, 152
  - system in Nigeria, 26
- mission education, 3
- schooling, 4
Forster, C.A. 43
Fraser, Garden Alexander 32
Free
- and Compulsory Universal Primary Education, (UPE), 112
- Church of Scotland 135-136
- Education, 64
- Universal primary and compulsory education, 63

G

Gelsthorpe, A, Morris 27, 43, 47-48
Gender
- balance in institutions, 82
- disparity in education in African, 112
- gap in Education ,112- 113
- revolution, 142

Index

Ghana Education Services 33
Ginigeme, Amos 135
Girl-child education, 113
Girl's Friendly Society of England, 156
Girls Education, 98
"Giving unto God", 120
George, Rufus Ada 49
Government Standard Six Examinations, 20
Guggisberg, Gordon 32
Gun-smithing – traditional occupation of Nkwerre people, 7

H

Historical
- biographies, 1,4
- style, 105

History of
- schooling, 2

Holy Ghost Fathers at Onitsha, 46
Holy Rosary College, Enugu 112
Home craft training-programme, 139
Honours, Award and Congratulatory messages, 273-274
Hope Waddell Training Institute, Calabar 20,46

I

Ibekwe, Janet Nwannedie a.k.a Daa Acha-Ama 13, 15-17
Ibekwe, Uzoma 13, 15-17, 106
Ibeneme, J. 11
Ibezim, Dick 12
Ibiam, Akanu 26
Ibiam, Endora 146
Ifiteana known as *Okika-na-ube* (*Umu-Okanube* or worshippers of Okanube), 29
Igbani, Madumere 12
Igbo
- civilisation, 28
- communities, 106

Iheanacho, F.O. 26
Iheanetu, Isaac 11
Ihedioha, Jimanze 94
Ihegboro, Eunice Eriaba (Da Eriaba), 151-152
Ihekwaba, Francis U. 9,93-94
Ihekwaba, J.O. 121
Ihekwoaba, John 94
Ihekwoaba, Lazarus 94
Iheme, Ethel 114

Iheme, Margaret 16
Ihetu, Jason, 49, 95
Ihezue, Dinah 149
Ihiekwe, Silas 20
Ike-Nwachukwu, Gen. rtd. 145
Ike-Nwachukwu, Gwendoline 145
Ikejo, Clement 44
Ikoku Committee, 69
Ikoku, Alvan 26-28, 54
Ikokwu, Margaret 160
Ikonne, Eze 122
Ikpeme, Affiong 145
Ikpeme, Iwo 145
Ilona, Martin Igwegbe 116
Ilona, Ntochukwu Obinna 116
Independence Constitution, 1960, 51
Information leaflet on the work of the Committee on Higher Education of the Joint Council of the Niger Group (Anglican), 236-239
International
- Council of Women 160
- Alliance of Women, 160

Interview with R.I. Uzoma conducted by Umezurike, I. Ifeanyi, P.N., Abamara and Ogidi, Anene of Orlu Zonal Educator, 212-219
Introduction of Christianity into West Africa, 3
Irochukwu, Prisicilla 145
Isong, Clement, 46
Isu Local Government, Area, 8
Isu Water Scheme 99
Ita, Eyo 26, 53-53, 66
Iweka, Gloria Nwoyibo 46
Iweka, Isaac 41,45
Iwuanyanwu, Emmanel, 118
Iwundu, Nwangborie 133-134
Iwunze, Wilfred 135
Iwuoha, Emmanuel Sir 126
Iwuoha, Oke 135

J

Jaja, E.R.D. 43
Jawara, Dawda , 33
Jeffrey, G.M. 35
John, T. 158

K

Kano, Aminu 61
Kashim, Shettima 62

Katsina
- Teacher College, now Barewa College, 58
- Higher College, 59

Kemmer, May (Mrs.Uwechia) 145
Kemmer, Violetta 145
King's College, Lagos 58
Koripamo, R.J.E. 53-54
Koripamo-Agary, Timiebi 54

L

Letter
- conveying approval for the naming of local Government Library as R.I. Uzoma Library, 308
- conveying naming of a Reuben Uzoma House at St. Augustine's Grammar School, Nkwerre, 1982, 309
- from Director of Education of West Sussex County Council, 313
- from Director, American Library USIS for his request for materials and books on life in America, 317
- from L.J. Acknowledging Receipt of Manuscript in Overseas Education, 315
- from L.J. Lewis as part of study in social survey at the Institute of Sociology, University of London, 316
- from Librarian of Royal Empire Society Northumberland Avenue, London while in the Institute of Education, University of London, 310
- from Mr. J.B. Davies Chairman UASC on award of OBE, 287
- from Rev. W.J. Wood, Education Adviser to the Protestant Missions, 1961 286
- from Rt. Rev. B.C. Nwanlenti requesting for input on state-controlled education system, 320
- from School of oriental and African Studies for payment in checking examination papers in Igbo language, 314
- from Secretary to the Government of the Federation on the award of Nigeria National Honour of Officer of the Order of the Federal Republic (OFR), 1965 277
- from Sir Louis Mbanefo, 1901 on conferment with the OBE, 285
- from University of London, conveying admission and registration for M.A. Degree in Geography as External student, 318-319
- from World Association for Adult Education to a request for education related research materials at the Institute for Education, University of London, 311-312
- in respect of appointment as provincial Administrator for Orlu 1967, 296-297
- of Appointment and of Recognition, 295-309
- of Appointment as a Member of State Educational Board (SEB), 304
- of Appointment as a member of the Council of Federal University of Technology, Owerri, Imo State, 306
- of appointment as a member of the Teacher's Service Commission, 1974 299-300
- of appointment as an Interim Member of the East Central State Public Service commission, 1975, 301
- of appointment as Chairman of Orlu Zonal Education Board, 305
- of appointment as Chairman, Nkwerre Divisional School Board, 298-299
- of Appointment as Chairman, Imo State Teachers Disciplinary Committee, 307
- of appointment as member of the Provisional Council of the University of Lagos, 295
- of appointment as permanent member of the East Central State Public Service Commission, 302
- of appointment from Etim O. Inyang on role on Police Community Relations Committee in Imo State, 294
- of appointment to the Public Service Commission of Imo State, 1976 303
- of Conferment of Honourary Degree, 1990 282
- of Congratulation from Amadi Ikwechegh on conferment with LLD Honoris causa by University of Nigeria, 1990 293
- of Recognition and Declaration of a Philanthropist, 281

Lewis, Herbert Rev. 46
Local community
- fundings, 80

Index

- Union, 154
London
- Intermediate Bachelors Degree (B.A.) class, 60
- Matriculation, 60
- Examination, 27
- University degree, 28

M

MacPherson Constitution, 19, 51, 47, 51-52, 61, 78
Madumere, Christopher 96
Madumere, Julius 96
Mahama, John Dramani 33
Manumihe, Victoria (Mrs. Amadi) 145
Mbanefo, A. 158
Mbang, Sunday 46
Mbonu, Wilfred 41
Melton, Andrew W. 44
Members of
- the House of Representatives (MHR), 51
- Regional Houses of Assembly (MHA), 51
Memo on Financing Imo State University, 1985 266-270
Memorandum
- by Nkwerre Community to Imo State Local Government, Agada Panel visiting Nkwerre, 1976 243-255
- to Anyaegbuena Local Government, Re-organization by Nkwerre Community 1971, 256-265
Merchants of Light Secondary School, Oba, 53
Merenu, Agbarakwe 12
Methodist
- Boys College, Uzuakoli (later Methodists Boys High School), 46
- Church Mission, 79
- Girls High School, Lagos, 112
- mission, 136
Methodists Uzuakoli 20
Miles, J.B. 44
Mills, John Evans Atta 33
Ministerial notes by R.I Uzoma on Eastern Regional Scholarship Awards, 1952 322-324
Mission
- education, 2
- Houses, 3
Missionary education, 3-4, 106
- system, 2
Modern childhood, 3

Mohammed, Murtala 8
Mokelu, Janet 161
Mothers' Union 155-156
Mugabe, Robert 33
Muna, S.T. 53,55

N

National
- Council of Nigeria and the Cameroons (NCNC), 46, 53-54
- Council of Women's Societies (NCWS), 159-162
- Youth Movement, 52
Nationalist pioneers, 59
New Era Ladies Club, Lagos, 58
New Okigwe/Orlu Diocese for inauguration of the new Diocese, 240-242
Ngowu, Emmanuel 118
Nguma Festival, 15
Ngwa
- College Rate, 75
- Educational Cultural Assembly, 73-74
- High School Model, Aba, 73-74
- High school, 80
- Women Association, 75
Niger Delta Area, 10
Niger Mission Area, 28
Niger-Delta Diocese, 87
Nigerian
- civil war, 5, 8, 13, 79, 73, 82, 88, 158
- Union of Teachers (NUT), 68
- Youth Movement (NYM), 53
Njemanze, Benjamin 145
Njemanze, Bobo 145
Njemanze, Mercy (Mrs. Iheanacho, 146
Njoku, G.U. 43
Nkemena, Idah 146
Nkrumah, Kwame 33
Nkwerre
- Aborigines Union (Women's Section), 18
- Aborigines Union (NAU), 9, 93-94, 97-100, 113, 121, 151, 153
- Chieftaincy Affair 120-125
- community, 111, 121, 123
- Divisional Education Board, 103
- *Opiaegbe*, 7
- *part of Nkwerre Ohuebe*, 7
- primary school, 20
- Town Union (NTU), 96

- Water Scheme, 98-99
- youths, 95

Nnadi, Grace 152
Nnadi, Timothy 96
Nnajuba, Joseph. O. 94
Nnamezie, Nonye (nee Onyedum), 345
Nnanano, 10
Nnanna, Christiana 145
Non-governmental social movements, 150
Northern-Ngwa Teacher Training College, Nsulu, Nbawsi, 80
Nosike, John 75
Nri civilisation, 28
Nsu communities, 133,138
Nuffield Foundation, 62
Nwachukwu,
- Abraham 49, 95-96
- B. 101
- Chief, 75
- Daniel Nwokocha 17
- Eze Daniel Nwokocha 131-133, 135-138, 141, 144
- Jemimah Chinyere (Mrs. Uzoma), 131-132, 137-139
- Joy Nkechinyere, 139
- Rebecca Chinuru 131, 138-139
- Ugo-Eze Rebecca Nwanyichukwu, 131 Nwadigo,
- Michael 135
- Eze Nwachukwu 132
- Nwachukwu 38,132, 134-135
- Nwonuhie Nwachukwu (nee Nwoku of Okpoetere of Onicha-Uboma), 132

Nwadinafor Chinyelu de Souza (ne Okediadi), 30
Nwagbo, Christiana 145
Nwaigwe, Chief 75
Nwakanma,
- Abel N. 93-94, 121
- Benson 96
- Nathan 96

Nwakiti, Benjamin 45
Nwana, O.C. 140
Nwangwu, Isaac 41
Nwankiti, Bishop 89,103,156
Nwankpa, Sunday 96
Nwannunu, Chief, 75
Nwanyichukwu Rebecca 138
Nwapa, Flora (Mrs. Nwakuche), 148
Nwelue, Nwadigo 132
Nwogu, John 94
Nwogu, Nze Emmanuel 121,124

Nwokorie, Luke 135
Nwopuru, Nwonyeoma 135
Nworisa, Florence Nwachi 152
Nwosu,
- B.C.E. 42
- Emma 100
- James Idiwogu 94
- Nwankpa 12
- S.M.O. 79

Nwosu, James Iheme 94
Nwosu-Iheme,
- Chioma 114
- Nze 99
- Sylvia 114
- Uzoma, 126

Nwozo, Eunice 146
Nzeduru, Ekeoba 134
Nzegwu, Dr. 145
Nzegwu, Nwachukwu 145
Nzimiro, May 160
Nzimiro, Priscilla 145
Nzuko Ekeukwu 150, 155

O

Obasanjo, Olusegun 46
Obasi, Okorie 138
Obi, Stella (late Nzegwu, Rebecca), 143-145
Obiajunwa, Ugoagwu 12-13
Obianyo, Elsie (nee Agugua), 114
Obiefule, Mark Achiegbu 11
Obinuhu Kindred 14-15,19
Obua, Felicia 160
Obuforibo, Abiye II, 49
Octivom, Reverend 135
Odiakosa, C.O. 44
Odinamadu, Oyibo Ekwilo16,160
Odogwu, Juliana 145
Offonry, H.K. 104
Ofonagoro, Walter Ibekwe 22
Ofonagoro,Gabriel Obioha–Ugochinyere of Amaigbo, 21-22
Ogbolu, Alfred 41
Ogbolu, Beatrice 145
Ogbonna,
- Aaron 135
- Benson 96
- J.N 75

Ogoni
- community, 77,79
- County Council, 79

Index

- Grammar School project, 78
- Representatives Assembly, 77-78

Ogori, R.D. 43
Oguntayo. T. 157
Ogwo, Sammy 44
Ogwuma, Mr. 75
Ohagwa, Thompson 20
Ohanka, S.N. 94
Oharka, S. 121
Ohayagba, Rose 152
Ohia, E.I. 43
Oihaeri, Nathaniel 44
Oji, Okwara 94
Ojike, Mbonu 43
Ojukwu, Odumegwu, 7, 99
Okagbue, Yenna 145
Okechukwu, Albert 43
Okechukwu, H.L.O. 43
Okediadi, Eunice Chinelo (nee Onyeabo), 30
Okediadi, Samuel Iyasele 29
Okeigwe, S. 121
Okeke,
- Albert O. 118
- Ebele 46
- James Chukwuma (ogbunechendo Nnewi), 46

Okeondarue, Ernest 43
Okigwe (Ecclesiastical) District, 11
Okigwe/Orlu Christian Association, 89-90
Okigwe/Orlu Diocese, Imo State, 88
Okocha Andrew C. 43
Okorie, Mary Akure (nee Nwokorie Ebo), 138-140
Okoro, B.C.I. 93, 125-126
Okoro, Elelaonu (nee Amadi) 145
Okoye, Madam 160
Okpala, Bertram Ikedinachukwu 39, 115
Okpara, Michael Iheonukara 46, 52-53
Okparaocha,

- Daniel Uju 12, 94
- James, 11
- Nwaigbe Sophia (nee Uzoma), 109
- Nzewuba 12, 109

Okpofabiri Mr. 98
Okpuala-Ngwa Native Authority, 73, 76
Okrika Grammar School
- (Known as Coastal Varsity), 48
- Okrika (OGS), 47-48, 95

Okure, U.U. 62
Okwara, Thomas 11

Okwuosa, Adaoha Chibuzo OON (nee Uzoma) 111, 126, 343-344
Oladipo, A.A. 158
Olaiya, C.O.K 158
Old Boys of Achimola College, 34
Oli, Enoch , I. 26, 28, 47, 53-54
Olisa, Helen Uzoamaka 146
Olum, Chief, 75
Oluwa, M. 158
Omoneghuzia, C.A. Jos 43
Omoniyu, Joy 158
Onagbesan, O.O. 158
Onejeme, Victoria Ayo (nee Ezenwa) 148
Oni, J.O. 66-67
Onuoha, Esther 158
Ononuju, Joy 161
Onubogu, Walter 41
Onubuogu, Andrew 20
Onumonu, Margaret (Mrs. Oputa), 145
Onuoha, Apati 135
Onuoha, D.I. 38, 101
Onuoha, Daniel Nwosu 20, 23
Onusa, 9
Onwuchekwa, B. 43
Onwuegbuzia, Daniel 44
Onwukwe, Timothy 20
Onwumere, Silas 96
Onwumere, Ugochi Eziaha (nee Uzoma), 115, 126
Onwuzuruigbo, Christian 152
Onyeabo, Alphanso Chukwuma 30
Onyeabor, A.C. 136
Onyeador, U. 160
Onyeagiri, James 94
Onyebula, Lawrence 49
Onyegbula, Godwin A. 8, 49, 96, 99-100, 118, 120-121
Onyegbula, Lawrence 96
Onyejiaka,
- Emmanuel 96
- Marcus 94
- Mary 114
- Willie 8

Onyekuru, Christie 158
Onyemelukwe, James 45
Onyia, J.B. 104
Oparaeke, Durochie 134
Organisation of African Unity (OAU) Humanitarian Relief Agency, 5
Orlu-Nigerian headquarter of the British Cheshire Home, 5
- province, 7

Oron Training Institute, 26
Osagie, S.U. 158
Osigwe, Uriah Anyiam 94
Osunkwo, Francis I. 94
Otagburuagu, John 101
Otubelu, Gidion 45
Oviuke, J. 88-89

P

Patterson, C.J. 43
Pam, Elizabeth 149
Pentecostal churches, 13
Pepple, Grace 146
Pikibo, William 49
Pivotal teachers, 143,149
Political
- competitiveness, 78
- developments, 65
- dispensations, 100
- independence, 63,112
- pressure, 69

Police Public Relations Committee, 101
Pollard, W.G. 77
Postgraduate Diploma Certificate, University of London, Institute of Education 1947, 273
Post-Retirement Public Service, 102-104
Public Service Commission (PSC), 103

Q

Quasi-federation arrangement, 51
Queen Amina College, Kano 112
Queen's College, Lagos, 58

R

R.I. Uzoma Educational Foundation (RIUEF), 125-129
- aims and objectives,- 126
- pioneer beneficiaries, 127-129
- Trust Fund, 118

Ransome-Kuti, Olikoye 146
Rawlings, Jerry John 33
Regional
- governments, 51
- Houses of Assembly, 62

Relevance of Continued Education — address to clergy of Okigwe/Orlu Diocese, 1986 220-223
Report of Committee on Higher Education to Joint Council of the Dioceses, East of the Niger, 228-235
Response to questionnaire interview by Orlu Zonal Students Association, University of Ibadan, 1988 204-211
Richardson, Reverend 135-136
Role of Church Missions, 3
Roman Catholic
- Church, 10-11,40
- missions, 68

Rule of law, 55
Rural development by community development organs, 83

S

Saronwiyor, Fiito N. 78
Second Memorandum on the Political Bureau 183-187
Second World War 147
Selected Correspondence, 310-324
Sermon Preached at 1989 Annual Thanksgiving and Dedication Service of DMGS Old Boys Association,193
St. Michael Cathedral, Aba, 1989 193-198
Seventh Day Adventist Mission (SDA), 12
Shagari, Shehu 148
Shodeinde Chief Alias 149
Shodeinde, Titi 160
Shonekan, W.I. 158
Short Memorandum on Future Political Arrangements for Nigeria, 176-182
Slave trade, 6
Social transformation, 4
Spiff, Clarice 145
St.
- Andrew's Teacher College, Oyo 26
- Anne's School, Molete Ibadan 112
- Augustine's Grammar School (SAGs) Nkwerre, 31, 82, 93, 96-97, 125
- Barnabas NDP Church Omoba 11
- Bartholomew's Primary School, Asata, Enugu 55
- Catherine's Girls Secondary School, Nkwerre, 16, 82, 97-98, 125, 152
- Charles Training College Onitsha, 26
- Paul Training College Awka, 26
- Paul's Anglican Church, Mbara-Nwakpa, 10-11, 13
- Paul's College, Awka 27-31
- Paul's Pro-Cathedral Church, Nkwerre, 91-92

Index

- Paul's University Awka, 31
- Paul's University College (of Theology), 28, 92
- Peter's School, Okrika 47-48

State Management of Schools, 271-272
Summer, Mary 155-156

T

Tamuno, Tekena Nitonye 49
Tax collectors, 122
Taylor, H. 41
Teachers Training College Katsina, 26
Teachers'
- Service Commission (TSC), 102-103
- Training Colleges, 79,113

Tertiary education, 82
Thompson, J.W.L. 44
Toro Teachers Training College, 26
Traditional
- education, 3
- four kindred group, 9-10

U

Ubani, M.W. 75
Ubani, Mary 75
Ubani-Ukoma, S.W., 53
Udechukwu, James 135
Udo, Anyiam Emeghara 123
Udogu, Ada Chinwuba 160
Udom, Grace 146
Udoma, Udo 46
Ugballa, Eze Ibenye 122
Ugochukwu,
- Angelina 152
- C.C. 101
- Eshi Eze J.O. 121
- J.O. 94, 123

Uju,
- Catherine Nwanu 151-152
- Chief 110

Ukaegbu, Nze D.I. 121
Ukegbu,
- Christiana Nwakwa 152
- Daniel Udeagwu 93-94
- Dickson 94
- Ndubueze 96

Ukpabi, E.N. 104
Ukwuoma, Billy G. 126
Umu-Durueshikaodu, 14

Una, S.J. 53
UNICEF, 112
United Nations Declaration of Human Rights and UNESCO's education plans for Nigeria, 112
Universal
- Primary Education (UPE), 63-64, 66-67, 80, 112
  - policy, 56
  - Proposal of R.I. Uzoma as Minister of Education – Education Policy for the Eastern Region, December, 1952 167-172
  - Review committee, 1958 69
- Schooling in Ngwe Clan of Aba Division, Uzoma, R.I. General Manager and supervisor Anglican Schools, 173-175

University
- College, Ibadan, 25
- Education, 25
- of London, 25
- of Nigerian, Nsukka 25

Upo Ritual, 14
Ururuka, Mr. 98
Uwechia, Azuka 145
Uwanaka, Adeline Dane 126
Uzoamaka, Grace 152
Uzoechi, Felicia Nwaigbe (Da Nwaigbe) 152
Uzoma
- Adaoha Chibuzo 18, 47, 109
- Anele Nwachukwu 18, 47, 109, 147
- Beatrice (Nwaobiaraku), 108, 111, 166
- Bertram (Azuatalam) 16, 49, 95, 108
- Blessing (Ikechi), 108
- Charles C. 126
- Christiana (Elechi), 108
- Chinyere Iheanacho 109
- Chukwukere Ihetu 18,109
- Comfort (Ahuzuru), 108
- Ebere Obioma 18
- Elewechi Uzonna 18

- Emilia (Nwanyimba or Nwamba), 108
- Eric Chinyere 17, 108
- Eunice (Ubakanwa), 108
- Eberechukwu Obioma 109
- House (in Okrika Grammar School (OGS), 50
- House (named after Uzoma, R.I. – in

Ngwa High School), 77
- Ijeuru Okwuchi 18, 109
- James Chikwe (Agbarakwe), 16, 108, 124
- Janet Nwannediya (Nwannedie) 108
- Jemimah Chinyere (Nee Nwachukwu), 17, 49, 82, 98,
  - As
    - a pivotal teacher, 147
    - Lay Canon of Diocese of Owerri, 156
    - teacher, Girls' Secondary School, Elelenwa, 148
  - at
    - St. Bartholomew's Primary School, Enugu, 147
    - Women's Training Centre (WTC), Umuahia, 148
    - Queens College, Lagos, 141-145
  - elected President of NAU Women's Section, 153
  - first Secretary and President, Nkwerre Aborigines, Union (Women's Section), 18
    - London Matriculation, 34
    - teacher at CMS Archdeacon Crowder Memorial Girls Secondary School, 34
  - founding member, Eastern Region National Council of Women's Societies, 160
  - from School-Mistress to Pivotal Teacher, 146-150
  - member, Governing Council of University of Ibadan, 161-163
  - President, Imo State YWCA Chapter, 157
  - Principal at Owerri-Nkworji Girls' Secondary School, 150
  - Prize for best graduating student in Community Medicine, 162
  - Service to Women, 150-154
  - Sponsored for Diploma Course in Social Psychology (Leadership) at Columbia University, New York, U.S.A., 149
- Teacher
  - at St. Silas Primary School, Old Umuahia, 148
  - at Uzii Lay-out Primary School, 149
  - Trustee, Imo State Endowment Fund Committee, 161
  - Vice President, Eastern Regional NCWS, 160-161
  - Vice Principal, St. Catherine's Girls Secondary School, Nkwerre, 150
- Johnson Nduweze 16, 108
- Margaret (Ikwuoma) 108, 111
- Ndubuisi Chigozie 18, 109
- Okechukwu Madueke 18, 109
- Onuoha Chijioke 18, 47, 109

Uzoma, Reuben Ibekwe1
- Sophia Nwaigbe 108
- Ugochi Eziaha 18, 109
- Ukachi Nwaobiara, 109
- Susanna (Nwanyiwunwa) 108, 111

Uzoma, Reuben Ibekwe
- Administrator, Orlu Province, 99-100
- Admission to CMS Teachers Training College (formerly Awka College), 27-31
- a.k.a bookworm, 61
- a.k.a. Nwanwa-Ukwu, 16
- appointed, Minister of Education, 56, 59, 148
- as
  - Commissioner, Public Service Commission, Imo State, 115
  - education secretary Delta Diocese and later Owerri Diocese, 31
  - elected member of Eastern Regional House of Assembly, 47
  - father and facilitator, Orlu/Okigwe Diocese of the Anglican Church of Nigeria, 86, 90, 102
  - General Manager and supervisor of Anglican Schools, 37
  - Ochonma-Oha of Orlu-Promoter of Public Good, 124
  - Onye-Nkuzi 26, 107
  - pioneer pupil of Nkweme Central School, 1, 19
  - Principal, Awka College Practicing School, 30, 60, 147
  - Principal, Okrika Grammar School (OGS), 1944-1946 47-50, 147
  - Public Service Commissioner, 104
  - Chairman, Nkwerre Divisional School Board, 102
  - pupil teacher, 23, 27, 37, 60

Index

- tutor in Awka College, 30
- at
    - at Achimota College, Gold Coast now Ghana), 32-34, 47, 114, 147
    - Awka College 106-107, 110, 114, 147
    - CMS Central School, Nkwerre, 105, 114
    - DMGS, 110
    - Ekwulobia Central School (ECS), Aguata, 38, 114
    - st. Paul's Ezeoke-Nsu CMS Central School, Ehime-Mbano, Imo State 37, 60
- baptism at St. Paul's Church Nkwerre 108
- beneficiary of CMS Mission Education system scholarships, 25
- birth and early childhood, 13
- Chairman,
    - Eastern Nigeria Rural Activities Committee ENRAC of CCN, 88-89
    - Orlu Zonal Education Board, 104
    - State Teachers' Disciplinary Committee, 104
    - 24-member Advisory Committee, 91
    - Zonal Education Management Board, 6
- childhood under care of his paternal grandmother "Baaba", 107
- children of, 18, 109
- commissioner in the Public Service commission, 86
- conferment of Honorary Doctor of Laws (L.L.D. *Honouris Causa*) by UNN, 124
- Education Secretary and
    - Supervisor of Schools in the Niger Delta Diocese, 70-72, 75-76, 80, 82, 101
    - Manager of Schools, 98
- elected, Secretary of NAU/Women's Section (NAU/WS), 151
- Elected, to Eastern Regional Assembly, 148
- External examiners for Igbo language examination at School of Oriental and African Studies, University of London, 36
- Fellow, Royal of the Geographical Society (FRGS), 36
- first Minister of Education in the Eastern Region, 8
- First University graduate from Old Orlu Province/Division, 16, 34, 60
- General Manager, Schools in Niger Delta Diocese, 87, 148
- Hometown, Nkwerre , 5-24
- In United Kingdom to study for Post-graduate Diploma in Education at Institute for Education, University of London, 34-37
- Interview with Editorial Board of Orlu Zonal "Educator" 107-108
- Knighthood of St. Christopher, Okigwe/Orlu Anglican Diocese, 117-118
- Lay Prince of the Anglican Church in Nigeria, 85
- Life Member of the Church Missionary Society (CMS), 85
- Magnificent Order of British Empire (OBE), 124
- Member
    - Christian Council of Nigeria (CCN) 87-88
    - inaugural governing council of Federal University of Technology, Owerri (FUTO), 104
    - Provincial Synod of the Province of West Africa, 87
- National Honour of Office of the Order of the Federal Republic of Nigeria (OFR), 123
- of Umunubo Kindred, 15
- on CMS scholarship to Achimota College Gold Coast Colony, 4, 34, 60, 114
- Onye-Nkuzi, Pupil Teacher, School Master, 37-39, 83
- pacesetter for educational scholarship, 5-6
- papers of, 165-324
- passed Cambridge School Certificate Examination, 34, 60
- Principal, member, Owerri Diocesan Synod, 103
- principal, Okrika Grammar School for Boys, 77,95
- publications, 74
- published work in Overseas Education, 37
- siblings of 16, 108

- silent philanthropy, 120
- tenure on Imo State Public Service commission, 104
- tutor,
  - at Awka College, 47-60
  - Dennis Memorial Grammar School (DMGS), Onitsha, 39-47, 60
- Ukeje I Nkwerre meaning "The One who is different from his peers" or "A First among Equals", 124-125

Uzoukwu, E.C.O. 118

V

Vernacular-based education, 40
Voice of Women 161-162
Voluntary
- agencies, 3, 31, 68-69, 79, 112
  - and churches, 64
- agency institutions, 79
- Christian Organisations, 111
- education system, 55
- organisations, 111
- schools, 38
- service Agencies, 102-103

W

Waboso, Mabel 145
Wachukwu, Maggie 145
Wachukwu, U. 160

Wadibia, Dorothy (Mrs. Mbanefo), 146
Wadibia-Anyanwu Nkem 146
Walter R.E. 43
Warrant Chiefs, 122
Warrant of Appointment under the Queen's signs manual, 280
Weekes, T. 43
Wesleyan Training Institute, 1928, 26
West African Frontier Force (WAFF), 132
Western Education 106, 107-108
 - in Nigeria, 4
Western Region Elections, 1952 54
Williams, Octavia 46
Wokoma, Constance 145
Women's empowerment, 156
World Association for Adult Education, 36
World Council of Churches 158

Y

Yar'Adua, Musa 46
Yirenki, R. 44
Young Women's' Christian Association (YWCA), 156-159

Z

Zikist Movement, 53
- of the NCNC, 52

About the Author

The author, Adaoha Chibuzo Okwuosa, OON (Nee Uzoma) graduated with a Double Honours degree in Politics and Sociology from the University of Sussex in 1966, after secondary education at Queen's School Enugu, Nigeria, and St. Michael's Public School for Girls in Limpsfield, Surrey, England. She subsequently obtained a D.Phil(cum laude) in Sociology of Development from the Albert-Ludwigs University, Freiburg, Germany, as a scholar of the Friedrich Ebert Foundation from 1971 to 1975.

Dr Adaoha Okwuosa had a successful career in lecturing and academics from 1976 to 1996, attaining the rank of Associate Professor and Head of Department. That career variously saw her at the University of Nigeria, Nsukka, Alvan Ikoku College (now University) of Education (AICE) in Owerri, and the former Centre for Democratic Studies under the Presidency in Abuja. This was followed by extensive experience in Public Service administration in the Federal Civil Service up to the level of Permanent Secretary, before she retired and was appointed to serve for five years in international diplomacy as Nigeria's pioneer Commissioner to the Economic Community of West African States (ECOWAS) Commission from 2007 to 2012.

Some instances from Dr Okwuosa's vast experience in Public Service administration and management, alongside lecturing and academics, include the following; Board Membership of the pioneer Directorate of Women Affairs in her home state, Imo State, Nigeria from 1989 to 1991; Before then, Membership of Justice Ukattah Judicial Panel for Review of Petitions Arising from Government White Papers in Imo State from 1985 – 1987; Membership of Governing Council of Alvan Ikoku College of Education (AICE) as Staff Representative from 1985 to 1987; Membership of Imo State Economic Consultative Committee from 1984 to 1986.

At the national level, Dr Okwuosa was no less busy. She served as National Research Coordinator in the Executive of the National Council of Women's Societies (NCWS) from 1995 to 1997, a capacity in which she was a member of the Nigerian delegation to the Fourth UN Conference on Women held in Beijing, China in 1995. In the mainstream Civil Service between 1996 and 2000, she was a Director of Planning, Research and Statistics (PRS) in the Federal Ministries of Justice, of Finance, and later in the States and Local Government Affairs Office under the Vice-President's Office, from 1999 to 2001. While serving as PRS Director in the Federal Ministry of Finance, Dr Okwuosa gained valuable experience as a Board Member of the Federal Inland Revenue Service (FIRS) from 1998 – 1999. However, it was from her subsequent position as Secretary/Director of the Federal Government Staff Housing Loans Board, in the Office of the Head of Civil Service of the Federation from 2001 to 2005 that she was appointed Permanent Secretary. It was this varied and extensive public service experience that gave Dr Okwuosa several Honours and Awards. Principal among these, are the 2007 Public Service Award on her retirement 'in Recognition of (her) Dedication and Outstanding Public Service Record of Excellence'. This followed in February 2008 with her National Honour decoration as Officer of the Order of the Niger (OON) by then Head of State; H.E President Umaru Yar'adua.

Okwuosa has written extensively on Gender Issues, Politics, Social Development and Democratisation. Her works include a four-volume publication on Democratisation in Africa, co-edited with Professor Omo Omoruyi, Dirk Berg-Schlosser and Adesina Sambo. Her chapter is on, 'Women in the Democratisation Process in Nigeria: Gains and Limitations'. The author also contributed a chapter on 'Sources of Women's Political Powerlessness in Nigeria' in the book Women in Politics in Nigeria edited by J.A.A. Ayoade, Elone J. Nwabuzor and Adesina Sambo. Dr. Okwuosa was also co-editor of the Nigerian Journal of Democracy Vol. 1, No. 1 1994, in which she contributed on 'Minority Rights and the Constitutional Question in Nigeria'.

Dr Adaoha Okwuosa married a fellow academic, Late Dr Bennett N. Okwuosa of Oguta, Imo State. They have four daughters and several grandchildren.

About the Co-Author

The co-author, Nonye Nnamezie (Nee Onyedum) obtained her first degree in History and later studied History and Strategic Studies for her Masters and Doctorate degrees all at the University of Lagos, Nigeria. Whilst carving a niche for herself in Gender related issues, she was awarded a scholarship for a Postgraduate Certificate in Gender Studies from the University of South Africa, Cape Town.

Her research and teaching interests have focused on African Children and Childhood History, African Urban History, Migration Studies, Biographies, Gender and Ethnic Studies. Her articles have appeared in local and international journals of repute such as the Journal of Social History, Vol. 49, No. 2 in which she contributed, the article, "Patriarchy and the Igbo Girl-Child; A Culture to Revisit."

Nonye is one of the few African historians whose research focus is on African Children and Childhood History. She has attended local and international conferences, presenting papers on issues bordering on children and the culture of childhood in Africa, including a paper titled "Reflecting Childhood in African History; A Study of Child Labour in South Africa" presented at the Southern Africa Historical Society Biennial Conference in June 2017, Wits University, Johannesburg. Nonye is an Associate Editor of the Hezekiah University *Journal of Humanities*, and a Member of the Historical Society of Nigeria, Historical Association of South Africa and the Lagos Studies Association. She is currently at work on Nigerian Migrants: Trends, Issues and Challenges.

Nonye is married with four children.

Made in the USA
Monee, IL
03 May 2026